Oxford AQA History

A LEVEL AND AS
Component 2

The American Dream: Reality and Illusion, 1945–1980

Mark Stacey

SERIES EDITOR
Sally Waller

OXFORD

973·91

Great Clarendon Street, Oxford, OX2 6DP, United Kingdom

Oxford University Press is a department of the University of Oxford. It furthers the University's objective of excellence in research, scholarship, and education by publishing worldwide. Oxford is a registered trade mark of Oxford University Press in the UK and in certain other countries

British Library Cataloguing in Publication Data Data available

978-0-19-835455-0

Kindle edition: 978-0-19-836401-6

10 9 8 7 6 5 4 3 2

Paper used in the production of this book is a natural, recyclable product made from wood grown in sustainable forests. The manufacturing process conforms to the environmental regulations of the country of origin.

Printed in India

Acknowledgements

From the author, Mark Stacey: To Abi, Ben and Lottie for giving me the peace and the time to write. I love you. To my students, for their determination that I should mention them by name. I admire your persistence.

The publisher would like to thank the following people for offering their contribution in the development of this book: Roy Whittle, Sally Waller and Indexing Specialists (UK) Ltd.

Approval message from AQA

This textbook has been approved by AQA for use with our qualification. This means that we have checked that it broadly covers the specification and we are satisfied with the overall quality. Full details of our approval process can be found on our website.

We approve textbooks because we know how important it is for teachers and students to have the right resources to support their teaching and learning. However, the publisher is ultimately responsible for the editorial control and quality of this book.

Please note that when teaching the AQA A Level History course, you must refer to AQA's specification as your definitive source of information. While this book has been written to match the specification, it does not provide complete coverage of every aspect of the course.

A wide range of other useful resources can be found on the relevant subject pages of our website: www.aqa.org.uk.

Please note that the Practice Questions in this book allow students a genuine attempt at practising exam skills, but they are not intended to replicate examination papers.

Contents

Contents (continued)

Introduction to features

The *Oxford AQA History* series has been developed by a team of expert history teachers and authors with examining experience. Written to match the new AQA specification, these new editions cover AS and A Level content together in each book.

How to use this book

The features in this book include:

TIMELINE

Key events are outlined at the beginning of the book to give you an overview of the chronology of this topic. Events are colour-coded so you can clearly see the categories of change.

LEARNING OBJECTIVES

At the beginning of each chapter, you will find a list of learning objectives linked to the requirements of the specification.

SOURCE   EXTRACT

Sources introduce you to material that is primary or contemporary to the period, and **Extracts** provide you with historical interpretations and the debate among historians on particular issues and developments. The accompanying activity questions support you in evaluating sources and extracts, analysing and assessing their value, and making judgements.

PRACTICE QUESTION

Focused questions to help you practise your history skills for both AS and A Level, including evaluating sources and extracts, and essay writing.

STUDY TIP

Hints to highlight key parts of **Practice Questions** or **Activities**.

ACTIVITY

Various activity types to provide you with opportunities to demonstrate both the content and skills you are learning. Some activities are designed to aid revision or to prompt further discussion; others are to stretch and challenge both your AS and A Level studies.

CROSS-REFERENCE

Links to related content within the book to offer you more detail on the subject in question.

A CLOSER LOOK

An in-depth look at a theme, event or development to deepen your understanding, or information to put further context around the subject under discussion.

KEY CHRONOLOGY

A short list of dates identifying key events to help you understand underlying developments.

KEY PROFILE

Details of a key person to extend your understanding and awareness of the individuals that have helped shape the period in question.

KEY TERM

A term that you will need to understand. The terms appear in bold, and they are also defined in the glossary.

AQA History specification overview

Part One content
Prosperity, inequality and Superpower status, 1945–1963

1. Truman and post-war America, 1945–1952
2. Eisenhower: Tranquility and crisis, 1952–1960
3. John F Kennedy and the 'New Frontier', 1960–1963

Part Two content
Challenges to the American Dream, 1963–1980

4. The Johnson presidency, 1963–1968
5. Republican reaction: the Nixon presidency, 1968–1974
6. The USA after Nixon, 1974–1980

AS examination papers will cover content from Part One only (you will only need to know the content in the blue box). A Level examination papers will cover content from both Part One and Part Two.

The examination papers

The grade you receive at the end of your AQA AS History course is based entirely on your performance in two examination papers, covering Breadth (Paper 1) and Depth (Paper 2). For your AQA A Level History course, you will also have to complete an Historical Investigation (Non-examined assessment).

Paper 2 Depth study

This book covers the content of a Depth study (Paper 2). You are assessed on the study in depth of a period of major historical change or development, and associated primary sources or sources contemporary to the period.

Exam paper	Questions and marks	Assessment Objective (AO)*	Timing	Marks
AS Paper 2: Depth Study	**Section A: Evaluating primary sources** One compulsory question linked to two primary sources or sources contemporary to the period (25 marks) • The compulsory question will ask you: *'with reference to these sources and your understanding of the historical context, which of these sources is more valuable in explaining why…'*	AO2	Written exam: 1 hour 30 minutes	50 marks (50% of AS)
	Section B: Essay writing One from a choice of two essay questions (25 marks) • The essay questions will contain a quotation advancing a judgement and <u>could</u> be followed by: *'explain why you agree or disagree with this view'.*	AO1		
A Level Paper 2: Depth Study	**Section A: Evaluating primary sources** One compulsory question linked to three primary sources or sources contemporary to the period. The sources will be of different types and views (30 marks) • The compulsory question will ask you: *'with reference to these sources and your understanding of the historical context, assess the value of these three sources to an historian studying…'*	AO2	Written exam: 2 hours 30 minutes	80 marks (40% of A Level)
	Section B: Essay writing Two from a choice of three essay questions (2 x 25 marks) • The essay questions require analysis and judgement, and <u>could</u> include: *'How successful…'* or *'To what extent…'* or *'How far…'* or a quotation offering a judgement followed by *'Assess the validity of this view'.*	AO1		

*AQA History examinations will test your ability to:

AO1: Demonstrate, organise and communicate **knowledge and understanding** to analyse and evaluate the key features related to the periods studied, **making substantiated judgements and exploring concepts**, as relevant, of cause, consequence, change, continuity, similarity, difference and significance.

AO2: **Analyse and evaluate** appropriate source material, primary and/or contemporary to the period, within the historical context.

AO3: **Analyse and evaluate**, in relation to the historical context, different ways in which aspects of the past have been interpreted.

Visit **www.aqa.org.uk** to help you prepare for your examinations. The website includes specimen examination papers and mark schemes.

Introduction to the *Oxford AQA History* series

Depth studies

The exploration of a short but significant historical period provides an opportunity to develop an 'in-depth' historical awareness. This book will help you to acquire a detailed knowledge of an exciting period of historical change, enabling you to become familiar with the personalities and ideas which shaped and dominated the time. In-depth study, as presented here, allows you to develop the enthusiasm that comes from knowing something really well.

However, 'depth' is not just about knowledge. Understanding history requires the piecing together of many different strands or themes, and depth studies demand an awareness of the interrelationship of a variety of perspectives, such as the political, economic, social and religious – as well as the influence of individuals and ideas within a relatively short period of time. Through an 'in-depth' study, a strong awareness of complex historical processes is developed, permitting deeper analysis, greater perception and well-informed judgement.

Whilst this book is therefore designed to impart a full and lively awareness of a significant period in history, far more is on offer from the pages that follow. With the help of the text and activities in this book, you will be encouraged to think historically, question developments in the past and undertake 'in-depth' analysis. You will develop your conceptual understanding and build up key historical skills that will increase your curiosity and prepare you, not only for A Level History examinations, but for any future studies.

Key Term, **Key Chronology** and **Key Profile** help you to consolidate historical knowledge about dates, events, people and places

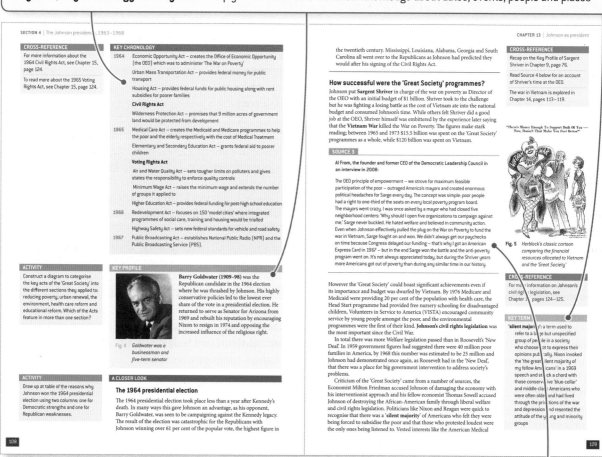

▲ American Dream: Reality and Illusion, 1945–1980

Source features support you with assessing the value of primary materials

This book also incorporates primary source material in the **Source** features. Primary sources are the building blocks of history, and you will be encouraged to reflect on their value to historians in trying to recreate the past. The accompanying questions are designed to develop your own historical skills, whilst suggestions for **Activities** will help you to engage with the past in a lively and stimulating manner. Throughout the book, you are encouraged to think about the material you are studying and to research further, in order to appreciate the ways in which historians seek to understand and interpret past events.

The chapters which follow are laid out according to the content of the AQA specification in six sections. Obviously, a secure chronological awareness and understanding of each section of content will be the first step in appreciating the historical period covered in this book. However, you are also encouraged to make links and comparisons between aspects of the period studied, and the activities will help you to relate to the key focus of your study and the key concepts that apply to it. Through intelligent use of this book, a deep and rewarding appreciation of an important period of history and the many influences within it will emerge.

Developing your study skills

You will need to be equipped with a paper file or electronic means of storing notes. Organised notes help to produce organised essays and sensible filing provides for efficient use of time. This book uses **Cross-References** to indicate where material in one chapter has relevance to that in another. By employing the same technique, you should find it easier to make the final leap towards piecing together your material to produce a holistic historical picture. The individual, group and research activities in this book are intended to guide you towards making selective and relevant notes with a specific purpose. Copying out sections of the book is to be discouraged, but recording material with a particular theme or question in mind will considerably aid your understanding.

There are plenty of examples of examination-style 'depth' **Practice Questions** for both AS Level, in Part One, and A Level in Parts One and Two of this book. There are also **Study Tips** to encourage you to think about historical perspectives, individuals, groups, ideas and ideology. You should also create your own timelines, charts and diagrams, for example to illustrate causation and

consequence, analyse the interrelationship of the differing perspectives, consider concepts and identify historical processes.

It is particularly important for you to have your own opinions and to be able to make informed judgements about the material you have studied. Some of the activities in this book encourage pair discussion or class debate, and you should make the most of such opportunities to voice and refine your own ideas. The beauty of history is that there is rarely a right or wrong answer, so this supplementary oral work should enable you to share your own opinions.

Writing and planning your essays

At both AS and A Level, you will be required to write essays and, although A Level questions are likely to be more complex, the basic qualities of good essay writing remain the same:

- **read the question carefully** to identify the key words and dates
- **plan out a logical and organised answer** with a clear judgement or view (several views if there are a number of issues to consider). Your essay should advance this judgement in the introduction, while also acknowledging alternative views and clarifying terms of reference, including the time span
- use the opening sentences of your paragraphs as stepping stones to take an argument forward, which allows you to **develop an evolving and balanced argument** throughout the essay and also makes for good style
- **support your comment or analysis** with precise detail; using dates, where appropriate, helps logical organisation
- **write a conclusion** which matches the view of the introduction and flows naturally from what has gone before.

Whilst these suggestions will help you develop a good style, essays should never be too rigid or mechanical.

This book will have fulfilled its purposes if it produces, as intended, students who think for themselves!

Sally Waller

Series Editor

Timeline

The colours represent different types of events, legislation and changes as follows:

- Blue: Economic
- Yellow: Social
- Red: Political
- Black: International (including foreign policy)
- Green: Religious

1945
- Democrat Franklin Roosevelt dies, replaced by Harry Truman
- Dropping of atomic bombs on Hiroshima and Nagasaki; Japan surrenders
- Recession hits US economy, unemployment reaches 5.2 per cent, GDP declines 12.7 per cent

1947
- Truman introduces 'Truman Doctrine'
- Construction of suburb of Levittown; New York begins process of suburbanisation
- Republicans take control of Senate and House

1948
- The Marshall Plan introduced

1949
- Chairman Mao pronounces communist takeover in China
- Democrats regain control of Senate and House

1954
- Brown v Board of Education decision by Supreme Court
- CIA overthrows Arbenz in a military coup in Guatemala

1955–56
- Montgomery Bus Boycott

1955
- Household television ownership exceeds 90 per cent

1956
- 'In God we trust' adopted as the official motto of the United States
- President Eisenhower signs Interstate Highway Act
- Southdale Centre opens as first US shopping mall

1963
- President John F Kennedy assassinated; Lyndon Johnson becomes president
- Betty Friedan publishes *The Feminine Mystique*
- CIA overthrows Bosch in a military coup in the Dominican Republic

1964
- Mississippi Freedom Summer
- CIA overthrows Goulart in a military coup in Brazil
- 1964–68 Major race riots in many US cities
- Civil Rights Act signed by Johnson

1965
- Voting Rights Act signed by Johnson
- César Chávez and United Farm Workers begin strike action
- Selma campaign
- Malcolm X assassinated in New York

1966
- National Organization of Women (NOW) founded

1971
- Richard Nixon declares a 'War on Drugs'
- US pulls out of Bretton-Woods Accord and abandons the gold standard

1972
- Nixon re-elected and makes historic visit to China
- Nixon and Brezhnev complete talks on Strategic Arms Limitation Treaty (SALT)
- Equal Rights Amendment passes Congress

1973
- *Roe v. Wade* decision by Supreme Court
- CIA overthrows Allende in a military coup in Chile
- OPEC raise oil price by 70 per cent
- Vietnam ceasefire agreement signed
- American Indian Movement seizes Wounded Knee, South Dakota

1974
- Inflation hits 11 per cent
- Nixon announces his resignation; Gerald Ford becomes president

1950
- Senator Joseph McCarthy launches campaign to expose communists in government

1951
- US tests first Hydrogen bomb

1952
- Republican Dwight Eisenhower elected as president

1950–54
- 1950–3 US forces fight in the Korean War
- 1953–4 Recession hits US economy, unemployment reaches 6.1 per cent, GDP declines 2.6 per cent
- 1953 CIA overthrows Mossadegh in a military coup in Iran

1957
- Little Rock Crisis

1960
- Sit-ins lead to the founding of the SNCC
- John F Kennedy elected as president
- Food and Drug Administration approve the use of the contraceptive pill
- 1960–61 Recession hits US economy, unemployment reaches 7.1 per cent, GDP declines 1.6 per cent

1961
- Freedom Rides begin
- CIA orchestrates failed Bay of Pigs invasion
- Building of Berlin Wall

1962
- Cuban missile crisis
- Rachel Carson publishes *Silent Spring*

1968
- Martin Luther King assassinated
- Assassination of Robert Kennedy by Palestinian nationalist Sirhan Sirhan
- Tet Offensive in Vietnam

1969
- Republican Party candidate Richard Nixon elected president
- Stonewall Rebellion in New York launches gay rights movement
- Women's movement protests at Miss America pageant in Atlantic City
- News of My Lai massacre reaches US

1969
- Woodstock music festival
- US astronaut Neil Armstrong becomes the first person to walk on the Moon
- 1969–70 Recession hits US economy, unemployment reaches 6.1 per cent, GDP declines 0.6 per cent
- 250,000 protesters march in Washington against the Vietnam War

1970
- Bombing of Cambodia begins
- Four students shot and killed at Kent State University during anti-war protests

1975
- Church Committee condemns CIA abuses

1976
- Democrat Jimmy Carter elected president

1979
- Three Mile Island incident
- Hostage crisis at US embassy in Tehran, Iran
- 'Moral Majority' founded as Christian political group
- Soviet Union invades Afghanistan; CIA begins funding guerrilla opposition

1980
- Recession hits US economy, unemployment reaches 7.8 per cent, GDP declines 2.2 per cent
- Republican Ronald Reagan elected president

This book will take you on a journey from the end of the Second World War to the start of the eighties, introducing you to a period of history in which the concept of the 'American Dream' became widely discussed both in the USA and abroad. At its most basic, the Dream stems from the Declaration of Independence which pronounced both that 'all men are created equal' and that they have a right to 'Life, liberty and the pursuit of happiness.' But the signatories to the declaration didn't count slaves as men, or give many rights to women. The phrase itself was only popularised when the historian James Truslow Adams wrote in 1931 *The Epic of America* that the Dream meant 'a better, richer, and happier life for all our citizens of every rank'. On the face of it, that promise seems a useful pledge for any government and people to aspire to but was nothing that would make the US unique in the world.

What set the US apart in 1945 was the **pluralist** nature of its society. Its population was incredibly diverse in terms of race, religion, culture and tradition. Many of these people were first or second generation immigrants whose ideas about government and rights clashed with the principles of the **Constitution**. Others were part of an **entrenched** system of prejudice between whites and other races whose roots stretched back beyond the constitution itself.

The period from 1945 to 1980 was a time of economic growth, of nuclear fear and of heroic movements for civil rights. Yet it was also a time when the presidency itself came under scrutiny from a growing media, a frustrated Congress and through the actions of, perhaps, the defining figure of the era, Richard Nixon, president between 1969 and 1974. The media became the lens through which Americans experienced their government, the products they could buy and the rest of the world and the growth of the various media outlets: TV, radio, film, magazines and newspapers is entwined with the political, social and economic events and changes in these years.

KEY TERM

pluralism: a form of society in which the members of minority groups maintain their independent cultural traditions

Constitution: the 'rule book' which states how a country or organisation is to be governed

entrenched: in political terms this means very well established and difficult to change, as in, 'the First Amendment is entrenched in the US Constitution'

Fig. 1 *US marines raise the American flag atop Iwo Jima, Japan, towards the end of the Second World War in 1945*

This book begins in 1945 when it was clear that the US and its allies were going to triumph in the war against the Nazis and Japanese. More precisely it begins with the death of Franklin Roosevelt on 12 April 1945 and the accession of his vice president Harry Truman. Truman inherited a nation that was accepted, both at home and abroad, as one of the two greatest powers in the world. But whereas Stalin could rule the Soviet Union as a dictator, the US president's power came from the people and was defined by the Constitution, the seven articles and 22 amendments (in 1945) of which form the backbone of the events of the period.

The Constitution defined how the different parts of government are elected, removed and their powers. It also establishes the rights of US citizens including the right to free speech, freedom of religion and a free press (Article 1), the right to bear arms (Article 2), the right not to self-incriminate (Article 5, source of the phrase 'take/plead the fifth'), the abolition of slavery (Article 13), right of citizenship (Article 14) and the right to vote regardless of colour or race (Article 15). The latter three were all introduced after the North won the Civil War of 1861–65.

This seems to imply that the Constitution was relatively easy to change but nothing could be further from the truth. Of the 27 amendments ratified (approved) since the first in 1791, 11 came in the first five years. Over 11,500 have subsequently been turned down. To change the US Constitution requires a proposal approved by either two thirds of Congress or two thirds of the states. Ratification, the final approval stage, then requires three quarters of the states to approve of the amendment.

Changes are therefore hard to achieve, not least because of the regularly changing make up of Congress and the presidency. The electoral merry-go-round involves:

- The president and the vice president being elected together in a presidential election held once every four years in November with the winner taking office in January of the following year.
- Elections to Congress taking place every two years. Congress has two chambers: the Senate and the House of Representatives.
  - The Senate has 100 members, two from each state, elected for a six-year term with one third being renewed every two years. The group of the Senate seats that is up for election during a given year is known as a 'class'; the three classes are staggered so that only one of the three groups is renewed every two years. It has a shared role in making the law with the House of Representatives but it can also act as a check on the larger house to prevent the most populous states becoming too powerful. The Senate also has sole power of approval on foreign treaties and cabinet and judicial nominations, including appointments to the Supreme Court.
  - The House of Representatives has 435 members, with the number of members from each state being dictated by the size of the population in that state, elected for a two-year term in single-seat constituencies. House of Representatives elections are held every two years on the first Tuesday after 1 November in even years. The House is responsible for initiating all revenue-based legislation which then goes to the Senate for review and approval. The House is also the only one of the two chambers that can begin impeachment proceedings.

The Supreme Court consists of a chief justice and eight associate justices who are nominated by the sitting president and then confirmed or rejected by the Senate. After being appointed, justices have life tenure unless they resign or retire.

Complicating matters further is the fact that the US is a federation meaning that the above system of Executive, Legislature and Judiciary (or president,

KEY TERM

National Guard: reserve soldiers of the US army who can be brought in by a state's governor in emergency situations or federalised by the president to act on his authority

Congress and Supreme Court) is reproduced at the state level meaning each state has an Executive (the Governor), a state legislature and a state Supreme Court who are elected in a similar way. States have control over many aspects of policy including education, sales tax, use of the death penalty, jury selection in trials and more recently gay marriage and use of medical marijuana. States also have an armed force, known as the **National Guard** which is under the command of the Governor but can be federalised (brought under the president's control) in an emergency.

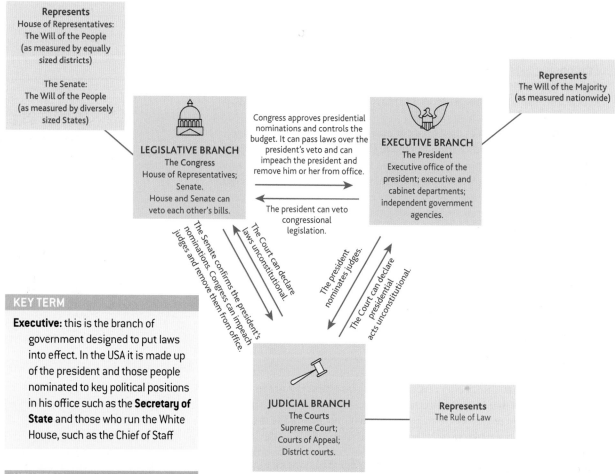

Fig. 2 *This diagram shows the US political system*

KEY TERM

Executive: this is the branch of government designed to put laws into effect. In the USA it is made up of the president and those people nominated to key political positions in his office such as the **Secretary of State** and those who run the White House, such as the Chief of Staff

KEY TERM

Secretary of State: a senior appointment in the office of the president primarily concerned with foreign affairs

KEY TERM

Manifest Destiny: a phrase first used by the journalist John O'Sullivan in 1845 which has come to mean both America's destiny to expand and spread its democratic capitalist identity and the special qualities of American people that enable it to do this

This seemingly cumbersome system had, in fact, served the country well in providing stability and economic success. In 1945 the USA was the third largest country in the world by area (after Russia and Canada) and by population (after India and China). One hundred and forty million people lived there, a figure that grew to over 227 million by 1980. It was also blessed with huge natural resources including substantial deposits of coal, oil and natural gas which meant that the US was virtually self-sufficient in meeting its energy needs in 1945. This natural bounty had given Americans a feeling of superiority that was enhanced by victory in the Second World War, a sense of a '**Manifest Destiny**' to lead the world and a belief that the USA was exceptional. In 1945 this belief was shared by much of the world with millions of people desperate to emigrate to the 'land of the free' from war shattered Europe and poverty stricken countries elsewhere.

However, all was not well in the USA itself. Though its natural resources were the envy of the world and its capitalist system allowed many to benefit through well paid jobs, many groups felt they had no access to the American Dream. Some of these groups had protested prior to the Second World War. Women had gained the right to vote in 1918 through a suffrage movement led by Elizabeth Cady Stanton and Susan B. Anthony and had played a key role in the manufacturing effort that had helped win the Second World War. This provided a sense of independence and fulfilment that was lost in the aftermath of the war. African-Americans had achieved freedom from slavery in 1865 but the defeated southern states had used their constitutional right to create their own laws to introduce segregation in schooling, transport and recreational facilities. Groups such as the National Association for the Advancement of Colored People (NAACP) had campaigned for black rights but a legal decision known as *Plessy v. Ferguson* of 1896 had established that the laws could remain provided 'separate but equal' facilities existed for blacks and whites. Meanwhile terror groups like the Ku Klux Klan kept the black population living in fear through violence and intimidation.

So in 1945, America was the effective leader of the free world and its people mostly felt that they lived in the best country on earth. However this feeling of superiority was under threat. The spectre of fascism had been defeated but the post-war territorial acquisitions of the communist Soviet Union in Eastern Europe made Americans fearful of the influence of 'reds'. An accusation of being a 'communist' could be levelled at anyone, sometimes for the most innocent opinions and this fear of communism persisted throughout the period, waxing and waning through McCarthy in the early 1950s to Nixon in the 1970s to Reagan after 1980.

What perplexed Americans about communism most was how it could possibly appeal. They saw the advantages of a free market that provided comforts unparalleled in the world from cars to fridges to Coca-Cola and the evolution of the American consumer is one of the key economic themes of this period. Advertising and manufacturing manipulated the newly wealthy into desiring material possessions above social goods like schools, libraries, highways and health care and while this consumption boosted the economy it also had harmful effects on the environment and on social cohesion. For those that could not afford the glittering array of new products, resentment grew through the 1950s and this was to explode in the decade that followed.

The 1960s saw protests emerge across America as noisy minorities sought to reclaim their share of the Dream. African-Americans sought political rights with first non-violence and later intimidation; women sought social and economic equality and young people sought to right the wrongs that the older generation were perceived to be committing in Vietnam and at home. All of these protests were covered by a media that had grown rapidly through TV, at the movie theatres and in local and national newspapers and magazines. The media's coverage of the protests and the reasons behind them forced politicians to respond and make sweeping promises about making the American Dream more accessible for the majority. But those making promises weren't immune to having their dreams shattered. First the glamorous young President John F Kennedy was shot dead in 1963, then the firebrand black radical Malcolm X in 1965. In the space of two months in 1968, Martin Luther King and the presidential hopeful Bobby Kennedy were both killed in the culmination of five years that had seen America's cities aflame with rioting and its proud reputation as the defender of peace fatally damaged by Vietnam.

The 1970s saw the cracks in the Dream further exposed as Vietnam dragged on, economic superiority was eroded by the defeated nations of the Second World War and protest movements were hampered by a lack of government money to address their demands. The nation needed hope and Richard Nixon seemed to offer it by appealing to the 'Silent Majority': the great

KEY CHRONOLOGY

Presidents of the United States, 1933–89 (D = Democrat, R = Republican)

March 1933–April 1945
Franklin Roosevelt (D)

April 1945–Jan 1953
Harry Truman (D)

Jan 1953–Jan 1961
Dwight Eisenhower (R)

Jan 1961–Nov 1963
John F Kennedy (D)

Nov 1963–Jan 1969
Lyndon Johnson (D)

Jan 1969–Aug 1974
Richard Nixon (R)

Aug 1974–Jan 1977
Gerald Ford (R)

Jan 1977–Jan 1981
Jimmy Carter (D)

Jan 1981–Jan 1989
Ronald Reagan (R)

A CLOSER LOOK

Presidential elections take place on the Tuesday after the first Monday in November in an election year. The 1933 20th Amendment states that the new or returning president begins their term at noon on the 20th January of the following year (unless the 20th is a Sunday, in which case it begins at noon on the 21st).

mass of Americans who still believed in the Dream and, more importantly, were willing to work for it. But Nixon's downfall in the Watergate Affair was a better story than any that Hollywood had produced and gave rise to a pessimism about America's future that tainted Nixon's two successors. They suffered further economic trials and succeeded only in swapping the jungles of Vietnam for the deserts of the Middle East when it came to foreign policy problems. By 1980 the Dream came full circle as Hollywood casting finally got its hands on the presidency and former B-movie actor Ronald Reagan could promise that he would make America great again.

This book will encourage you to reflect on what the 'American Dream' meant in the years 1945 to 1980 and how perceptions of the Dream changed. It will also require you to think about how the relationship between the government and the people differed for different groups at different times. In the course of your journey through these years of US history, you will come to appreciate how difficult it can be to strike a balance between personal freedom and the responsibilities of individuals to society as a whole. You will also come to understand how the role of business, the media, the Church and the wider world can affect the decisions people make both at the ballot box and in the streets – one of the many issues thrown up by this period of history that continues to be relevant today.

The thirty-five years that followed the Second World War saw changes in America that rippled out across the world. Partly this came through economic strength, partly from the size and power of the US military machine and its arsenal of nuclear weapons, but it also came from the actions of individual Americans. This may have been collectively as they campaigned for their rights, or individually as they bought fast-food, suburban homes, new cars and music that encouraged them to challenge authority. There is much to fascinate and much to think about in this book and whatever conclusions you reach on the events, ideas and developments that you will read about, remember that whatever the setbacks, the errors and the excesses, this was a time when the US you recognise today was born.

1 | Truman and post-war America, 1945–1952

1 | The United States in 1945

SOURCE 1

President Truman announces the surrender of Japan in a radio address to the American people, 1 September 1945:

Liberty does not make all men perfect nor all society secure. But it has provided more solid progress and happiness and decency for more people than any other philosophy of government in history. We know that we can meet the hard problems of peace which have come upon us. America can build for itself a future of employment and security. Together with the United Nations, it can build a world of peace founded on justice, fair dealing, and tolerance. From this day we move forward. We move toward a new era of security at home. With the other United Nations we move toward a new and better world of cooperation, of peace and international good will and cooperation. God's help has brought us to this day of victory. With His help we will attain that peace and prosperity for ourselves and all the world in the years ahead.

ACTIVITY

Evaluating primary sources

1. What reasons does Truman give in Source 1 for US success in the Second World War?
2. Why might an historian find this source valuable in understanding Truman's goals?

The legacies of the Second World War

For the American people the experience of war between 1941 and 1945 had been different from all the other nations involved. Outside the USA the legacy of war included mass destruction, massive casualties, huge social disruption and serious economic hardship. Millions of people in Europe and the Far East suffered bombings, food shortages and rationing as well as occupation by foreign armies. None of this happened to the American people. No foreign soldier set foot on American soil and American pride was enhanced by the size and success of the war effort with many Americans, military or civilian, strongly believing that the Second World War was a 'good war'.

Country	Military	Civilian	Total
Soviet Union	10,000,000	10,000,000	20,000,000
Germany	3,500,000	700,000	4,200,000
Japan	2,000,000	350,000	2,350,000
France	250,000	350,000	600,000
UK	326,000	62,000	388,000
USA	400,000	6	400,000

Table 1. *Estimated deaths in the Second World War.*

LEARNING OBJECTIVES

In this chapter you will learn about:

- the legacies of the Second World War
- powers of the US president
- the main American political parties
- the state of the US economy and American post-war prosperity
- the regional, ethnic and social divisions in the USA.

KEY PROFILE

Fig. 1 *Truman saw the US through the end of the Second World War*

Harry S Truman (1884–1972), the 33rd president, had been vice president under Franklin Delano Roosevelt (FDR) for less than three months when FDR died. Dealing with the post-war fall out, communism at home and abroad, as well as civil rights issues and an economy in transition, Truman plumbed depths of unpopularity in opinion polls. However, his uncompromising and honest approach (he had a sign on his desk that read 'the buck stops here') saw him re-evaluated on his death in 1972.

KEY TERM

American exceptionalism: the idea that America is unique or exceptional which has become a popular part of conservative American thinking

KEY PROFILE

Fig. 3   *Roosevelt led the US in a time of economic depression and total war*

Franklin Delano Roosevelt (1882–1945) was born to wealthy New York-based parents. He was the fifth cousin of Teddy Roosevelt, the 26th President. He became president after three years as Governor of New York and his 'New Deal' policies of large-scale government intervention and spending on infrastructure projects are often credited with bringing the country out of the Great Depression. Roosevelt contracted polio at the age of 39 but was careful never to allow his lack of mobility to be seen by the public.

Fig. 2   *New York City in the 1940s. While the capitals of Europe smouldered, the US thrived*

By the start of 1945 the USA was clearly in the strongest position of any country. With a mere 7 per cent of the global population, the US had 42 per cent of the world's income, 62 per cent of its discovered oil, 50 per cent of its manufacturing output, 80 per cent of its cars and 33 million households owned a radio. The war in Europe was drawing to a close and the USA was in the ascendency in the Pacific. The ideas of '**American exceptionalism**' and the country's 'manifest destiny' had grown in many minds. The economy had recovered strongly from the Great Depression thanks partly to war spending, there was a strong sense of national unity, President Roosevelt was popular and there was little criticism of the political system.

The political scene

On 12 April 1945 the 32nd president of the United States, **Franklin Delano Roosevelt** died following a stroke, bringing to an end his 12 years as president. He is still the longest-serving president, being in office for 1500 days longer than any other. Roosevelt had presided over two major crises: the Great Depression that followed the Wall Street Crash of 1929 and the Second World War and his approval rating at the time of his death stood at 70 per cent, having never dipped below 48 per cent.

His successor and Vice President Harry S Truman (his middle name was just S) therefore had a difficult act to follow, not least because the wars in Europe and the Pacific were still going on and because he was seen by many as a compromise candidate for the vice presidency and not up to the top job.

When Truman offered his consolations to the widowed Eleanor Roosevelt, saying, 'Is there anything I can do for you?' Mrs Roosevelt responded, 'Is there anything we can do for you? For you are the one in trouble now.'

Powers of the presidency

Though the US president is often described as the most powerful person in the world, one of the principles of the American political system is that of 'checks and balances'.

In this system the president is prevented from having too much power both by a Congress that can refuse to co-operate and a Supreme Court that can rule the president's actions as unconstitutional. The president, meanwhile, can veto congressional proposals for laws and gets to appoint new members of the Supreme Court. Congress's power comes from the ability to introduce new proposals for laws, control the budget, approve or disapprove of presidential nominations to the Supreme Court and **impeach** the president if he is accused of a crime. In this way each part of the government can 'check' the other parts meaning no part can become too powerful; a sensible system for a new country eager, in 1787 when the **Constitution** was written, to avoid the mistakes of Europe.

Truman lacked the **political capital** of Roosevelt, and Mrs Roosevelt was right to suggest that he was in trouble as the complicated set up of the US political system could easily leave a weak president faced with an uncooperative Congress and Supreme Court, along with uncooperative individual states. This system was designed to prevent the kind of dictatorships that had developed in Europe but it also served to create tension between the states and the Federal government, between Congress and the president and between the president and the Supreme Court. In addition, with the system of elections for president, the House of Representatives and the Senate overlapping it was possible to have a Republican president and a Democrat controlled Congress and vice versa, leading to **intransigence** in the passing of legislation with both Congress and the president blaming each other.

ACTIVITY

Try to watch some episodes of the US television show *The West Wing*. Though it deals with a contemporary presidency it provides excellent, if idealistic, insights into the workings of the presidency and relations with Congress, the Supreme Court and the Press.

SOURCE 2

Supreme Court Judge Thurgood Marshall, the great grandson of a slave, commenting on the US Constitution, in its bicentennial year, 1987. Marshall was one of few willing to criticise the Constitution and the Framers (the Founding Fathers who wrote the Constitution):

I do not believe that the meaning of the Constitution was forever 'fixed' at the Philadelphia **Convention**. Nor do I find the wisdom, foresight, and sense of justice exhibited by the Framers particularly profound. To the contrary, the government they devised was defective from the start, requiring several amendments, a civil war, and momentous social transformation to attain the system of constitutional government, and its respect for the individual freedoms and human rights, we hold as fundamental today. When contemporary Americans cite 'The Constitution,' they invoke a concept that is vastly different from what the Framers barely began to construct two centuries ago.

Truman also had to face up to the fact that both Congress and the individual states felt that Roosevelt had increased **Executive** power at their expense. With the coming of peace and an inexperienced new president there was every reason to believe that Executive power would be challenged repeatedly at home. However the Constitution made little reference to the powers that the president could exercise in Foreign Affairs, and the role of the president in international diplomacy had expanded in the early twentieth century. As a result, Truman found it considerably easier to wield power internationally than at home.

KEY TERM

impeach: meaning to charge the holder of a public office, such as the president, with misconduct

CROSS-REFERENCE

For more details of the American political system and Constitution, see pages xii–xiii in the Introduction.

KEY TERM

political capital: this refers to the trust and influence a politician has with the public and other politicians which forms a kind of currency that politicians can 'spend' to get things done

intransigence: refusal to change one's views about something

ACTIVITY

Evaluating primary sources

What argument is Source 2 trying to make? What tone does it use?

KEY TERM

Convention: a formal meeting of a political party in the US for the purposes of choosing candidates and establishing policies

ACTIVITY

Construct a table identifying the strengths and weaknesses of the president's role.

The main American political parties

There were two major political parties in the USA: The Democrats and the Republicans. All presidents and all but eight members of the Senate and House of Representatives came from one of these two parties in the period from 1945 to 1980. Independent candidates could stand in presidential elections, as Strom Thurmond did in 1948 and George Wallace in 1968, but political success was primarily dependent on being part of one of the two parties.

There are several reasons behind the advantage of being either a Democrat or a Republican. Firstly the US electoral system is a 'winner takes all' system. There are no seats in Congress or re-use of votes for the party or candidate that comes second, and either the Democrats or the Republicans always won. As a result there is no incentive to form or support a party that is popular but cannot win. In addition, the USA has mostly single member districts meaning that each legislative district sends only one member to Congress, in contrast to some countries where multiple-member districts (or constituencies) make it easier for minor parties to succeed because there are more members winning seats in the legislature. Finally, this system was so entrenched by 1945 that there was no incentive to change it. As a result, the Democrats and Republicans could benefit from access to financial resources that smaller parties could never dream of and could also adopt policies that the electorate approved of.

KEY TERM

segregationist: someone who supported the separation of races

Dixiecrat: a portmanteau term (word formed from combining two others) for Southern Democrats, 'Dixie' was a common name for the South

non-intervention: an ideological attitude where the government tries to minimise its involvement in the everyday lives of the population

small government: non-intervention should lead to small government, meaning a limited number of administrators and hence a lower cost in taxation

emancipation: the freeing of slaves by government order and the abolition of slavery

ACTIVITY

Extension

Research the two principal political parties and try to come up with five words that define each one.

A CLOSER LOOK

The Democratic Party

The Modern Democratic Party in the US was founded in 1828 and its traditional stronghold had always been in the South where Democrats and pursued **segregationist** policies. The Administrations of Woodrow Wilson and FDR had created a more liberal and interventionist platform and, in 1945, the party was split between 'New Deal liberals' and **Dixiecrats** who would often vote with Republicans in Congress on matters connected to race.

A CLOSER LOOK

The Republican Party

Founded in 1854 by anti-slavery activists and traditionally strong in the North, Midwest and New England, the Republicans tended to support **non-intervention** and **small government** along with a conservative attitude to civil rights. They were largely despised in the South owing to Lincoln's role in **emancipation** of the slaves but, following the 1964 Civil Rights Act, the Southern states have voted for the Republican party consistently.

Post-war prosperity

The first and perhaps most important impact of the war was to fully restore the American economy. It is often claimed that it was not the '**New Deal**' that pulled the USA out of the Great Depression but rather that it was the war that kick-started real economic recovery. In 1940, unemployment still stood at nearly 8 million. In the war years there was full employment, and even some shortages of workers in certain areas of the economy, especially agriculture.

The 'New Deal' (1933–8)

A series of domestic programs introduced by President Roosevelt to kick-start the economy and provide jobs. The programs were a pro-active response to the Great Depression, and focused on providing jobs for the unemployed and poor, restoring economic activity and reforming the financial system with the government borrowing money to invest in various programmes. In Roosevelt's 12 years in office, the US economy enjoyed an average annual GDP growth of 8.5 per cent, the highest growth rate in the history of any industrialised country.

Fig. 4 *A female worker working on the interior of a B17. By the middle of the Second World War, aircraft were being produced at the rate of 1000 a day, providing new jobs and generating large amounts of money for the US economy*

While the USA had emerged as a prosperous nation, its rivals such as the British Empire, Germany, Japan, France and the Soviet Union had been badly damaged by the war. This gave the USA a huge advantage in trade in the years that immediately followed. Other countries needed goods and raw material to rebuild and the USA was in a position to supply them. The country also benefitted from the repayment of loans it had made to the Allied powers and the reparations it had received in the post-war settlements. These included patents of German inventions such as the soft drink 'Fanta'.

In this climate of economic advantage and undamaged industry, the US economy flourished and the average American benefitted not least because of the growth of the major trades union organisations during the war. The American Federation of Labour (AFL) and, even more so, the Congress of Industrial Organisations (CIO) had defended worker's rights and campaigned for pay rises which were difficult to turn down in the war years.

Write three sentences about the post-war economic situation in the USA, two should be true and one should be false. A partner should then guess the false statement, or, if possible, argue that it is actually true.

The regional, ethnic and social divisions of the USA

Regional Divisions

The huge size of the US made for significant differences in climate, industry and population density. The North East was the traditional political, financial and educational powerhouse incorporating Washington DC, New York and Boston. It saw itself as more sophisticated than the rest of the country and more responsible for the success of the US; 18 of the 32 presidents up to FDR had come from north-eastern states. The eastern states and the northern cities of Chicago and Detroit could also lay claim to the most sophisticated industry, especially the automobile industry in Detroit supplied by the raw material richness of Pennsylvania and the Carolinas.

The Midwest was sparsely populated and lacked major cities, which reduced its influence in national politics. However, the region had huge agricultural riches stretching from Ohio to the Rocky Mountains which produced sufficient wheat, corn and even rice to feed the population and profitably export. The South was seen as more traditional than the rest of the country. Segregation was still embraced and rural communities focused on plantation crops such as cotton, sugar and tobacco which dominated. The South's legacy of slavery and its defeat in the Civil War influenced Southern political attitudes towards the rest of the country. On the border with Mexico were the hot, dry states of Texas, New Mexico, Arizona and Southern California. These states were oil rich and were experiencing a population explosion caused by an influx of Hispanic immigrants and white Americans who were moving away from the colder North; although the population in these areas remained small and their political influence was limited.

> **ACTIVITY**
>
> Label a map of the USA with the key criteria from this section, such as ethnic groups, relative wealth, population, major cities and major industries. What are the implications of such diversity within such a large country?

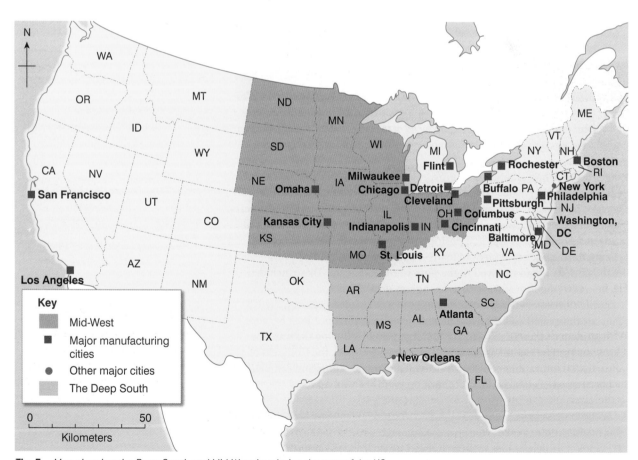

Fig. 5 *Map showing the Deep South and Mid-West in relation the rest of the US*

Finally on the West Coast was the giant state of California, permanently associated with the American Dream and home to major cities like Los Angeles and San Francisco. California saw itself as more relaxed, liberal and glamourous than the traditional East Coast but resented its perceived lack of political influence.

Ethnic divisions

At the base of the Statue of Liberty is a quote from a poem by Emma Lazarus that reads 'Give me your tired, your poor / Your huddled masses yearning to breathe free.' For over 200 years those huddled masses had been arriving to take up residence in the USA from all over the world.

In 1945 white people dominated the US population with over 130 million people according to census reports but many still identified themselves with the country of their ancestors' origins. Irish-Americans, Polish-Americans and Italian-Americans were proud of their heritage, German-Americans always had been proud but their willingness to assert their German origins declined significantly during the war years.

Asian-Americans were a much smaller part of the population with just over 250,000 being registered in the 1940 census and only 320,000 by 1950. The Immigration and Nationality Act of 1952, known as the McCarran-Walter Act, made immigration easier from Asia. As a result, by 1980 there were 3.5 million Asian Americans. Of these, most were Chinese who had come to the country in waves since the mid-nineteenth century to work on the railways and had stayed predominantly in the west of the country. Japanese-Americans made up a smaller group but had suffered greatly from racism since the 1920s. Many Americans were troubled by the way the treatment of Japanese-Americans conflicted with the national myth about all kinds of people becoming Americans in the 'melting pot' of integration, which was so firm a part of the idea of 'American exceptionalism'.

Fig. 6 *Japanese-Americans imprisoned in Tule Lake camp in Northern California, 1944*

African-American was the largest ethnic group after white, amounting to 14 million people, about 10 per cent of the population as a whole. They were concentrated in the South owing to the legacy of slavery and plantation work but had been moving north and west for over 30 years in a demographic shift known as the '**Great Migration**'. Most moved to large industrial cities such as Detroit and Los Angeles, driven by the injustice of '**Jim Crow' Laws**, increased mechanisation of agriculture in the South and the lure of far higher wages in the service sector and industry which had been boosted by the war and Roosevelt's **FEPC**.

ACTIVITY

What questions does this image make you want to ask about the imprisonment of Japanese-Americans in the Second World War?

CROSS-REFERENCE

The position of African-Americans will be explored in detail in Chapter 4.

For more detail on Jim Crow Laws, see the Closer Look in Chapter 4, page 30.

KEY TERM

Great Migration: the movement of over 6 million African-Americans out of the rural South to the urban Northeast, Midwest, and West that occurred between 1910 and 1970

The Fair Employment Practices Commission (FEPC)

Established by an **Executive Order** of Roosevelt, this Commission monitored the hiring practices of any company that held a government contract and required them not to discriminate on the basis of race or religion. The enormous purchasing power of the Federal Government should have been a highly effective way of ensuring desegregation of employers but the FEPC lacked sufficient funding to be truly effective.

KEY TERM

Executive Order: an order issued by the president, with the full force of law, even though Congress approval is not necessary

KEY TERM

social mobility: a term meaning people's ability to move between classes in society, i.e. to go from being poor to becoming wealthier

CROSS-REFERENCE

The GI Bill was a scheme set up in 1944 by President Roosevelt to help returning soldiers. It provided low-cost mortgages, low-interest loans to start a business and funded university tuition. It is explained in more detail on page 21 of Chapter 3.

Jim Crow Laws are featured in a Closer Look in Chapter 4, page 30.

Hispanics were the next largest group constituting nearly 2 million citizens in 1945, mainly concentrated in the South West in the states near the Mexican border. Native Americans made up the smallest and most neglected of the ethnic groups, with barely 350,000 members spread widely between tribes that were often unwilling to work together. Several commentators expected the Native American population to simply die out over the subsequent decades, but were to see their numbers increase.

Social divisions

The period from the Wall Street Crash in 1929 to the end of the Second World War in 1945 had levelled out many of the inequalities in US society that had been prevalent in the early years of the century. The Crash and subsequent Great Depression reduced the wealth of the middle classes and created a culture of 'thrift' and hard work. The very rich survived the Crash and Depression with their wealth largely intact. However, for the rest of society there was little difference in wealth between the managerial professions and 'blue collar' industrial workers whose rights were well protected by Trade Unions, known as 'Organized Labour'. However this relatively equitable situation did not apply if you were part of a minority group. African-Americans and Native Americans were at the bottom of the social and economic hierarchy and were far more likely to live in poverty and lack good quality education, healthcare and housing. They were joined in the ranks of those for whom the American Dream was less attainable by Hispanic-Americans and, to a lesser extent, Asian-Americans. Poor white people could also be found, often living in rural areas such as the Appalachian Mountains and in farming towns in the Midwest and South. In these areas, however, poverty went unseen until the 1960s owing to the growing abundance of cheap food and clothing in the post-war boom.

The war had led to an increase in **social mobility**. Many young men who served in the armed forces left their home districts for the first time and large numbers of jobs were therefore freed up in agriculture for other groups including women and African-Americans. Many women were also employed in the munitions industry and parts of the economy that were previously dominated by men. By 1944, 36 per cent of the workforce was female.

However, the social changes brought about by the war posed a hidden threat; 12 million American soldiers returned from Europe and the Pacific expecting jobs, meaning that women who had been liberated by war work would face exclusion from the workforce. African-American soldiers who had served in segregated units in a war against a racist power returned home to the South to find that **Jim Crow Laws** were still in place and the **GI Bill** was not applied equally to them. By 1946, only one fifth of the 100,000 black men who had applied for the educational fund had succeeded in registering for college.

A perceived threat also existed in terms of communism. As Stalin's armies were encamped in Europe, the fear of communism began to grow and any group or figure suspected of leaning to the left became a source of suspicion. Many Congressmen saw the increasing power of Trade Unions or 'Organized Labor' as the first stirrings of a communist threat to the USA itself and it was to this problem, at home and abroad, that Truman would dedicate much of the rest of his presidency.

EXTRACT 1

The war not only put the United States in a position to dominate much of the world; it created conditions for effective control at home. The unemployment, the economic distress, and the consequent turmoil that had marked the thirties, only partly relieved by 'New Deal' measures, had been pacified, overcome by the greater turmoil of the war. The war brought higher prices for farmers, higher wages, enough prosperity for enough of the population to assure against the rebellions that so threatened the thirties. As Lawrence Wittner writes, 'The war rejuvenated American capitalism.' The biggest gains were in corporate profits, which rose from $6.4 billion in 1940 to $10.8 billion in 1944. But enough went to workers and farmers to make them feel the system was doing well for them.

A People's History of the USA by Howard Zinn (Harper, 2003)

Summary

The US emerged from the war as the most powerful country in the world with an economy whose dominance would inevitably be eroded as other nations recovered. Nevertheless, the head start the US had in terms of wealth, technological excellence, a united population and an established political system made it the envy of the rest of the world. Its strength however was enhanced by the decimation of its rivals in Europe and Asia; only the USA had seen the living standards of its population rise during the war and continue to rise after it. While there were tensions geographically, economically and racially in 1945, the US was clearly the pre-eminent Superpower.

 PRACTICE QUESTION

'The USA was a divided society in 1945.' Explain why you agree or disagree with this view.

 PRACTICE QUESTION

'In 1945 the USA, domestically, was stable and prosperous.' Assess the validity of this view.

ACTIVITY

Evaluating historical extracts

How closely does Extract 1 reflect what you have learnt in this chapter about the legacy of the Second World War?

STUDY TIP

A 'divided society' invites you to consider society as a whole and the divisions within groups; these might include issues of race, wealth, political allegiance, gender and even age.

STUDY TIP

For for/against questions, it can be useful to create a table as a planning tool. You should look at issues like political stability, the extent to which prosperity was evenly distributed, and perhaps compare the state of the US with that of rival countries.

ACTIVITY

Evaluating primary sources

What message is Churchill trying to give to Truman in this extract from the speech?

KEY PROFILE

Winston Churchill (1874–1965) was the British prime minister during the Second World War. He was hugely admired in the US even after his defeat in the 1945 General Election. He followed this defeat with tours of the US, and his ideas about the potential threat from Moscow carried enormous weight given his stature as a statesman. He was profoundly pro-empire and had a tense relationship with Stalin, who did not trust him.

KEY TERM

'Iron Curtain': Churchill's metaphor describing the border between the Soviet-controlled Eastern European states and the states of Western Europe

CROSS-REFERENCE

See Chapter 1, page 5 for details of Roosevelt's 'New Deal'.

SOURCE 1

From Winston Churchill's 'Iron Curtain' speech delivered in Fulton, Missouri, on 5 March 1946. Truman was sitting behind him on the platform while the speech was delivered:

From what I have seen of our Russian friends and Allies during the war, I am convinced that there is nothing they admire so much as strength, and there is nothing for which they have less respect than for weakness, especially military weakness. For that reason the old doctrine of a balance of power is unsound. We cannot afford, if we can help it, to work on narrow margins, offering temptations to a trial of strength. If the Western Democracies stand together in strict adherence to the principles of the United Nations Charter, their influence for furthering those principles will be immense and no one is likely to molest them. If however they become divided or falter in their duty and if these all important years are allowed to slip away then indeed catastrophe may overwhelm us all.

Truman's character and policies

Truman was a plain-Speaking Southerner who was hard-working, just and willing to take responsibility. He was appointed as vice president on 20 January 1945 and within 82 days he succeeded Roosevelt. He barely had chance to formulate an extensive range of policies before holding office. His presidency was characterised by a desire to continue the success of Roosevelt's **'New Deal'** at home whilst easing the transition from the wartime economy. He had a reputation as a staunch anti-communist, partly because this was a politically popular stance but also because he had no experience of international relations and the compromises which are required. This made him far less willing to deal with **Stalin** than his predecessor, and far more inclined to lean on the advice of those he respected such as his Secretary of State **Dean Acheson** and Churchill. As a result his foreign policy aims evolved quickly into a desire to contain Soviet expansion and ensure the security of US allies and trading partners.

KEY PROFILE

Josef Stalin (1878–1953) was born Ioseb Jughashvili in Georgia. He took the name of 'Stalin' (Man of Steel) in 1910 and succeeded Lenin as leader of communist **USSR**. Consolidating his rule through propaganda and brutality Stalin held off the Nazi advance after 1941 and then push on to Berlin. A fearsome negotiator and dictator, his grip on the USSR tightened after 1945 until his death in 1953.

Dean Acheson (1893–1971) was a Yale graduate, lawyer and Democrat. He was an early believer in both the Truman Doctrine and the 'domino theory': the idea that communism spreads from country to country like falling dominos. Truman appointed him Secretary of State in 1949 and he was part of the study group that produced **NSC-68**.

Fig. 1 *Acheson shaped American foreign policy during the Cold War*

NSC-68

NSC-68 (National Security Council Report 68) was a top secret security policy document ordered by Truman and issued in April 1950 after the Soviet Union successfully tested a nuclear device in August 1949. It suggested an increase in defence spending to $50 billion per year from the original $13 billion set for 1950. This was in order to carry out Kennan's policy of containment and it also stressed that the destruction of civilisation was at stake if the US failed to prevent the spread of communism.

USSR/Soviet Union: The USSR (Union of Soviet Socialist Republics) included Russia and several other large states, notably Ukraine, Belarus, Estonia, Latvia and Lithuania in the west and Kazakhstan and others in the south. Russia and its capital Moscow dominated, but this book will use the terms USSR and Soviet Union, rather than Russia

Post-war peace making

The Yalta Conference (4–11 February 1945)

At the Russian resort town of Yalta, before the war was over, loose agreements were made to split Germany into four zones (to be controlled by the US, USSR, France and Britain). This was to allow free elections in liberated countries in Eastern Europe and for the USSR to join the war against Japan after Germany's defeat. Stalin was also invited to join the **United Nations**, which Roosevelt had discussed setting up in a meeting with Churchill in 1941, the aim of which was to preserve world peace. Stalin had a deep distrust of the West and Churchill in particular so Roosevelt took responsibility for the handling of the Soviet leader. Despite these differences, Yalta was hailed as a success by Roosevelt who described it as a start on the road to a world of peace.

The Potsdam Conference (17 July–2 August 1945)

At Potsdam, President Truman was determined to stand up to Stalin and to establish his reputation on the world stage, but the resulting tension between the two meant that little was agreed. Poland's frontiers were discussed but with Soviet troops in place Stalin had to be persuaded into conceding free elections. There were some definite outcomes though, such as German disarmament and reparations and a decision was made to hold trials of leading Nazis. Perhaps of most importance was Truman's failure to alert Stalin to the US's atomic bombs before the end of the conference. Four days later the first bomb was dropped on Hiroshima, partly to prevent the need for the promised Soviet aid in the war against the Japanese, therefore denying them a place at any negotiations over the future of Japan. The nuclear age had become a reality.

The United Nations

The United Nations organisation was born out of a desire to maintain international security and peace. At Yalta in 1945 the structure and voting principles of the new organisation were established. The United Nations officially came into existence on 24 October 1945, when the Charter had been ratified by China, France, the Soviet Union, the UK, the USA and by a majority of other signatories. These named five ensured their influence by making up the permanent membership of the Security Council.

Table 1 *Decisions at Yalta and Potsdam*

Yalta, February 1945	Potsdam, July–August 1945
• Divide Germany into four 'zones', one each for Britain, France, the USA and the USSR. • Put Nazi war criminals on trial. • Set up a Polish Provisional Government of National Unity and hold free elections in Poland. • Help the people of Europe set up democratic and self-governing countries. • Set up a commission to look into reparations. • Stalin also promised that Russia would join the war in the Pacific, in return for occupation zones in North Korea and Manchuria, and would join the United Nations.	• Confirmed the setting up of four 'zones of occupation' in Germany. • The Nazi Party, government and laws were to be eliminated and an effort would be made to de-Nazify German education and institutions. • Confirmed the plan to bring Nazi war criminals to trial. • Confirmed the plan to hold 'free and unfettered elections as soon as possible' in Poland. • Russia was allowed to take reparations from the Soviet 'zone of occupation' and 10 per cent of the industrial equipment of the western zones as reparations. • The US and Britain could take reparations from their zones.

Extension

Consider the two conferences at the end of the Second World War. What do you think mattered most to the USA? Can you identify potential areas of disagreement between the Allies?

Pairs Task

In pairs, consider the arguments for and against Truman's decision to drop atomic bombs on Japan. Do you think it can be justified?

The atmosphere at Yalta in February 1945 was much more agreeable than it was five months later at Potsdam and this is reflected in the scope of the agreements made at the two conferences. By the time the Potsdam Conference took place, tensions had grown and personnel had changed leading to major disagreements over the details of Soviet policy in Eastern Europe, and over Stalin's desire to use reparations to cripple Germany.

Despite his inexperience, Truman was aware at Potsdam that the new atomic bomb had been tested successfully and was ready for use against Japan. The bomb had cost $2 billion to develop and was a result of the fear that Nazi scientists would achieve the technology first. Tests had shown its destructive power but Truman had a difficult decision over whether to use the bomb. On the positive side it could end the war without the need for a bloody land invasion of Japan, it would act as a warning to the Soviet Union about US power, and it would go some way to justifying the huge cost of development. On the negative side the civilian losses would be enormous and no one was clear about the long-term environmental consequences. In addition, US army intelligence suggested that the Japanese were on the verge of surrender.

The Cold War: 'Containment' in Europe

Truman's presidency had therefore begun with a rapid alienation of Stalin that was to have profound consequences for the rest of the world but Stalin had reasons to be paranoid about the West, other than the secret development of the bomb:

- Britain and the US had supported the communists' opponents in the Russian Civil War 1918–22. Churchill even went as far as saying communism should be 'strangled in its cradle'.
- In the Second World War, Stalin had frequently demanded that the Allies relieve pressure on Soviet troops by invading France and thus splitting the German army. Roosevelt and Churchill resisted this pressure until 1944. Stalin felt this was because Churchill and Roosevelt were content for the Nazis to kill communists.

Fig. 3 *Kennan was a diplomat and historian*

George Kennan (1904–2005) was a US diplomat who had experience of both Eastern Europe and the USSR through the 1920s and 30s. In 1946 he wrote a defining analysis for the Secretary of State James Byrnes, which advocated standing up to communism throughout the world. This policy became known as 'containment' and was highly influential until the disastrous outcome of the Vietnam War.

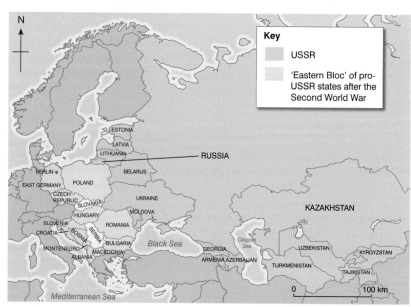

Fig. 2 *Soviet influence in Europe and along its southern border at the end of the Second World War*

Truman Doctrine and Marshall Plan

Truman chose profoundly anti-communist advisers, such as Dean Acheson. He was further influenced, in February 1945, by a telegram from **George Kennan**, a diplomat in Moscow who was seen as the leading expert on the USSR.

SOURCE 2

Extract from Kennan's 'Long Telegram' to US Secretary of State James Byrnes advising on how to handle communist Foreign Policy, February 1945:

Soviet power, unlike that of Hitlerite Germany, is neither schematic nor adventurous. It does not work by fixed plans. It does not take unnecessary risks. It is impervious to the logic of reason, and it is highly sensitive to the logic of force. For this reason it can easily withdraw – and usually does when strong resistance is encountered at any point. Thus, if the adversary has sufficient force and makes clear his readiness to use it, he rarely has to do so. If situations are properly handled there need be no prestige-engaging showdowns. Gauged against the Western world as a whole, Soviets are still by far the weaker force. Thus, their success will really depend on the degree of cohesion, firmness and vigor which the Western world can muster.

 PRACTICE QUESTION

Evaluating primary sources

With reference to Sources 1 and 2 and your understanding of the historical context, which of these two sources is more valuable in explaining Truman's attitude to the Soviet Union?

The implications of Kennan's analysis may have been on Truman's mind when he attended a speech (see Source 1), entitled 'The Sinews of Peace', in his home state of Missouri. While Truman sat directly behind him, Churchill claimed that an 'Iron Curtain' had descended across Europe and counselled Truman 'I do not believe that Soviet Russia desires war. What they desire is the fruits of war and the indefinite expansion of their power and doctrines.'

To Truman these two messages rang loud and clear, as Soviet control over the countries on its western borders increased over the next year. After Soviet troops failed to leave Iran despite Stalin having promised to withdraw them, and Greek communists backed by the USSR had destabilised the Greek monarchy, Truman formulated a policy to put before Congress. On 12 March 1947 he asked for $400 million in military and economic assistance for Greece and Turkey declaring that US policy was to 'support free peoples who are resisting attempted subjugation by armed minorities or by outside pressures'. This policy, implicitly referring to communist forces, was viewed throughout the world as a commitment to oppose the spread of communism. The **Truman Doctrine**, backed by the increase in defence spending promised in NSC-68, was to inform US Foreign policy for the next 40 years.

The Truman Doctrine was a military commitment to defend any country that was faced with takeover by an armed minority, although it did not specify that this minority should be communist. Meanwhile after touring Europe, new Secretary of State George Marshall convinced Truman to also offer financial aid to help the countries rebuild their shattered economies. Congress was initially reluctant but after the Communist Party seized power in Czechoslovakia in February 1948, the **Marshall Plan** was approved and offered to all European countries including those who were communist.

Fig. 4 *The city of Berlin in 1945 shows the extent of rebuilding required throughout much of Europe at the end of the Second World War*

Officially known as the European Recovery Program (ERP), the plan gave $17 billion ($160 billion in 2014 terms) in support to help rebuild the European economies with the bulk of the money going to the UK, France, Germany and Italy for four years from April 1948. These four years saw the fastest period of growth in European history with industrial production rising 35 per cent,

Fig. 5 *Marshall Plan aid to Europe, 1948–52 in relative accounts*

austerity measures being relaxed and the European market for American goods being restored. Perhaps more importantly it established the USA as the protector of Europe whilst further alienating Stalin who wanted to ensure that Germany should never be able to recover the economic and military strength that had seen it invade Russia twice between 1914 and 1941. Together the Truman Doctrine and Marshall Plan helped to establish the parameters of the **Cold War**, but the first military test, and the first example of the **brinksmanship** that was to be a feature of the Cold War, was to come in Berlin.

Berlin airlift

In early 1948 the USA, Britain and France embarked on discussions with a view to creating a West German government by combining their zones and reforming the currency to create a new common unit, the *Deutschmark*. Within the divided city of Berlin, people could cross from East to West easily and the presence of wealthy West Berliners in communist East Berlin eroded Stalin's control. On 25 March 1948 Stalin took the opportunity to cut the Allies out of the Eastern bloc by blockading Berlin citing 'technical difficulties' as a reason for shutting down routes into the city.

Stalin was able to blockade Berlin without breaking international laws on a technicality; there was nothing written down promising surface access to Berlin in any post-war agreement. Any attempt to enter Berlin on the ground would involve US troops invading East Germany and Stalin was sure Truman would not risk this. Truman responded with an act of political brinksmanship; he asserted not only his commitment to the Doctrine he had espoused the previous year, but also gave an overwhelming demonstration of American wealth and military capacity by taking the decision to supply the needs of a city of 2.5 million people entirely by air. With the assistance of the RAF, he ordered 1.5 million tons of supplies, in 275,000 flights, to be flown into Berlin over the next 324 days.

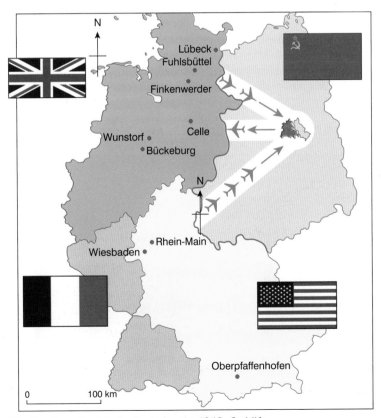

Fig. 6 *Air routes into Berlin during the 1948–9 airlift*

NATO

The North Atlantic Treaty Organisation signed a collective defence agreement in April 1949 which pledged that an attack on one of its members constituted an attack on all. The presence of the US within NATO, along with Belgium, the Netherlands, Luxembourg, France, the UK, Canada, Portugal, Italy, Norway, Denmark and Iceland effectively meant that the USSR could not risk attacking a Western European country without declaring war on the US.

Use the 'Diamond Nine' template below to prioritise the following factors in terms of their importance to the policy of containment in Europe: NATO; the Berlin Blockade; the Truman Doctrine; the Marshall Plan; the Greek Civil War; the communist takeover in Czechoslovakia; the Iron Curtain speech; the Potsdam Conference; Kennan's long telegram.

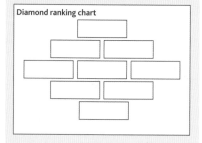

Diamond ranking chart

Fig. 7   MacArthur was one of only five men ever to become General of the Army

Douglas MacArthur (1880–1964) was a five star US General, the top rank in the armed forces, who fought in the First World War, and commanded the US Army in the Far East in the Second World War where he earned the Medal of Honor, as his father had before him. MacArthur accepted the official Japanese surrender on the USS *Missouri* on 2 September 1945 and then oversaw the occupation of Japan from 1945 to 1951. He was in command of UN forces in Korea until removed from the position by Truman in 1951 despite his status as an American hero.

It was clear that the only way Stalin could stop the airlift was by attacking the planes directly, so on 12 May 1949 Stalin lifted the blockade. This was Truman's finest hour in foreign policy. Not only had he comprehensively won both the moral and the propaganda victory but he had also succeeded in justifying the creation of **NATO** and the deployment of B-29 bombers (which were capable of carrying a nuclear device) in Europe. He had also entrenched the Truman Doctrine as the basis of US foreign policy and seen the citizens of Berlin, who four short years previously had been vilified as Nazis, reinvented as brave heroes defying the 'tyrannous' Soviet leader through their resilience during the blockade.

The Cold War: 'Containment' in Asia

The occupation of Japan

In a radio broadcast on 14 August 1945, five days after the second atomic bomb had been dropped on Hiroshima, Emperor Hirohito announced the Japanese surrender. 350,000 US troops poured into Japan and **General Douglas MacArthur** was given dictatorial powers to transform the country from a militaristic state into a modern democracy in the image of the USA but without the economic power. Between 1949 and 1952:

- communists were banned from government posts
- Article 9 of the new constitution renounced war as an instrument of policy
- a democratically elected government was constituted with votes for women.

However, policy towards Japan changed after **Mao Zedong's** victory in China in 1949 (see below) and a stronger and more economically powerful Japan became desirable as a balance to China and to make up for the loss of Chinese markets. In addition, Truman feared that a poor Japan would be easy prey for communism which then might spread through the country. When the Korean War broke out in 1950, Japan's utility as a base for US operations led to substantial military spending which boosted the Japanese economy.

Though resentment remained both amongst the Japanese in the areas near the bases and amongst the American allies in Asia that had suffered the brutal occupation of the Japanese, the occupation ended in 1952 and within a decade the country had re-industrialised and was competing with the US in many industries.

The establishment of communist China

Mao Zedong (1893–1976) was born into a relatively wealthy peasant farming family. He converted to Marxism-Leninism, and went on to found the Communist Party of China, which was based on 'Mao Zedong Thought'. Mao proclaimed a communist China, the People's Republic of China, on 1 October 1949. He then ruled for 27 years.

Fig. 8   Mao is a controversial historical figure, viewed by some as a dictator

An invasion of China by Japan in 1931 had seen communist and nationalist factions working together to repel the invader. However after working together to defeat the Japanese, the leaders of the Nationalist and Communist parties, **Jiang Jieshi** and Mao Zedong, met for talks on the formation of a post-war government. The truce they came to was fragile, and despite the efforts of General George Marshall to broker an agreement, by 1946 the two sides were fighting a civil war.

In the USA, Truman was unconvinced of the strategic importance of supporting the Nationalists given their inability to create a stable China in the decades prior to the Second World War, but he was keenly aware of the potential political impact of allowing the 'loss' of China to communism. Because of this, limited military and financial aid to the Nationalists continued but it was insufficient. Jiang Jieshi and the Nationalists fled to Taiwan taking much of the gold supply with them and on 1 October 1949 Mao Zedong proclaimed the establishment of the People's Republic of China (PRC). Both the largest country on earth and the most populous had become communist.

Involvement in Indo-China

Elsewhere in Southeast Asia Truman's policies were focused on containing the rise of communism in the former French Empire. Prior to the Second World War, the area which is Laos, Cambodia and Vietnam today was part of the French Empire. During the war the Japanese had occupied it and found themselves fighting a **guerrilla** force organised by **Ho Chi Minh** who had formed the Indo-Chinese Communist Party in 1930 to fight for independence from France.

After the Japanese were defeated, Ho Chi Minh expected US support for Vietnamese independence given the United States' professed commitment to **self-determination**. Instead, Truman gave support to the French to the extent of covering 78 per cent of the costs of French involvement in Indo-China. With the loss of China to communism fresh in his memory, Truman saw the situation in Vietnam as part of the Cold War, believing Ho Chi Minh to be a puppet of Stalin. In a memo to Dean Acheson, John Ohley, a senior Defense Department official, predicted that 'We are gradually increasing our stake in the outcome of the struggle [between the Vietminh and the French] we are dangerously close to the point of being so deeply committed that we may find ourselves completely committed to direct intervention. These situations, unfortunately, have a way of snowballing.'

War in Korea

Extract from a letter by General MacArthur to Joseph William Martin, Jr, the Republican leader in the House of Representatives, read aloud on the floor of the House on 5 April 1951:

It seems strangely difficult for some to realize that here in Asia is where the communist conspirators have elected to make their play for global conquest, and that we have joined the issue thus raised on the battlefield; that here we fight Europe's war with arms while the diplomats there still fight it with words; that if we lose the war to communism in Asia the fall of Europe is inevitable, win it and Europe most probably would avoid war and yet preserve freedom. As you pointed out, we must win. There is no substitute for victory.

As happened in Germany, after the Second World War Korea was divided between the powers that helped liberate it: the Soviet Union from the

Jiang Jieshi (1887–1975) established the Republic of China on Taiwan after being defeated by Mao's Communist Party. The lack of support from Truman to retake China disappointed Jiang but he cultivated good relations with the US and Japan as a defence against China's attempt to retake Taiwan. He ruled as a dictator using accusations of anti-communism to justify the arrest of thousands of citizens in the period 1949–87, known as the 'White Terror'.

See Chapter 14, page 114 for a map of Indo-China (during the Vietnam war).

guerrilla: a form of warfare involving irregular fighting, especially against a larger force

self-determination: the idea of letting the people of a nation decide on their own government

Ho Chi Minh (1890–1969) travelled extensively in the USA and UK before moving to Paris where he campaigned for Vietnamese independence during negotiations at Versailles in 1919. Here he joined the Communist Party before moving to Moscow for training then on to China. Arriving back in Vietnam in 1941 he led a 10,000 strong guerrilla force (the Vietminh) in their fight for independence from France, then against the Japanese in the Second World War and finally against the Americans.

Thinking point

Consider why the fall of China to communism was such a damaging blow to Truman's foreign policy.

Evaluating primary sources

List the arguments given in Source 3 by General MacArthur for the need to wholeheartedly pursue victory in Korea.

North and the US from the South along an arbitrary line known as the 38th Parallel. Efforts to unify the country through the UN were blocked by the USSR so the US held elections in the South leading to the election of Syngman Rhee. The Soviets installed Kim Il Sung in the North in 1948 where he ruled until 1994.

US troops were removed so when 100,000 North Korea troops invaded the South on 25 June 1950 they faced little opposition. Truman felt he had to act, not only to contain communism but to offset criticism that he was 'losing' Asia. To avoid debate with an uncooperative Congress Truman took the issue to the UN and a US-led UN intervention began in July 1950.

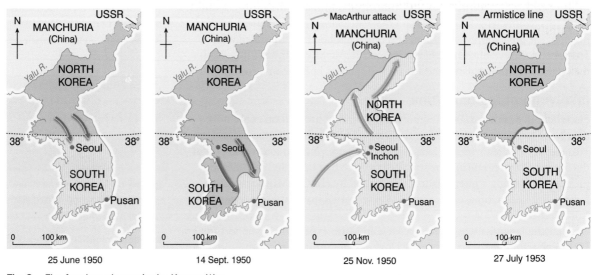

25 June 1950   14 Sept. 1950   25 Nov. 1950   27 July 1953

Fig. 9   *The four key phases in the Korean War*

The map above illustrates the futility of the war, MacArthur's initial success with an invasion at Inchon led to an overstretch that alarmed the Chinese whose substantial aid resulted in the war being fought to a stalemate close to the 38th Parallel. In the process Mao's eldest son Mao Anying was killed. By 1951 MacArthur was calling for Truman to use the atomic bomb and was complaining about his handling of the war, leaving Truman with no choice but to remove him from command.

Korea showed Truman was willing to use American military force to back up the policies of containment but in many ways it was a futile war costing 14 per cent of US GDP in its final year and resulting in 138,000 US dead and injured. Truman's decision not to stand for re-election in 1952 was partly due to the damage the stalemate in Korea had done to his standing in the opinion polls. His approval rating was only 22 per cent as the final year of his presidency began. However, Truman's actions in Korea were put into perspective by the difficulties the US was to face in Vietnam a little over a decade later.

This is a question that will lean heavily on your 'understanding of the historical context'. You will need to consider the provenance of each of the sources and the intention behind each of the texts when they were created. What influence did the authors of the sources have over Truman? You should consider their standing and role at the time.

A LEVEL PRACTICE QUESTION

Evaluating primary sources

With reference to Sources 1, 2 and 3 and your understanding of the historical context, assess the value of these three sources to an historian studying the US policy of containment.

Summary

For a president with limited foreign policy experience Truman perhaps faced more significant problems than any of his peers before or since. He relied heavily on his advisors who have become known as 'the wise men', of whom Acheson and Kennan were key. Truman also leaned on the experience and diplomatic skill of General George Marshall, a man described by Truman himself as 'the greatest American'. However not all of the decisions Truman made were right, and the right decisions were not necessarily made for the right reasons. Many of the problems encountered in US foreign policy in the subsequent six decades can be traced back to Truman.

ACTIVITY

Summary

Copy and complete the following table to explain whether you feel Truman succeeded or failed in his foreign policies.

	Were Truman's policies successes or failures?	
	Success	Failure
Europe		
Berlin		
Japan		
China		
Indo-China (Vietnam)		
Korea		

 PRACTICE QUESTION

To what extent was Truman's foreign policy in the years 1945 to 1952 a disastrous failure?

STUDY TIP

This question makes a significant assertion. A balanced answer is required that assesses the successes and failures of Truman's foreign policy both at the time and in the light of subsequent events and the change in attitude of subsequent leaders.

3 Truman and post-war reconstruction

LEARNING OBJECTIVES
In this chapter you will learn about:

- how effectively Truman dealt with the American economy
- the political divisions Truman faced
- the domestic problems Truman faced
- anti-communism and the rise of McCarthyism.

ACTIVITY

Evaluating primary sources

What can you infer from the statement by Keynes in Source 1 about how leaders approach the running of national economies?

KEY PROFILE

Fig. 1   Keynes was a key figure in economics

John Maynard Keynes (1883–1946) was a British economist. During his lifetime he produced some of the most enduring theories about economics and he is often held up as one of the two most influential economists of the twentieth century. Keynes led the British delegation in the 1944 negotiations that established the Bretton-Woods system.

CROSS-REFERENCE

See Chapter 1, pages 4–5 for more on the US economy after the Second World War.

The economy

SOURCE 1

Adapted from John Maynard Keynes' 1936 book *The General Theory of Employment, Interest and Money*:

The ideas of economists and political philosophers, both when they are right and when they are wrong, are more powerful than is commonly understood. Indeed the world is ruled by little else. Practical men, who believe themselves to be quite immune from any intellectual influence, are usually the slaves of some long dead economist. Madmen in authority, who hear voices in the air, are taking their frenzy from some academic scribbler of a few years back. I am sure that the power of the established companies and government is vastly exaggerated compared with the gradual encroachment of ideas.

One of economist John Keynes' theories explained how to encourage a national economy out of recession or depression by using government financial muscle to borrow money and spend it on large scale projects that stimulated industry and created jobs. This philosophy was employed by FDR in his 'New Deal'. Truman was more sceptical of Keynesian economics but he wanted to continue with the liberal social programmes that had been so popular before the war. Massed against him, in his pursuit of a domestic programme which could be compared to that of his predecessor, was an economy set for decline and a country and population that had been remade by the war.

The USA and the global economy

The USA was the single dominant force in the global economy at the end of the Second World War. However, to retain this pre-eminence it needed to return to peaceful trading with partners in Europe and the Pacific, and this was one of the factors that influenced Truman's post-war thinking when it came to foreign affairs. Growing economies in Europe and Asia would also allow Britain, France and China to pay back their substantial war loans from the US; $31 billion for Britain, $3.2 billion for France and $1.6 billion for China.

A CLOSER LOOK

The Bretton-Woods System

On 1 July 1944 representatives of the 44 Allied nations met in Bretton Woods, New Hampshire, USA to design a system of monetary management for the post-war world. The discussions led to the establishment of the International Monetary Fund (IMF) and the World Bank as well as obliging countries to adopt a monetary policy that tied their currencies to the US dollar. The system also promised that the IMF would step in to help countries in financial trouble.

However, measures taken towards the end of the war in preparation for a return to global trade had given the US a key advantage. The introduction of the Bretton-Woods System and with it the **IMF and World Bank**, both of which were headquartered in New York, promised that the new world economic order would be based around an American conception of

capitalism and trade. Truman merely needed to keep things ticking over for the first few post-war years and the pick up in the world economy should inevitably have followed.

The US economy under Truman

Truman's ambitions for his presidency were mainly domestic and it is ironic that he has become most associated with international problems. Principal amongst the domestic ambitions were a desire to continue with the liberal legislative programme of the 'New Deal' and to smooth the transition of the economy from wartime to peacetime. Truman called this policy the **'Fair Deal'** and it was designed to address the problems of poverty that had carried over from the Great Depression, such as inequalities in education and healthcare, along with the problems of unemployment. With 12 million former soldiers about to rejoin the job market, cushioning the inevitable problems they would face was imperative. Truman took the decision to **demobilise** nine million of them in 1945 but keep an army of three million given the dangerous state of the global political situation. In 1946 the army was further reduced in size to 1.5 million men. This gradual reintroduction to the civilian workforce prompted some short-term unemployment but nothing on the scale of the Great Depression, indeed the Truman presidency never saw unemployment run higher than 5 per cent.

Businesses also faced a transition from the demands of wartime production to those of peacetime. However, the confidence from having gained victory and the influx of men returning home led to a consumer boom which produced an **inflation** rate of 25 per cent in 1945 to 1946. This contributed in no small part to the Democrats' defeat in the 1946 midterm congressional elections. Truman proposed a Price Control Bill in 1946 but it was watered down by a Congress convinced the president was too weak to push it through. Later that year, Truman suggested the creation of a Council of Economic Advisors (CEA) to advise the government and this did get approval along with an Employment Act which committed the country to 'maximum employment'.

The post-war economy was also helped by the demand for housing and Roosevelt's 1944 GI Bill. The latter provided government help in getting a 90 per cent mortgage, along with a guaranteed 52 weeks of unemployment benefit and loans for college education. In the subsequent decade, the government invested $20 billion through the GI Bill, stimulating several key sectors of the economy and providing a golden age for social mobility. In addition the **'baby boom'** of 1945 to 1950 created a huge new market for goods and services as well as stimulating housing. The housing boom led to the development of suburban housing sites such as Levittown in Long Island, New York, where workers could have far larger houses for less money than in the city and still get to work thanks to booming car sales which rose from 2.1 million in 1946 to 7.9 million by 1955.

By the time Truman had been re-elected in 1948 the economy was improving and demand was growing. This was helped too by the maturing of the $185 billion of war bonds purchased by US citizens since 1941, injecting money into the economy which could fuel the consumer boom. By 1952 Truman could boast in an economic report to Congress that total output had increased by almost 90 per cent on 1939 levels, that industrial output had approximately doubled, agricultural output had increased by a third and that business investment had risen from an annual rate of $14 billion to almost $38 billion. Employment had also risen despite the demobilisation of the army, growing from 46 million to an average of about 61 million during the same period. Most impressively, the per capita (per person) income of Americans had risen about 40 per cent.

KEY TERM

IMF and World Bank: these two organisations, headquartered in New York, were set up after the Second World War to provide assistance to countries who faced an economic crisis

capitalism: an economic and political system in which trade and industry are controlled by private organisations who aim to make a profit, rather than by the government

CROSS-REFERENCE

Truman's Fair Deal policies (see pages 24–25 in this chapter) also had an impact on the US economy.

For a recap on international problems faced by Truman, revisit Chapter 2.

KEY TERM

demobilise: to take troops out of active service, usually after a war

inflation: the rise in the price of goods or services from one year to the next

KEY TERM

baby boom: a term that refers to the rapid rise in the population that followed the Second World War in the US; there were nearly a million live births per year more in 1947 than in 1945

Pairs task

In pairs hold a timed three minute debate with one student arguing that Truman's economic policies were successful and the other arguing that his policies were a failure.

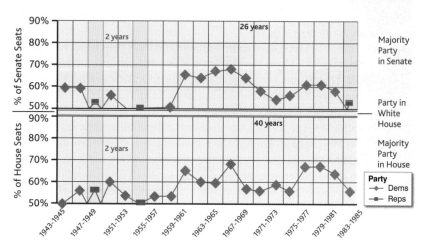

Fig. 2 *Control of Congress in the years 1944 to 1982; note how rare Republican control was*

CROSS-REFERENCE

Eisenhower later became president and his time in office is covered in Chapters 5–8. See page 37 in Chapter 5 for his Key Profile.

KEY TERM

States' rights: the rights granted to the Governor and legislature of individual states to make decisions on matters such as education, sales taxes or the use of the death penalty

campaign: the process of persuading people to vote for a party or individual

political gridlock: when opposite parties control the White House and Congress it often makes bills very difficult to pass because of the 'checks and balances' the US Constitution provides to prevent any branch of government becoming too strong. This can mean both sides blame each other for the failure to make progress on key issues

Political divisions

Truman's economic problems led to political trouble in the midterm congressional elections of 1946. Republicans highlighted the problems of reconversion from a war economy with slogans that hit home, particularly 'To Err is Truman', and won control of both the House and Senate. With opposition from Congress came the likelihood of political gridlock leading up to the presidential election of 1948.

The election, when it came, was the greatest upset in US political history and a triumph for the underdog Truman who had seemed beaten throughout. Indeed Truman had proposed that **General Dwight Eisenhower** be invited to become the Democratic presidential nominee with himself as the vice president (Eisenhower declined both the Democrats and the Republicans that year). The Democrats seemed in disarray with former Vice President Henry Wallace breaking away to form a Progressive Party and Democrat Senator for South Carolina, Strom Thurmond, standing as an independent candidate on a platform of **States' rights.** Truman's opponent, the Republican Governor of New York, Thomas Dewey, ran a cautious and aloof **campaign**, while Truman toured the country remorselessly railing at the **political gridlock** resulting from the Republican controlled Congress and earning the nickname 'Give 'em hell, Harry.'

Truman's hard earned victory coincided with the Democrats regaining control of both Houses of Congress and, with an improving economy and a hard-line stance against the Soviet Union, Truman was able to complete his next term with more domestic cooperation. Constitutionally, Truman could have stood in 1952 as the 22nd Amendment, limiting presidents to two terms, had only been passed in 1951 and did not apply to him. However his lack of popularity prompted him to stand aside in favour of Adlai Stevenson who was unable to repeat the shock result of 1948 in 1952.

Fig. 3 *Truman celebrates victory with a copy of the Chicago Tribune that had gone to press early believing he had lost*

 PRACTICE QUESTION

'Truman's victory in the 1948 presidential election was the result of Republican failings.' Explain why you agree or disagree with this view.

Domestic problems

The years following the Second World War led to a spike in the birth rate which had a significant effect on society. Women increasingly had to stay at home to look after children and there was increased demand for housing in the suburbs and increased pressure on the school system. At the same time, demand from the government for war materials had ended and so jobs were threatened. Fortunately for Truman the US economy adapted to this to some extent and factories changed what they produced to serve a new market for consumer goods such as clothing, cars and household appliances. However, unemployment did rise to 5 per cent by 1950 and those worst affected were minority groups and women who all received little protection or encouragement from the Trade Unions, who found themselves increasingly under pressure for their left-wing sympathies.

The role of organised labour

SOURCE 2

From a speech by John L Lewis in 1937 entitled *Labor and the Nation.* Lewis was addressing accusations that the Trade Union movement was a form of communism:

Unionization, as opposed to communism, presupposes the relation of employment; it is based upon the wage system and it recognizes fully and unreservedly the institution of private property and the right to investment profit. It is based upon the fuller development of collective bargaining, the wider expansion of the labor movement, the increased influence of labor in

ACTIVITY

The 1948 presidential election saw four parties compete and gain over one million votes each. Why didn't this lead to multi-party democracy in the US?

STUDY TIP

This requires a balanced answer that deals with the issue of Republican failings on the one hand and on the other covers other reasons why Truman won. When looking at reasons for success in presidential elections the health of the economy is always key. Consider also the other factors that contribute to success, criticisms of opponents' failings or mistakes and the issue of how united the party is.

CROSS-REFERENCE

For more detail on the baby boom read Chapter 6, page 48

ACTIVITY

Class debate

The change in demographics created by the 'baby boom' also led to huge social change. What implications, other than those mentioned in the paragraph to the left, might an increased birth rate have had, both positive and negative?

ACTIVITY

Evaluating primary sources

What message is Lewis trying to give in this source? Why might he feel he needs to give this message?

Fig. 4 *Lewis was a constant thorn in the side of the Truman Administration*

John L Lewis (1880–1969) was a leader of Miners' trade unions who founded the Congress of Industrial Organisations (CIO) in 1938. He supported FDR and the 'New Deal' and his CIO was open to African-Americans. After the Second World War he led mine workers' strikes in 1945, 1946, 1948 and 1949–50.

KEY TERM

State of the Union Address: a speech presented annually in January by the President of the United States to a joint session of the United States Congress (Senate and House of Representatives). The speech outlines the challenges facing the US (the Union) and the legislation the president would like to introduce

lynching: a form of trial and execution carried out by an unofficial group or mob usually involving death by hanging

CROSS-REFERENCE

See Chapter 4 for more information on African-Americans in northern cities.

our national councils, that the perpetuity of our democratic institutions must largely depend. The organized workers of America, free in their industrial life, conscious partners in production, secure in their homes and enjoying a decent standard of living, will prove the finest bulwark against the intrusion of alien doctrines of government.

A traditional supporter of the Democrat Party, organised labour, the US equivalent of Trade Unions, gave Truman the most headaches. In August 1945, Truman announced that he would maintain price controls but that unions could pursue higher wages. Beginning in late 1945 and lasting throughout 1946, a wave of strikes hit the steel, coal, auto and railroad industries, debilitating key sectors of the American economy and stifling production of certain consumer goods. Truman remained steadfast in the face of labour's demands. To end the strikes and restore industrial peace, he recommended compulsory mediation and arbitration, he warned that the government would draft striking railroad workers, and even took a union, the United Mine Workers, to court. The unions backed down and returned to work, for the most part with healthy gains. But by taking such a hard line, Truman had damaged his relationship with an important element of his party's support base.

The 'Fair Deal'

In September 1945, Truman presented to Congress a 21-point programme incorporating economic and social measures to tackle domestic problems that he wished to see the legislature draft and pass. However owing to the conservative majority in Congress few of the measures were ever passed. As a result, in his **State of the Union Address** in January 1949, buoyed by the legitimacy his victory in the previous year's election gave him, Truman stated that every part of the population had the right to expect a fair deal from the government and introduced a revised series of measures that became known as 'The Fair Deal'. These measures included:

- federal aid to education
- tax cuts for low-income earners and an increase in public housing
- the abolition of poll taxes
- anti-**lynching** laws
- a permanent FEPC (see Chapter 4)
- the establishment of a new Department of Welfare
- an increase in the minimum wage from 40 to 75 cents an hour
- national health insurance and expanded Social Security coverage.

Truman's programme of social change lacked the fierce economic necessity that had allowed Roosevelt to push through the 'New Deal' and so it was never implemented in a wholesale fashion. Nevertheless, substantial social and economic progress did take place under Truman. By 1953, 62 million Americans were employed, an increase of 11 million under Truman and unemployment was virtually zero. Income from agriculture, share dividends and businesses were at all-time highs, and no bank had failed in nearly nine years. The minimum wage had also been increased and Social Security benefits had been doubled, whilst 7.8 million veterans had taken advantage of the GI Bill. Millions of new homes had been financed through government programs, and a start had been made in clearing inner city slums (ironically this made housing worse for **African-Americans in the northern cities** as the cleared slums were not replaced with affordable housing quickly enough, causing rents to skyrocket). Poverty had also been reduced, with one estimate suggesting that the percentage of Americans living in poverty had fallen from 33 per cent of the population in 1949 to 28 per cent by 1952.

Yet Truman was profoundly unpopular with the electorate for much of his second term with a Gallup poll in February 1952 giving him only a 22 per cent approval rate. Part of this was the result of the prolonged war in Korea which had not provided a quick victory and had led to inflation, but the Truman Administration was also affected by scandal. When dozens of **IRS** officials were forced to resign in 1951 over alleged corruption it was easy to make links with a president who was derisively known as the 'Senator from Pendergast' thanks to his relationship with an influential Missouri politician, Tom Pendergast, earlier in his career.

The rise of McCarthyism

In January 1950 **Joseph McCarthy** was a little-known Senator from Wisconsin, the following month he was catapulted to the forefront of American politics after claiming to have a list of 205 Communist Party members who were working in the US State Department. McCarthy's accusations tapped into a widespread fear of communism that had existed in the US since the Russian Revolution of 1917. This fear can, and has been attributed to a number of factors:

- economic fear of the consequences of communism amongst the rich
- military fear of the size and aggression of the Soviet and Chinese armies following the creation of the 'Iron Curtain' and the 'fall' of China to communism
- the rise of Organised Labour during the Second World War
- the successful Soviet nuclear test in August 1949
- the political value to ambitious politicians of exaggerating a threat (Richard Nixon first came to national attention as a member of **HUAC** in 1948 after pursuing Alger Hiss)
- the psychological need for the US to have an enemy in order to define itself against.

ACTIVITY

Using a stopwatch, try and talk to a partner for one minute on the subject of the 'Fair Deal'. If you hesitate, your partner should take over.

KEY TERM

IRS: the Internal Revenue Service is the US government agency responsible for tax collection and tax law enforcement

KEY TERM

HUAC: the House Un-American Activities Committee was formed in 1938 to monitor extremist groups

Fig. 5 *Joseph McCarthy making the case for the proliferation of communism in the USA*

KEY PROFILE

Joseph McCarthy (1908–57) became Senator for Wisconsin in 1947, after serving in the Second World War, before his accusations about widespread communist conspiracies catapulted him to national attention. His efforts led to the coining of the word **'McCarthyism'** as a term for making broad accusations of treason without evidence. McCarthy never proved any of his accusations and was eventually censured by the Senate in 1954 before dying of alcoholism in 1957.

Evaluating primary sources

1. What do you think McCarthy means by a 'great conspiracy'?
2. How do the events covered in the previous chapter agree or disagree with this idea?
3. Why did McCarthy refer to his campaign in this way?

KEY TERM

appeasement: giving in to the demands of others as a way of stopping them becoming more aggressive

SOURCE 3

Adapted from a speech delivered by Senator Joseph McCarthy to the Senate on 14 June, 1951. McCarthy described his campaign by saying 'McCarthyism is Americanism with its sleeves rolled':

Six years ago this summer America stood at what Churchill described as the 'highest pinnacle of her power and fame'. What do we find in the summer of 1951? The influence of Moscow runs to upwards of 900 millions of people – a good 40 per cent of all men living. During all this time the Administration preaches a gospel of fear and Acheson and Marshall expound a foreign policy in the East based upon cowardly, whimpering **appeasement**. How can we account for our present situation unless we believe that men high in this Government are concerting to deliver us to disaster? This must be the product of a great conspiracy, a conspiracy on a scale so immense as to dwarf any previous such venture in the history of man. It cannot be attributed to incompetence.

Anti-communism permeated all aspects of American society despite the fact that the Communist Party of the United States had less than 80,000 members. The Truman Doctrine and Marshall Plan had established the USSR as the new enemy and HUAC began investigating Hollywood actors and writers. Comic book heroes like Captain America, created in 1941, changed their enemies from Nazis to communists in storylines with titles like 'Captain America, Commie Smasher!'. Perhaps more worryingly there was a string of cases of arrests of officials and scientists who were alleged to have divulged nuclear secrets to the Soviets including **Alger Hiss** and **Ethel and Julius Rosenberg**.

A CLOSER LOOK

Hiss and the Rosenbergs

Alger Hiss, a high-ranking State Department official was convicted of perjury in 1948 after being accused of passing secrets to the USSR; a young Richard Nixon played a key role in the case. Ethel and Julius Rosenberg had worked on the atomic bomb project during the war and were executed in 1953 for passing nuclear secrets to the Russians.

STUDY TIP

In AS source questions it is important to look carefully at both the provenance and the content of the source as well as understanding the context in which they were written. Look first at the dates and consider what else was happening nationally and internationally at the time. Then look at the audience hearing these speeches; where were they and why were they being addressed? Finally, consider the agenda of the speakers; would they have any reason to alter the truth for their own purposes?

McCarthy exploited the public fear of nuclear war and was encouraged by a Republican party desperate for any issue that could weaken the Democrats' 20-year grip on the presidency. Although McCarthy had an erratic personal history, his message struck a chord with an America that was stuttering in Korea and whose opinion of former ally 'Uncle Joe' Stalin had been recast in order to justify measures like the Truman Doctrine, Marshall Plan and Executive Order 9835 which established Federal loyalty boards designed to root out communist sympathisers in the federal government.

 PRACTICE QUESTION

Evaluating primary sources

With reference to Sources 2 and 3 and your own understanding of the historical context, which of these two sources is more valuable in explaining attitudes towards communism in the USA?

Truman's attempts to veto a 1952 Internal Security Act which allowed communists to be denied passports saw only 58 members of Congress support him as the Truman Administration entered the '**lame duck**' phase of its time in power. McCarthy seemed to wield more power than the most powerful man in the world with few willing to confront him for fear of being accused themselves.

Summary

Truman kept a plaque on his desk which read 'The buck stops here' and, for all of his failings and inadequacies, he was a man who took responsibility. His domestic agenda may have been affected by political manoeuvrings, the development of the Cold War, and the inevitable initial decline in the post-war economy, but Truman also managed to establish valuable precedents in civil rights, social welfare and union relations as well as foreign policy.

 PRACTICE QUESTION

'Truman failed to address the domestic problems of the USA because he was too preoccupied by foreign affairs.' Explain why you agree or disagree with this view.

KEY TERM

'lame duck' presidency: as a president approaches the end of their second term (or if they have announced they won't seek re-election) their ability to carry out policy is often hampered by a lack of co-operation from others or outright dissent

ACTIVITY

Look back over this chapter at the domestic measures Truman tried to introduce. Draw up a table that analyses where he succeeded and where he failed.

STUDY TIP

This question makes an assertion which you can challenge. Did Truman in fact 'fail to address the domestic problems of the USA'? You might also like to challenge the idea that he was 'preoccupied' by foreign affairs. It is important to look at Truman's domestic problems in the economy and society, particularly divisions and inequality in society, and balance your answer.

4 African-Americans in the North and South

ACTIVITY

Evaluating primary sources

Look carefully at the wording of Source 1. Why was desegregation of the army seen as highly important in the quest for African-American civil rights? Are there any problems with the wording?

KEY TERM

de jure: a Latin term meaning 'in law/ legally'

SOURCE 1

Extract from Executive Order 9981, 26 July 1948, in which Truman declared the abolition *de jure* of the practice of segregation in the US armed forces:

By virtue of the authority vested in me as President of the United States, by the Constitution and the statutes of the United States, and as Commander in Chief of the armed services, it is hereby ordered as follows:

1. It is hereby declared to be the policy of the president that there shall be equality of treatment and opportunity for all persons in the armed services without regard to race, color, religion or national origin. This policy shall be put into effect as rapidly as possible, having due regard to the time required to effectuate any necessary changes without impairing efficiency or morale.

2. There shall be created in the National Military Establishment an advisory committee to be known as the President's Committee on Equality of Treatment and Opportunity in the Armed Services, which shall be composed of seven members to be designated by the president.

The impact of the Second World War

For many black Americans, both at home and in the army, the irony of their opponents in the Second World War was painfully clear. A brutal, ideological enemy committed to ideas of racial superiority was something many were used to in the small towns of the South.

The experience of soldiers

Before 1940 army units had been segregated and during the Second World War African-American soldiers largely served in logistics rather than on the frontline. The Red Cross wouldn't accept blood donations from black people and when black and white soldiers were stationed in British towns ahead of the D-Day invasions they were kept strictly segregated. Fights frequently broke out between black and white American servicemen and British locals would join in on the black soldiers' side.

A CLOSER LOOK

The reception of black soldiers in Europe

Many black servicemen were astonished by the reception they received when stationed in the UK and as troops made their way across Europe. Europeans saw Americans as liberators regardless of colour and the status of black soldiers was enhanced by their courtesy, relative wealth in terms of wages and supplies and the music and culture they brought with them. For young black men, especially those raised in southern towns perpetually in fear, this was a revelation.

The experience at home

Meanwhile, at home the demands of the wartime economy increased the 'Great Migration' of black workers north into the major cities where government contracts had created huge demand across a variety of industries. With steady jobs, good wages and a concentration of black families in areas of cities like Detroit, Chicago and Cleveland, came political influence in the election of city mayors and even members of Congress.

Black newspapers like the *Chicago Defender* become more popular and were active in their campaigns, notably the 'Double V' campaign which explicitly linked victory over the Nazis to victory over racism at home. The black newspapers contributed to increased political awareness and this, coupled with the growing wealth of some African-Americans, led to a rise in the membership of the National Association for the Advancement of Colored People (NAACP, founded in 1909). By the time Eisenhower came to power membership had reached over a million and this provided funding for its ambitious legal campaigns. A second civil rights group, Congress of Racial Equality (CORE), was founded in 1942. It focused on the North and together with the union movement, led by **A Philip Randolph's** Brotherhood of Sleeping Car Porters, and began to adopt a more proactive but peaceful approach to civil rights.

The impact of the Second World War undoubtedly led to advances for African-Americans, but there were also severe racial tensions, including a 1943 race riot in Detroit involving 100,000 which led to 34 deaths. Army leaders became so concerned that the army commissioned the Hollywood director, Frank Capra, to make *The Negro Soldier* (1944), a film intended to reduce prejudice.

It is difficult to assess the extent of social change during and because of the Second World War even for historians. Adam Fairclough for instance argues that no breakthrough emerged whereas Robert Cook suggests that the war did more than any other event to drag the South into the twentieth century. Although extensive shifts in wealth and demographics took place, they often proved temporary and did not fundamentally change attitudes.

KEY PROFILE

A Philip Randolph (1889–1979)
was born in Florida. In 1917 he founded a political magazine, *The Messenger*, before going on to found the black trade union Brotherhood of Sleeping Car Porters in 1925.
He successfully used his influence to push Roosevelt to found the FEPC and Truman to desegregate the military. He also co-organised the 1963 March on Washington and gave the first speech there.

Fig. 1 *Randolph was a leading figure in the Civil Rights Movement*

African-Americans in the South in the Truman years

In contrast to the North most African-Americans in the South lived in small rural towns. Here they worked in agricultural occupations or in menial service roles all the while under the close watch of the white population and under the jurisdiction of **Jim Crow Laws**. Education was segregated and African-Americans were kept from voting using a variety of borderline illegal methods. The Church was an extremely powerful unifying force and black preachers were afforded more respect than ordinary African-Americans by the white population, which led to many being content not to challenge segregation. The threat of violence from the legacy of the lynchings of the 1920s and 1930s hung heavily over the black population and, for many, standing up against segregation would mean harassment and violence for their families and the possible loss of their jobs if news reached their white employers.

Fig. 2 *Allegiances at the time of the Civil War (1861–65) which was largely fought over the issue of slavery, which the Southern (or Confederate) states wanted to maintain and the Northern (or Union) states wanted to abolish*

A CLOSER LOOK

Jim Crow Laws

These were laws enacted in the South from 1876 to 1965 at the state or local level which made it illegal for black people to use the same water fountains, waiting rooms, bus seats, cinemas, libraries and other public facilities as white people. They derived their legality from the 1896 Supreme Court case *Plessy v. Ferguson* that established that states could provide segregated facilities provided they were 'separate but equal.' In reality, facilities for black people were inferior.

African-Americans in the North in the Truman years

ACTIVITY

Evaluating primary sources

Evaluate the provenance, tone, emphasis, content and argument of Source 2.

SOURCE 2

Taken from *The Autobiography of Malcolm X*. Co-authored with the journalist Alex Haley and published in 1965, it recounts Malcolm's life from his time as a hustler to his conversion to Islam:

I was astounded to find in the nation's capital, just a few blocks from Capitol Hill, thousands of Negroes living worse than any I'd ever seen in the poorest sections of Roxbury [the area of Boston where Malcolm X lived]; in dirt-floor shacks along unspeakably filthy lanes with names like Pig Alley and Goat Alley. I had seen a lot, but never such a dense concentration of stumblebums, pushers, hookers, public crap-shooters, even little kids running around at midnight begging for pennies, half-naked and barefooted. Some of the railroad cooks and waiters had told me to be very careful, because muggings, knifings and robberies went on every night among these Negroes [...] just a few blocks from the White House.

A CLOSER LOOK

The Nation of Islam

Established in 1930 to improve the spiritual, mental, social and economic condition of African-Americans, from 1934 the Nation of Islam was led by Elijah Muhammed. Its doctrines include the beliefs that the original men were black, and white men had been created by an evil scientist named Yakub. The movement also preached self-reliance and self-respect, encouraging black people to reject drink and drugs and shop only in black-controlled shops. After the death of Malcolm X in 1965 the movement declined but remains active to this day.

Prejudice existed in the North however it wasn't enforced by Jim Crow Laws but a combination of economic segregation, social pressure and **ghettoisation**. Black populations in Northern cities were a relatively recent addition, only 8 per cent of African-Americans lived outside the South in 1900 but 'The Great Migration' caused substantial dislocation of the Southern black population. This was brought on by various factors: fear of the revived **Ku Klux Klan**, the mechanisation of agriculture, the Great Depression and the creation of huge numbers of factory jobs all provided incentives to leave the South. In the 1940s 1.4 million black citizens did just that and they were followed in the 1950s by a further 1.1 million.

A CLOSER LOOK

The **Ku Klux Klan** was a secret society that flourished in the 1950s and espoused an ideology of racial purity. They employed violent tactics against those that disagreed with their views. The third Klan was a loose collection of groups in the South but was responsible for several murders and countless acts of intimidation.

Fig. 3   *Malcolm X was a Muslim Minister and human rights activist*

Malcolm X (1925–65) was born Malcolm Little in Nebraska. He joined the Nation of Islam in 1948 during his time in prison for robbery. His charismatic style made him nationally infamous after his appearance in a TV documentary called *The Hate that Hate Produced* in 1959 where he espoused a confrontational attitude towards white people. He was assassinated in 1965 after breaking away from the Nation.

ghettoisation: the process of certain areas of cities becoming dominated by one ethnic group as others move out; this is usually linked to a decline in facilities like education, healthcare and housing

Fig. 4   *An African-American woman having been evicted from her apartment in New York in 1950*

KEY PROFILE

Fig. 5   *Powell was a politician and civil rights leader*

Adam Clayton Powell (1908–72) was a former Baptist preacher turned politician who represented Harlem in the House of Representatives from 1945 to 1971. He was a key spokesman for African-Americans in the North. In 1961 he became Chair of the House Education and Labor Committee which put him in a key position to aid the progress of the social legislation of Presidents Kennedy and Johnson.

ACTIVITY

Evaluating primary sources

What difficulties does Truman highlight in this speech in Source 3, that had prevented a successful attack on 'prejudice and discrimination'?

After moving to the North, from the 1940s most African-Americans lived in cramped apartments in the centre of cities. Rents were often high and landlords could afford to neglect property owing to demand always exceeding supply. Even though many were in work they were prevented from moving out to the growing suburbs by the 'restricted covenants' and ***de facto*** segregation operated by realtors (estate agents). Though black people faced prejudice in housing, education and employment there were benefits to their concentration in the cities. As white people left for the new suburbs, black political power grew, enabling black members of the House of Representatives to be elected such as William L Dawson in Chicago and **Adam Clayton Powell** in Harlem. As well as some political influence, the proximity of the black population made it easier to organise and groups such as the NAACP (started in Baltimore in 1909), CORE (started in Chicago in 1942), the Urban League (started in New York in 1910) and the Nation of Islam (started in Detroit in 1930) grew in membership during and after the war years.

Jobs were available too although they were often poorly paid except for in the automobile industry around Detroit. However black artists and sportsmen could gain recognition and wealth. Jackie Robinson had become the first black baseball player in Major League Baseball in 1947 and was awarded Most Valuable Player (MVP) by 1949. In addition, Joe Louis had held the World Heavyweight Boxing title for 12 years by 1949, while Louis Armstrong, Miles Davis, Charlie Parker, Billie Holiday and many others had established well paid careers in the clubs of the northern cities.

Although not on the same scale as in the South, relations with white people were tense and none more so than with the police who would often resort to violence in their dealings with the black population. The justice system was far harsher on black defendants than white ones as Malcolm X was to discover in 1946 when he began an eight- to ten-year sentence for burglary.

ACTIVITY

Draw a Venn diagram that illustrates the problems faced by African-Americans in the North and the South and the problems they shared.

The campaigns for civil rights

SOURCE 3

Extract from President Truman's address to the NAACP at the Lincoln Memorial, June 1947:

We can no longer afford the luxury of a leisurely attack upon prejudice and discrimination. There is much that state and local governments can do in providing positive safeguards for civil rights. But we cannot, any longer, await the growth of a will to action in the slowest state or the most backward community. Our national government must show the way. This is a difficult and complex undertaking. Federal laws and administrative machineries must be improved and expanded. We must provide the government with better tools to do the job.

The immediate post-war period saw a more proactive approach from the major civil rights groups. While the Urban League and the Nation of Islam concentrated their efforts in the North, CORE and the NAACP found success in the southern states.

A CLOSER LOOK

'Journey of Reconciliation'

On 10 April 1947 CORE organised a group of eight white and eight black men on what was to be a two-week bus trip through Virginia, North Carolina, Tennessee, and Kentucky in an effort to end segregation in interstate travel. CORE called it the 'Journey of Reconciliation' and although the group were arrested and jailed repeatedly they succeeded in generating substantial media interest in the issue of desegregation.

The most successful civil rights group in the Truman years was the NAACP. Their long-term tactic of seeking to challenge segregation through the courts had begun to pay dividends. Many of the NAACP's cases were focused on undermining a Supreme Court decision from 1896, *Plessy v. Ferguson*. Here the Supreme Court declared that Homer Plessy had not been discriminated against in terms of his 14th Amendment rights when he was asked to sit in the coloured carriage of a train, establishing a principle that 'separate but equal' facilities were acceptable and legitimising segregation in any state that chose to enact Jim Crow Laws.

After establishing a Legal Defence Fund in 1939 the NAACP began to raise money to take on cases that would challenge the principle of *Plessy v. Ferguson*, with this money they were able to hire the best black lawyers, notably Robert Carter, Charles Hamilton Houston and his protégée, **Thurgood Marshall**. From 1944 to 1950 the NAACP won a series of cases before the Supreme Court which challenged different aspects of segregation, including:

- 1944 – *Smith v. Allwright* – a voting rights case which allowed African-Americans in Texas to vote in Primaries (elections used by political parties to choose a candidate).
- 1946 – *Morgan v. Virginia* – a transport-related case which ruled that segregation on interstate buses was illegal.
- 1948 – *Shelley v. Kramer* – a housing-related case that said estate agents could not refuse to show and sell houses to black clients if the seller had placed a 'restrictive covenant' on the property.
- 1950 – *Henderson v. US* – a transport case where the Supreme Court ruled that segregation in railway dining cars was illegal.
- 1950 – *McLaurin v. Oklahoma State* – an education case. George McLaurin was allowed to enter the University of Oklahoma to pursue a PhD but was kept segregated from other students.
- 1950 – *Sweatt v. Painter* – a second education case; the Court ruled that the provision of a 'separate but equal' Law School for Heman Sweatt and others to attend was not equal to the white University of Texas Law School.

The success of these cases emboldened the NAACP and brought substantial donations to its fundraising arm, all of which prepared the way for the biggest court case since the organisation was founded in 1909. The 1954 **Brown v. Board of Education case**, first argued in the Supreme Court in the last month of Truman's presidency was to prove pivotal to the Civil Rights Movement.

KEY PROFILE

Thurgood Marshall (1908–93) was a lawyer for the NAACP who won a series of cases before the Supreme Court, notably *Brown v. Board of Education* in 1954, a decision that desegregated public schools. Kennedy promoted him to the United States Court of Appeals. President Johnson nominated him to the United States Supreme Court in 1967.

CROSS-REFERENCE

For more information on the *Brown v. Board of Education* case's impact on the Civial Rights Movement, see Chapter 8, page 65

ACTIVITY

Draw a diagram showing the areas of segregation these cases were focused on and why these areas were targeted by the NAACP.

Fig. 6 *George McLaurin sits outside a classroom gaining 'separate but equal' access to the teaching. He also had a separate desk in the library and a separate table in the cafe*

The responses of the federal and state authorities to civil rights

Civil rights campaigners expected little from Truman given his southern background. He came from a small town in the former slave state of Missouri where Jim Crow Laws were still enforced. Despite all this, Truman believed in fairness. While serving in Jackson County public office, he saw the problems faced by African-Americans in urban areas and in 1940 he gave a remarkably brave speech in Sedalia, Missouri, while seeking re-election declaring that he believed in the 'brotherhood' of black and white men before the law.

Truman also proclaimed his horror at the treatment of black soldiers returning from the war; some had been thrown out of trucks and beaten in Mississippi. A growing media was providing more coverage of racially motivated beatings and murders and Truman felt that something had to be done. In 1946, he established 'The President's Committee on Civil Rights' and told its members that he wanted the **Bill of Rights** to be become a reality.

'To Secure these Rights'

The committee released its report entitled 'To Secure These Rights' in 1947. It was a scathing attack on all aspects of discrimination both in the North but particularly in the South, citing education, housing, public facilities (such as parks, water fountains, waiting rooms) and voting rights as the prime areas of discrimination. Truman responded by giving a radical civil rights speech to a joint session of Congress in February 1948 asking Congress to support measures including federal protection against lynching, protection of the right to vote, and a permanent and better funded FEPC. The proposals were electorally risky given the presence of many Dixiecrat congressmen and were never successfully implemented. They may even have contributed to the narrowness of his election victory later that year by dividing the party over the issue of race.

Opposition from fellow Democrats

The opposition from fellow Democrats was a key factor hampering Truman. As a Democrat he was nominally the head of the Democratic Party which covered a broad spectrum of beliefs. Members of the party included extreme racists such as James O Eastland, a Senator for Mississippi, and Strom Thurmond,

> **KEY TERM**
>
> **Bill of Rights:** the collective term for the first ten Amendments of the US constitution, laying out the rights of all Americans

a Senator for South Carolina as well as Governors like Fielding L Wright in Mississippi and Herman Talmadge in Georgia. Southern politicians, keenly aware of the importance of segregation to the voters to whom they were accountable, largely balked at the idea of any concessions to the fledgling Civil Rights Movement. In the absence of widespread media coverage and with much of the campaigning coming via the NAACP's efforts in the courts, Truman's putative attempts to push the issue of civil rights was met with obstruction and delay by southern politicians who covered their racism behind a veneer of defending the rights of their states from federal interference.

The wider political context

The Republican Party saw no need to engage with the Civil Rights Movement, Eisenhower barely mentioned the issue in his 1952 campaign. However, internationally segregationist attitudes were damaging the US's reputation. Added to this, the collapse of the European empires was creating independent new countries in Africa and Asia who would hold influence at the UN and were being wooed by the Soviet Union, increasing the pressure on the president to be seen to act.

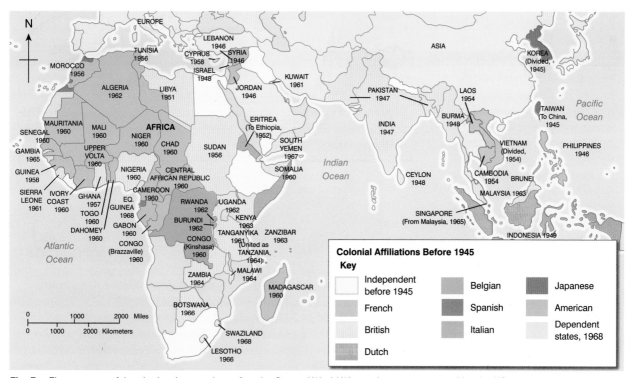

Fig. 7 *The process of decolonisation sped up after the Second World War and was encouraged by the US*

A CLOSER LOOK

The international situation

For Truman, racial issues were not just a matter of North and South but they had international implications. The end of the Second World War had led not only to the formation of the UN but also to increased agitation for independence amongst the colonies of France, Belgium, the Netherlands and, especially, Britain. Truman was aware of how segregation and violence in the South looked overseas and with newly independent countries also being entitled to a seat at the United Nations the danger of alienating the African states in particular was very real.

ACTIVITY

1. Draw a spider diagram which covers the policies Truman enacted to help black people in the areas of voting, jobs, housing, education and healthcare from the 'Fair Deal'.

2. Hold a class debate with the motion 'This house believes that Truman did all he could to address the issue of black civil rights.'

Summary

In 1946 Truman described discrimination as a disease and cited the opportunity to vote, find employment and have access to quality housing, education and medical care as the cure. There is clear evidence in this chapter of how he attempted to address each of these areas, despite the considerable strains on his presidency.

Truman may not have achieved the landmark legislation of Johnson, nor the heroic status of Kennedy when it comes to popular interpretations of the Civil Rights Movement's key figures, but his efforts laid the groundwork for their successes and continued in the traditions established by Roosevelt.

 PRACTICE QUESTION

'Truman's failure to address African-American civil rights effectively was a result of political pressure.' Assess the validity of this view.

 PRACTICE QUESTION

Evaluating primary sources

With reference to Sources 1 and 2 and your understanding of the historical context, which of these two sources is more valuable in explaining the problems affecting African-Americans?

STUDY TIP

You will need to consider how far, if at all, Truman addressed the issue of civil rights and also explain how political pressure affected him. Remember that political pressure can encompass a desire for re-election, pressure from members of his own party, from the Republican Party, from the states and from overseas issues. You may also want to consider whether economic issues played a role.

STUDY TIP

You should aim to engage with the sources' different perspectives. What did it mean for the president to pass an Executive Order like this for African-Americans? What does Malcolm X's surprise suggest about the situation in Washington and what kind of problems does his account highlight?

5 The presidency under Eisenhower

Eisenhower's personality

Fig. 1 *Eisenhower arriving at the Republican Party Convention in 1952*

KEY PROFILE

Fig. 2 *Many of Stevenson's policies formed the basis of the Kennedy campaign*

KEY PROFILE

Dwight D Eisenhower (1890–1969), also known as 'Ike', became the 34th president of the United States in January 1953. In many ways Eisenhower was a classic Republican. But he was far from a stereotypical soldier despite his being a five-star general who served as Supreme Commander of the Allies in Europe in the Second World War and as supreme commander of NATO. Although a Republican he was committed to the USA above all and sought to lead without infringing on the rights of the states and with minimal government involvement.

In 1952 Dwight D Eisenhower ended 20 years of Democratic presidents with a landslide election victory over **Adlai Stevenson**. Eisenhower was an American hero. He was honourable, affable and gregarious as a man, and as a soldier he commanded respect and inspired confidence in his troops. His biographer Peter Lyon argues that Eisenhower was distressed when people didn't like him and he refused to speak ill of anyone. Eisenhower was devoted to his wife, Mamie, with whom he had two children though only John survived into adulthood. Of the couple's four grandchildren Eisenhower doted on David after whom the Presidential retreat 'Camp David' is named and who married Nixon's daughter Julie in 1968.

Adlai Stevenson (1900–65) served as Governor of Illinois before being nominated as the Democratic candidate in 1952. After being resoundingly beaten he stood and lost again in 1956 as no other Democrats felt they could beat Eisenhower. JFK appointed him as Ambassador to the UN in 1961.

KEY PROFILE

Fig. 4   Nixon was the thirty-seventh President of the United States

Richard Nixon (1913–94) entered Congress at the age of 34 and by 37 was Senator for California. He made his name during the Alger Hiss spy case but lost a very tight election to Kennedy in 1960. Circumstances helped him recover and he defeated Hubert Humphrey to become President in 1968. His first term saw some foreign policy success in Vietnam and a resounding re-election before he was brought down by the Watergate Scandal.

CROSS-REFERENCE

See Chapter 7, pages 56–58 and pages 60–61 for information on the crises in Hungary and Egypt.

Eisenhower had shown little interest in politics in his early life and had never cast a vote in an election until 1948. He didn't even commit to a party prior to 1951 having twice turned down Truman's overtures that he should become the Democratic candidate in 1947 and 1951. He appealed to the American electorate like no other candidate could, his election slogan simply read 'I like Ike' and 55 per cent of the electorate agreed.

Two-election victories

Fig. 3   Eisenhower chose to run with 39-year-old Senator Richard Nixon. This was a sensible choice for a president with no political experience; the two had only met six times before the campaign began and they were to have an uneasy relationship both during and after Eisenhower's presidency

Eisenhower was persuaded to stand by friends and colleagues in the Republican party in 1952 and he ran a clever election campaign ignoring Stevenson and attacking Truman as part of a formula for victory, K1C2 (Korea, communism, corruption). His promise to go to Korea to end the war resonated with the public despite an inflated corruption scandal involving Nixon (see below).

Eisenhower made his own mistakes during the campaign, choosing not to defend General George C Marshall who McCarthy had denounced as part of a Communist conspiracy. Marshall was possibly an even greater hero than Eisenhower himself and this smacked of cowardice. In the end though nothing could stop the war hero who even did well in the Dixiecrat South, taking a larger percentage of the popular vote than any previous Republican candidate and winning Virginia, Florida, Tennessee and Texas.

Eisenhower's successful first term brought economic growth and an end to the Korean War which made him a firm favourite in the 1956 election, despite his suffering a major heart attack in September 1955. In the run up to the election Eisenhower dealt effectively with **crises in both Hungary and Egypt** which confirmed for many the quality and calm of his leadership in a dangerous world and on election day, Eisenhower crushed Stevenson again. However it was Eisenhower that the electorate wanted, not the Republicans and the Democrats retained control of Congress, which they had secured in the midterm elections of 1954. Eisenhower became the first candidate since 1848 to win the presidency without having his party gain a majority of seats in either the House or the Senate.

Eisenhower's policies of dynamic conservatism

As a former soldier it was always clear that Eisenhower's speciality would be foreign affairs but Ike had big plans for his domestic program, seeing it as a chance to implement '**dynamic conservatism**'. He was obviously hampered by the lack of a supportive Congress, only having a Republican majority from his first election up to 1954.

A CLOSER LOOK

'Dynamic conservatism' or 'modern republicanism.'

Eisenhower described himself as 'conservative when it comes to money, liberal when it comes to human beings' and this was the essence of his 'dynamic conservatism'. Eisenhower recognised the popularity of the 'New Deal' and the credit Roosevelt received for kick-starting the economy after the Great Depression. Eisenhower therefore intervened to stimulate the economy: he introduced an enormous highway building programme, raised the minimum wage and expanded benefits. In this way he differed from previous and subsequent Republican presidents.

Eisenhower emphasised the need for a balanced budget, which he achieved in 1956, 1957 and 1960, and in giving responsibility to states and local governments but also favoured an expansion of the limited welfare state in the US at the expense of the armed forces.

SOURCE 1

An extract from Eisenhower's 'A Chance for Peace' speech delivered on 16 April, 1953 to the American Society of Newspaper Editors, in Washington, DC. The speech came shortly after the death of Stalin, with the end of the Korean War in sight and after the successful test of a Soviet nuclear bomb:

Every gun that is made, every warship launched, every rocket fired signifies, in the final sense, a theft from those who hunger and are not fed, those who are cold and are not clothed. This world in arms is not spending money alone. It is spending the sweat of its laborers, the genius of its scientists, the hopes of its children. The cost of one modern heavy bomber is this: a modern brick school in more than 30 cities. It is two electric power plants, each serving a town with a 60,000 population. It is two fine, fully equipped hospitals. It is some fifty miles of concrete pavement. We pay for a single fighter with a half-million bushels of wheat. We pay for a single destroyer with new homes that could have housed more than 8,000 people […] This is not a way of life at all, in any true sense. Under the cloud of threatening war, it is humanity hanging from a cross of iron.

ACTIVITY

Evaluating primary sources

How valuable would this speech be for an historian studying Eisenhower's policies?

Among Eisenhower's most successful domestic policies were:

- the creation of the new Department of Health, Education and Welfare
- the expansion of social security benefit to cover 10 million Americans, a policy that broke away from traditional Republican ideas and reflected how Eisenhower was conscious of those at the bottom of society
- an increase in the minimum wage by 25 per cent, which challenged the Republican ideas of the 'free market'
- $500 million was made available for low-income public housing. Though this amount was insufficient to deal with all the problems in housing it once again showed Eisenhower's willingness to involve the federal government in addressing the problems of the poor

CROSS-REFERENCE

Eisenhower's civil rights policies are covered in Chapter 8, pages 68–70.

CROSS-REFERENCE

The American economy, including the three recessions, is examined in Chapter 6.

KEY TERM

recession: the financial year is divided into quarters (periods of three months) during which time, economists calculate whether the economy has grown; if the figures for two consecutive quarters are negative, i.e. the economy has shrunk, the country is said to be in recession

KEY TERM

big government: a critical term often used by right-wing politicians to describe a government that they feel is too large or too inefficient or spends excessively. It is a term often attributed to both Roosevelt's 'New Deal' and Truman's 'Fair Deal'

rolled back: to move back to a previous state in terms of expenditure or bureaucratic expansion

CROSS-REFERENCE

For a contrast, revisit the Key Term definition of 'small government' in Chapter 1, page 4.

- the Federal Aid Highway Act of 1956 became the largest peacetime public works project in American history, 41,000 miles of Interstate Highways were built over a 20 year period
- establishing a 'soil bank', which paid farmers to withdraw lands from production in the interest of maintaining food prices and conserving agricultural resources
- admitting Alaska and Hawaii as States
- introducing **two civil rights** acts in 1957 and 1960.

As can be seen from this policy agenda Eisenhower was far more willing to intervene on behalf of the Federal government than later Republican presidents. In education, health, housing and benefits he was proactive in addressing the problems of those excluded from the American dream although, admittedly, he was starting from a low base.

However the Eisenhower years were not a total success when it came to domestic policy. Eisenhower faced important and, at times, controversial issues in domestic affairs including the **management of the economy** through three **recessions** and problems, the growth of civil rights campaigns and dealing with McCarthy. Eisenhower's status protected him from the usual levels of criticism heaped on politicians and he often enjoyed approval ratings of over 70 per cent in the polls, in stark contrast to the other presidents between 1945 and 1980.

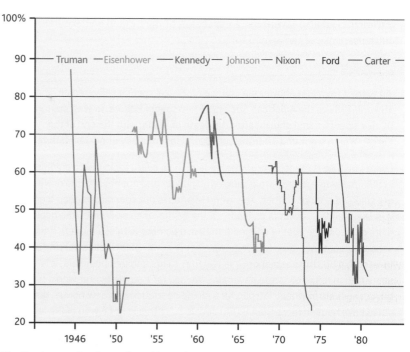

Fig. 5 *Approval ratings of presidents from 1945 to 1980, compiled from different polling companies*

Yet Eisenhower also had critics. In Congress in particular there were those who believed that he had not used his powers as president effectively to protect individual freedom and ensure justice. Eisenhower had criticised the **big government** programmes of Truman's 'Fair Deal' but didn't want to go as far as some Republicans who believed government should be 'rolled back' allowing the private sector to take a bigger role.

Eisenhower's plan was to lead the US down a middle path between big government intervention and rampant capitalism and this enabled him to work with Congress despite it being dominated by the Democrats for six of his eight years as president. In that time only ten of the 83 bills he sent to Congress were rejected. In his final years as president however the Republicans performed badly in the midterm elections of 1958 with only 34 of 98 Senators and 154 of 436 seats in the House of Representatives. The Eisenhower Administration was blamed for a second recession in eight years and for a perceived defeat in the **space race** to the Soviet Union when, in quick succession, Moscow succeeding in putting a satellite, 'sputnik' (October 1957), then a dog, Laika (November 1957), into space.

Eisenhower had also struggled with his promise to reduce spending. Domestic spending rose from 31 per cent of the budget in 1953 to 49 per cent in 1961 but in spite of this, and the consumer boom, many Americans did not share in the new prosperity. One in every four, (forty million in total) were living in poverty and didn't benefit either from the growth of **the economy** or the increase in the minimum wage and Social Security.

CROSS-REFERENCE

See Chapter 7, page 55 for more on the space race.

CROSS-REFERENCE

The economy is the focus of Chapter 6.

SOURCE 2

Extract from *The Other America* by the sociologist Michael Harrington, published in 1962 and based on his travels around the US in the late 1950s:

Poverty is off the beaten track. It always has been. Now the American city has been transformed, the poor still inhabit the miserable housing in the central area, but they are increasingly isolated from contact with, or sight of, anybody else. In short, the development of the American city has removed poverty from the living, emotional experience of millions of middle-class Americans. Living out in the suburbs, it is easy to assume that ours is, indeed, an affluent society. Clothes make the poor invisible too; America has the best-dressed poverty in the world. For a variety of reasons, the benefits of mass production have been spread much more evenly in this area than in many others. It is much easier in the United States to be decently dressed than it is to be decently housed, fed, or doctored. The people of the other America do not belong to unions, to organizations, or to political parties. They are without lobbies of their own; they put forward no legislative program. They have no face; they have no voice.

ACTIVITY

Evaluating primary sources

1. Create a spider diagram to show the ways in which Harrington suggests that the poor are concealed from the rest of society.
2. Suggest reasons for each development and make a note of these on your diagram.
3. In what ways would this source be of value to an historian investigating American society in the 1950s?

 PRACTICE QUESTION

Evaluating primary sources

With reference to Sources 1 and 2 and your understanding of the historical context, which of these two sources is more valuable in explaining why there was poverty in the USA in the 1950s?

STUDY TIP

Consider the different angles of the sources. In assessing their relative value you must look at how broadly the sources explain why poverty existed and the context in which they were produced.

The South was home to almost half of the country's poor, black and white alike, yet in the North, poverty was largely the preserve of African-Americans in the inner cities and Native Americans whom the Eisenhower government unsuccessfully tried to assimilate into mainstream American society. This was attempted through the Indian Relocation Act of 1956, which encouraged them to move from reservations to the cities. While Harrington's book had an effect on some, the majority either did not see the poverty it described or felt little sympathy having come through the difficulties of the Great Depression period themselves.

One area where Eisenhower significantly changed the direction of US politics was in the relationship he developed with religious leaders. In 1957 66 per cent of the US population identified themselves as Protestant (with 26 per cent as Catholic and 3 per cent as Jewish). Amongst those over 50 this figure was even higher at 74 per cent. However the US is a constitutionally secular state where religion has no role in government. Eisenhower's

ACTIVITY

Class debate

A criticism of dynamic conservatism was that Eisenhower appeared to argue that he would 'strongly recommend the building of a great many schools […] but not provide the money'. Discuss whether it is ever possible for a government to improve the quality of citizens' lives without increasing its spending.

CROSS-REFERENCE

Billy Graham is the subject of a Key Profile in Chapter 17, page 141.

ACTIVITY

Thinking point

Aside from the issue of Eisenhower's personal beliefs, what reasons can you think of that would make a closer association with the Church a sensible idea?

KEY TERM

the ticket: this refers to a pair (or more) of candidates that will be elected in a single vote. In the US the presidential elections serve to elect both a president and a vice president. Together they form 'the ticket'. The vice president is sometimes also referred to as a 'running mate'

ACTIVITY

Evaluating primary sources

Nixon's 'Checker's speech' is legendary in US politics for demonstrating both the power of television as a medium for addressing the American people and highlighting the use of a 'straw man' argument to win a political point. A 'straw man' argument is where the speaker creates the impression of having defeated an opponent's point by replacing it with a different proposition. How does Nixon use this technique in this speech?

KEY TERM

GOP: standing for 'Grand Old Party' it is an alternative, informal name for the Republicans

CROSS-REFERENCE

See Chapter 4, page 32 for the Key Term definition of *de facto*.

Administration drew closer to the Church than any other before him. He attended church regularly, proclaimed national days of prayer and invited the evangelist **Billy Graham** to the White House. The Administration also added the words 'under God' to the Pledge of Allegiance, and Congress made the phrase 'In God We Trust' the national motto. The inter-relationship between the Protestant Church and the Republican Party was to be a feature of the rest of the century.

Nixon as vice president and the Republican Party

Nixon had first come to the public's attention as the dogged congressman who had pursued the Alger Hiss case, but Eisenhower chose him to balance **the ticket**, bringing in a talented political operator to offset his own lack of experience. It quickly became clear that for all his talents Nixon also brought baggage in the form of a tense relationship with the media and a whiff of corruption that jarred with Eisenhower's promise that his Administration would be as 'clean as a hound's tooth'.

Nixon had acquired a reputation as 'Tricky Dicky' from his campaign in the California Senate elections in 1950 and he was definitely a cunning politician. However his career at the highest level was almost stillborn after accusations that he had used $18,000 of political donations for personal use. Nixon brilliantly extricated himself by giving a televised speech explaining his actions. The public responded to 'The Checkers Speech' (Checkers was Nixon's family dog) with enthusiasm for Nixon, and Eisenhower decided to keep him on the ticket.

SOURCE 3

Extract from 'The Checkers Speech', a 30 minute TV address on 23 September 1952. Nixon made an explicit defence citing his whole financial history and invoking his wife, Pat and children and the family dog:

We did get something, a gift, after the election. A man down in Texas heard Pat on the radio mention the fact that our two youngsters would like to have a dog. And believe it or not, the day before we left on this campaign trip we got a message from Union Station in Baltimore, saying they had a package for us. We went down to get it. You know what it was? It was a little Cocker Spaniel dog in a crate that he'd sent all the way from Texas, black and white, spotted. And our little girl Tricia, the six-year-old, named it 'Checkers.' And you know, the kids, like all kids, love the dog, and I just want to say this, right now, that regardless of what they say about it, we're gonna keep it.

The historian Irwin Gellman credits Nixon with being the first modern vice president. He chaired the cabinet and National Security Council in Eisenhower's absence, travelled widely, including to Saigon and presided over the presidency when Eisenhower was incapacitated for six weeks by a heart attack. Eisenhower's personal popularity didn't translate into Republican popularity and it is interesting to note that given Eisenhower's ambivalence to party politics there hadn't be a truly committed and successful Republican president since Theodore Roosevelt left the White House in 1909. The **GOP** won control of Congress in 1952, but only by narrow majorities – three seats in the House of Representatives, one seat in the Senate and some senior figures in the party lost their seats, including Henry Cabot Lodge who lost his Senate seat to John F Kennedy.

The *de facto* leadership of the Republican Party fell to Nixon and this is the most likely explanation for the failure of Eisenhower's version of 'modern republicanism' to become the long-term party platform. The loss of both houses in 1954 kept the party from control of the Senate until 1980 and from control of the House until 1994. Historian David Reinhard concluded that 'voters liked Ike – but not the GOP'. Eisenhower's support in 1952 had come from the grass roots, a 'Citizens for Eisenhower' movement canvassed and got the vote out but Eisenhower's willingness to ignore their efforts to create a wider, more inclusive party led to a backlash and more **conservative Republicans** came to the fore led by Barry Goldwater.

CROSS-REFERENCE

For the Key Profile of Barry Goldwater, look ahead to Chapter 13, page 108.

The end of McCarthyism

Fig. 6 *Senator Joseph McCarthy addresses the nation on the 'communist threat'*

Truman had failed to deal with the paranoia of McCarthyism, whose accusations had also tainted Adlai Stevenson's presidential bid, though Eisenhower's status as a war hero had protected him. Nevertheless Eisenhower was not immune from McCarthy's influence. Opinion polls in 1953 suggested half the population were in favour of McCarthy's crusade despite not a single indictment or conviction resulting from his allegations. Eisenhower feared that a direct confrontation would weaken his prestige or be turned to McCarthy's advantage, but in 1954, the situation was brought to a head when McCarthy held televised hearings on communist influence in the army. Eisenhower was outraged but, fortunately McCarthy effectively self-destructed on television when Joseph Welch, a lawyer working for the army, put to the senator: 'Have you no sense of decency, sir, at long last?'

By the end of 1954, the Senate voted to censure McCarthy for conduct unbecoming a senator. McCarthy continued to serve for the next two and a half years but was a pariah in Washington, a situation Eisenhower described as 'McCarthywasm'. By 1957 McCarthy was dead of alcoholism, his replacement described him as 'a disgrace to Wisconsin, to the Senate, and to America'.

ACTIVITY

Extension

The 2005 George Clooney film *Good Night and Good Luck* deals with the efforts of CBS's Edward Morrow to bring attention to the holes in McCarthy's arguments. Discuss how far we can trust different forms of media to give us a true picture of the past.

ACTIVITY

Write a newspaper editorial piece summarising the McCarthyist campaign, perhaps highlighting the difficulty for those who wanted to speak out.

A CLOSER LOOK

Appraisal of McCarthy

McCarthy remains a controversial figure. However, recent research by conservative authors such as Medford Stanton Evans and historians including Arthur Herman, using released Soviet espionage archives, suggest that of the 159 people identified on McCarthy's lists, nine had aided Soviet espionage efforts. Even figures such as George Kennan saw that infiltration of the US government by Soviet agents was real. Perhaps therefore, a more nuanced interpretation of McCarthy is due: his motives were correct but his black and white approach to any dissent caused untold damage.

Summary

Eisenhower's presidency saw substantial changes that had long-term effects in America including highway building, expansion of the USA to include Hawaii in 1959 and the decision to stick with Nixon. For many Americans the Eisenhower period is seen as a golden time of peace, growing economic security and moral correctness, but Eisenhower is usually seen as a modest success rather than a truly great president. The lack of ambition shown in his domestic programme goes some way to explain this, and his failure to confront McCarthy will long be held against him.

ACTIVITY

Summary

Draw a spider diagram that explains why Eisenhower was so politically successful.

STUDY TIP

For an A Level question you should look at not only the short-term consequences of the politics of dynamic conservatism but also their long-term impact. For this it is important to see which policies were kept on by subsequent presidents and which were removed. It is important to remember that Nixon was Eisenhower's vice president and went on to be president himself. How far was he influenced by 'dynamic conservatism'? A sensible way to look at this might be to consider the positive, negative and neutral impact of the policies in the short- and long-term.

 PRACTICE QUESTION

'Eisenhower's dynamic conservatism had a positive impact on the USA.' Assess the validity of this view.

6 The economy in the 1950s and the consumer society

The growth of the American economy in the 1950s

SOURCE 1

From the script of a nationwide TV broadcast in 1956 during Eisenhower's campaign for a second term. Parties purchased time for political broadcasts in blocks of 30 minutes:

There's no such thing as a 'common' man to President Eisenhower. You're an individual with rights privileges and responsibilities. And one of your basic rights is the security that your national government is sincerely and honestly working for your best interests. It is your right to bring children into the world in the secure knowledge that their future is clear and uncluttered by staggering debt or overwhelming inflation. He thinks that you're entitled to a steady job and that you shouldn't have to surrender the major part of your earnings back to the government in taxes. And what does Ike think of your future? Well, he's a man who looks toward tomorrow with confidence and excitement.

In many ways Eisenhower was a lucky president. Much of the sting had been taken out of the Cold War by the events of 1945 to 1952 and the death of Stalin in 1953 meant that his foreign adversary was a relatively inexperienced newcomer. At home too the problems of the post-war years had begun to settle down, not least in terms of an economy that had, by 1953, completed the transition from its dependence on war to be booming in its own right. In 1950 **Gross Domestic Product** (GDP) had been $355 billion, by the end of Eisenhower's Second term in 1960 it stood at $488 billion. The healthy **macroeconomic** picture was also reflected in micro-economic terms. Wages were rising, hours were falling and **per capita income** rose from $1720 in 1940 to $2699 in 1960.

Overall the economy grew by 37 per cent during the 1950s and by 1960 the typical American family had 30 per cent more purchasing power than at the beginning of the decade. Inflation was kept low because of Eisenhower's obsession with balancing the federal budget and his regime of low taxes and increases in public spending kept the economy healthy. Cheap oil from US wells helped to keep industry running and the slow recovery of competitors in Europe and Asia kept the US as the major supplier of manufactured goods worldwide. In addition, Eisenhower was able to use his status as a former general to reassure the American people that there was no need to carry on increasing the defence budget excessively.

Reasons for economic growth

A number of factors helped encourage what has become known as the Eisenhower boom. There was the maturing of war bonds, an investment scheme put in place by the government during the Second World War which paid out in the years that followed. There was government spending on both the **GI Bill**, which led to a boost in housebuilding and an increase in the numbers of educated people in the population, and $40 billion annually on the burgeoning military sector. The latter benefitted from the decisions taken by the Truman Administration to heed Kennan's encouragement that a strong military was the best way to discourage Soviet expansion. However, most significant was the role of business in promoting a consumer lifestyle to a larger audience.

LEARNING OBJECTIVES

In this chapter you will learn about:

- how the economy recovered and grew after 1952
- why the consumer society developed and its impact.

ACTIVITY

Evaluating primary sources

With reference to Source 1, try to summarise Eisenhower's economic aims as he campaigned for a second term. How is this message in keeping with how Eisenhower was seen by the public?

CROSS-REFERENCE

Look at Chapter 7, page 55 for more information on the impact of Stalin's death.

KEY TERM

Gross Domestic Product (GDP): the total value of all goods and services produced within a country. Usually measured over a year, it is a useful indicator of the relative wealth of a country

macroeconomics and microeconomics: macroeconomics is the study of the whole economy, microeconomics looks at the financial state of individuals or small groups

per capita income: the amount of money an individual earns in a year

CROSS-REFERENCE

For a recap on the GI Bill, revisit Chapter 1, page 8.

'Eisenhower Answers America'

Before 1952 the use of television by politicians had been limited and dull, with candidates buying time to show full half-hour speeches. Advertising executive Rosser Reeves convinced Eisenhower that advertising within TV shows like *I Love Lucy* would be cheaper and more effective. The 'Eisenhower Answers America' campaign saw Ike responding to questions from ordinary people. Eisenhower's responses helped establish him as a straight talker, in touch with America.

The growth of the media and advertising

For those who had grown up with the austerity of the Great Depression and the limited amount of consumer goods during the Second World War this was a new and exciting world. The abundant resources of the US and the explosion of advertising across newspapers, radio and television had created a desire for glitz and glamour. Where the older generation had had to make do and mend, those who came of age in the 1950s became 'consumers'. Their purchasing desires were driven by advertising which grew enormously from $6 billion annually in 1950 to more than $13 billion by 1963. Robert Sarnoff, President of the National Broadcasting Company, said advertising's effect on the economy 'Advertising is the foot on the accelerator, the hand on the throttle'.

Businesses were investing heavily, converting plants that had been used to make military equipment to produce consumer goods in huge numbers. These consumer goods included those that made use of new technology and, in particular, television. The increased sales of televisions also created a captive market for advertisers who began to build on the work of public relations expert **Edward Bernays** to sell their products to a growing population with increased leisure time. Politicians also began to use advertising techniques more effectively such as in Eisenhower's 1952 **'Eisenhower Answers America'** campaign ads.

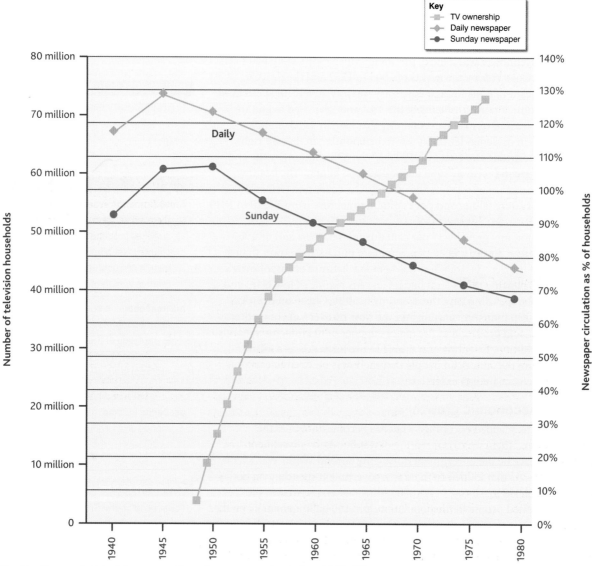

Fig. 1 *Figures for television ownership and newspaper circulation, 1940–80*

Good job for a girl—
Good girl for the job !

Meet Mary, your Bell Telephone Operator. She's the cheerful, efficient girl who's always on hand to speed your calls and help you in times of emergency.

Her job takes intelligence, alertness, and a true spirit of service. Mary has them all.

Telephone work is interesting and it has many other attractive features. Full pay while learning, regular increases, vacations with pay, sickness and accident benefits, even a pension plan that costs her nothing. And the chance to advance—a very important advantage for women in telephone work.

Mary likes her work and she's typical of the many telephone women—single and married—who are proud to be part of a company that gives such important service to everyone.

Telephone men and women
know it's a good place
to work . . . **Bell Telephone System**

Fig. 2 *A 1950s advert for Bell Telephone System operators*

Increased availability of credit

Eisenhower focused much of his attention on balancing the federal budget, but America's consumers were less thrifty and were lured by cheap credit. This came in housing through the Federal Housing Administration and the Veteran's Administration which both offered low-interest loans to allow families to buy new homes. **A building boom** followed with large suburbs being built such as Levittown in New York where standardising plot sizes and appearance enabled the cheap mass production of housing for 80,000 families at a cost of around $8000 per home featuring all the modern conveniences that Nixon boasted about when he met Khrushchev in Moscow. Levittown also operated restricted covenants, meaning African-Americans couldn't buy property there.

Cheap credit was also helped by the first credit card, from the Diner's Club which launched in 1950. Initially intended for restaurant payments, the idea caught on and others were launched including American Express in 1958. As a result, private debt more than doubled from $104.8 billion to $263.3 billion by 1960 as consumers borrowed to buy cars, refrigerators, televisions and vacuum cleaners. The growth in debt further stimulated the economy and created jobs in manufacturing.

The baby boom

Demand was also stimulated by the baby boom which added millions of new Americans to the population between 1946 and 1959. An explosion in sales of baby food, toys, nappies and other associated products followed and as the late 1950s rolled around and the first of the boomers entered their teenage years, the creation of an entirely new demographic became increasingly clear. Teenagers became a powerful economic force. *Life* magazine ran an article in August 1959 describing them as a '$10 billion power' citing their spending on food, cosmetics and entertainment.

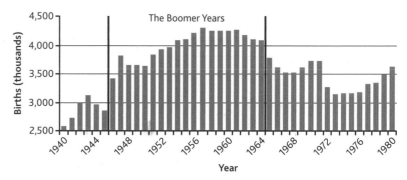

Fig. 3   *Birth rates in the USA, 1940–80*

The impact of the 'consumer society'

By 1960 Americans owned nearly half of the cars and telephones in the world and 90 per cent of families had a television while virtually all workers enjoyed at least two weeks of paid holidays each year. A more obvious manifestation of growing prosperity was the growth of the suburbs prompted by the increase in credit to buy housing, for many Americans this was a key constituent of the 'American Dream'.

Access to the suburbs was made possible by the boom in sales of cars. Cheap gasoline from domestic production allowed the sales of General Motors, Chrysler and Ford to jump from 5.1 million vehicles per annum in 1949 to 7.9 million by 1955. Eisenhower's Interstate Highway Act of 1956, inspired by Hitler's autobahns that he had seen in Germany, further stimulated demand and jobs. The $26 billion of federal budget allocated to highway construction also reflected a departure in Republican priorities towards a period of more pronounced federal intervention, although the initial justification was as a civilian evacuation aid in case of nuclear attack. By 1959 the American standard of living was unparalleled in the rest of the world and the American Dream was increasingly promoted as part of Cold War propaganda.

In 1959 Vice President Nixon and the Soviet Leader Khrushchev held an impromptu 'Kitchen Debate' in Moscow about the merits of American capitalism versus Soviet style communism. On a return trip to the US in September 1959, Eisenhower arranged for Khrushchev to take a helicopter trip over busy roads, parking lots and malls to witness the success of the US economy first hand. Chastened by the experience, Khrushchev returned

Fig. 4 *The Levittown housing development in New York State*

to the USSR and demanded a rapid increase in the production of consumer goods.

SOURCE 2

Extract from the 'Kitchen Debate' which took place in a model American kitchen at the American National Exhibition in Moscow, 1959. The Soviet news agency Pravda had criticised the exhibition as unrepresentative of the average American worker. The debate was broadcast in both the US and USSR:

Nixon: I want to show you this kitchen. It is like those of our houses in California.
    [Nixon points to dishwasher.]
Khrushchev: We have such things. Your capitalistic attitude toward women does not occur under communism.
Nixon: This house can be bought for $14,000, and most Americans can buy a home in the bracket of $10,000 to $15,000. Any steelworker could buy this

Evaluating primary sources

With reference to Source 2 explain how Nixon argues that American capitalism helped improve the lives of average Americans. How valuable is this source as proof that the lives of people in the US were improving?

house. They earn $3 an hour. This house costs about $100 a month to buy on a 25 year contract.

Khrushchev: We have steelworkers who can afford to spend $14,000 for a house. Your American houses are built to last only 20 years so builders could sell new houses at the end. We build firmly. I have read much about America and American houses, and I do not think that this exhibit and what you say is strictly accurate.

SOURCE 3

An extract from the 1958 book *The Affluent Society* by Harvard economist JK Galbraith, who was an adviser to Roosevelt, Truman, Kennedy and Johnson:

In a community where public services have failed to keep abreast of private consumption things are very different. Here, in an atmosphere of private opulence and public squalor, the private goods have full sway. Schools do not compete with television and the movies. Moreover, in a society which sets large store by production, and which has highly effective machinery for providing what the public wants, there are strong pressures to have as many wage earners in the family as possible. As always, all social behaviour is of a piece. If both parents are engaged in private production, the burden on the public services is further increased. Children, in effect, become the charge of the community for an appreciable part of the time. If the services of the community do not keep pace, this will be another source of disorder.

Entertainment and leisure

Galbraith's warnings did little to stem the flow of consumer goods and services. Automation of manufacturing and farming led to an increase in the **tertiary sector** of the economy and demand for entertainment grew. Live sport and music became more popular and television played its part in popularising both. However this came at the expense of cinema where attendances began a slow decline that was to last until the mid 1980s. One exception was the Disney Company whose films remained enormously popular and who opened the first of its theme parks in Anaheim, California, in 1955. Disney quickly realised the importance of souvenirs and additional sales and their products contributed to the growth of toys and games as consumer items. Disney also played its part in the **homogenising** of the American experience as an entire nation began to experience the world in a similar way.

Housing had been homogenised by the growth of the suburbs, products had gone the same way through advertising and as the decade progressed, other experiences such as shopping, eating and listening to music also began to be indistinguishable from the East to the West Coast.

The first climate-controlled indoor shopping mall opened in Edina, Minnesota, in October 1956, defying the harsh temperatures of the North and providing covered access to 72 stores with 5200 parking spaces. The Southdale Center was soon being replicated across the US with restaurants and childcare facilities, making it a single destination for consumers. The growth of out-of-town malls also contributed to the rapid development of the fast food industry which had been pioneered by the White Castle brand in the 1920s but was joined by **Ray Kroc's** McDonald's and Burger King in 1954 which popularised the idea of drive-through dining.

KEY TERM

tertiary sector: the services sector of the economy where jobs are in finance, government, the media, hospitality, education and retail as opposed to primary (farming, etc.) and secondary (manufacturing) sectors

homogenising: a word used to describe a process that makes things the same for wider and wider groups. Television and advertising in America meant the same products were sold and consumed nationwide, from Oregon to Florida and the same TV shows and films were watched, reducing the previous differences between South and North East, West Coast and Midwest.

In 1954 **Ray Kroc (1902–84)** correctly identified that the popular drive-through hamburger restaurant owned by the McDonald brothers Richard and Maurice in San Bernardino, had the potential to be a model for a chain of restaurants. He persuaded the brothers to allow him to franchise their model. By 1961 McDonald's boasted 228 restaurants in the US and Kroc bought out the McDonald brothers for $2.7 million.

Fig. 5   *Kroc was a Czech-American businessman*

ACTIVITY

Extension

In groups research the top ten most popular songs, TV shows and films of the 1950s. Present to the class on what they suggest about the Eisenhower era.

The entertainment industry of the USA in the 1950s seems very tame by today's standards. Shows like *I Love Lucy* and artists like Elvis Presley and Perry Como hardly seem like the kind of thing that would alarm a government. However other artists, musicians, writers and actors were breaking through who would form the backdrop to the youth rebellion of the 1960s. Those born during the baby boom would enter their late teens in that decade filled with a sense of injustice and anger. Artists like Jackson Pollock, writers like Jack Kerouac and Allen Ginsberg and musicians like Bob Dylan were either beginning their careers or coming to wider attention whilst the films of James Dean and Marlon Brando were providing a template for teenage behaviour.

Limitations of the consumer boom

The prosperity of the Eisenhower years didn't reach all Americans. A quarter still lived in poverty, defined as an annual income under $3000 for a family of four, which was exposed by **Michael Harrington** in his book, *The Other America*. This invisible poverty was easy to ignore and for most Americans Eisenhower seemed to have successfully piloted the country through the difficulties of the post-war years.

However, the Eisenhower years saw two recessions. A minor one in 1954 and a more serious one in 1958 which saw 5 million Americans unemployed and production fall by 14 per cent. This damaged the Republican reputation for financial probity and was heavily exploited by Kennedy in his 1960 election campaign. On average however, in Eisenhower's presidency, unemployment remained low, bottoming out at 4.5 per cent in 1957. Inflation also remained low and averaged 2 per cent. Eisenhower's focus on balancing the budget was largely achieved with surpluses in 1956 and 1957 and again in 1960.

The achievement of balanced budgets came with Eisenhower's scaling-back of aspects of the 'New Deal'. Federal subsidies to the Tennessee Valley Authority (TVA) were dramatically reduced for example, from $185 million in 1952 to just $12 million in 1960 and Eisenhower went further and

Fig. 6   *Harrington was one of the most renowned left-wingers in America*

Michael Harrington (1928–89) was a Yale Law School graduate who became an atheist campaigner, socialist, author Professor of Political Science. His book *The Other America* had a substantial influence on the anti-poverty programmes of Kennedy and Johnson. He was described by the historian Arthur Schlesinger as 'the only responsible radical in America' for his willingness not only to debate with right-wing figures but also to challenge the ideas of radical young left-wingers.

CROSS-REFERENCE

The Soil Bank is covered on page 40 in Chapter 5.

KEY TERM

subsidy: money granted by the government to help an industry or business keep the price of a commodity or service low.

changed many aspects of the energy generation industry. He sold off power plants and allowed the money from drilling rights to go to the states rather than to the federal government, a popular move in the southern states which had coastlines on the Gulf of Mexico. Despite this cutting, privatising and redeploying, Eisenhower struggled to control government spending which rose by 11 per cent during his presidency due to the pressure to increase military spending and compete with the Russians in the Space Race.

The increased productivity of agriculture created problems leading to the setting up of a **Soil Bank** as the real prices of food dropped, requiring the government to provide **subsidies** to farmers of $5.1 billion per year in 1960, up from $1 billion in 1951 in order to avoid a dangerous crash in prices. The lessons of the Great Depression made these measures necessary and acceptable to a Republican party which was usually uncomfortable with such heavy handed government intervention.

The effects of the consumer boom were not uniform across society with some groups benefitting disproportionately to others. Teenagers gained huge freedoms and opportunities, with part-time work allowing them to have considerable disposable income to spend on music, movies and clothes. The middle class as a whole grew with an increase in employment brought about by consumption and a more comfortable life in the growing suburbs. The rich grew richer with the wealthiest families such as the Gettys, Rockefellers and Mellons taking advantage of investment opportunities in growth industries, while entrepreneurs like Ray Kroc in fast food, Lucille Ball in the media and Sam Walton in retail began to amass fortunes. For others though, the consumer boom merely highlighted the inaccessibility of the 'American Dream'. Many women had lost their war jobs to accommodate returning men and were now trapped in a suffocating suburban world that provided no challenges. The elderly became increasingly isolated as families moved out of towns and into nuclear family units such as those at Levittown. For ethnic minorities the situation was worse. As industrialisation made manual jobs redundant many lost their employment status at the very time money began to bring enormous consumer opportunities. Coupled with this was the fact that employment practices were still often racist and ethnic minority workers would be the first to be fired in the event of a downturn.

ACTIVITY

Construct a spider diagram showing the positive and negative effects of the consumer boom under the four principal categories of Economic effects, political effects, social effects and the effects on military spending.

Summary

The 1950s saw a dramatic change in the nature of the American economy, creating a commercial landscape far closer to the one we see today. The growth in consumer spending led to wholesale changes to both society and the landscape as suburbs grew and cities were hollowed out as whites moved out and left minority groups in the inner cities. This in turn led to a **decline in services** such as health and education along with a reduction in the availability of work and quality housing. Culture became increasingly homogenised with the same television shows airing nationwide and the same products in every store.

It is easy to be cynical about this period in American history but many looked back on the Eisenhower period with huge affection as the epitome

CROSS-REFERENCE

Revisit Chapter 4 for detail on the decline in services and housing.

of the American Dream. Ike was a comforting figure, a hero that could be trusted, who stood up to Khrushchev, ended the Korean war, avoided further wars, presided over economic growth, more jobs, huge leaps forward in terms of quality of life and an end to the McCarthy witch-hunts.

 PRACTICE QUESTION

'During Eisenhower's presidency, American society was transformed.' Assess the validity of this view.

STUDY TIP

Questions on changes in society can be difficult to address as societal change is difficult to measure. One way to approach these questions is to take a snapshot of where society was at the start of a period and where it was at the end. Of course things don't change for everyone in the same way so by breaking the issue of societal change down into demographics you can achieve a more nuanced answer. Useful demographics to think of are age (young people, the middle-aged, the elderly), gender, class (the rich, the workers, those in poverty) and race.

 PRACTICE QUESTION

Evaluating primary sources

With reference to Sources 2 and 3 and your understanding of the historical context, which of these two sources is more valuable in explaining whether the consumer boom had a positive effect?

STUDY TIP

The issue of provenance is key here. Galbraith is an economist who had advised former presidents. Nixon is engaged in a spur of the moment debate with an ideological rival which is being broadcast. The question also asks you to decide what was a positive effect. Galbraith's account suggested that there were negatives to the consumer boom; does Khrushchev make any valid points?

LEARNING OBJECTIVES

In this chapter you will learn about:

- Superpower rivalry and conflict with the USSR

- the ways in which Eisenhower and the US responded to developments in Western and Eastern Europe

- the US reaction to the rise of communism in Asia

- the US response to the crises in the Middle East.

SOURCE 1

An extract from Eisenhower's Farewell Address to the Nation on 17 January 1961, broadcast on television. Three days later he left the presidency and was allowed to reinstate his rank of Five-Star General, the top rank in the US Army:

Until the latest of our world conflicts, the United States had no armaments industry. But now we can no longer risk emergency improvisation of national defense; we have been compelled to create a permanent armaments industry of vast proportions. Added to this, three and a half million men and women are directly engaged in the defense establishment. We annually spend on military security more than the net income of all United States corporations. This conjunction of an immense military establishment and a large arms industry is new in the American experience. The total influence – economic, political, even spiritual – is felt in every city, every State house, every office of the Federal government. In the councils of government, we must guard against the acquisition of unwarranted influence, whether sought or unsought, by the military-industrial complex. Only an alert and knowledgeable citizenry can ensure the huge industrial and military machinery of defense serves with our peaceful methods and goals, so that security and liberty may prosper together.

ACTIVITY

Evaluating primary sources

1. Summarise Eisenhower's speech in Source 1 in one sentence.
2. Share your summary with a partner and discuss whether you feel Eisenhower's speech conveyed a significant argument.
3. What would the value of this speech be for an historian studying Eisenhower's attitudes as president?

KEY TERM

'massive retaliation': used in a 1954 speech by John Foster Dulles where he referred to 'the deterrent of massive retaliatory power', the term suggested the US would respond to provocation from both the Soviet Union and China with extreme force

As Supreme Allied Commander in Europe during the war President Eisenhower was expected to cope well with foreign relations. Eisenhower had a reputation for organisation from his time in the military and was determined to make the Department of State work better. He appointed **John Foster Dulles** as his Secretary of State, an anti-communist and advocate of **'massive retaliation'**, who drew a clear distinction between policy, the remit of the National Security Council (NSC) and day-to-day operations, which he felt should be in the hands of the Department of State. Dulles also believed that some issues, such as covert operations, were too sensitive to be discussed by the full NSC.

CROSS-REFERENCE

See Chapter 2, page 11 for details on the NSC (National Security Council).

CROSS-REFERENCE

See the Key Profile on Allen Dulles in this chapter, page 58.

To recap on brinksmanship, go back to the Key Term in Chapter 2, page 15.

KEY PROFILE

John Foster Dulles (1888–1959) was legal counsel to Wilson at the Treaty of Versailles and was later appointed Secretary of State by Eisenhower. He became a highly significant influence on foreign policy. A staunch anti-communist, trained lawyer and older brother of the Director of the CIA **Allen Dulles**, he advocated both 'massive retaliation' and **'brinksmanship'** as well as the support of the French in their war against Vietnam.

Fig. 1 *Dulles advocated an aggressive stance against communism*

Superpower rivalry and conflict with the USSR

On 5 March 1953 Stalin died. Almost immediately protests broke out in East Germany which had to be suppressed while the power vacuum was addressed by the **Kremlin**. It took several years before **Nikita Khrushchev** emerged as the undisputed new leader of the USSR.

KEY PROFILE

Nikita Khrushchev (1894–1971) was an early member of the Communist Party. He worked his way up the party ranks before emerging victorious from the power struggle after Stalin's death. In 1956 he delivered a 'Secret Speech' in which he denounced Stalin's cult of personality and called for 'peaceful co-existence' with the West. Nevertheless his actions precipitated both the Hungarian Crisis of 1956 and the Cuban Missile Crisis.

The Space Race

While conventional wars had always been fought between protagonists on a battlefield, the advent of Mutually Assured Destruction (MAD) made the Cold War morph into other spheres. Principal amongst these was the space race with all its connotations of technological superiority and the prospect of whether the Moon, Mars or 'Space' itself would 'go red.' On 4 October 1957 the Soviet Union put the first man-made object in space. Sputnik was a 58cm polished metal sphere that orbited earth until 5 January 1958. The response in the US was immediate. Eisenhower had known about the project but underestimated the blow of being beaten into space by the Russians; America's position as the technological leader of the world suddenly looked shaky. This blow was compounded when the Soviets launched a second craft, sputnik 2, on 3 November 1958, containing a dog, Laika. The US Vanguard TV3 rocket satellite then blew up after only climbing 4ft in a televised launch leading US newspapers to christen it 'Flopnik', 'Dudnik', and best of all, 'Kaputnik'. The blow to US prestige was tangible and forced the Eisenhower Administration to rely more heavily on **Werner von Braun** and his team to develop more reliable rocket technologies.

KEY PROFILE

Werner von Braun (1912–1977) was a brilliant aerospace engineer who was an ambivalent member of the Nazi party. He surrendered to US forces at the end of the war and was soon employed by the Army to develop rocket technology. He became a US citizen in 1955 and Eisenhower transferred him to NASA in 1958 where he led the development of the Saturn series of rockets that eventually put 12 Americans in total on the moon.

The Arms Race

Following the detonation of the atomic bombs over Hiroshima and Nagasaki in 1945 the US and the USSR had been locked in a race to develop more powerful bombs with greater range and accuracy. The rocket technology required also aided the space race. By 1953 hydrogen bombs with a destructive power seven times that unleashed on Hiroshima had been developed by both sides and by 1955, the US was keeping a third of its nuclear bombers ready to fly at 15 minutes' notice.

KEY TERM

Kremlin: the name, meaning 'fortress inside a city' given to the seat of the leader of the Soviet Union since the Bolshevik Revolution in 1917. In the heart of Moscow, is often used as a synonym for the Soviet or Russian leadership in the way the White House is used for the US presidency

ACTIVITY

Use the 'Diamond Nine' template below to prioritise as many reasons as you can think of as to why the death of Stalin was significant for the USA.

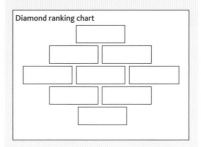

Diamond ranking chart

Date	Name	Yield (kT)*	Country	Significance
1952	*Ivy Mike*	10,400	USA	First thermonuclear weapon
1952	*Ivy King*	500	USA	Largest pure-fission weapon ever tested
1953	*Joe 4*	400	USSR	First fusion weapon test by the USSR
1954	*Castle Bravo*	15,000	USA	Largest nuclear detonation conducted by USA
1955	*RDS-37*	1,600	USSR	First thermonuclear weapon test by USSR
1961	*Tsar Bomba*	50,000	USSR	Largest thermonuclear weapon ever tested

Fig. 2 *Development of nuclear weapons by the USA and USSR (*1kt is the equivalent of 1000 tonnes of TNT)*

> **KEY TERM**
>
> **missile gap:** the name given to the perception that grew in the US after 1957 that the Soviets had surpassed the USA in terms of the number, range and power of their missile capability; U-2 spy flights suggested this was incorrect

In 1957 the USA had a stockpile of 5543 nuclear weapons compared to the USSR's 650, making Kennedy's later suggestion that there was a **missile gap** seem ludicrous. However, the USSR had succeeded in launching sputnik into space in October 1957. More significantly, the development of Intercontinental Ballistic Missiles (ICBMs) which could fly thousands of miles before hitting a target, began to make the locating of missile bases near to the US a serious concern for the Eisenhower government.

Dulles therefore persuaded Eisenhower to embrace the build-up of a nuclear arsenal as part of a policy known as the 'New Look' and popularly known as 'more bang for the buck'. The 'New Look' proposed a cost-effective response to communist aggression by balancing Cold War military commitments with the nation's financial resources to ensure the economy was never overstretched. Dulles argued that the US and its allies must be willing and able to respond vigorously to a communist threat and that the very real threat of 'massive retaliation' alongside conventional forces provided 'more basic security at less cost'.

Responses to developments in Western and Eastern Europe

Hungary

> **KEY TERM**
>
> **destalinisation:** the process of trying to remove the influence of Stalin after his death by revising his policies and dislodging the cult of personality surrounding him
>
> **Warsaw Pact:** a collective defence agreement concluded between the Soviet-controlled countries of Eastern Europe in 1955 promising to respond collectively if one was attacked. Its creation was prompted by West Germany joining NATO

By 1956 Khrushchev had control of the USSR and at the Twentieth Party Congress he gave a speech entitled 'On the Cult of Personality and its Consequences' denouncing Stalin's methods. Otherwise known as the 'Secret Speech' it began a process of **destalinisation** in the USSR under Khrushchev. The reaction in Eastern Europe was immediate as news of the speech leaked out, helped, allegedly, by the **CIA**, and people realised they were potentially free of Stalinist oppression. There were riots in Poland against the communist government. Protests in Hungary then led to the withdrawal of the hard-line leader Rakosi and his replacement with Imre Nagy who promised free elections, the restoration of farmland to private property and neutrality in the Cold War. Nagy also declared that Hungary would leave the **Warsaw Pact**.

The CIA

Established by Truman as part of the National Security Act of 1947, the Central Intelligence Agency (CIA) has a remit involving gathering intelligence about foreign governments, corporations and individuals, analysing the evidence and feeding the analysis to policymakers. In 1948 they were given further authority to carry out covert operations. In the 1950s alone the CIA was involved in covert operations in Cuba, Hungary, Laos, Guatemala, Iran and North Vietnam.

There was a widespread belief in Budapest that not only was Khrushchev amenable to a gradual relaxation of Stalinist control but also that Eisenhower, the great liberator of Europe, would support Hungary. However the prospect of a hole being created in the Iron Curtain by Hungarian secession from the Warsaw Pact was too much for Khrushchev who sent troops and tanks to Budapest in November of 1956. 3000 Hungarians were killed in bloody fighting while 200,000 fled across the border into Austria, and hence into the West.

CROSS-REFERENCE

For information on the Iron Curtain see Chapter 2, page 10.

Fig. 3 *A Hungarian man chops up a toppled statue of Stalin at the start of the Hungarian revolution of 1956*

Khrushchev quickly re-established control by installing János Kádár who crushed resistance. Eisenhower was able to claim that nothing in the containment policy or Truman Doctrine warranted going to war over a state rebelling against communist control but the failure of the USA to come to the aid of Hungary in 1956 made it abundantly clear that the world was to be divided into the two spheres for a considerable time.

SOURCE 2

An extract from a note by the Executive Secretary to the NSC on US Policy towards the Soviet Satellites in Eastern Europe, 3 July 1956:

Soviet domination of the Eastern European satellites remains firm and there appears little immediate prospect of basic change in this regard. While the satellite regimes have not been able to overcome widespread popular dissatisfaction with their communistic program and with their inclusion within

Evaluating primary sources

Highlight and annotate Sources 1 and 2 with your contextual knowledge. For example you might highlight 'satellite regimes' and provide the context of which countries this refers to.

KEY PROFILE

Fig. 4 *Allen Dulles was the brother of Secretary of State John Foster Dulles*

Allen Dulles (1893–1969) served as the Director of the CIA from 1953 to 1961 when Kennedy removed him following the **Bay of Pigs** fiasco. He commissioned the U-2 Spy plane and was involved in the *coups d'état* in Iran and Guatemala. He later sat on the Warren Commission investigation into Kennedy's assassination.

CROSS-REFERENCE

See Chapter 10, page 82 for details on the Bay of Pigs.

For more information on the Korean War see Chapter 2 pages 17–18.

the Soviet world, nevertheless there are no known underground groups capable of coordinated, sustained resistance activities to the governments in power in any of the countries concerned. As long as a Moscow-dominated communist leadership remains in power in these countries and is backed by Soviet military force or threat of force, it is unlikely that Soviet ability to exercise effective control over and to exploit the resources of the European satellites can be appreciably reduced.

Berlin

Khrushchev felt that he had won the battle over Hungary and began to look to Berlin and the long-term aim of removing the West from their enclave in East Germany. On 10 November 1958, Khrushchev demanded that the Western powers pull their forces out of West Berlin within six months. Eisenhower was aware that a repeat of the Berlin Airlift was impossible given the growth of the city in the decade since 1948 but Berlin was symbolic of the fight against communism. For Khrushchev, the lack of a border meant 20 per cent of the population of East Germany had escaped to the West by 1961. Eisenhower was determined not to give in to Soviet demands so a foreign minister's conference was held in Geneva in 1959. Progress was limited but sufficient for Eisenhower to invite Khrushchev to the US for further talks. Khrushchev arrived in the US on 15 September 1959 for an 11-day tour. The Soviet leader met with Eisenhower at Camp David where the two agreed that there would be no firm deadline to solve the question of Berlin but did agree that Eisenhower would visit Moscow the following year.

The U-2 Crisis, 1960

The visit became diplomatically impossible after the Soviet Union shot down an American U-2 spy plane on 1 May 1960. Khrushchev, who felt he had a close personal bond with Eisenhower, thought that **Allen Dulles** was responsible for the flights, especially as the US, assuming the pilot to have been killed, announced that a weather plane had been lost near the Turkish-Soviet border. When Khrushchev produced the pilot, Gary Powers, alive on 5 May, Eisenhower was forced to admit that he had ordered the spying missions, calling them a 'distasteful necessity'. A proposed conference between the two in Paris broke down when Khrushchev arrived, made his demands and then suggested the conference should be postponed for six months ensuring Eisenhower would be gone and a new US president would be in place. The Berlin problem would then pass to a new Administration.

Reactions to the rise of communism in Asia

Ending the war in Korea

Eisenhower went to **Korea** on 2 December 1952 and decided that drastic action was required. Combining diplomacy with a clear statement of intent about US military power over the next seven months brought the protagonists to the negotiating table and on 27 July 1953 an armistice was signed leaving the Korean Peninsula divided into north and south at the 38th parallel. In a 1956 *Life* magazine interview, Dulles described how he had intimated to China and North Korea that the US was prepared to use atomic weapons. His ruse was helped by the belligerent attitude of McArthur earlier in the war. Dulles claimed that his policy, which became known as 'brinksmanship' ended the war while avoiding a larger conflict.

Eisenhower's success strengthened his hand both at home and in foreign affairs. His effective use of aggression, coming so soon after Stalin's death in March 1953, re-established him on the world stage and gave heart to the NATO alliance. The effectiveness of brinksmanship as a policy also ensured that the military build-up called for by NSC-68 could continue.

Taiwan

The outbreak of the Korean War had made Taiwan strategically important for the US despite the fact that Mao claimed it was part of China and Truman had been willing to let it be retaken. Jiang Jieshi's willingness to allow Taiwan to be used as a base for US Naval operations ensured a degree of protection for the island which was vital when Mao ordered the shelling of two islands controlled by Taiwan but close to the Chinese mainland in 1954.

Eisenhower reacted to the shelling of the islands, Quemoy and Matsu, by securing the Formosa Resolution in January 1955 with only six of 494 members of Congress voting against it. The resolution provided for the defence of Taiwan. John Foster Dulles followed this up by suggesting that the US was seriously considering a nuclear attack on China. On 1 May the Chinese ceased the shelling prompting a belief, in Dulles' mind at least, that the strong stance had succeeded in containing China.

Fig. 5 *Eisenhower with Jiang Jieshi on a visit to Taiwan in 1960*

Vietnam

By 1954 the war in Vietnam between Ho Chi Minh's forces and the French had clearly turned against the Europeans with French public support slipping. Eisenhower agreed to covert air support being provided by American B-26 bombers, whilst Dulles suggested providing the French with a nuclear device. Eisenhower also gave orders to plan for Operation Vulture, a US intervention in Vietnam, which had the support of Vice President Richard Nixon but was eventually rejected by Eisenhower himself.

Ho Chi Minh was in a strong position when peace talks began in Geneva in May after a crushing defeat of the French at Dien Bien Phu. On 20 July 1954 a decision was reached to partition Vietnam into two states, North and South with a promise to hold a general election in both by June 1956. However when Ngô Đình Diệm, a committed anti-communist took power in fraudulent elections in 1955, the US supported his regime, turning a blind eye to injustices against the Buddhist population because of Diệm's strong anti-communist beliefs.

ACTIVITY

Draw up a 3 by 3 grid and in each box put the following terms – Hungary, Berlin, civil rights, Stalin's death, nuclear weapons, U-2 Crisis, Dulles, Khrushchev, Eisenhower. See how many coherent sentences you can make that connect three of these people or developments together.

CROSS-REFERENCE

Jiang Jieshi is profiled in Chapter 2, page 17.

ACTIVITY

Hold an in-class competition to see who can find the most pictures of Eisenhower meeting with dictators from Asia (or elsewhere). Discuss as a class whether it is right for the US president to meet with leaders of distasteful regimes.

CROSS-REFERENCE

For more information on the situation in Vietnam, see Chapter 2, page 17.

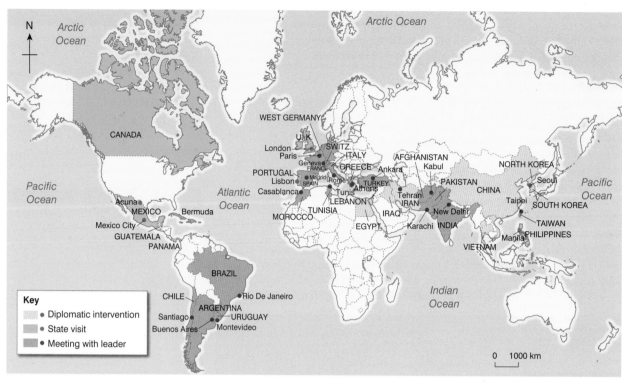

Fig. 6 *Eisenhower's overseas visits and interventions, 1952–60*

Eisenhower had avoided military intervention in Vietnam and hoped that **SEATO** would be sufficient to contain communism in Asia. However another unsatisfactory partition agreement suggested that Vietnam, like Korea and Germany was an issue that was likely to return for a future president.

KEY TERM

SEATO: a South East Asian version of NATO, created by John Foster Dulles in September 1954, that aimed to prevent further communist gains in South East Asia. Members included Australia, France, New Zealand, Pakistan, Bangladesh, the Philippines, Thailand, the UK and the US

KEY TERM

non-aligned: a term used to describe a state that did not consider itself to be part of either the US or the Soviet sphere of influence. The original meaning of the term 'Third World' also referred to these non-aligned states

Responses to crises in the Middle East

Truman's recognition of the new state of Israel in May 1948 had stoked tensions in the Middle East because the land from which the new country was formed had previously belonged to the Arab dominated state of Palestine. These tensions were worsened by the increasing dependence of the Western powers on Middle Eastern oil. The area was also strategically key to Dulles' plan to encircle and contain the Soviet Union with a series of Treaty Organisations. NATO had served this purpose to good effect in Europe where there had been no significant tension since the Berlin Blockade, SEATO was designed to achieve similar goals in South East Asia, which left the Middle East as the only area not covered by a treaty organisation backed by US military power. In the Middle East left-leaning leaders like the democratically elected leader of Iran, Prime Minister Mohammad Mosaddegh, were seen to be susceptible to communist influence. This led Dulles to approve a CIA plot to depose Mossadegh in 1953, following his decision to nationalise the oil industry. In 1955 Dulles was able to create the Central Treaty Organization (CENTO) a second NATO parallel made up of Iran, Iraq, the United Kingdom, Pakistan and Turkey. However Dulles' policy foundered when the Iraqi monarchy was overthrown in 1958 and the Soviets began to develop friendly relations with the new **non-aligned** Iraq along with Egypt, Syria and Libya.

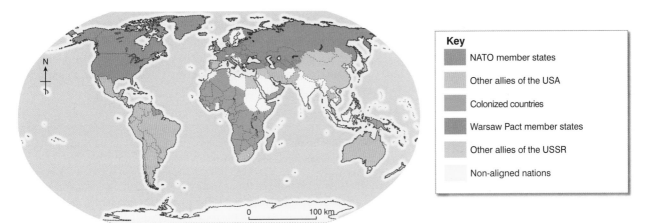

Fig. 7 *The alignment of states by 1959*

Suez Crisis

In July 1956 the Egyptian leader Nasser nationalised the Suez Canal, the key waterway built and run by the British and the French which provided access for ships travelling between Europe and Asia. Nasser's plan was that taking control of the canal on Egypt's behalf would enable him to use the money raised by the Canal to fund the Aswan Dam. This was a key part of his plan to further industrialisation in Egypt. Britain and France retaliated by striking a secret deal with Israel whereby the latter would attack Egypt, the European powers would call for a ceasefire and when it was not forthcoming would begin to bomb Cairo under the pretext of trying to force peace.

All three powers were convinced they would have the support of Eisenhower but with a re-election campaign in full swing and tensions with the Soviets elsewhere, Eisenhower didn't want to be seen to be supporting imperialism and instead used financial pressures to force the British and French into a humiliating withdrawal. Nasser's clever decision not to side with either the Soviets or the USA meant both were willing to help him with arms sales and aid and he hoped to get US financial help to build the dam.

EXTRACT 1

When the British–French–Israeli invasion forced them to choose, Eisenhower and Dulles came down, with instant decisiveness, on the side of the Egyptians. They preferred alignment with Arab nationalism, even if it meant alienating pro-Israeli voters on the eve of a Presidential Election in the United States, even if it meant throwing the NATO alliance into its most divisive crisis yet, even if it meant risking whatever was left of the Anglo-American 'special relationship', even if it meant voting with the Soviet Union in the United Nations Security Council at a time when the Russians, themselves, were invading Hungary and crushing – far more brutally than anything that happened in Egypt – a rebellion against their own authority there. The fact that the Eisenhower Administration itself applied crushing economic pressure to the British and French to disengage from Suez might have been expected to gain the United States the lasting gratitude of Nasser, the Egyptians and the Arab world. Instead, the Americans lost influence in the Middle East as a result of Suez, while the Russians gained it.

We Now Know by John Lewis Gaddis (Clarendon Press, 1998)

ACTIVITY

Evaluating primary sources

Gaddis was the pre-eminent Cold War historian during the period. In 1998, with the benefit of material from the Soviet archives, he revisited the topic, producing a new interpretation of the events of 1945–63.

What reasons does Gaddis give to explain why he believes Eisenhower should have sided with the British, French and Israelis during the Suez Crisis?

ACTIVITY

Evaluating primary sources

On the basis of Source 3 and your understanding of the Truman Doctrine, how did the Eisenhower Doctrine differ? What might the consequences of these differences be?

CROSS-REFERENCE

For more details on the Truman Doctrine, read Chapter 2, pages 13–14.

To avoid a repetition of the issues of 1956 in Hungary, in January 1957 Eisenhower issued the 'Eisenhower Doctrine' which committed the USA to assist any nation requesting assistance against armed aggression from any country controlled by international communism. Congress agreed to provide $200 million to fund such aid.

SOURCE 3

Extract from Eisenhower's Special Message to the Congress on the Situation in the Middle East, 5 January 1957:

Russia's rulers have long sought to dominate the Middle East. That was true of the Czars and it is true of the Bolsheviks. The reasons are not hard to find. The reason for Russia's interest in the Middle East is solely that of power politics. Considering her announced purpose of Communizing the world, it is easy to understand her hope of dominating the Middle East. It contains about two thirds of the presently known oil deposits of the world and it normally supplies the petroleum needs of many nations of Europe, Asia and Africa. It is now essential that the United States should manifest through joint action of the president and the Congress our determination to assist those nations of the Mid East area, which desire that assistance.

Summary

During the Eisenhower years, the USA consolidated the policy of containment, whilst attempting, largely through Dulles, to have a robust foreign policy that left the Soviet union in no doubt as to their willingness to use 'massive retaliation'. The USA ratified a series of treaties designed to encircle the Soviet Union through CENTO, SEATO and security treaties with Japan, South Korea, Taiwan and the Philippines. However in Eisenhower's handling of Khrushchev an opportunity was missed, the new Soviet premier had talked of 'peaceful co-existence' with the West, but ended the decade being increasingly antagonistic to the US and awaiting a new president, either the tough anti-communist Nixon, or the untested Kennedy.

STUDY TIP

Use your contextual knowledge here. Which of the two areas had the most importance for Eisenhower and the US and which situation was the most stable? In addition you might consider how willing Eisenhower was to intervene and commit troops.

 PRACTICE QUESTION

Evaluating primary sources

With reference to Sources 1, 2 and 3 and your understanding of the historical context, assess the value of these three sources to an historian studying Eisenhower's foreign policy priorities.

STUDY TIP

By drawing up a quick table as a plan, you should be able to show where Eisenhower lived up to or failed to live up to his promise in his foreign policy. Complete the table with countries and dates and you have the basis of a plan that will lead to a focused answer.

 PRACTICE QUESTION

'Eisenhower lived up to his 1952 promise to show no weakness in foreign policy.' Explain why you agree or disagree with this view.

8 African-Americans in the North and South, 1953–1960

Fig. 1 *A properly segregated social event: an annual barbeque on an Alabama plantation*

LEARNING OBJECTIVES

In this chapter you will learn about:

- the emergence of the Civil Rights Movement
- the policies and attitudes of the main political parties
- the responses of the state and federal authorities.

The position of African-Americans

The situation in the North

In the North *de facto* segregation remained the norm despite the limited efforts of the Truman Administration. Organisations like the National Urban League (NUL) continued to campaign for change but without creating spectacles like the **Bus Boycott** and the **Little Rock Crisis** that were taking place in the South. The NUL pushed tirelessly for integration in the racist trade unions and CORE, which had grown to 53 national chapters by the end of the Eisenhower presidency, was beginning to challenge *de facto* segregation in Chicago schools and elsewhere, taking on the powerful Democratic Mayor of Chicago, Richard Daley.

The problems of inner city areas remained the same as under Truman. White flight to the suburbs left the inner cities ethnically homogeneous and often dividing lines between white and black areas were clear such as the 8 Mile Road in Detroit. Black residents who lacked access to cars had to shop at local stores where prices were higher. Rents were increased by landlords aware of the fact that real estate agents could prevent wealthier African-Americans from moving out. Over all of this hung the threat of police violence and intimidation, while the promise of work, which had drawn many to the cities, had resolved into a series of low-paid and non-unionised service jobs.

In the House of Representatives Adam Clayton Powell and William Dawson were joined by Charles Diggs representing Michigan and Robert Nix Sr representing Pennsylvania but the Senate remained entirely white.

Into this combustible environment came Malcolm X in the most incendiary event in the Civil Rights Movement in the North, when in July 1959, a TV show aired called *The Hate that Hate Produced* which covered the **Nation of Islam** (NOI). It began with an extract from a speech by Louis X, later Louis Farrakhan, who had been the assistant minister to Malcolm X at the Harlem NOI Temple.

CROSS-REFERENCE

See later in this chapter, pages 66–67, for more information on the Bus Boycott and the Little Rock Crisis.

CROSS-REFERENCE

for more detail on Malcolm X and the Nation of Islam go back to Chapter 4, page 31.

SOURCE 1

An extract from a play called *The Trial* written by Louis X and shown in *The Hate That Hate Produced* television show of July 1959, in which a minister of the Nation of Islam delivers the speech as if it were a sermon:

I charge the white man with being the greatest liar on earth! I charge the white man with being the greatest drunkard on earth […] I charge the white man with being the greatest gambler on earth. I charge the white man, ladies and gentlemen of the jury, with being the greatest murderer on earth. I charge the white man with being the greatest peace-breaker on earth […] I charge the white man with being the greatest robber on earth. I charge the white man with being the greatest deceiver on earth. I charge the white man with being the greatest trouble-maker on earth. So therefore, ladies and gentlemen of the jury, I ask you, bring back a verdict of guilty as charged!

The effect of the programme was to terrify white viewers. Most powerfully a national audience was introduced to Malcolm X whose uncompromising erudite militancy, not to mention height and good looks immediately made him a celebrity figure. It became remarkably easy for a media which was hungry for stories to begin to cast Malcolm as the antithesis of **Martin Luther King, Jr** and as the spokesman for black people in the North.

CROSS-REFERENCE

See page 67 in this chapter for a Key Profile of Martin Luther King, Jr.

ACTIVITY

Make three lists of reasons why the Civil Rights Movement developed in the South in the way it did under the headings 'Political reasons', 'Social reasons' and 'Economic reasons'. Were these reasons less pressing in the North?

Fig. 2   *The Cuban leader Fidel Castro meeting Malcolm X in 1960 when the former had come to New York for a UN meeting*

ACTIVITY

What does the image above suggest about the tactics of Malcolm X in his campaign for civil rights?

The situation in the South

The war had heightened black awareness of injustice but it was not until the Eisenhower Administration that the Civil Rights Movement in the South began to gather momentum to tackle these injustices. A combination of **court victories for the NAACP** against Jim Crow Laws, the *Plessy v. Ferguson* decision of 1896 and the emergence of popular new figureheads like King was vital, but perhaps most important was the role of the media as television became more popular. Over half of US households owned a television by 1955 and could therefore see first hand the realities of segregation, particularly in the pivotal *Brown v. Board of Education* case.

CROSS-REFERENCE

Revisit the court victories for the NAACP in Chapter 4, page 33.

The emergence of the Civil Rights Movement

Education

While schools in the North were *de facto* segregated through the economic inequalities that led to ghettos, schools in the South were *de jure* segregated by Jim Crow Laws and the 1896 *Plessy v. Ferguson* ruling, which allowed states to provide separate facilities for black and white people, such as schools and water fountains, provided they were of equal quality.

Eisenhower was aware of the progress of the court case that has become known as *Brown v. Board of Education* of Topeka Kansas and in early 1953 *Brown* and five other cases reached the Supreme Court. Here the NAACP's legal team headed by Thurgood Marshall presented compelling legal and psychological evidence that separate school facilities were inherently unequal. On 17 May 1954 **Chief Justice Earl Warren** announced that the court had unanimously ruled in favour of *Brown*.

Fig. 3   *Warren helped end segregation in schools*

Earl Warren (1891–1974) was a three-time Republican Governor of California and, from 1953, Chief Justice of the Supreme Court renowned for presiding over a series of Liberal decisions. Warren also headed the investigation into the assassination of JFK which concluded that it was the work of one man: Lee Harvey-Oswald.

SOURCE 2

Adapted from the majority opinion of the Supreme Court in the *Brown* case, decided 17 May 1954. Chief Justice Earl Warren pushed for a unanimous decision from the other eight justices:

Today, education is perhaps the most important function of state and local governments. In these days, it is doubtful that any child may reasonably be expected to succeed in life if he is denied the opportunity of an education. Such an opportunity, where the state has undertaken to provide it, is a right which must be made available to all on equal terms. To separate children from others of similar age and qualifications solely because of their race generates a feeling of inferiority as to their status in the community that may affect their hearts and minds in a way unlikely to ever be undone. Whatever may have been the extent of psychological knowledge at the time of *Plessy v. Ferguson*, this finding is amply supported by modern authority. We conclude that in the field of public education the doctrine of 'separate but equal' has no place. Separate educational facilities are inherently unequal. Therefore, we hold that the plaintiffs and other similarly situated are deprived of the equal protection of the laws guaranteed by the 14th Amendment.

ACTIVITY

Evaluating primary sources

What reasons are given in Source 2 for the decision of the court? How might a Dixiecrat have sought to undermine these reasons?

CROSS-REFERENCE

See Chapter 4, page 31 for more detail on the Ku Klux Klan.

ACTIVITY

Examine the events covered in this chapter and draw up a table summarising the use of 'lawful means' to obstruct desegregation.

KEY TERM

manifesto: a published declaration of intentions usually produced by a political party. This term made the Southern Manifesto more alarming as it raised the possibility of the Southern Dixiecrat politicians splitting the Democratic Party

The victory was a landmark in US legal history and a triumph for the NAACP, vindicating their gradualist approach. But it also created problems for Eisenhower, who later said that appointing Warren as Chief Justice after the death of Chief Justice Fred Vinson in September 1953 was 'the biggest damned-fool mistake I ever made'.

Shortly after the case, opponents of desegregation began to retaliate. White Citizen's Councils were formed and by 1956 boasted 250,000 members. The **Ku Klux Klan** was revitalised and began to grow in membership and in brutality. More significantly for Eisenhower was the signing of The Southern **Manifesto**, a document drawn up and signed by 101 Dixiecrat Congressmen which threatened to use 'all lawful means' to oppose the Supreme Court's decision on the grounds of it infringing state's rights.

Eisenhower was faced with a potentially explosive situation with echoes of the 1861–5 Civil War. He was reluctant to use Federal power to enforce the decision and tried as far as possible to avoid commenting on subsequent events – including the brutal murder of a 14-year-old black Chicagoan, **Emmett Till**, in Money, Mississippi. This led to accusations that Eisenhower was against desegregation but a simpler explanation was that he did not want to have to deal with it. However the issue wouldn't go away. In 1956 the University of Alabama expelled its first black student, Autherine Lucy, despite

The murder of Emmett Till

On 28 August 1955 the body of a 14-year-old African-American boy from Chicago was found in Mississippi. The boy, Emmett Till, had been visiting relatives and had made a flirtatious comment to a white woman whose husband then sought him out to teach him a lesson. Till's mother decided to hold an open casket funeral for Emmett so the press could show how badly disfigured he was, and this caused a sensation in the media.

Orval Faubus (1910–84) served as Governor of Arkansas from 1955 to 1967 and famously used the Little Rock incident to establish a reputation as a tough pre-segregation candidate in contrast to his earlier moderate leanings. Faubus became the epitome of the 'all lawful means' promise of the Southern Manifesto.

Evaluating primary sources

Find one of the many famous images of Elizabeth Eckford's arrival at Little Rock Central High School and use Source 3 to write thought bubbles for the different people in the picture.

the NAACP having won a court case, *Lucy v. Adams*, in 1955 to secure her place. Eisenhower's refusal to intervene heartened the segregationists who were about to force his hand at Little Rock in Arkansas.

The Little Rock Crisis

In 1955 the Supreme Court had been forced to follow up the original *Brown* decision with a second, known as *Brown 2* when the NAACP sought to establish a timescale for desegregation of schools. The court's ruling, that desegregation should occur 'with all deliberate speed', left room for the southern state officials to implement delaying tactics. This was most obvious in Virginia where Senator Harry Byrd urged committed segregationists to adopt a strategy of 'Massive Resistance', including closing down schools completely.

Despite the opposition, desegregation of schools began, in Tennessee Governor Frank Clement vetoed a bill introduced in the state legislature to preserve integration and in September 1956 used the National Guard to protect the first black students to enter Clinton High School. In September 1957 Central High School in Little Rock, the capital of Arkansas, was due to accept its first nine black students. The Governor, **Orval Faubus** had already desegregated the bus system but decided to encourage opposition to the NAACP organised entry of the 'Little Rock Nine' to reinforce his segregationist credentials with voters. Faubus appeared on TV to warn that a riot might occur when Little Rock was integrated but this served to bring protesters out to block the students leading to controversial scenes and Faubus mobilised the National Guard to turn the students away. The scenes played out on national television and became a source of embarrassment for Eisenhower internationally, forcing him to federalise the National Guard and then dispatch the 101st Airborne to protect the students, becoming the first president to send troops into the South since the Civil War.

The soldiers escorted the nine students day by day at school but could not stop the intimidation, which included stabbings, throwing of acid and a threat to burn a student alive. The following year Faubus closed all of the public (state) schools in Little Rock claiming the city had to assert its rights against federal decisions. This period became known as 'The Lost Year' as no African-Americans could afford to attend the private schools which were opened. After the crisis Faubus was re-elected as Governor four times and later voted one of the ten most admired men in America in a 1958 Gallup poll. Harry Ashmore, the editor of the *Arkansas Gazette*, who won a 1958 Pulitzer Prize for his coverage of the crisis maintained that Faubus had manufactured the crisis, for political advantage and his manoeuvrings had made him a he ro to segregationists but Eisenhower had reinforced a vital precedent, that presidents had to support Supreme Court decisions.

Elizabeth Eckford, one of the Little Rock Nine, recalls her first day at Central High School in Little Rock. Due to a miscommunication Eckford arrived alone and was caught up in the violent anti-integration protest:

When I was able to steady my knees, I walked up to the guard who had let the white students in. When I tried to squeeze past him, he raised his bayonet and then the other guards closed in and raised their bayonets. They glared at me with a mean look and I was very frightened and didn't know what to do. I turned around and the crowd came toward me. Somebody started yelling 'Lynch her!' I tried to see a friendly face somewhere in the mob. I looked into the face of an old woman and it seemed a kind face, but when I looked at her again she spat on me. They came closer, shouting, 'No nigger bitch is going to get into our school.'

The Montgomery Bus Boycott

SOURCE 4

Address by **Martin Luther King, Jr** to 5000 black citizens in Holt Street Baptist Church, Montgomery, 5 December 1955:

The great glory of American democracy is the right to protest for right. My friends, don't let anybody make us feel that we are to be compared in our actions with the Ku Klux Klan or with the White Citizens Council. There will be no crosses burned at any bus stops in Montgomery. There will be no white persons pulled out of their homes and taken out on some distant road and lynched for not cooperating. There will be nobody among us who will stand up and defy the Constitution of this nation. And we are not wrong in what we are doing. If we are wrong, the Supreme Court of this nation is wrong. If we are wrong, the Constitution of the United States is wrong. If we are wrong, God Almighty is wrong. If we are wrong, justice is a lie. Love has no meaning. And we are determined here in Montgomery to work and fight until justice runs down like water, and righteousness like a mighty stream.

Following the arrest of **Rosa Parks**, an NAACP activist in Montgomery, Alabama for sitting in the white section of a city bus, a boycott was organised. It was based on a much shorter but successful boycott in Baton Rouge, Louisiana in 1953. A minister new to the city, the Revd Martin Luther King, Jr was asked to lead the boycott and succeeded in prolonging it past the original plan of a single day, to 381 days in which black citizens walked or shared cars rather than used the buses, costing the bus company 80 per cent of their costs per day. Whilst the boycott continued, the NAACP took another case to the Supreme Court, known as *Browder v. Gayle*, in which the court ruled in December 1956 that bus segregation was unconstitutional under the 14th Amendment.

KEY PROFILE

Rosa Parks (1913–2005) was seen as the mother of the Civil Rights Movement. Parks was a seamstress and NAACP activist whose arrest in 1954 for sitting down in a white's only seat, because she was 'tired of giving in', sparked the Montgomery Bus Boycott. Parks was a key heroine in the burgeoning movement.

Fig. 5   *Parks has been named 'the first lady of civil rights'*

ACTIVITY

Evaluating primary sources

Explain the ways in which King attempts to establish the bus **boycott** as having the moral high ground in Source 4?

KEY PROFILE

Fig. 4   *King became a civil rights activist early in his career*

Martin Luther King, Jr (1929–68) was born in Atlanta, Georgia, the son of a Baptist Minister. King moved to Montgomery in 1954. Through his powerful speeches and strong belief in non-violent protest, pioneered by Mahatma Gandhi, King became the public face of the Civil Rights Movement. In 1957, he founded the Southern Christian Leadership Conference (SCLC) and took part in many major protests. He won the Nobel Peace Prize in 1964 but was assassinated in 1968 in Memphis prompting riots in over 100 cities across the US.

KEY TERM

boycott: the refusal to purchase the products of an individual or company as a means to pressurise them to change

The Montgomery Bus Boycott of 1955 to 1956 has gained a status in the history of civil rights that is perhaps beyond that which it deserves. Though it did elevate King to a position of national prominence, make a heroine of Rosa Parks, highlight the economic power black citizens could wield when united and show how non-violent protest could be a model for successful opposition, it was again largely ignored by Eisenhower and only partly influenced the two civil rights acts of 1957 and 1960, which achieved very little for the movement.

Class debate

Rosa Parks is often portrayed as a tired, respectable woman who happened to take a stand, but actually she was a committed activist who was looking for an opportunity to protest. Does she deserve her reputation as a heroine of the Civil Rights Movement? Prepare an answer in groups and debate your views.

Policies and attitudes of the main political parties

With Eisenhower born and raised in Kansas and a Republican like the 'Great Emancipator' Abraham Lincoln, there were numerous reasons to believe that civil rights could progress significantly under him. Not least of which was because the president had been very clear in how damaging media coverage of segregation was to the US's moral leadership in the Cold War.

However Eisenhower was aware of how divisive an issue civil rights was. He had not won any of the states in the Deep South in the 1952 election so was not dependent on the Dixiecrats in the same way that a Democratic president would be, but he feared large-scale intervention both ideologically and in terms of the conflict it might bring. He believed that 'It is difficult through law and through force to change a man's heart' and assured his speech writer that his call for equality of opportunity did not mean that the races 'had to mingle socially – or that a Negro could court my daughter'. This fear of **miscegenation** was one of several factors behind the resistance to desegregation.

KEY TERM

miscegenation: the mixing of different races through marriage, cohabitation or procreation

Civil rights legislation

Eisenhower introduced two civil rights acts in the later years of his presidency aimed at increasing black voter registration in the South. He had been appalled to discover that only 7000 of Mississippi's 900,000 African-Americans were able to vote, but had a clear eye on the political capital that could be gained in the run up to the 1956 presidential election.

KEY TERM

filibustering: a tactic used to delay a vote in Congress by prolonged speechmaking

KEY PROFILE

Strom Thurmond (1902–2003) served as Senator for South Carolina for 48 years, switching parties from Democrat to Republican after the 1964 Civil Rights Act. He ran for president against Truman in 1948 as a 'State's Rights' candidate. He co-wrote the first draft of the Southern Manifesto and filibustered for over 24 hours in an attempt to derail Eisenhower's 1957 Civil Rights Bill. Six months after his death it was revealed that he had a mixed race daughter who had kept his secret for 78 years.

A CLOSER LOOK

The issue of black votes

Southern states used a variety of techniques to prevent black people from voting. These included literacy tests with impossible questions such as 'How many bubbles are in a bar of soap?' or obscure questions on the state's constitution. 'Grandfather clauses' enabled illiterate white people to vote as they could demonstrate their grandfathers had been registered. Poll taxes were also used as were arbitrary opening times for registration offices.

Vice President Richard Nixon had met Martin Luther King, Jr in March 1957 in Ghana, as the country celebrated its independence, and the two had got on well with Nixon inviting King to his office to discuss the bill on their return. On the same trip Nixon had found himself sitting beside a man and turned to ask him how it felt to be free. 'I wouldn't know, sir,' the man replied. 'I'm from Alabama.' The two incidents encouraged Nixon to work hard on the bill, setting himself against staunch segregationists like Richard Russell, the Dixiecrat Senator for Georgia. King later wrote to Nixon to express his thanks for Nixon's work on the Bill. Nixon's attitude was a sharp contrast to that of Eisenhower, who publicly admitted that he didn't understand the detail of the bill.

However, the 1957 Bill was undermined by Dixiecrats both in Congressional Committees and by **filibustering**, indeed **Strom Thurmond** filibustered for

24 hours and 18 minutes to obstruct it. The weakened legislation did little for African-Americans, adding only 3 per cent more black voters in the South by 1960. Eisenhower was to claim that 'there were certain phrases I did not really understand' and he failed to protect the bill as he had failed Autherine Lucy in 1956. Historian David Nichols stresses that Eisenhower had introduced the first civil rights legislation since the post Civil War Reconstruction, and that Adam Clayton Powell had called the bill 'the second emancipation' but it was the symbolism of this move that was most important.

A CLOSER LOOK

Congressional Committees

Congressional Committees examine bills that are passing through Congress and debate and revise their terms. The majority leader (the leader of the party with the majority in each house) decides which is the most appropriate committee for a bill to be examined by. The heads of these Committees are chosen on longevity of experience, meaning a well established Senator or Representative often gets to head important committees.

Eisenhower's second Civil Rights Bill took shape from 1958 as the second term president began to look to his legacy and became increasingly worried by the sporadic violence in the Deep South including bombings of black schools, homes and churches. The bill was again watered down at the committee stage and little was done to enforce its elevation of obstructing desegregation into a federal crime, but Eisenhower had created a precedent which was to be taken on by Kennedy and Johnson in the years to come.

The responses of the state and federal authorities

Fig. 6 *A group protesting admission of the 'Little Rock Nine' to Central High School, State Capitol Little Rock, Arkansas, 20 August 1959*

Eisenhower believed in a gradual response to the civil rights campaigns and was unwilling to put his political weight behind the campaigners, refusing to comment on the Till case and the *Brown* decision or condemn the Southern Manifesto and only becoming involved at Little Rock when it appeared the issue of state versus federal authority was in question. Unlike the Democrats

ACTIVITY

Use a Venn diagram to illustrate the problems faced by African-Americans both in the North and in the South. What problems did they have in common?

KEY TERM

rhetoric: persuasive speech making or writing; the history of civil rights is full of great examples of rhetoric, from King's effective use of repetition and biblical imagery, to the barely constrained anger of Malcolm X

STUDY TIP

Provenance is important here: a minister of the Nation of Islam addressing a crowd of Northern black people, a young girl whose life was threatened when she tried to go to a segregated school, and Martin Luther King, Jr preaching to a congregation in Montgomery. Consider how the provenance might affect the speaker's judgements about attitude. In addition, consider other events that might be pertinent.

STUDY TIP

Comparison questions demand a balanced response. A quick table before you start writing will pay dividends. List Truman's and Eisenhower's achievements in the table and in your response try to evaluate them with reference to their effectiveness and the precedents they set. You might also consider how politically difficult it was for the presidents to act in each case.

he did not need to court the support of the South, he only won Louisiana out of the seven states of the Deep South in either of his election victories. This refusal to engage allowed Dixiecrats in Washington to obstruct his bills, issue the Southern Manifesto and effectively eliminate the already limited influence of black congressmen. In addition it suggested Eisenhower was turning a blind eye to the actions of State authorities who proceeded to obstruct the integration that should have followed *Brown* with impunity. The closure of schools, continued use of Jim Crow Laws and the political popularity of governors like Faubus and Marvin Griffin, who became Governor of Georgia after running a segregationist campaign, suggested that it would take more than the actions of the Supreme Court and a lukewarm president to force the states to abandon 'separate but equal'.

Summary

By the end of the 1950s progress had been made in getting more rights for African-Americans. The *Brown* decision had quashed the 1896 *Plessy v. Ferguson* verdict and the Bus Boycott had helped to erode Jim Crow Laws. New leaders had emerged including King and X, as well as more politicians like Diggs. Heroes were in more plentiful supply too: Rosa Parks, Emmett Till and black players in the National Hockey League and National Basketball Association (NBA). Nat King Cole got a TV show, Motown Records was founded in 1959 capping a decade which had begun with Ralph Bunche becoming the first person of colour to win a Nobel Peace Prize.

Yet there were still huge barriers. King admitted in 1959 that little was achieved by the SCLC in its first two years. A US census report revealed that 56 per cent of black citizens in 1959 lived below the poverty line compared to only 18 per cent of white citizens. Eisenhower's legislation had been 'a small crumb from Congress' according to Roy Wilkins of the NAACP. While King had established the effectiveness of non-violence, the press had found a counterweight to that in the belligerent **rhetoric** of Malcolm X. Meanwhile, in the cities, tensions continued to be ratcheted up by the police and the lack of education and opportunity.

 PRACTICE QUESTION

Evaluating primary sources

Using Sources 1, 3 and 4 and your understanding of the historical context, assess the value of these three sources to an historian studying the attitude of black people towards white people in the 1950s.

A LEVEL PRACTICE QUESTION

'Eisenhower achieved far less for African-American civil rights in his presidency than Truman achieved before him.' Assess the validity of this view.

3 John F Kennedy and the 'New Frontier', 1960–1963

9 The presidential election of 1960

The 1960 presidential election

SOURCE 1

This extract from Theodore White's 1960 book *Making of the President* which charted Kennedy's election campaign describes the first ever televised debate between presidential hopefuls, Kennedy and Nixon, before the 1960 presidential election. Kennedy was seen as the victor by those who watched on TV, Nixon by those who listened on radio:

It was the sight of the two men side by side that carried the punch. There was, first and above all, the crude, overwhelming impression that side by side the two seemed evenly matched – and this even matching in the popular imagination was for Kennedy a major victory. Until the cameras opened on the Senator [Kennedy] and the Vice President [Nixon], Kennedy had been the boy under assault and attack by the Vice President as immature, young and inexperienced. Now, obviously, in flesh and behaviour he was the Vice President's equal. Tonight Kennedy was calm and nerveless in appearance. The Vice President by contrast, was tense, almost frightened and, occasionally, haggard looking to the point of sickness, his 'lazy-shave' powder faintly streaked with sweat, his eyes exaggerated hollows of blackness, his jaw, jowls and face dropping with the strain. It is impossible to look again at the still photographs of Nixon in his ordeal and to recollect the circumstances without utmost sympathy. For everything that could have gone wrong that night went wrong.

ACTIVITY

Evaluating primary sources

How does Source 1 suggest that Kennedy benefitted from the televised debate with Nixon?

KEY PROFILE

John Fitzgerald Kennedy (JFK) (1917–63) was the son of Irish catholic businessman Joseph Kennedy. JFK's older brother Joe died in the Second World War and his father turned his attention to JFK to fulfil his ambition to have a son become president. Kennedy also served in the Second World War before being elected to the House of Representatives in 1947, the Senate in 1953 and the White House in 1960 through a combination of charisma, political savvy and his father's vast wealth.

Fig. 1   *JFK was famously assassinated in November 1963*

LEARNING OBJECTIVES

In this chapter you will learn about:

- the reasons behind Kennedy's victory in the 1960 presidential election

- the policies and personalities of the Kennedy Administration

- the ideas behind the 'New Frontier'.

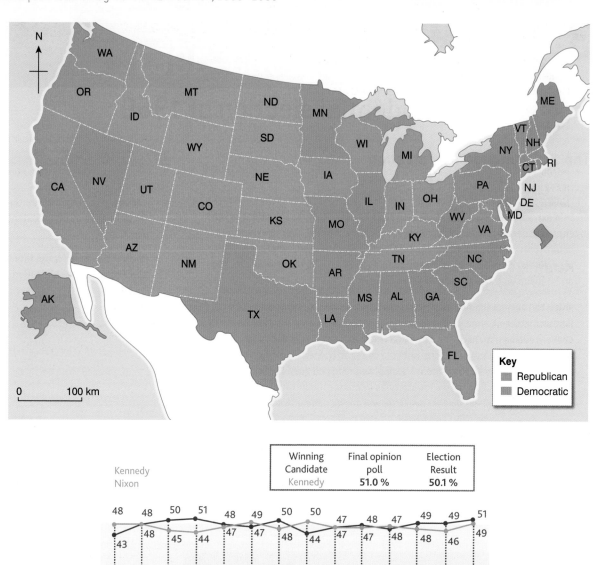

Fig. 2 *Final results and opinion polls of the 1960 election; the letters on the map represent states/constituencies*

The results of the 1960 presidential election:

Candidate	Party	Popular Votes
John F Kennedy	Democratic	34,227,096
Richard M Nixon	Republican	34,107,646
Harry F Byrd	Democratic	116,248

The presidential election of 1960 was the closest of the twentieth century with only 119,450 votes separating the candidates; a winning margin for Kennedy of just 0.17 per cent of the popular vote. Kennedy's opponent, Vice President Richard Nixon was only 47, Kennedy, a Senator from Massachusetts was 43. Both candidates had particular strengths they played to.

Nixon's strengths	Kennedy's strengths
• 13 years' experience in Congress including eight as vice president to Eisenhower • his reputation as a staunch anti-communist (see Chapter 19) • his extensive foreign policy experience including visits to Africa, South America, Vietnam and Moscow • his non-privileged background • he pledged to campaign in every state • he chose Henry Cabot Lodge, a former Massachusetts senator as his vice president • he had strong support from California (his home state)	• he had been a war hero • he was young, handsome and tall (since 1904 the taller candidate had won all but two presidential elections) • 13 years' experience in Congress including seven in the Senate • he had strong support from Northern Democrats and Catholics • he chose Lyndon B Johnson, an experienced Texas senator, as his vice president • he appealed to African-American voters with targeted promises (see Chapter 11) • his father's wealth and political connections bankrolled his campaign

A CLOSER LOOK

Kennedy the war hero

While Kennedy was serving in the Navy, a Japanese destroyer rammed his ship. Kennedy rescued several of his crewmates then swam from island to island until he found some friendly natives. He gave them a coconut shell carved with a message to deliver to the naval base at Rendova so he and his crew would be rescued. (Kennedy later had the coconut shell encased in wood and plastic and used it as a paperweight on his desk in the Oval Office.)

Kennedy tried to address some of his weaknesses, and in particular his Catholicism which threatened to derail his campaign in the '**Bible Belt**'. He spoke to a group of Protestant ministers in Houston two months before the election where he promised a solid commitment to the separation of Church and State. However despite his assurances, **psephologists** believe Kennedy's Catholicism cost him 1.5 million votes.

SOURCE 2

Extract from the address of Senator John F Kennedy to the Greater Houston Ministerial Association, 12 September 1960. The Protestant audience was chosen to alleviate concerns about Kennedy's Catholicism:

While the so-called religious issue is necessarily and properly the chief topic here tonight, I want to emphasize from the outset that we have far more critical issues to face in the 1960 election; the spread of Communist influence, until it now festers 90 miles off the coast of Florida – the humiliating treatment of our President and Vice President by those who no longer respect our power – the hungry children I saw in West Virginia, the old people who cannot pay their doctor bills, the families forced to give up their farms – an America with too many slums, with too few schools, and too late to the moon and outer space. But because I am a Catholic, and no Catholic has ever been elected president, the real issues in this campaign have been obscured – perhaps deliberately, in some quarters less responsible than this.

Unusually Nixon, who was no stranger to using dirty tricks in an election campaign, focused on Kennedy's inexperience rather than his Catholicism. Nixon stressed his anti-communist pedigree stemming from **the Hiss case**. Kennedy stressed his character and Second World War heroism, assisted by a friendly press whose support Kennedy's father assiduously courted. Here Kennedy had a distinct advantage as Nixon's war service had not led

ACTIVITY

If you were advising the candidates how would you play up your candidate's strengths and criticise your opponent? How could your opponent's advantages be used against them?

KEY TERM

Bible Belt: an informal term referring to the prevailing socially conservative and protestant leanings of the Southern states and parts of the Midwest

psephology: a branch of political studies which focuses on statistical analysis of voting patterns and habits across different demographics. It seeks to correlate this with factors like campaign spending, opinion polls and the influence of pressure groups and the media

CROSS-REFERENCE

See Chapter 3, page 26 for more on the Alger Hiss case.

him into combat but instead he had worked in logistics, receiving several commendations for efficiency but nothing in the way of heroic stories involving Pacific islands, coconuts and sinking ships.

Fig. 3 *Kennedy's relative youth made him appeal to young people and younger voters; here he is shaking hands with a young Bill Clinton*

There was little difference in policies between the two candidates so much of the campaign came down to presentation. The key differences were over the economy and the growth in Cold War tension. Kennedy made considerable effort to portray Nixon and Eisenhower as having neglected America's defences by allowing a 'missile gap' to develop between the United States and Soviet Union, in other words that the Soviets had built a numerical and technical superiority in nuclear capability. Though later research showed this to be untrue, it served to undermine Nixon's profile as a skilled politician when it came to foreign policy.

Differences over the economy were more nuanced, a key issue was how to extend the prosperity of the 1950s to all sections of society, particularly minority groups. Nixon allowed himself to be dragged into this debate rather than emphasising the economic success of the Eisenhower Administration. Eisenhower, who had not been involved in the Nixon campaign despite the huge popularity he still had, became increasingly vocal in his support of the Vice President and his intervention helped to erode some of the gains Kennedy had made in the televised debates. As 8 November drew closer, the candidates were impossible to separate.

Why did Kennedy win?

Two incidents are often credited with making the difference to the Kennedy campaign. One of these was the call Kennedy placed to **Martin Luther King, Jr's** wife when he was imprisoned during a **sit-in** in Atlanta. This was part of an orchestrated campaign to win the African-American vote and was heavily promoted in the black press. In the end Kennedy took the black vote by 70:30.

However the biggest factor in the Kennedy victory was believed to be the first ever televised debate, six weeks before the election. Kennedy's team prepared for this obsessively ensuring he had no other appointments on the day and had

CROSS-REFERENCE

See Chapter 11, pages 87–88 for information on King's imprisonment during a sit-in in Atlanta.

been campaigning in Florida prior to the debate so he appeared well-tanned. Kennedy's blue suit was chosen to contrast with the grey TV background where Nixon's grey suit blended into the backdrop. Nixon was recovering from a knee injury and flu he had developed during a tireless campaign, he sweated profusely under the hot lights, and could not seem to find a make-up artist that could hide his stubble. While radio listeners to the first of the four debates narrowly thought Nixon had won, the larger television audience of 74 million believed Kennedy to be the victor by a wide margin.

Four days after the election Kennedy admitted 'It was the TV more than anything else that turned the tide.' Research by David L Vancil and Sue D Pendell has suggested that the impact of the debates was less significant than has been perceived but one aspect that they did highlight was the growing importance of effective marketing. Here Kennedy benefitted from snappy party political broadcasts which used jingles like 'Kennedy For Me' and a huge range of merchandise. Pin badges, posters, hats, flags, pennants in their thousands were distributed by the campaign and clever photo opportunities showed Kennedy meeting a range of people and often included his glamorous wife, Jackie. On a darker side there were allegations of voter fraud in Texas, Johnson's home state, and in Chicago where Democrat Mayor Richard Daley had a reputation for guaranteeing landslide results. Eisenhower encouraged Nixon to challenge the result in the courts but magnanimously Nixon elected not to, saying that it would cause a constitutional crisis, and suggest that he was a sore loser.

The policies and personalities of the Kennedy Administration

The Kennedy victory was greeted as a new dawn for America by his supporters. A handsome young president with a beautiful wife and children, a gifted orator coming to power at the start of a new decade and with a new vision of America rooted in strength and service. Kennedy was eminently quotable, his inaugural speech included lines like 'the torch has been passed to a new generation of Americans', and challenges to his fellow Americans, 'Ask not what your country can do for you – ask what you can do for your country.'

ACTIVITY

Construct a spider-diagram giving the reasons why Kennedy won the 1960 election and remember to include the reasons Nixon lost. Which of these reasons were most significant?

SOURCE 3

Extract from an interview with Harris Wofford. Wofford was a campaign worker who was tasked, alongside **Sargent Shriver**, with going outside of the political scene to find talented individuals who could help the Administration:

As soon as the election was over, Kennedy started this talent search, of which I was a part, to find the so-called 'best and brightest' and bring them into the Administration. He wanted people like himself; perhaps not exactly like himself, but people that were on balance young and vigorous and tough. That was one of the words he liked to use. He wanted them to have a sense of humour and to be committed to public service. He didn't want people who were bureaucratic, and he certainly didn't want just politicians. We were to scour the country – academia, the professions, business, unions, the party, people who'd been in the campaign – to see who should be called. At the same time that this sort of hunt was going on, people were offering themselves in large numbers because there was excitement in the government, and Washington was a magnet, as it had been with Teddy Roosevelt and with Franklin Roosevelt and with Wilson.

ACTIVITY

Evaluating primary sources

Kennedy clearly felt that new blood was needed in politics. What does Source 3 tell you about Kennedy's reasoning for this and can you speculate on any problems that might emerge from bringing outsiders into government?

Fig. 4   *Shriver: a devout Catholic and Kennedy's brother-in-law*

Sargent Shriver (1915–2011) was a trained lawyer. A key part of the tight-knit group around the president, he was the driving force behind the Peace Corps and continued to serve under Lyndon B Johnson as one of the architects of the 'War on Poverty'. He was Ambassador to France (1968–70) and ran as vice presidential candidate in George McGovern's 1972 presidential bid.

Robert McNamara (1916–2009) was headhunted from his role as president of Ford by Sargent Shriver to form part of a group around Kennedy. His previous career teaching accountancy at Harvard made him a devotee of statistical analysis. His role as head of the Department of Defense made him favour military intervention and he was far more exuberant and persuasive than Rusk. He was kept on by Johnson after Kennedy's death.

Dean Rusk (1909–94) was Secretary of State under both Kennedy and Johnson. He was involved in foreign affairs for a considerable time but was always seen as second choice. He had a fractious relationship with Kennedy who felt the state department offered little. Johnson kept him on despite his offer to resign both after Kennedy's death and when his daughter Peggy became engaged to an African-American man in 1967. Johnson refused on both occasions.

Fig. 5   *Dean Rusk, President Johnson and Robert McNamara*

Lyndon Baines Johnson (LBJ) (1908–73) served for 24 years in Congress before Kennedy chose him as vice president after Johnson's failure to win the Democratic nomination. This balanced the Democratic ticket between North and South and experience and youth. After Kennedy's assassination Johnson tried to focus on addressing poverty but got bogged down in the Vietnam War. He won the 1964 election with ease but chose not to stand in 1968 due to protests over Vietnam.

Bobby Kennedy (1925–68) was John's younger brother who ran his election campaign before serving him and then Johnson as Attorney General. Bobby stood for one of the Senate seats for New York in the 1964 presidential election, serving as Senator from 1965 to 1968 before being assassinated whilst campaigning for the presidency in 1968.

Fig. 6   *Kennedy was more engaged with civil rights than his brother*

McGeorge Bundy (1919–66) was a former intelligence officer in the Second World War and Professor of Government at Harvard. Bundy served as a United States National Security Advisor to Kennedy and Johnson from 1961 to 1966. He was involved in the Bay of Pigs decision and the Cuban Missile Crisis but is primarily known for his role in advocating escalating US involvement in Vietnam to both Kennedy and Johnson.

The ideas behind the 'New Frontier'

Kennedy saw himself as a foreign policy president and was determined to make his name on the global stage. He did, however, have ambitious plans domestically. He had made a number of promises to African-Americans to gain their support in his campaign. He also saw himself as part of the liberal Democrat tradition of FDR in terms of raising the quality of lives of the poor through a rise in the minimum wage and new health insurance legislation. Kennedy also wanted to take measures to address the environment and channel new money into education. These liberal policies were summed up in his phrase the '**New Frontier**'.

SOURCE 4

Extract from John F Kennedy's speech entitled 'The New Frontier' delivered on 15 July 1960, at Memorial Coliseum, Los Angeles, to the Democratic National Convention as Kennedy accepted the nomination of the party to run as their candidate for president:

The New Frontier is here whether we seek it or not. Beyond that frontier are uncharted areas of science and space, unsolved problems of peace and war, unconquered problems of ignorance and prejudice, unanswered questions of poverty and surplus. It would be easier to shrink from that New Frontier, to look to the safe mediocrity of the past, to be lulled by good intentions and high rhetoric – and those who prefer that course should not vote for me or the Democratic Party. But I believe that the times require imagination and courage and perseverance. I'm asking each of you to be pioneers towards that New Frontier. My call is to the young in heart, regardless of age, to the stout in spirit, regardless of Party, to all who respond to the scriptural call: 'Be strong and of a good courage; be not afraid, neither be [thou] dismayed.'

Key provisions of the 'New Frontier'

The 'New Frontier' addressed a huge range of areas. More legislation was approved and passed into law than at any time since the 'New Deal', and by 1963, 35 of the 58 bills that Kennedy had submitted for congressional approval had been passed.

Economy	Kennedy attempted to galvanise the US economy with a huge stimulus package based around the creation of jobs that were better paying. He instructed all federal agencies to speed up their own construction projects and introduced a new Housing Act that created 420,000 construction jobs. Alongside this the increased minimum wage put $175 million into American workers' pockets. $200 million was spent on extra welfare benefits that applied to 750,000 children, while $780 million in increased unemployment benefits helped three million unemployed Americans get back on their feet. All of this would be funded by the effects of the most significant tax reforms since Roosevelt. By cutting both corporate and individual taxes Kennedy attempted to stimulate investment and spending which would in turn create more jobs.
Workers	Kennedy wanted to ensure that workers were protected in his 'New Frontier'. He began with a 1962 Executive Order, which provided federal employees with collective bargaining rights, and the 1962 Contract Work Hours and Safety Standards Act, which established standards for working hours and safety. These were followed by the 1961 Fair Labor Standards Act. Programmes placed young people in jobs and training to protect them from being underpaid in the service and retail industries. The salaries of nearly two million jobs were brought under the protection of the act.
Welfare	The clearest example of Kennedy's attempt to eradicate poverty came with changes to welfare. Social security benefits were increased by 20 per cent and a School Lunch Act provided free lunches and free milk for poor schoolchildren. A food stamp programme was launched which fed a quarter of a million people. Federal retirement benefits were linked to the consumer price index, which was a huge bonus for retired government workers. There was also increased funding for foster care and the disabled. In total, the benefits system was extended to cover five million more Americans.
Health	Kennedy went further than any president before him in moving towards a system of universal healthcare. A new universal Healthcare Bill for the elderly (Medicare) was introduced along with funding for nursing homes and healthcare for migrant workers. Millions of children were vaccinated through the Social Security Act of 1963, and more attention was given to those with learning difficulties and physical disabilities. Kennedy also introduced the Food, Drug and Cosmetic Act of 1963, which tightened federal regulations on therapeutic drugs – another example of those in most danger being offered protection and support from the state.

Education	A third of 'New Frontier' legislation had an educational aspect with increases in vocational training with the Vocational Education Act of 1963, and the expansion of scholarships and student loans. Money was also provided to aid the use of television in education through the Educational Television Facilities Act of 1962, and targeted programming improved education for those with disabilities. The government also provided grants to construct new facilities for those training to be healthcare providers and supplied loans of $2000 per annum for this training.
Housing	Kennedy's housing programme was another enormous undertaking: $3.19 billion was spent, with a focus on middle- and low-income families and the retired. Urban renewal grants went up from $2 million to $4 million, 100,000 new homes were constructed while urban open spaces were protected and public mass transit systems were supported.
Environment	Kennedy passed a Clean Air Act in 1963 and expanded the National Park System. He also doubled the funding for the prevention of water pollution.
Women's rights	Kennedy established the Presidential Commission on the Status of Women in December 1961 and invited Eleanor Roosevelt to chair it. The commission's final report, 'American Woman', was issued in 1963 and highlighted the degree of discrimination against women in the workplace. It recommended paid maternity leave, affordable childcare provision and hiring practices that promoted equality. Kennedy signed the Equal Pay Act into law in June 1963 (four months before the report) which allowed 171,000 women to reclaim pay amounting to $84 million over the next ten years.
Civil rights	A Civil Rights Bill was introduced in 1963, a Voter Education project was launched in April 1962, a new government agency, the Committee on Equal Employment Opportunity (CEEO), was established. Discrimination in public housing was prohibited and the Interstate Commerce Commission (ICC) was forced to **desegregate interstate** travel.
The Space Race	Kennedy arranged for an additional $9 billion to be given to NASA for the purpose of putting a man on the moon by the end of the sixties. During Kennedy's presidency, astronauts Alan Shepard, Gus Grissom, John Glenn and three others were safely put into space.

CROSS-REFERENCE

For more information on the desegregation of interstate travel see Chapter 11, page 89.

ACTIVITY

Create a character and make a list of how many of Kennedy's 'New Frontier' policies they might have benefitted from. For example you might choose an unemployed black labourer with two children from a small Southern town, a single migrant worker from Texas or Arizona, or a single waitress in a city diner with a child to support.

Fig. 7 *The Presidential Commission on the Status of Women is established by President John F Kennedy in 1961*

Kennedy's 'New Frontier' programme and the attack on poverty that it clearly demonstrated were both wide ranging and committed but Kennedy lacked the advantages that had allowed FDR to make such a success of the 'New Deal':

- **Foreign policy** concerns in Cuba, Berlin and Vietnam dominated much of his time.
- He was a first-term president with a close-run election victory.
- He was a Northern Democrat aware of the dangers of splitting his party over civil rights.

CROSS-REFERENCE

Kennedy's foreign policy is examined in Chapter 10.

- The Executive lacked influence over key figures in Congress that would have enabled Kennedy to call in favours to get bills passed.
- His team of advisers, drawn from across a variety of disciplines and often young and idealistic became frustrated with the slow pace of change.

It is obviously difficult to judge Kennedy's success given his premature death in November 1963, but the Kennedy presidency tends to be remembered as a triumph of style over substance. It was really left to Johnson to use the legacy of Kennedy in getting key bills like the Civil Rights Bill past Congress and reinventing the 'New Frontier' as the 'Great Society'.

Summary

The 35th president served only a total of 1036 days before he was assassinated in November 1963. In the popular mind, Kennedy was a great president in the making, tragically cut short before he had the chance to reach the level of the Roosevelts, Lincoln or the Founding Fathers. However, much of his reputation rests on his successful resolution of the Cuban Missile Crisis and his involvement in other matters of foreign affairs. In domestic affairs Kennedy had some moderate success and adopted a highly liberal and interventionist stance whilst trying to cut taxes to stimulate the economy. As with many aspects of domestic policy results tend to take years to become clear. With such a short presidency, it is difficult to judge Kennedy's effectiveness, particularly given the fact that many of the most important bills he introduced were actually forced through later by Johnson, who exploited the public sentiment following the assassination to gain the approval of a Congress that had never fully supported the Massachusetts senator.

 A LEVEL PRACTICE QUESTION

'The Kennedy Administration achieved more in domestic affairs in 1000 days than Eisenhower's did between 1953 and 1960.' Assess the validity of this view.

AS LEVEL PRACTICE QUESTION

Evaluating primary sources

With reference to Sources 1 and 2 and your understanding of the historical context, which of these two sources is more valuable in explaining why Kennedy won the 1960 election?

Ranking the presidents

JFK occupies an almost sacred position in the hearts of many Americans. However, historians view him as a 'nearly man'. In 1948 the historian Arthur Schlesinger carried out a poll of historians to rank the presidents in order of success. Whilst subsequent polls have used different methodologies and surveyed different groups they are a useful way of understanding how president's can be assessed.

ACTIVITY

Extension

How far does Kennedy differ from the two presidents who came before him? Draw up a table with two columns for Personality and Policies and rows for Differences and Similarities with Truman and Eisenhower.

STUDY TIP

You could attempt to analyse Kennedy's successes and failures and then Eisenhower's or you could look at the areas of domestic policy and compare the two within each paragraph. A key part of the question is the comparison between relative achievements in the timescale; here you might also consider other factors that explain underachievement, such as the international situation.

STUDY TIP

One way of considering the usefulness of sources is to assess four factors: origin (i.e. who wrote them and when), purpose (i.e. intended audience and the message of the author/speaker), value (i.e. what they tell us) and limitations (i.e. what are the problems in terms of reliability). Try to analyse each of the sources in this way before attempting the Practice Question.

10 Challenges to American power

ACTIVITY

Evaluating primary sources

In what ways does this foreign policy statement in Source 1 from Kennedy differ from the policies pursued by Eisenhower and Truman?

KEY CHRONOLOGY

November 1960	900 US troops in Vietnam in advisory capacity
April 1961	Kennedy orders Bay of Pigs invasion
August 1961	Berlin Wall built
April 1962	Strategic Hamlet Programme begins, US troop numbers reach 11,000
October 1962	Cuban Missile Crisis
June 1963	Kennedy visits Berlin, delivers 'Ich bin ein Berliner' speech
October 1963	Partial Nuclear Test Ban Treaty signed with USSR
November 1963	Diệm overthrown and executed in Vietnam

CROSS-REFERENCE

Revisit the Key Profile of Dean Rusk in Chapter 9, page 76.

SOURCE 1

An extract from Kennedy's inaugural address, 20 January 1961. A Kennedy aide was detailed to read all the previous inaugural addresses and focus on what made the memorable ones memorable:

In the long history of the world, only a few generations have been granted the role of defending freedom in its hour of maximum danger. I do not shrink from this responsibility – I welcome it. I do not believe that any of us would exchange places with any other people or any other generation. The energy, the faith, the devotion which we bring to this endeavor will light our country and all who serve it. And the glow from that fire can truly light the world. And so, my fellow Americans, ask not what your country can do for you; ask what you can do for your country. My fellow citizens of the world, ask not what America will do for you, but what together we can do for the freedom of man.

The legacy of the crises over Berlin and relations with Khrushchev

Kennedy and Khrushchev met for the first time at a summit in Vienna in June 1961. On the table for discussion was the ongoing problem of Berlin, which Eisenhower had failed to settle, the situation in Cuba and the situation in Laos where US support of a right-wing government was directed at holding back the communist organisation the Pathet Lao. Berlin had been a bone of contention between the Superpowers since Stalin's failed blockade of 1948 to 1949.

Kennedy stood firm on all three issues but privately confided that Khrushchev had 'savaged' him. The Soviet leader felt confident that Kennedy was likeable but naive and hence decided on a solution to his problem in Berlin where 30,000 more East Germans had escaped to the West in July alone. On 13 August 1961 a barbed wire barrier was erected along the border between East and West Berlin, followed by a wall which was built over the subsequent days. Moving between East and West Berlin was strictly controlled and anyone caught without a permit faced imprisonment, while those trying to cross illicitly were shot.

Kennedy was relatively calm about construction of the wall, saying that it showed that Khrushchev did not intend to seize the whole of Berlin and that a wall was better than a war. He was not criticised by either the media or the Republican party, indeed the crisis was only seen as a crisis in Germany, whereas Kennedy instructed **Dean Rusk** to exploit the situation for propaganda as far as was possible. In stark contrast Khrushchev saw Kennedy's lack of belligerence as proof of the impression he had got at Vienna; that Kennedy was a coward when it came to international issues and could be pushed around to the advantage of the Soviet Union.

In June 1963 Kennedy travelled to West Berlin to reiterate the US commitment to the city and gave one of his most famous speeches, stressing the US commitment to freedom across the world. Berlin, however, was to remain divided for the next 36 years but the building of the wall reduced tensions in Europe by effectively creating a status quo acceptable to both sides at the same time as other areas began to become more dangerous. In August 1963 Khrushchev summarised how Berlin featured in his planning in a speech in Yugoslavia declaring "Berlin is the testicle of the West. When I want the West to scream, I squeeze on Berlin."

Fig. 1 *Residents of West Berlin showing grandchildren to their parents in the East, 1961*

A CLOSER LOOK

Ich bin ein Berliner

Two years after the wall was built Kennedy addressed a crowd of 450,000 people telling them 'Ich bin ein Berliner' meaning that he, and by extension all Westerners, were committed to the protection of Berlin. Incorrect suggestions that his key phrase actually means 'I am a jam donut' have obscured the importance of the speech and how it reaffirmed the US commitment to West Germany.

ACTIVITY

Evaluating primary sources

This is an emotive source but can you actually describe the kind of peace Kennedy means? Is it different from the peace Truman and Eisenhower sought?

SOURCE 2

Extract from Kennedy's Address to students beginning their courses at American University, 10 June 1963:

What kind of peace do I mean and what kind of a peace do we seek? Not a Pax Americana enforced on the world by American weapons of war. Not the peace of the grave or the security of the slave. I am talking about genuine peace, the kind of peace that makes life on earth worth living, that enables men and nations to grow and build a better life for their children. I speak of peace because of the new face of war. Total war makes no sense in an age where a single nuclear weapon contains almost ten times the explosive force delivered by all the allied air forces in the Second World War. It makes no sense in an age when the deadly poisons produced by a nuclear exchange would be carried by wind and water and soil and seed to the far corners of the globe and to generations yet unborn.

The challenge of Castro's Cuba

A CLOSER LOOK

Fidel Castro and Cuba

In January 1959 **Fidel Castro** deposed Fulgencio Batista, the US backed dictator of Cuba. This meant that a socialist country was less than 100 miles from Florida. Castro nationalised hundreds of American businesses and Cuban allies of the Batista regime fled to the US. Castro feared an American attempt to depose him, as the CIA had done to the Guatemalan President Jacob Árbenz in 1954, after Árbenz's land redistribution policies had angered the US company United Fruit.

KEY PROFILE

Fig. 2 *Castro was Prime Minister of Cuba from 1959 to 1976*

Fidel Castro (b. 1926) fought with Che Guevara against dictatorships in the Dominican Republic and Colombia. Back in Cuba his guerrilla forces took power and he converted to communism, developing close relations with the USSR. A 2006 Channel 4 documentary alleges that there have been over 600 attempts on his life, many organised by the CIA.

Eisenhower had failed to address Cuba to any effect but had instructed the CIA to work on a plot to overthrow Castro using Cuban exiles who had fled to Florida. However, this was not before Castro had humiliated the US by travelling to New York for the General Assembly Meeting of the United Nations and met with Khrushchev, the new Soviet leader, Egyptian President Gamal Abdel Nasser and Indian Premier Jawaharlal Nehru as well as Malcolm X with whom he took a tour around Harlem. Castro's success was embarrassing for Eisenhower and Dulles as were his outspoken comments against poverty and racism in the US but with only three months of his presidency left, Eisenhower was willing to leave the situation.

Kennedy inherited Eisenhower's CIA plan and authorised it as a show of strength. The invasion, at a location called Bay of Pigs, in April 1961 was a fiasco as the majority of the exiles were captured and those that escaped failed to persuade the local population to rise up against Castro who was considerably more popular than Batista. The debacle put Kennedy on the defensive when it came to foreign policy and made Khrushchev think he was naive and could be pushed around. This feeling was confirmed when Kennedy failed to take action over the **Berlin Wall**, encouraging Khrushchev to push a little harder. He did so by forming a closer trading relationship with Castro and, by October 1962, placing Soviet missiles on Cuba bringing US cities in range of soviet missiles for the first time.

The Cuban Missile Crisis

The Cuban Missile Crisis is often described as the closest the world has come to nuclear war and the 13 days in the latter half of October 1962 when the crisis took place were certainly astonishingly tense for the people of the US. The speed with which the crisis unfolded is a measure of how seriously the events were seen at the time.

Ex-Comm: a group convened to manage the Cuban Missile Crisis including, both Kennedys, Johnson, Rusk, McNamara, McGeorge Bundy and top officials from the CIA and Department of Defense. The groups meetings were secretly recorded by JFK

ACTIVITY

On discovering the missiles, Kennedy had a number of options that were discussed intensively at the Ex-Comm meetings. These were: to ignore the missiles, to launch a military invasion of Cuba, to launch air strikes against the Cuban bases, to request that the Russians remove the missiles or to quarantine the island and ensure no further missiles arrived while negotiating. Discuss the pros and cons of each of these courses of action as a way of understanding why Kennedy made the decision he did.

KEY CHRONOLOGY	
15 October 1962	A U-2 spy plane discovers evidence of missiles in Cuba.
18 October	Robert Kennedy meets with Soviet Foreign Minister Andrei Gromyko who tells Kennedy that the only help the Soviet Union is giving to Cuba is assistance growing crops and missiles that are only for defence.
19 October	**Ex-Comm** suggests quarantining Cuba.
22 October	President Kennedy gives a **televised speech to the nation**.
23 October	Soviet ships on their way to Cuba are stopped 750 miles away under Khrushchev's orders.
24 October	Khrushchev refuses to remove the missiles from Cuba.
25 October	Kennedy orders flights over Cuba to be increased from once to twice per day.
26 October	Ex-comm begins discussions about invading Cuba. Khrushchev sends a telegram, offering to dismantle the sites if Kennedy promises not to invade Cuba.
27 October	A U-2 plane is shot down over Cuba. Kennedy receives a second telegram, demanding that he also dismantle American missile bases in Turkey. Kennedy agrees to the proposal in the first telegram. He also secretly agrees to remove US missiles from Turkey.
28 October	Khrushchev gives a speech saying he has agreed to Kennedy's arrangement.

OVER THE GARDEN WALL

Fig. 3 *This cartoon called 'Over the Garden Wall' appeared in* Punch *magazine in 1962*

SOURCE 3

Extract from Kennedy's televised address to the American public, 22 October 1962:

I call upon Chairman Khrushchev to halt and eliminate this clandestine, reckless, and provocative threat to world peace and to stabilise relations between our two nations. I call upon him further to abandon this course of world domination, and to join in an historic effort to end the perilous arms race and to transform the history of man. He has an opportunity now to move the world back from the abyss of destruction by returning to his government's own words that it had no need to station missiles outside its own territory, and withdrawing these weapons from Cuba by refraining from any action which will widen or deepen the present crisis, and then by participating in a search for peaceful and permanent solutions.

SOURCE 4

Robert McNamara, Secretary of State for Defense talking in the 2003 film *Fog of War: Eleven Lessons from the Life of Robert McNamara* about the Cuban Missile Crisis. McNamara was part of the Ex-Comm group that advised Kennedy on how to handle the crisis:

I want to say, and this is very important: at the end we lucked out. It was luck that prevented nuclear war. We came that close to nuclear war at the end. Rational individuals: Kennedy was rational; Khrushchev was rational; Castro was rational. Rational individuals came that close to total destruction of their societies. And that danger exists today. The major lesson of the Cuban missile crisis is this: the indefinite combination of human fallibility and nuclear weapons will destroy nations. Is it right and proper that today there are 7500 strategic offensive nuclear warheads, of which 2500 are on 15 minute alert, to be launched by the decision of one human being?

KEY TERM

Doomsday Clock: a symbolic clock face which hangs on a wall in the University of Chicago and represents a countdown to global catastrophe. The closer the clock is set to midnight, the closer the world is to global disaster

DEFCON: meaning Defense Readiness Condition, this is a measure used to estimate the imminence of nuclear conflict by the US armed forces ranging from 1 (nuclear war is imminent) to 5 (the lowest state of imminence)

KEY TERM

Third World: originally a term to distinguish between those nations that were neither aligned with NATO or with the Warsaw Pact. Its later use was related to the developing countries of Africa, Asia and Latin America

domino theory: the idea that once one country fell to communism surrounding countries would inevitably fall 'like dominos'

Vietminh: meaning 'League for Vietnamese Independence' it was formed in 1941 and led by Ho Chi Minh and Võ Nguyên Giáp. With training from the OSS (the forerunner to the CIA) they fought a guerrilla war against the Japanese from 1941–5 and then against the French from 1945–54. Following the division of Vietnam many of the Vietminh became involved in the running of North Vietnam, but some remained in the South and became the core of the Vietcong

General Curtis Le May told Kennedy he considered Cuba to be 'the greatest defeat in our history' as the public were not made aware of the withdrawal of US missiles from both Turkey and Italy as a result of the negotiations. But with the crisis averted Kennedy basked in public adulation for the first time since before the Bay of Pigs. The missiles were removed from Cuba within two months and a hotline was set up between the White House and the Kremlin to allow for easier communication between the two nations' leaders at a time of crisis. Khrushchev however was weakened by the crisis and communist hardliners in his government began to erode his power; within two years of the crisis coming to an end he had been deposed.

A CLOSER LOOK

How dangerous was the Cuban Missile Crisis?

The **Doomsday Clock** registered the crisis as having a rating of twelve minutes to midnight, whereas the US military rated it at **DEFCON** 2, the highest state of military readiness ever. It is an event that has been pored over perhaps as exhaustively as any in the Cold War, with peripheral participants like Johnny Prokov or Vasili Arkhipov being credited as 'the man who saved the world' by lazy journalists. But the danger felt very real and, as the events unfolded, many thought that the end of the world was nigh.

Deepening involvement in Vietnam

With the building of the Berlin Wall resolving the European situation, Kennedy's foreign policy team felt that the Cold War would now be fought in what was then known as the '**Third World**'. The situation in Vietnam was a clear example. Here was a country bordering China, with two further neighbours, in one of whom, Laos, the US was also supporting a government against communist insurgency. The leader of South Vietnam, a Catholic called Ngô Đình Diệm, had American support but was hated by the people for his persecution of the Buddhist majority. By 1960, this mistreatment led the communist North to encourage rebellion in the South in the hope of ousting Diệm and re-unifying the country. The implications for the **domino theory** were obvious. In addition there was an established guerrilla force, the **Vietminh**, who had proven effective in conflict against both the Japanese and the French.

However the Kennedys paid little attention to Vietnam initially. After the journalist Stanley Karnow warned about the ominous situation in Vietnam in 1961, Bobby Kennedy replied, 'Vietnam, Vietnam […] we have thirty Vietnams a day here.' As a result, and with the acquiescence of Robert McNamara, Kennedy saw Vietnam as a military rather than a diplomatic problem and sanctioned the build up of advisors there and the provision of further aid to Diệm.

Fig. 4 *This picture of the self-immolation of Thích Quảng Đức was distributed worldwide and became symbolic of US imperialism*

At the start of Kennedy's Administration there were 800 American military advisers in South Vietnam but by 1963 there were 23,000 in addition to the 250,000 strong South Vietnamese army under Diệm. Though the US advisers never engaged in combat, but rather sought to bolster and train the South Vietnamese army in their fight against the **Vietcong**, the fact the combined forces couldn't defeat approximately 12,000 Vietcong opposing them should have been a clear warning of the different nature of the guerrilla warfare that was the norm in the jungles of Vietnam. With **Robert McNamara**, a committed devotee of statistical analysis, at the heart of policymaking, the figures merely seemed to make a US victory that much more inevitable.

To counteract the guerrilla warfare employed by the Vietcong, Kennedy adopted a tactic of 'flexible response' using different fighting and propaganda methods. Amongst these was an ill thought out tactic known as 'strategic hamlets' which involved moving Vietnamese peasants from their villages to fortified villages protected by the South Vietnamese military and away from the influence of the Vietcong. However this was resented by the peasants and Vietcong influence in the hamlets occurred anyway. The Vietcong also succeeded in getting the support of the peasants by paying for food and treating them respectfully, employing similar tactics to Mao's People's Liberation Army during the Chinese Civil War.

Diệm's persecution of the Buddhist majority resulted in the **self-immolation** of Thích Quảng Đức, a Buddhist monk in 1963. This brought international criticism of the US's role in supporting Diệm. The image shocked Kennedy. When the CIA discovered that one of Diệm's own generals, Dương Văn Minh, was planning to assassinate him they failed to intervene and Diệm was killed a few weeks before Kennedy himself. General William Westmoreland, who took over as Commander in Vietnam on the advice of McNamara in January 1964, stressed that the US's complicity in the assassination of Diệm obliged them to stay in Vietnam to sort out the mess they had created.

Kennedy ignored the advice of Harold Macmillan, the Prime Minister of Britain and Charles de Gaulle, the French leader, not to become further entangled in Vietnam. The need to show himself as a strong leader, reassure other non-communist states in Asia, and stand up to Soviet and Chinese aggression, along with the advice of technocrats like McNamara drew Kennedy further into Vietnam, leaving Johnson the most poisoned of chalices.

KEY TERM

Vietcong or **VC:** a Communist guerrilla force which operated in South Vietnam and was supported by North Vietnam

CROSS-REFERENCE

Look back to the Key Profile of Robert McNamara in Chapter 9, page 76.

KEY TERM

self-immolation: to offer oneself as a sacrifice, especially by burning

ACTIVITY

Draw up a table of reasons for increasing involvement in Vietnam and reasons against as far as JFK was concerned.

Summary

Kennedy's popular legacy is dominated by his perceived victory in the Cuban Missile Crisis. This is helped by imagery burnished in the popular media such as Dean Rusk's quote when the Soviet ships turned around on 23 October, 'We're eyeball to eyeball, and I think the other fellow just blinked.' But Cuba was an initial failure for Kennedy at the Bay of Pigs, as was much of his Latin American policy. Even the results of the Missile Crisis are not clear cut. Khrushchev succeeded in getting US missiles removed from Italy and Turkey and ensuring his client state of Cuba was preserved, all for the limited cost of a few clandestine boat trips. The strategic advantage of potentially having nuclear missiles in Cuba was also being eroded by developments in technology.

Elsewhere Berlin was a symbolic and propaganda success for Kennedy, especially in terms of his speeches, but it is in Vietnam where his actions had the longest shadow. Seduced by McNamara and the military into thinking the US were invincible, he developed the situation into a much more serious one than Eisenhower had allowed. Ironically the great General's fear of the Military-Industrial Complex prevented him feeding it. It was his successor, with his willingness to invest in nuclear capability and put increased US presence on the ground, who really contributed to the massive build up of the military which made the Vietnam War inevitable.

STUDY TIP

Both sources are from public addresses but the dates are different; coming at both ends of JFK's presidency. Think of what had happened between 1961 and 1963 to inform your answer.

 PRACTICE QUESTION

Evaluating primary sources

With reference to Sources 1 and 2 and your understanding of the historical context, which of these two sources is more valuable in explaining Kennedy's attitude to foreign policy?

STUDY TIP

This is an awkward question as it asks you to evaluate two things about Kennedy's foreign policy, his promises and his achievements. Try to consider the context of Kennedy's promises. The best way to approach this is to look at the key events and then try to come up with arguments for why they could be considered both a success and a failure.

 PRACTICE QUESTION

'Kennedy's foreign policy promised far more than it delivered.' Assess the validity of this view.

STUDY TIP

For A level source questions you must look at the provenance, content and argument and the tone and emphasis of the sources. For these three sources that will involve looking at the audience, the time in which the sources were made and the purposes of the messages given.

 PRACTICE QUESTION

Evaluating primary sources

With reference to Sources 1, 3 and 4 and your understanding of the historical context assess the value of these three sources to an historian studying how Kennedy's foreign policy changed during his presidency.

11 African-Americans in the North and South

President Kennedy was never likely to be embraced by Democrats in the South with his courting of the black vote in the 1960 election campaign. His narrow election victory also made it politically risky for him to alienate southern Democrats. Nevertheless he was responsible for introducing some of the most far-reaching legislation to affect African-Americans along with presiding over some of the most potent events in the history of the movement. In addition, Kennedy used his executive power effectively, creating five black federal judges, including Thurgood Marshall, while Robert Kennedy at the Justice Department brought 57 suits against violations of black voting rights in the South compared to the six brought in Eisenhower's eight years. Kennedy also used his Executive power to create a new body, the Equal Employment Opportunity Commission (EEOC) to encourage companies with federal contracts to employ more black people.

LEARNING OBJECTIVES

In this chapter you will learn about:

- the rise and development of the Civil Rights Movement

- how opposition to civil rights developed and changed, including within the Democratic Party

- Kennedy's policies in response to the pressure for change.

A CLOSER LOOK

Kennedy's courting of 'the black vote'

In 1961 Andrew Hatcher became the first black employee in the White House Press Office. In interviews with black newspapers Kennedy promised to abolish racial discrimination in federally aided housing but, perhaps most effectively, Kennedy publicly intervened when King was convicted for a probation violation after a sit-in in Atlanta. Kennedy called Coretta Scott King to offer sympathy while Bobby made calls to get King out of jail.

The rise of the Civil Rights Movement

The success of *Brown*, the **Montgomery Bus Boycott** and **Little Rock** had not been maintained in the last years of Eisenhower's presidency. The NAACP had continued to bring cases to the Supreme Court, and win them, but the movement seemed to be treading water. King had founded his own organisation, the Southern Christian Leadership Conference (SCLC), in 1957, which drew on the success of the evangelist Billy Graham's crusades. Graham and King had become friends after King appeared at a Graham crusade in New York in 1957. However the SCLC's tactics which sought to use black churches to promote the organisation of non-violent protest faced resistance from the police, the White Citizens' Council, the Klan and some black church leaders who feared white retaliation. In this climate King struggled to make an impact and the next move forward had to come from a different source.

The sit-ins

By 1960 the promise of desegregation that followed *Brown* had almost evaporated. Jim Crow Laws still operated throughout the South, preventing African-Americans accessing education, transport and even restaurants on an equal basis. In response to the lack of progress, young people, for whom *Brown* had been seen as a breakthrough, began to take matters into their own hands. They were uniquely well-suited to the task; as students they lacked the financial commitments of supporting a family that affected older people and were often willing to put themselves in danger for their beliefs. Lacking legal experience or the authority of the Church, they began to protest using the weapons they had: their bodies and their wallets. Their tactics were simple. They would go to a segregated restaurant, sit in a 'whites only' seat, and ask

CROSS-REFERENCE

For a recap on *Brown*, the Bus Boycott and Little Rock, revisit Chapter 8, pages 65–67.

CROSS-REFERENCE

For more detail on Jim Crow Laws, see Chapter 4, page 30.

Fig. 1 *Baker worked alongside some of the most famous civil rights leader of the twentieth century*

Ella Baker (1903-86) was a radical activist. She joined the NAACP as a secretary in 1940, travelling and lobbying for a greater say for the ordinary people within the organisation until her resignation in 1953. She joined the SCLC in 1957 as Executive Director organising the Conference that led to the founding of the SNCC. After the decline of the SNCC from 1967 she worked for women's rights groups.

to be served. These sit-ins had begun on 1 February 1960, whilst Eisenhower was still president. Four black students from North Carolina A&T College: Joseph McNeil, Izell Blair, Franklin McCain and David Richmond, purchased several items in a Woolworths store then sat at the counter reserved for white customers and tried to order food, remaining for an hour until the store closed.

The sit-ins electrified the Civil Rights Movement. Within a month 50,000 students in 30 venues across seven states had replicated the protest, drawing media attention and violent reactions from local white people, particularly in the most organised example in Nashville. Idealistic students had less to lose in terms of economics, no children to support or jobs to hold down, and many of them had been told after *Brown* in 1954 that things were changing, only to spend their teenage years suffering more of the same. The tactic of using sit-ins became well established during the Kennedy years and was used at Albany, Birmingham and Selma as part of orchestrated campaigns. The sit-ins also gave birth to a new group, the Student Non-Violent Co-ordinating Committee (SNCC) which emerged from a meeting organised by **Ella Baker**. Eisenhower had offered sympathy with the ideals of the students but it was Kennedy who made the most political capital, securing King's release after he was sentenced for a month of hard labour after having been persuaded to take part in a sit-in in October 1960. The Kennedys' clear eye on the black vote was evident from the start of their involvement with the movement.

Fig. 2 *A volunteer being prepared for the type of abuse he might receive on a sit-on*

The Freedom Rides

In the spring of 1961 CORE sought to push the movement further by repeating their own 1947 Journey of Reconciliation, which had attempted to integrate interstate bus travel. The bus service was widely used to travel long distances in the US and changing buses in major cities required restaurants and waiting rooms. In the North these were integrated but in the South they remained segregated despite the Supreme Court precedents of *Morgan v. Virginia* from 1946 and *Boynton v. Virginia* from 1960. Thirteen riders, seven black and six white, led by CORE Director James Farmer, set out from Washington to New Orleans to test the success of the court's decision. If they reached New Orleans without incident it would prove progress was being made. If they faced hostility it would force a new president to confront the issue of civil rights early in his term by exposing the hypocrisy of the South both to the national media and to the communist press in the USSR, Eastern Europe and China.

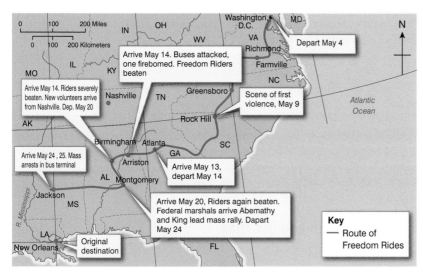

Fig. 3 *Route of the 1961 Freedom Rides from Washington DC, through the Deep South to the intended destination of New Orleans*

The ride prompted violence and intimidation, particularly at Aniston. TV images of defiant but badly beaten riders, like Jim Zwerg and James Peck, were broadcast globally and with particular glee in the Soviet Union. **Attorney General** Robert Kennedy called for a cooling off period but the rides continued unabated. After having forced the Democrat Governor of Alabama John Patterson to protect the riders, and striking similar deals with Democrat Governors of Mississippi and Louisiana to let the initial ride through, Robert Kennedy demanded that the Interstate Commerce Commission (ICC) enforce their own 1955 ruling on desegregation of interstate buses. As the ICC deliberated, 60 further rides involving 300 riders, 75 per cent of whom were male, made their way to Jackson, Mississippi, where everyone was arrested.

On 1 November 1961 the ICC issued instructions ending segregation in interstate travel and facilities. The CORE campaign had been a huge success gaining international attention, leveraging grassroots activism and the power of the media through the provocation of Southern white people. Here too the Kennedy Administration had delivered on its promises to black voters, perhaps not with a spectacular gesture but with consistent and reliable support by Bobby Kennedy.

> **KEY TERM**
>
> **Attorney General:** best summarised as the Chief Lawyer and Chief Law Enforcement Officer of the US government, the Attorney General's official role is as head of the Department of Justice

ACTIVITY

Create a poster encouraging students to join either the sit-ins or the Freedom Rides.

The Albany Campaign

The success of the sit-ins led SNCC campaigners to think bigger and three of them headed to Albany, Georgia, to challenge segregation there. Charles Sherrod, Cordell Reagon and Charles Jones had big ideas but their movement lacked the focus of the restaurant sit-ins by targeting not only restaurants, but libraries, parks and buses and using marches and boycotts, too. They also came into conflict with established civil rights groups and fell foul of the local police chief, Laurie Pritchett. Having studied the movement's tactics Pritchett saw that provoking violence led to media attention which led to presidential involvement. He therefore gave instructions to his officers to:

- police the marches fairly and protect the demonstrators
- contact local jails in a 40 mile radius to ensure that if arrests had to be made then jail space would be available and African-Americans wouldn't be crowded into single cells
- treat King, if and when he arrived, with considerable care.

Pritchett's tactics frustrated the SNCC campaigners and the protests stagnated, leading local groups to invite King. He answered the call to the annoyance of the SNCC who felt King was sweeping in to take the glory. King was arrested when taking part in a march and, when offered the choice of a $178 fine or jail, chose jail. Pritchett saw the potential for media attention and swiftly and discreetly arranged for King's fine to be paid and he was released with little fuss. King left town to concentrate on other campaigns but had learnt valuable lessons about the importance of unity, choosing target cities carefully and having a clear goal. While the role Albany was to play in the national campaign effectively ended with King's departure Charles Sherrod and the SNCC stayed and within a year Albany had removed all segregation laws from its books.

James Meredith and Ole Miss

SOURCE 1

Extract from a letter from James Meredith to the Justice Department of the US Government, 7 February 1961, explaining that he has applied to be enrolled at the University of Mississippi:

America is a great nation. It has led the world in freedom for a long time. I feel that we can and we must continue to lead in this respect. However I feel that a greater use can be made of the Negro potential. In my state, this is generally impossible under the present set-up. A Negro born in Mississippi can write himself off of the potential list of all of the professions, except teaching and preaching, nearly all of the technical fields and trades and off of the Commissioned Officers roll. At the present time much is being said by the radio and press about a Negro wanting to go to the University of Mississippi. Much is being made of prior attempts by Negroes to go to 'all white' Mississippi schools. They elaborate on the fate of these individuals; for instance, the last one to try is now serving a seven-year prison term on trumped-up charges subsequent to his attempt to go to the school.

James Meredith had served in the US Air Force from 1951 to 60, taking advantage of the GI Bill and inspired by Kennedy's **inauguration** speech he decided to apply to the University of Mississippi. After a series of NAACP led court cases, followed by underhand attempts by the Democrat Governor of Mississippi Ross Barnett to prevent Meredith's entry, he successfully enrolled on 1 October 1962. Riots followed in which two people were killed and Robert Kennedy had 500 US Marshals supported by the 70th Army Engineer Combat Battalion brought in to maintain order, one third of the Marshals and 40 soldiers were also injured. Meredith graduated in August 1963 with a degree in Political Science having endured abuse and isolation throughout his time at 'Ole Miss'. Nevertheless, once again, when provoked, the Kennedys had stood up for an African-American in the South.

Other southern Governors were quick to see the political advantage in continued opposition and being forced to acquiesce by the Kennedys. In June 1963, George Wallace, Democrat Governor of Alabama who had promised 'segregation now, segregation tomorrow, segregation forever' in his inaugural speech, blocked the access of two black students to the University of Alabama, which had already been integrated by **Autherine Lucy**. The 'Stand in the Schoolhouse Door' was **grandstanding** by Wallace, not for the first or last time, but again forced the Executive into action and Kennedy federalised the Alabama National Guard to force Wallace to step aside.

ACTIVITY

Evaluating primary sources

Summarise the argument of this letter from James Meredith to the Justice Department.

KEY TERM

inauguration: a formal ceremony to mark the beginning of a leader's office. Usually a speech will be given in which the president or governor will lay out the guiding ideals on which they plan to base their decision-making

CROSS-REFERENCE

Revisit the detail on Autherine Lucy in Chapter 8, pages 65–66.

KEY TERM

grandstanding: seeking to attract praise or favourable attention from spectators or the media

Birmingham

The lessons from Albany prompted a much more proactive campaign by the SCLC in Birmingham in April 1963. The city, one of the most racist in the South and nicknamed 'Bombingham' for its Klan activity, was in the midst of a disputed mayoral election in which the moderate Albert Boutwell defeated the segregationist commissioner of public safety, Eugene 'Bull' Connor, who had allowed the Klan to beat the Freedom Riders when they arrived in Birmingham in 1961.

Fig. 4 *Bull Connor authorised the use of fire hoses and clubs on the young, non-violent protesters; some hoses were so powerful they could strip bark from trees*

ACTIVITY

Imagine you are a journalist working for one of the major Soviet newspapers, *Pravda* or *Izvestiya*. How would you portray the situation in Birmingham to gain the maximum propaganda value?

A concerted SCLC campaign of marches, sit-ins and boycotts followed but the SCLC lacked the money to cover bail so when King was arrested after violating an anti-protest injunction and was kept in solitary confinement, his leadership of the campaign was challenged. During this time King penned the 'Letter from Birmingham Jail', in reaction to a statement in *The Birmingham News* condemning the protests. King's wife, Coretta Scott King, contacted the Kennedy administration and King was released on 20 April 1963.

King's absence had caused the campaign to stagnate leading SCLC organiser James Bevel to propose using young children in demonstrations, as they lacked the responsibilities of adult protesters and were far more media friendly. King was uneasy but the plan worked to amazing effect with Connor directing local police to arrest the children using clubs and dogs if necessary and the fire service to use high-pressure fire hoses. The images were shocking and made front page news across the world. While the media piled on political pressure, the economic damage of the campaign to local businesses was also beginning to tell. Robert Kennedy sent Burke Marshall, his chief civil rights assistant, to negotiate and an agreement was reached to start desegregating facilities.

ACTIVITY

How do the tactics the SCLC used in Birmingham demonstrate that they had learned from the mistakes of Albany?

ACTIVITY

Evaluating primary sources

Find six or more different reasons that Kennedy gives in Source 3 for his decision to introduce civil rights legislation.

KEY PROFILE

Fig. 5 *Wilkins was frequently referred to as the 'Senior Statesman' of the Civil Rights Movement*

Roy Wilkins (1901–81) was a former journalist who was assistant NAACP Secretary under Walter White. Wilkins served as Executive Director of the NAACP from 1955 to 77. In this role he was called on by Kennedy, Johnson, Nixon, Ford and Carter for advice and counsel and praised for his balanced and erudite approach.

A CLOSER LOOK

The aftermath of Birmingham

That night King's motel was bombed and Kennedy was forced to act ordering 3000 federal troops into position near Birmingham and making preparations to federalise the Alabama National Guard which stabilised the situation and allowed desegregation to continue. However four months later, on 15 September, Ku Klux Klan members bombed Birmingham's 16th Street Baptist Church, killing four young girls.

SOURCE 2

Adapted from a speech given by President Kennedy to Congress on 28 February 1963:

One hundred years ago, the Emancipation Proclamation was signed by a president who believed in the equal worth of every human being. That proclamation was only the first step. While slavery has vanished, progress for the Negro has been too often blocked and delayed. Equality before the law has not always meant equal treatment and opportunity. And the harmful, wasteful and wrongful results of discrimination and segregation still appear in virtually every aspect of national life. Racial discrimination hampers our economic growth by preventing the maximum development of our manpower. It hampers our world leadership by contradicting at home the message we preach abroad. It damages the atmosphere of a united and classless society in which the nation rose to greatness. It increases the costs of public welfare, crime, delinquency and disorder. Above all, it is wrong.

The march on Washington

On Tuesday 27 August 1963 over 200,000 marchers descended on Washington DC in the largest rally for civil rights in American history. The march was envisaged by Bayard Rustin and A Philip Randolph and co-organised with the 'Big Six' leaders, James Farmer of CORE, John Lewis of the SNCC, Martin Luther King, Jr of the SCLC, **Roy Wilkins** of the NAACP, Whitney Young of the Urban League and Randolph himself as head of the Brotherhood of Sleeping Car Porters. The goal of the march was to further increase pressure on the Kennedy Administration to press ahead with civil rights legislation but also to highlight the economic prejudice faced by African-Americans, hence the subtitle of 'For Jobs and Freedom'. Kennedy was initially wary of the march fearing the potential for violence but when it was clear that the organisers planned to go ahead regardless he was willing to endorse the march whilst ensuring 19,000 troops were stationed in the suburbs in the event of trouble. In the end no marchers were arrested.

The high point of the march came when King took to the podium as the second from last speaker. His *I Have a Dream* speech is widely regarded as one of the finest ever delivered and deployed many of his rhetorical tricks. He used rhythm and repetition to considerable effect and drew on both biblical and constitutional texts while using all the experience of countless sermons delivered during his career. King went on to be named *Time Magazine*'s Man of the Year for 1963 and to be awarded the Nobel Peace Prize in 1964.

Fig. 6 *Crowds gather at the Lincoln Memorial to hear speeches at the conclusion of the March on Washington*

The celebrity factor

The March on Washington is famous for King's speech but it also marked a point when celebrities came out in force in demanding civil rights. The singers Joan Baez, Bob Dylan and Harry Belafonte performed, as did gospel legend Mahalia Jackson. Baseball star Jackie Robinson, and actors Marlon Brando, Charlton Heston, Burt Lancaster, Paul Newman and Sammy Davis, Jr, were all in attendance, along with the writer James Baldwin.

The situation in the North

SOURCE 3

Extract from Michael Harrington's *Other America* published in 1962 which looked at poverty in the USA and had a significant influence on Kennedy and Johnson:

In New York City, some of my friends call 80, Warren Street 'the slave market'. It is a big building in downtown Manhattan. Its corridors are lined with employment agency offices; they provide the workforce for the dishwashers and day workers, the fly-by-night jobs. It is made up of Puerto Ricans, Negroes, alcoholics, drifters and disturbed people. Some of them will pay a flat fee (usually around 10 per cent) for a day's work. If all goes well they will make their wage. If not they will have a legal right to come back and get their half dollar. But many of them don't know that. Helpers in restaurant kitchens shift jobs rapidly and are hard to organize, this makes it a perfect place for labour and management racketeers. The dishonest union man would demand a pay off from the dishonest restaurateur. In return for this money the unionist would allow management to pay well below the prevailing minimum wage.

KEY TERM

disenfranchise: to be disenfranchised means to be denied the vote either through legal means, such as Jim Crow Laws, or by social or economic pressure. More widely it can refer to being disengaged from the political system through apathy or lack of education

CROSS-REFERENCE

The Hate that Hate Produced is covered in Chapter 8, pages 63–64.

Look ahead to Chapter 18, page 153 for detail on Malcolm X and Cassius Clay (who later changed his name to Muhammed Ali).

For more on Nasser and the nationalising of the Suez Canal, see Chapter 7, page 61.

CROSS-REFERENCE

For more on the Klan see Chapter 4, page 31.

The 1960 Civil Rights Commission estimated that 57 per cent of black housing was of substandard quality and said black life expectancy was seven years less than for white people while the infant mortality rate was twice as high. But while progress was being made in the South with African-Americans getting access to *de jure* rights the *de facto* situation in the North remained the same. A vicious cycle of poverty was maintained through poor housing, poor schooling and local **disenfranchisement**.

The Nation of Islam had been boosted by the exposure Malcolm X had gained in the 1959 television documentary *The Hate that Hate Produced*. Its media exposure had been further enhanced by the friendship between **Malcolm X and Cassius Clay**. However there were few concrete successes and Malcolm X was most notable in the period for his criticisms of King whom he called a 'chump' and events like the March on Washington or 'the Farce on Washington' as Malcolm X called it. His profile was sufficient however to meet with several world leaders at the 1960 United Nations meeting including Castro and **Nasser**.

Opponents of civil rights

Opposition to the Civil Rights Movement can be roughly divided into four groups:

- **The general population**, unaligned with an active organisation. These were people who would turn into a mob when riled or manipulated by politicians or the press, often the source of racist chanting and catnip to the media. People like Hazel Massery, who was pictured hurling abuse at Elizabeth Eckford during the Little Rock Crisis, or William Zantzinger, whose murder of a black waitress was immortalised in the Bob Dylan song *The Lonesome Death of Hattie Carroll*, expressed to varying degrees the latent racism of the South and were the kind of people other opponents depended upon to form mobs.
- **White Citizens' Councils** were known informally as the 'Country Club Klan'. The first Citizens' Council was formed in Greenwood, Mississippi, in July 1954 by Robert B Patterson and within a few years membership nationwide reached 60,000. Local and State politicians were more willing to join the Councils than the Klan and this brought considerable influence in state and local politics. In addition the middle-class nature of the Councils whose members included local businessmen, bank managers and even newspaper proprietors, enabled them to exert economic and propaganda influence, encouraging their employees not to join a march or organisation with blatant hints about their jobs status or reprinting stories from the Citizens' Council's newsletter.
- The **Third Ku Klux Klan** was directly responsible for a number of deaths including that of NAACP organiser Medgar Evers in Mississippi in 1963, and the bombing of the 16th Street Baptist Church in Birmingham, Alabama in the same year.

A CLOSER LOOK

The early Klan

The First Klan (1865–74), was a highly localised vigilante group formed after the Civil War. The Second, formed in 1915 in Atlanta, was far more influential with five million members and a national structure. The popular 1915 film *The Birth of a Nation* portrayed the Klan as defenders against the ethnically or religiously impure and instigated many of its myths including the burning cross and white hoods.

- Perhaps the most powerful of the opponents of civil rights were the **Dixiecrats**, the loose group of Democrat politicians whose political careers and inclinations were directed at obstructing desegregation in a variety of ways. These included filibustering, savaging bills in committee and in the States themselves and rousing popular sentiment against desegregation. Amongst the senators the most vociferous were James Eastland of Mississippi, Strom Thurmond of South Carolina, Richard Russell of Georgia, Harry Byrd of Virginia and Sam Ervin of North Carolina. State governors also used their powers to obstruct the movement and the president's attempts to enforce the Supreme Court rulings, most notably Orval Faubus in Arkansas, George Wallace in Alabama and Ross Barnett in Mississippi.

ACTIVITY

Draw up a table analysing the potential effectiveness of each of these groups, what were their strengths and weaknesses when it came to obstructing civil rights?

Kennedy's policies in response to the pressures for change

The events in Birmingham and Washington prompted Kennedy to draft a Civil Rights Bill far more comprehensive in its scope than either of Eisenhower's Civil Rights Acts of 1957 and 1960. It included a promise to give everyone 'the right to be served in facilities which are open to the public'. The eventual bill was strengthened in the Committee stage where Emmanuel Celler, a Democrat from New York added provisions that banned racial discrimination in employment, eliminated segregation in all publicly owned facilities (not just schools), and strengthened the anti-segregation clauses regarding public facilities, such as lunch counters. However in early November the bill moved from Celler's committee to Virginia Dixiecrat Howard W Smith's committee. Smith immediately made it clear he would do all he could to delay the bill and this is where the bill was languishing when Kennedy was shot.

Summary

The Kennedy Administration is sometimes criticised for having promised much but delivered little when it came to civil rights. No legislation was enacted, although a Civil Rights Bill was introduced. Government action was often reactive in the face of national and international media pressure. However no previous president made as many black appointments within the federal bureaucracy and Kennedy was also skilled at media-friendly gestures, inviting more African-Americans to the White House than any previous president, as well as forcing the Washington Redskins American Football team to hire black players.

Nevertheless, Kennedy's legacy was not flawless. He failed to keep his promises on housing, ignored events at Albany, did not give the EEOC the financial support it required and continued to appoint judges with deeply segregationist views in the South. It is always difficult to assess Kennedy's intentions, since his opportunity for action was cut short by his assassination. A second term could have brought a legislative breakthrough and a more proactive policy. However, the events of 22 November 1963 mean the question of how effective Kennedy might have been can never be answered.

AS LEVEL | PRACTICE QUESTION

'Divisions between King and the SNCC were the main reason why the Albany Campaign failed.' Explain why you agree or disagree with this view.

STUDY TIP

You should try to consider how Pritchett's tactics and other factors affected how the Campaign unfolded. You could then weigh these points against the problems that the divisions in the civil rights groups brought.

STUDY TIP

These two sources are taken from different areas and deal with the different aspects of the job market. Harrington is focused on the North, Meredith on the South. Meredith is discussing jobs in the professions, Harrington is discussing low-level service jobs. However both sources focus on the prejudice against black workers, but Meredith's has an agenda that relates to his attempt to gain entry to Ole Miss whereas Harrington's quote is taken from an academic text.

 PRACTICE QUESTION

Evaluating primary sources

With reference to Sources 2 and 4 and your understanding of the historical context, which of these two sources is more valuable in explaining the difficulties African-Americans found in gaining employment?

STUDY TIP

The structure here is clearly suggested by the question, what promises did Kennedy make and how would you evaluate his success with these? The problem will come with the vagueness of some of the promises and here you will have to look at how civil rights groups interpreted these promises and draw conclusions about how fair these interpretations were.

 PRACTICE QUESTION

'Kennedy failed to live up to his promises regarding civil rights.' Assess the validity of this statement.

12 The USA by 1963

Fig. 1 *Kennedy's body lying in state in the Capitol Rotunda, November 1963*

SOURCE 1

An extract from the eulogy delivered by Supreme Court Justice Earl Warren, on 24 November 1963. Warren was appointed by LBJ to head the Warren Commission investigation into the death of Kennedy:

John Fitzgerald Kennedy, a great and good president, the friend of all men of good will, a believer in the dignity and equality of all human beings, a fighter for justice, an apostle of peace, has been snatched from our midst by the bullet of an assassin. What moved some misguided wretch to do this horrible deed may never be known to us, but we do know that such acts are commonly stimulated by forces of hatred and malevolence, such as today are eating their way into the bloodstream of American life. It has been said that the only thing we learn from history is that we do not learn. But surely we can learn if we have the will to do so. Is it too much to hope that the martyrdom of our beloved president might even soften the hearts of those who do not shrink from spreading the venom which kindles thoughts of it in others? We can all be better Americans because John Fitzgerald Kennedy has passed our way.

ACTIVITY

Extension

In this eulogy Warren paraphrases the philosopher Hegel's dictum 'The only thing we learn from history is that we learn nothing from history'. What did Kennedy learn from his three predecessors in his conduct of the presidency?

KEY TERM

First Lady: the wife of the president

On 22 November 1963, President Kennedy and the **First Lady** were in Dallas on a campaign trip. As the motorcade moved through Dealey Plaza, the open-top presidential limousine was fired upon. Governor Connally was wounded and Kennedy was killed. The shots had been fired from a nearby warehouse and some hours after the assassination, police arrested warehouse employee Lee Harvey Oswald. Oswald was a former marine who had defected to the Soviet Union in 1959 but then returned to the US in 1962. Two days after the arrest, while being transferred to another jail, Oswald was shot by Jack Ruby, a Dallas nightclub owner with mafia connections. Ruby was tried and convicted of murder and died of cancer in January 1967, while awaiting a retrial in prison. The whirlwind of events that followed Kennedy's shooting led many to wonder whether a conspiracy was at the root of the problem, particularly given Oswald's Soviet links and Ruby's mafia ones.

Who killed JFK?

Johnson arranged a commission to investigate the assassination, chaired by Earl Warren. Its report confirmed that Oswald had acted alone. Conspiracy theories about Kennedy's assassination were boosted by the Watergate Scandal which revealed covert actions within US government. In 1991 Oliver Stone showed his film *JFK* to Congress, leading to the passage of the Assassination Materials Disclosure Act of 1992, the Act states that all records pertaining to the assassination should be published by 2017.

ACTIVITY

Extension

Watch the Oliver Stone film *JFK* for a broader picture of the situation in the US after the death of Kennedy.

On 24 November 1963, hundreds of thousands of people filed past Kennedy's coffin in the rotunda of the Capitol and an estimated one million people lined the streets of Washington DC to observe the funeral procession the next day. For many Americans, the murder of John F Kennedy would remain one of the most wrenching public events of their lifetimes.

The USA's position as a world power

Kennedy's 'victory' in the Cuban Missile crisis changed the Cold War. While the US media crowed about how Khrushchev had 'blinked first' Khrushchev's rivals in the Kremlin began to see his leadership and his policy of 'peaceful co-existence' with the West as flawed. Relations with Khrushchev improved after the Missile Crisis, leading to the signing of a Limited Test Ban Treaty, ratified by Congress in October 1963, which banned testing nuclear weapons in the atmosphere, in space and underwater. But US triumphalism cost them a potentially more malleable relationship with Khrushchev and by October of 1964 he had been replaced by Brezhnev.

Outside of direct confrontation between the Superpowers, their rivalry was morphing into other areas. Kennedy's attempts to rebuild relations with Latin America to prevent Soviet inroads had several strands including the creation of the Peace Corps by Sargent Shriver and the Alliance for Progress. The latter was signed in Uruguay in 1961 and promised $20 billion of US aid over ten years with a goal of increasing per capita income by 2.5 per cent, establishing democratic governments, eliminating adult illiteracy and promoting land reform. Though the programme saw some positive effects it was underfunded and Nixon reduced its budget drastically.

Trade was also becoming a key part of Superpower rivalry both in terms of economics and as a propaganda tool. The Kennedy White House sought to improve the image of the USA with programmes like 'Food for Peace' which built on Eisenhower's 1954 Agricultural Trade Development and Assistance Act allowing poorer countries to buy surplus US crops in their own currency. Kennedy framed the Act as 'Food for Peace' and switched the focus to broader humanitarian goals. The programme continues to operate today and has helped over 3 billion people in 150 countries.

Kennedy also expanded the scope of the Cold War beyond earth. Shortly before he departed to meet Khrushchev in Vienna, Kennedy had given a televised speech asking for an extra $1,700 million for landing an American on the Moon by 1970, prompted by the Soviet success of Yuri Gagarin's orbit of the earth on 12 April 1961. Kennedy's promise was to become part of his legacy and was achieved when Neil Armstrong set foot on the moon on 21 July 1969.

The Peace Corps

Formed in 1961 the corps encouraged young people to volunteer to work in poorer areas of the world, especially in Latin America, teaching English, providing medical supplies and improving sanitation. It had a clear altruistic goal but was also a propaganda tool for the US government as well as fitting with the Kennedy image of a reliance on youth and an alternative to the measures of the past.

ACTIVITY

Thinking point

How far does the Peace Corps fit into the ideology of Kennedy's foreign policy? Was it just window dressing for a hard-line policy of containment or was it a central plank in his goal of peace?

Finally from the very visible promise of a lunar landing the covert nature of the Cold War had also expanded under Kennedy. The CIA became active with numerous operations including:

- in September 1960, under Eisenhower, the CIA orchestrated the removal of the democratically elected Patrice Lumumba in Congo owing to his clear leanings toward the Soviet Union and talk of pan-Africanism, he was eventually killed three days before Kennedy was inaugurated
- in April 1961 the failed CIA-organised Bay of Pigs attack led Kennedy to fire Allen Dulles as the head of the organisation
- in May 1961 the CIA removed Rafael Trujillo in the Dominican Republic and later forced the democratically elected President Jose Velasco in Ecuador to resign
- in 1963 the CIA overthrew the democratically elected Juan Bosch, Trujillo's replacement in a military *coup d'état*, and in Brazil opposed the election of President Joao Goulart owing to his policies of land reform.

Much of the CIA's work was under the radar of the Federal government, but this veil of secrecy and dependence on covert operations eroded faith in the US and made Kennedy's talk of a global effort for peace seem hypocritical.

In standing up to Khrushchev, Kennedy had precipitated the latter's demise and followed in the footsteps of Truman and Kennan. He had secured the battle lines in Europe, contained communism in the Caribbean but also profoundly misjudged the situation in Laos and Vietnam, beginning the proxy war which would tear down the perception of US military invincibility in the most humiliating way imaginable.

> **ACTIVITY**
>
> Draw up a table to evaluate the extent of US influence worldwide by the end of Kennedy's presidency. Your table should include columns for Political and Economic influence and rows for Latin America, Africa, Europe, the Soviet Bloc and East Asia.

Economic prosperity by late 1963

Kennedy and the economy

Kennedy had benefitted from the recessions of 1958 and 1960, which had damaged the Republican reputation for economic competence. One of his slogans promised a Kennedy Administration would focus on 'getting America moving again' but he inherited a slow recovery and 6.8 per cent unemployment. The American Dream clearly needed to be kick-started after the Eisenhower years.

Kennedy's relationship with business had been a difficult one. A public dispute with the president of US Steel Roger Blough over an increase in steel prices, had reinforced the impression that Kennedy was anti-business. US Steel hit back by increasing prices the following year whilst also announcing that it would explore the possibility of building new factories abroad. By the end of 1962, economic issues seemed to be the main area of weakness in Kennedy's campaign for re-election in 1964. Unemployment stubbornly remained at 6 per cent and the stock market had failed to recover after losing a quarter of its value in the last two years. JFK also ignored advice about the costs of pressing ahead with Medicare, a decision that led several Democrats to turn against the bill, ensuring its defeat in the Senate.

Kennedy decided that it was time to be bold and declared that the absence of recession was not equivalent to economic growth in a dig at those Republicans who said he could learn from Eisenhower. Kennedy proposed a huge cut in income tax in 1963 from a range of 20–91 per cent to 14–65 per cent, whilst also proposing a cut in the corporate tax rate from 52 per cent to 47 per cent. The effect was swift with growth returning in 1963, despite **bipartisan** Republicans and conservative Democrats in Congress insisting that reducing taxes without making spending cuts was unrealistic. Kennedy disagreed, claiming that the increased spending from reducing

> **KEY TERM**
>
> **bipartisan:** a term usually associated with a two party governmental system this refers to when common ground is found between traditionally opposite sides, for example opposition to communism was a bipartisan policy in Congress

taxes would make tax receipts rise too, claiming 'a rising tide lifts all boats'. The battle over the tax cut and the federal deficit continued until the end of 1963 but opinion polls showed that over 60 per cent of Americans favoured the tax cuts.

A CLOSER LOOK

The Council of Economic Advisers (CEA)

First set up as part of the Employment Act of 1946 the CEA's aim was to offer presidents objective economic analysis and advice on the development and implementation of economic policy. Under Eisenhower and Kennedy the CEA advocated a largely Keynesian approach to economic policy, combining public works programmes with providing cheap credit and reducing taxes.

The CEA encouraged Kennedy to adopt a 'New Deal' style spending plan but this raised concerns about the potential implications of running a large deficit when the 1964 presidential election was taking place. Instead Kennedy's 'New Frontier' policies encouraged employment without spending heavily on major public works and succeeded in bringing unemployment down to 6 per cent where it stayed until 1963.

SOURCE 2

An extract from an interview with Carl Oglesby, a technical writer for the defence contractor Bendix Aerospace Systems Division. Oglesby later left Bendix and became the President of Students for a Democratic Society (SDS), a student activist movement prominent between 1965 and 1969:

In this one office they had the scotch (whiskey) out. The ripple of excitement, the thrill that ran through Bendix Systems Division when the word came of Kennedy's death, and with it the implicit word that now we got Johnson. It was like – I don't know how to describe it. It was almost a physical tremor. Before, there was gloom, because for one thing Kennedy had cancelled out a big contract we had. We were building something called the Eagle Missile that was supposed to go on a certain airplane. Well, the airplane didn't exist, and it wasn't going to exist either. So Kennedy logically figured why build the missile? But this didn't seem reasonable to 'corporate headquarters', which was really fed up at having lost the Eagle Missile system. Well that was the mood people were in. The next minute Kennedy gets popped. A minute after that, the scotch is out, because the contracts are coming back. And they did! By God, they did. I couldn't shrug that off.

ACTIVITY

Evaluating primary sources

What does the Source 2 tell you about the relationship between the Kennedy Administration and business?

CROSS-REFERENCE

To revisit Galbraith's *The Affluent Society*, look back to Chapter 6, page 50.

Kennedy had pledged to 'get America moving again', and at the time of his death it appeared to be on an upward trajectory. Heavily influenced by his friend JK Galbraith's 1958 book ***The Affluent Society*** Kennedy sought to combine growth with social justice. An employment boom was beginning and stocks were soaring. By 1966 the measures Kennedy began saw the economy growing at a rate of 6.6 per cent and the unemployment rate had fallen to 3.8 per cent. Kennedy had increased the minimum wage, expanded unemployment benefits and continued Eisenhower's spending on highway construction whilst also lowering taxes. In 1962, speaking at the Economic Club of New York, Kennedy said he was committed to cutting personal and corporate income taxes as he believed the tax system took away too much purchasing power from individuals and businesses which therefore didn't help

Fig. 2 *Kennedy addresses the nation on the topic of the economy in 1962*

the economy. In the fiscal year after Kennedy's death, the federal budget deficit did indeed shrink while between 1962 and 1966, the **Dow Jones Industrial Average** nearly doubled.

Historian Allen Matusow argues that Kennedy's tax cuts changed future economic policy for both parties and in particular have been used by Republicans in subsequent Administrations to argue that tax cuts lead to prosperity. Kennedy also succeeded in keeping inflation low throughout his short presidency but Matusow argues that the Medicare programme Kennedy introduced had unintended consequences for the very people it was trying to help. This is because medical costs were driven up by hospitals who knew they would get reimbursed by government.

Growing pressures for social change

The successes of the Civil Rights Movement prompted other groups to begin to campaign for their rights using techniques pioneered by African-American activists. The National Congress of American Indians (NCAI) had been founded in 1944 to campaign for Native American rights but in 1961 Clyde Warrior, Melvin Thom and Herbert Blatchford formed the National Indian Youth Council (NIYC). They were scathing in their assessment of federal treatment of Native Americans and adapted the tactics of the Civil Rights Movement to their situation, organising 'fish-ins' to assert fishing rights given to their ancestors in the nineteenth century but ignored by landowners. A Hispanic rights movement also emerged in 1962 when Cesar Chavez formed the United Farm Workers union to allow Mexican-American labourers to protest against their working conditions. However it was to be the feminist movement that was most significant in the Kennedy presidency.

Women

In 1960 the former First Lady Eleanor Roosevelt persuaded Kennedy to set up the Presidential Commission of the Status of Women. The commission reported in 1963 that, although women made up half the workforce, 95 per cent of managers were men and only 4 per cent of lawyers and 7 per cent of doctors were women. Even more damning was the fact that women earned around 55 per cent of the wages of men when doing the same work.

KEY TERM

Dow Jones Industrial Average: an average generated from the stock market performances of 30 top US companies, over a standard day's trading. The average is seen as representative of the wider economic situation

ACTIVITY

Draw up a table of successes and failures of Kennedy's economic policies. Why is it difficult to draw accurate conclusions?

Further evidence of the poor treatment of half the American population began to emerge. This was epitomised by Congresswoman Martha Griffiths' critical questioning of the personnel manager of National Airlines after their policy of firing stewardesses if they married or reached the age of 32 became evident.

Fig. 3 *A Kenwood Chef advert, 1961; during the Second World War images of women in advertising had highlighted their strength and contribution to the war effort, but by the early 1960s advertising executives had reverted to portraying women as passive homemakers*

The most significant development in the feminist movement under Kennedy was the publishing of a book by **Betty Friedan** called *The Feminine Mystique*. In it Friedan questioned why educated women were so disillusioned in the US.

SOURCE 3

Taken from Betty Friedan's 1963 book, *The Feminine Mystique*, chapter one 'The Problem That Has No Name'. The publication of the book is often seen as the start of the Second Wave of feminism in the US:

The problem lay buried, unspoken for many years in the minds of American women. It was a strange stirring, a sense of dissatisfaction, a yearning that women suffered in the middle of the twentieth century in the United States. Each suburban housewife struggled with it alone. As she made the beds, shopped for groceries, matched slipcover material, ate peanut butter sandwiches with her children, chauffeured Cub Scouts and Brownies, lay beside her husband at night, she was afraid to ask even of herself the silent question – "Is this all?" The American housewife, freed by science and labor-saving appliances from the drudgery, the dangers of childbirth, and the illnesses of her grandmother had found true feminine fulfilment. But strange new problems are being reported in the growing generations of children whose mothers were always there, driving them around, helping them with their homework, an inability to endure pain or discipline or pursue any self-sustained goal of any sort, a devastating boredom with life.

ACTIVITY

Evaluating primary sources

Construct a spider-diagram covering the reasons that some women were dissatisfied with their roles in the early 1960s. Use Friedan's ideas in Source 4 and your own knowledge. You might like to look at political, economic and social reasons.

Betty Friedan (1921–2006) is credited with starting the Second Wave of American Feminism with the 1963 publication of her book *The Feminine Mystique*. In 1966 she founded the National Organisation for Women (NOW) which aimed to bring women into equal partnership with men. She was a campaigner for abortion rights, for an Equal Rights Amendment to the US Constitution and for increased political representation for women.

Fig. 4 *Friedan is regarded as an influential author and intellectual*

Friedan had succeeded in articulating a problem at the root of the lives of many American women. While the Second World War had seen empowerment, a place in the job market and independence, the return of soldiers from overseas led to women being removed from the workforce to provide jobs for men. The resulting baby boom also meant that many women had very little time or energy to think through what they had lost at the end of the war. Friedan's rallying cry was to have profound effects on American society in the decades that followed although she was at pains to point out that this was not **misandry**, and that sexism was a societal rather than a male problem.

Kennedy introduced an Equal Pay Act as part of his 'New Frontier' legislation and this was signed into law in June 1963. The Act banned sexual discrimination in many, but not all, professions in terms of wages but made no mention of the Equal Rights Amendment which continued to be a key issue for feminists, as it had been since it was first proposed in 1923.

Youth

The growth of young people as a demographic was the result of the consumer boom, offering increased independence through part-time jobs and a voice, in the form of music, film and fashion, to express their discontent. Gangs began to develop in the major cities, sometimes linked by ethnicity as in the black gangs in Los Angeles and Harlem. They were also linked by fashion such as the Greasers, a working class youth subculture that originated among teenagers in the north-eastern and southern US who were most memorably portrayed in the 1978 film *Grease*.

These 1950s youth movements were largely apolitical but the formation of the SNCC in 1960 was one of the first instances of organised youth protest and the politicisation of many young people was a feature of the Kennedy presidency. Kennedy's own youth and rhetorical skill created an environment in which it seemed anything was possible, in addition there was the sense of change that always comes with the start of a new decade. However the memorable youth challenges to the status quo were to come under Johnson who, in many ways, seemed to be the antithesis of Kennedy's sense of hope.

Kennedy inspired many groups to make demands that he lacked both the political capital and the time to fulfil. The success of the Kennedy Administration in addressing the issues of minority groups is mixed at best but the atmosphere created by '**Camelot**' served to uncork a genie that would not return to its bottle despite the efforts of Johnson to assuage it and Nixon

The Equal Rights Amendment (ERA)

The ERA (equality of rights for both sexes under the law) was introduced in every congressional session between 1923 and 1970 but rarely made the floor of the House. Problems emerged because of the belief that full equality would lead to erosion of legislative protection that was unique to women. The Civil Rights Act of 1964 banned workplace discrimination not only on the basis of race but also on the basis of sex and pressure built to adopt the ERA. Congress finally did so in 1972 but ratification from the States was slow and the deadline eventually passed. To date there is no Equal Rights Amendment to the US Constitution.

misandry: the hatred of men; the equivalent term for women is misogyny

Construct a Venn diagram showing where the issues that faced the different groups overlapped and where they were different.

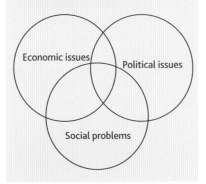

Camelot: an admiring term given to JFK's circle comparing it to the court of King Arthur

to silence it. Kennedy's real achievement in addressing social issues in the US was to create an environment in which the fact that the US had social issues could be addressed. In many ways his Administration highlighted just how far away the American Dream was from at least half of the American population.

Summary

Kennedy's legacy was the handing on of a host of problems. Vietnam and civil rights were the major source of these issues but women's rights, Native American and Hispanic rights, along with relations with the USSR, in the Middle East and in Latin America were all to become more protracted for the next four presidents. In addition, J Edgar Hoover's brooding power at the **FBI** along with the growing independence of the CIA began to chip away at presidential power.

Kennedy's biographer Robert Dallek titled his book about JFK, *An Unfinished Life*, a reference both to his early death and to the measures put in place during his first term and the potential achievements of his second that were partly addressed by Johnson. It is fair to say that he was the first president who really understood the media, that he left the economy in a healthy state, that he began the process of addressing the many social problems that the US faced and that he brought an optimism to the presidency and the country that was not seen again until the early days of Reagan. For many Americans the decade that followed Kennedy's assassination was what burnished his legacy, and made the era of JFK seem like the last great manifestation of the American Dream.

KEY TERM

FBI (Federal Bureau of Investigation): the domestic intelligence and security service in the USA

STUDY TIP

It is important to consider the type of source in this question. A eulogy will often be very forgiving of the flaws of the person it is about. Source 2 suggests that Kennedy was anti-business but can this be seen as reflecting the opinion of all business leaders? Source 3 should also be treated carefully.

 PRACTICE QUESTION

Evaluating primary sources

Look back at Sources 1, 2 and 3. With reference to these sources and your understanding of the historical context, assess the value of these sources to an historian studying Kennedy's presidency.

STUDY TIP

A balanced response will need to consider what Kennedy's achievements were and what can be defined as his mistakes. Aim to use your contextual knowledge to examine the various areas of Kennedy's policy, as well as the effects that his decisions had on America and on his legacy.

 PRACTICE QUESTION

'Kennedy's achievements were outweighed by his mistakes.' Assess the validity of this view.

The Johnson presidency, 1963–1968

13 Johnson as president

Johnson as president: his personality and policies

At 6'3" Johnson was the second tallest president after Lincoln and a big man in every way. Hugely ambitious and politically brilliant he was capable of enormous compassion and great cruelty. He loved practical jokes and delighted in pretending that his brakes didn't work as he and his terrified passengers rolled toward a lake, little knowing that Johnson owned an amphibious car. His two children were both christened so they shared his initials, even his wife, Claudia, changed her name to Lady Bird Johnson. He entered politics in 1930 at the age of 22, quickly fostering connections and winning a seat in the House of Representatives in 1937. During the war he served in the Navy and after the war ran for a senate seat. Winning the Democratic nomination amongst allegations of voter fraud, he trounced his Republican opponent and earned the nickname 'landslide Lyndon'.

In Washington his political skill came to the fore and he quickly rose to become the Democratic majority leader in the Senate, leading Kennedy to choose him as a running mate in the 1960 presidential election despite Johnson having sought the nomination himself. In particular Johnson excelled at intimidation. His physical presence enabled him to intimidate friends and opponents with 'the Johnson treatment' and he was also known for making aides uncomfortable by conducting briefings whilst on the toilet, exposing himself and berating his staff. But Johnson's work ethic was greater than any other president despite his having suffered a huge heart attack in 1955 and suffering from ill health throughout his presidency. He attacked the job, passing over 60 pieces of legislation during the 89th Congress and conducting both domestic and foreign policy with a forensic attention to detail and utter commitment. His ability to get bills passed is reflected in the fact that he needed to use **Executive Orders** far less extensively than Kennedy before him or the next Democratic President, Jimmy Carter despite the controversial nature of many of his proposals.

LEARNING OBJECTIVES

In this chapter you will learn about:

- the personality and policies of President Johnson
- Johnson's pursuit of the 'Great Society'
- the impact of the Kennedy legacy
- economic developments during Johnson's presidency.

ACTIVITY

The author Robert Dallek entitled one of his biographies of Johnson *Flawed Giant*. What do you think he meant by this?

CROSS-REFERENCE

See the Key Term for Executive Order in Chapter 1, page 8.

SOURCE 1

An adapted extract from Rowland Evans and Robert Novak's 1966 book: *Lyndon B Johnson: The Exercise of Power*:

Johnson's method for getting his way became known as 'the Johnson treatment' and took the form of supplication, accusation, persuasion, exuberance, scorn, tears, complaint, the hint of threat. It was all these together. It ran the range of human emotions. Its speed and force was breathtaking, and it was all in one direction. Interjections from the target were rare. Johnson anticipated them before they could be spoken. He moved in close, his face a scant millimeter from his target, his eyes widening and narrowing, his eyebrows rising and falling. From his pockets poured clippings, memos, statistics. Mimicry, humor, and the genius of analogy made The Treatment an almost hypnotic experience and rendered the target stunned and helpless.

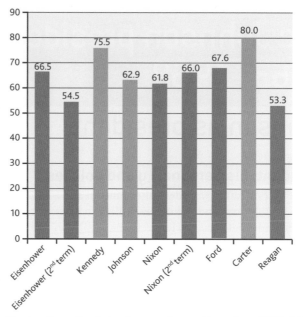

Fig. 1 *Executive Orders by term for presidents from 1945–80*

Fig. 2 *The Johnson technique in action; here, LBJ, the Majority Leader, puts the strong-arm on Theodore Green, a 90-year-old senator*

ACTIVITY

Discuss the aspects of Johnson's personality and background that would potentially make him an effective president. Are there any drawbacks?

CROSS-REFERENCE

See Chapter 9, pages 76–79 for details on Kennedy's 'New Frontier' programme.

Johnson's foreign policies are explored in Chapter 14.

Johnson's policies

Unlike other presidents, Johnson's policies were largely domestic and often a continuation of those of his predecessor. He sought to address the problems of poverty for all through his 'Great Society' programme (see below) which was an extension of Kennedy's **New Frontier**' but did not intend to raise taxes to pay for this. **Overseas** he remained committed to the Truman Doctrine and the principle of containment.

Johnson's pursuit of the 'Great Society'

The problems exposed by Michael Harrington in his 1962 book *The Other America* were the principal focus of Johnson's 'Great Society', a name adapted from **Walter Lippmann's** book 'The Good Society. The

'Great Society' was a programme of legislation designed to address the issues that had always been close to Johnson's heart. In his January 1964 State of the Union address Johnson had announced an 'unconditional war on poverty in America' and he intended the 'Great Society' to also encompass urban renewal, the environment, healthcare reform and educational reform.

KEY PROFILE

Walter Lippmann (1889–1974) was a Jewish-American writer, journalist and political commentator who won the Pulitzer Prize twice. Lippmann served in the First World War and was an adviser to Wilson. He was the foremost Liberal thinker in the US after Henry Wallace lost the vice presidency and was an adviser to Johnson until the two argued over Lippmann's criticism of the handling of the Vietnam War.

Fig. 3 *Lippmann introduced the concept of 'Cold War'*

SOURCE 2

President Johnson's **commencement address** at the University of Michigan, 1964. This was the first time he mentioned the 'Great Society':

It is harder and harder to live the good life in American cities today. The catalog of ills is long: there is the decay of the centers and the despoiling of the suburbs. There is not enough housing for our people or transportation for our traffic. Open land is vanishing and old landmarks are violated. Worst of all, expansion is eroding the precious and time honored values of community with neighbors and communion with nature. The loss of these values breeds loneliness and boredom and indifference. Our society will never be great until our cities are great. Today the frontier of imagination and innovation is inside those cities and not beyond their borders. New experiments are already going on. It will be the task of your generation to make the American city a place where future generations will come, not only to live but to live the good life.

KEY TERM

commencement address: a speech given to graduating students at US Universities, usually by a speaker of considerable note. All US presidents in this period delivered several commencement speeches and often used them to introduce new policies because of the optimistic nature of the occasion

Johnson was uniquely well-suited to getting through an ambitious programme of domestic reform. His political skill and ability to identify the things that mattered to individuals in Congress gave him a huge advantage. He once told his assistant Harry McPherson 'I understand power, whatever else may be said about me. I know where to look for it and how to use it.'

The 'Great Society' Programmes

The forerunners of the 'Great Society' were Roosevelt's **New Deal** and Kennedy's **New Frontier** which had both sought to address the disconnect between the American Dream that many still believed in and the reality of poverty and disenfranchisement which the Soviet media gleefully drew on when trying to damage the US's reputation. Johnson's landslide victory over **Barry Goldwater** in the 1964 presidential election gave him the mandate to pursue the 'Great Society' programmes.

CROSS-REFERENCE

See Chapter 1, page 5 for a reminder on the 'New Deal'.

CROSS-REFERENCE

For more information about the 1964 Civil Rights Act, see Chapter 15, page 124.

To read more about the 1965 Voting Rights Act, see Chapter 15, page 124.

KEY CHRONOLOGY

1964 Economic Opportunity Act – creates the Office of Economic Opportunity (the OEO) which was to administer 'The War on Poverty'

Urban Mass Transportation Act – provides federal money for public transport

Housing Act – provides federal funds for public housing along with rent subsidies for poorer families

Civil Rights Act

Wilderness Protection Act – promises that 9 million acres of government land would be protected from development

1965 Medical Care Act – creates the Medicaid and Medicare programmes to help the poor and the elderly respectively with the cost of Medical Treatment

Elementary and Secondary Education Act – grants federal aid to poorer children

Voting Rights Act

Air and Water Quality Act – sets tougher limits on polluters and gives states the responsibility to enforce quality controls

Minimum Wage Act – raises the minimum wage and extends the number of groups it applied to

Higher Education Act – provides federal funding for post-high school education

1966 Redevelopment Act – focuses on 150 'model cities' where integrated programmes of social care, training and housing would be trialled

Highway Safety Act – sets new federal standards for vehicle and road safety

1967 Public Broadcasting Act – establishes National Public Radio (NPR) and the Public Broadcasting Service (PBS).

ACTIVITY

Construct a diagram to categorise the key acts of the 'Great Society' into the different sections they applied to: reducing poverty, urban renewal, the environment, health care reform and educational reform. Which of the Acts feature in more than one section?

KEY PROFILE

Barry Goldwater (1909–98) was the Republican candidate in the 1964 election where he was thrashed by Johnson. His highly conservative policies led to the lowest ever share of the vote in a presidential election. He returned to serve as Senator for Arizona from 1969 and rebuilt his reputation by encouraging Nixon to resign in 1974 and opposing the increased influence of the religious right.

Fig. 4 *Goldwater was a businessman and five-term senator*

ACTIVITY

Draw up at table of the reasons why Johnson won the 1964 presidential election using two columns: one for Democratic strengths and one for Republican weaknesses.

A CLOSER LOOK

The 1964 presidential election

The 1964 presidential election took place less than a year after Kennedy's death. In many ways this gave Johnson an advantage, as his opponent, Barry Goldwater, was seen to be campaigning against the Kennedy legacy. The result of the election was catastrophic for the Republicans with Johnson winning over 61 per cent of the popular vote, the highest figure in the twentieth century. Mississippi, Louisiana, Alabama, Georgia and South Carolina all went over to the Republicans as Johnson had predicted they would after his signing of the Civil Rights Act.

How successful were the 'Great Society' programmes?

Johnson put **Sargent Shriver** in charge of the war on poverty as Director of the OEO with an initial budget of $1 billion. Shriver took to the challenge but he was fighting a losing battle as the cost of Vietnam ate into the national budget and consumed Johnson's time. While others felt Shriver did a good job at the OEO, Shriver himself was embittered by the experience later saying that the **Vietnam War** killed the War on Poverty. The figures make stark reading; between 1965 and 1973 $15.5 billion was spent on the 'Great Society' programmes as a whole, while $120 billion was spent on Vietnam.

CROSS-REFERENCE

Recap on the Key Profile of Sargent Shriver in Chapter 9, page 76.

Read Source 4 below for an account of Shriver's time at the OEO.

The war in Vietnam is explored in Chapter 14, pages 113–119.

SOURCE 3

Al From, the founder and former CEO of the Democratic Leadership Council in an interview in 2008:

The OEO principle of empowerment – we strove for maximum feasible participation of the poor – outraged America's mayors and created enormous political headaches for Sarge every day. The concept was simple: poor people had a right to one-third of the seats on every local poverty program board. The mayors went crazy. I was once asked by a mayor who had closed five neighborhood centers: 'Why should I open five organizations to campaign against me.' Sarge never buckled. He hated welfare and believed in community action. Even when Johnson effectively pulled the plug on the War on Poverty to fund the war in Vietnam, Sarge fought on and won. We didn't always get our paychecks on time because Congress delayed our funding – that's why I got an American Express Card in 1967 – but in the end Sarge won the battle and the anti-poverty program went on. It's not always appreciated today, but during the Shriver years more Americans got out of poverty than during any similar time in our history.

"There's Money Enough To Support Both Of You — Now, Doesn't That Make You Feel Better?"

Fig. 5 *Herblock's classic cartoon comparing the financial resources allocated to Vietnam and the 'Great Society'*

However the 'Great Society' could boast significant achievements even if its importance and budget was dwarfed by Vietnam. By 1976 Medicare and Medicaid were providing 20 per cent of the population with health care, the Head Start programme had provided free nursery schooling for disadvantaged children, Volunteers in Service to America (VISTA) encouraged community service by young people amongst the poor, and the environmental programmes were the first of their kind. **Johnson's civil rights legislation** was the most important since the Civil War.

In total there was more Welfare legislation passed than in Roosevelt's 'New Deal'. In 1959 government figures had suggested there were 40 million poor families in America, by 1968 this number was estimated to be 25 million and Johnson had demonstrated once again, as Roosevelt had in the 'New Deal', that there was a place for big government intervention to address society's problems.

Criticism of the 'Great Society' came from a number of sources, the Economist Milton Friedman accused Johnson of damaging the economy with his interventionist approach and his fellow economist Thomas Sowell accused Johnson of destroying the African-American family through liberal welfare and civil rights legislation. Politicians like Nixon and Reagan were quick to recognise that there was a '**silent majority**' of Americans who felt they were being forced to subsidise the poor and that those who protested loudest were the only ones being listened to. Vested interests like the American Medical

CROSS-REFERENCE

For more information on Johnson's civil rights legislation, see Chapter 15, pages 124–125.

KEY TERM

'**silent majority**': a term used to refer to a large but unspecified group of people in a society who choose not to express their opinions publically. Nixon invoked the 'the great silent majority of my fellow Americans' in a 1969 speech and struck a chord with those conservative 'blue-collar' and middle-class Americans who were often older and had lived through the privations of the war and depression and resented the attitude of the young and minority groups

Association (AMA) and local politicians were fearful of the erosion of their power through the extension of federal involvement, meanwhile King was damning in his comparison that in 1966 the government was spending $500,000 to kill one Vietcong soldier when only $35 were made available for each poor American.

The impact of the Kennedy legacy

After Kennedy's assassination, Johnson found himself in a similar position to that of Truman 19 years before, after the death in office of Roosevelt. The country was in shock and the cabinet was largely chosen by Kennedy. Things looked tough as the northern liberal members of the Democratic Party saw him as an unreconstructed southerner, and the Dixiecrat members were suspicious of his failure to sign the **Southern Manifesto**. But Johnson was alert to the problems and possibilities and he also understood that he had been given the opportunity he had dreamed of since he was 12 years old, when he had told his classmates that one day he would be president.

CROSS-REFERENCE

Revisit the Key Term definition of the Southern Manifesto in Chapter 8, page 65.

ACTIVITY

Make a list of problems that Johnson faced when he became president then categorise them into International, Economic, Political and Social.

Fig. 6 *Johnson being sworn in as President aboard Air Force One on the runway at Dallas' Love Field*

CROSS-REFERENCE

Recap on the Key Profiles in Chapter 9, page 76.

Johnson kept the bulk of Kennedy's team in place, including **Bobby Kennedy** as Attorney General despite the antipathy between the two, **Robert McNamara** as Defense and **Dean Rusk** as Secretary of State. Johnson also continued with many of Kennedy's policies including his tax cut, Civil Rights Bill and 'New Frontier' which he renamed the '**Great Society**'. In addition Johnson issued an Executive Order on 29 November for the renaming of NASA's launch centre at Cape Canaveral in Florida as the John F Kennedy Space Centre. In this way Johnson managed to appease the Kennedy camp, honour the previous president's legacy and pass substantial amounts of controversial legislation before he achieved a mandate of his own with a landslide victory in the 1964 Presidential Election.

Johnson was also alert to the public's demand for answers as to why Kennedy had been killed. He ordered Earl Warren to head a Commission into the assassination which reported in September 1964. Johnson handled the death of Kennedy as well as could have been expected and used his death to build a legacy for which Kennedy often gets credit. Nevertheless the assassination remains both controversial and distorted in the popular imagination.

The Warren Commission report

The report concluded that Lee Harvey Oswald had acted alone in killing Kennedy and that Jack Ruby, the Dallas Nightclub owner who had shot and killed Oswald, had also acted alone. Ruby himself died of lung cancer in 1967 but his links both to organised crime and Cuba have contributed to the proliferation of **conspiracy theories** around the death of Kennedy.

conspiracy theory: a term used to describe a theory that suggests a group, organisation, government department or secret society of having covered up, through secret planning and deliberate action, an illegal or harmful event or situation

Extension

In groups research the evidence that there was a conspiracy behind the assassination of the president. Are any of the theories credible?

Economic developments

President Johnson inherited a strong economy from Kennedy and took steps to augment both the economic recovery from the Eisenhower recessions and his own reputation as a safe pair of hands economically. White House press releases stressed how Johnson emphasised turning off the lights in every room at night, causing the press to briefly rechristen LBJ as Light-Bulb Johnson. More pertinently Johnson pushed through Kennedy's proposed tax cut which stimulated the economy and gave Johnson $4–5 billion in extra revenues to spend in his first two years. During this time inflation also stayed relatively low at just under 2 per cent but in late 1965 it began to pick up slightly, a pattern that was to continue, leaving Nixon with an inflation problem in 1968.

Gross National Product (GNP) grew by $9 billion and unemployment stood at 1.4 per cent which served to mask the problems with inflation and gave Johnson the confidence that he could fund a short-term war in Vietnam and the extravagant agenda of the 'Great Society'. Even as late as the winter of 1966 growth was at 9 per cent however unemployment had begun to rise, reaching 3.8 per cent by the start of 1967, a result of a mini-recession that had chilled the country in 1966. By this stage the Johnson Administration was becoming increasingly concerned with inflation. On 3 August Johnson asked Congress to impose a temporary 6 per cent income tax surcharge but Congress insisted this was tied to a $6 billion budget reduction in domestic spending which bit into the 'Great Society' budget, angering liberals. Overall during Johnson's presidency the average growth rate for the economy was 4.1 per cent per year and the National Debt was down to around 40 per cent from the 60.4 per cent that Kennedy had inherited. However with inflation at 4.7 per cent and rising, and an increasingly expensive overseas war to fight, Johnson could easily be excused form economic irresponsibility despite managing to get through his presidency without a significant recession.

Gross National Product (GNP): the total value of goods and services provided by a country, equal to GDP plus income from foreign investments

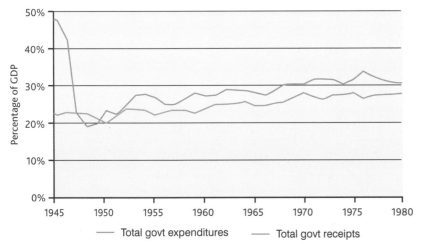

Fig. 7 *US government tax receipt versus expenditure as a percentage of GDP, 1940–80*

Using the list of 'Great Society' legislation and the information about Johnson's handling of the economy draw up a table showing which of his policies were unique to him and which were part of Kennedy's legacy.

ACTIVITY

Summary

Draw up a table of Johnson's successes and failures as a domestic president. Your headings might include Political Success, Economic success and Successes with Social Policies.

CROSS-REFERENCE

For Johnson's handling of the Vietnam War, see Chapter 14.

Summary

Johnson inherited a complex domestic situation and, in many ways handled it well. In surveys of historians Johnson usually ranks in the top third for the progress he made in welfare and civil rights. However his failures in handling the **war in Vietnam** are often used to suggest that overall his presidency was a disaster for the US.

The humourist PJ O'Rourke argues that 'Giving money and power to government is like giving whiskey and car keys to teenage boys'. In the case of Johnson, domestically at least, he seemed to use the power that came upon him in dramatic circumstances to good effect, targeting the groups in society that he felt had been marginalised. Nevertheless, this proactive effort to address the problems of those without a political voice, whilst also engaged in a costly foreign war, only served to marginalise those who, beforehand, had held the key to political success; Nixon's 'Silent Majority'. Perhaps Johnson's greatest failing on the domestic front was not his fine intentions but rather his inability to realise those intentions and demonstrate the value they had for American society as a whole. The death of Kennedy and the problems of the two presidents that followed him made many feel that the American Dream they had so believed in had been revealed as an illusion.

STUDY TIP

These sources provide considerable evidence on the problems facing Johnson and it is worth reading them with an eye for political, economic and social problems. Lack of representation in the political process is mentioned both at the local and national level, as are foreign entanglements and their consequences. Your understanding of the historical context will also be important.

 PRACTICE QUESTION

Evaluating primary sources

With reference to Sources 2 and 3 and your understanding of the historical context, assess the value of these sources to an historian studying the problems facing Johnson in the 1960s.

STUDY TIP

This question makes a significant assertion that requires unpacking. You must consider the aims of the 'Great Society' in order to judge whether it was a success or not but bear in mind that it is rare for any political programme to achieve all its goals. Dividing the 'Great Society' into its key areas might be a useful way to structure your response but remember to make a judgement about the programme as a whole in the conclusion.

 PRACTICE QUESTION

'The "Great Society" failed.' Assess the validity of this view.

14 Maintaining American world power

Following Eisenhower's decision to draw up military plans for an invasion of Vietnam, and Kennedy's decision to dispatch military advisers, it came as no surprise that US involvement increased in the area under Johnson. With an increasingly confident China and communist rebels in Laos and Cambodia enjoying success against US-backed regimes, the prospect of a 'red' South East Asia was too much for the Johnson Administration to contemplate but it took an incident off the coast of Vietnam to provoke the US into action.

Escalation of the war in Vietnam, 1964

One of Johnson's first actions in regard to Vietnam was to appoint **General William Westmoreland** to command military operations. At this stage, however, US troops were not fighting in Vietnam and neither was there a substantial air campaign. That was to change in August 1964 when Johnson asked Congress for a resolution of support to address reports that two US ships, the *Maddox* and the *Turner Joy* had been attacked in the Gulf of Tonkin, known as the Tonkin Incident. The resolution was passed by a unanimous vote in the House and a vote of 98:2 in the Senate. Only the Democratic Senators Wayne Morse from Oregon and Ernest Gruening from Alaska stood against the escalation.

SOURCE 1

Adapted extract from a speech by Johnson to the American people, 4 August 1964 after the Gulf of Tonkin incident:

In the larger sense this new act of aggression [the Tonkin incident], brings home to all of us the importance of the struggle for peace and security in south-east Asia. Aggression by terror against the peaceful villagers of South Vietnam has now been joined by open aggression on the high seas against the United States of America. The determination of all Americans to carry out our full commitment to the people and to the government of South Vietnam will be redoubled by this outrage. Yet our response, for the present, will be limited and fitting. We Americans know, although others appear to forget, the risks of spreading conflict. We still seek no wider war. I have instructed the Secretary of State to make this position totally clear to friends and to adversaries and, indeed, to all.

ACTIVITY

Evaluating primary sources

Using the speech above and your own knowledge, outline Johnson's reasons for escalating US involvement in Vietnam. When you have finished working through this chapter come back to this speech and highlight all of the promises Johnson goes on to break.

In the summer of 1964 Johnson had been campaigning on a peace platform and had warned that 'Some others are eager to enlarge the conflict. They call upon the US to supply American boys to do the job that Asian boys should do. We are not about to send American boys nine or ten thousand miles away from home to do what Asian boys ought to be doing for themselves,' Johnson went on. 'We don't want to get […] tied down to a land war in Asia'.

LEARNING OBJECTIVES

In this chapter you will learn about:

- the reasons behind the escalation of the war in Vietnam
- the political effect of the Vietnam War
- relations between the USA and its Western allies.

KEY PROFILE

Fig. 1   *Westmoreland adopted a strategy of attrition in the Vietnam War*

William Westmoreland (1914–2005) fought in the Second World War and rose to become a four-star General. Renowned as both tough and fair to his troops he brought a business-like attitude to the running of the Vietnam War. Convinced that his strategy of attrition was producing 'positive indicators' of progress, he was undermined by the Tet Offensive and replaced by General Creighton Abrams in June 1968.

KEY TERM

attrition: the process of reducing something's strength through sustained attack

Despite this, Johnson was torn; both Truman and Eisenhower had approved involvement in Vietnam through military advisers and Kennedy had increased the number of advisors to around 20,000 by the time he was assassinated in 1963.

Fig. 2 *This map shows the major actions of the Vietnam War, 1954–75*

A CLOSER LOOK

Operation Rolling Thunder

Operation Rolling Thunder was a sustained bombing campaign against North Vietnamese positions designed to disrupt supplies and destroy infrastructure in North Vietnam while boosting morale in the South. In the three years of Rolling Thunder, from 1965 to 1968, 864,000 tonnes of bombs were dropped on North Vietnam. However it failed to disrupt Vietcong supply lines and was a propaganda tool for the North.

The USA was committed to maintaining an independent South Vietnam as part of the policy of containment and Johnson was keenly aware that his place in history depended on how effectively he stood up to the communist threat. Nevertheless Johnson's interests, unlike the presidents who came before and after him, were focused on domestic affairs. As a result he kept on Kennedy's Defence Secretary McNamara and National Security Adviser McGeorge Bundy whilst also approving NSAM 273, a national security agency memorandum, on 26 November 1963. It directed the US government 'to assist the people and Government of South Vietnam to win their contest against the externally directed and supported Communist conspiracy'. In so doing he committed himself to a policy that was to prove disastrous and undermined his election commitments to peace.

A series of measures designed to damage North Vietnam and masterminded by the CIA had failed in early 1964 so Johnson approved NSAM 288 in late March 1964 which called for a greater use of US force. This included air strikes against North Vietnam and so when the Tonkin resolution was passed everything was in place for rapid escalation. On 13 February 1965, Johnson authorised Operation Rolling Thunder, a bombing campaign against

North Vietnam and on 8 March 1965, 3500 marines came ashore near Da Nang with orders to shoot only if fired upon. On 3 April Johnson sent two additional marine battalions and one marine air squadron, and an increase in logistical support units of 20,000 men whilst also approving active 'search and destroy' missions. Within a year of his election victory there were 175,000 US troops in Vietnam and a quarter of a million by the following year.

Johnson feared escalation would potentially bring in China and the Soviet Union, allies of communist North Vietnam, and widen the war. However, escalation was politically popular. In a speech in 1967 to Congress Westmoreland asserted thatus Army's 'Achilles heel' was its determination to fight. The speech was interrupted 19 times by applause and spelled out Westmoreland's belief that a policy of attrition in Vietnam would bring results. The use of high technology weaponry against the poor peasants of the North was already being exploited by the communist powers as part of a propaganda campaign. This was designed to bring developing countries into the communist orbit and put pressure on the USA both in the UN and the rest of the world. This propaganda was enhanced by the huge media coverage of the war facilitated by the growth in television ownership and newspaper purchasing worldwide. Johnson's advisers also failed to appreciate the effectiveness of the guerrilla tactics employed by the Vietcong and the willingness of the North to absorb the massive levels of damage in the belief that eventually the USA would end support for the South.

By the end of Johnson's presidency in 1968, the USA had 548,000 troops in Vietnam and 30,000 Americans had died there. Johnson's approval ratings had dropped from 70 per cent in mid 1965 to below 40 per cent by 1967. He expressed concern to his wife over what to do, he couldn't withdraw troops and couldn't win the war unless troop numbers increased. Johnson had tried to steer a compromise course of action between the **hawks** in Congress and the Executive who advocated greater aggression and **doves** like his Vice President **Hubert Humphrey** who counselled negotiation with Hanoi to clear a path to the eventual unification of Vietnam which the USA had agreed to under Eisenhower.

ACTIVITY

Draw up a table with two columns, one headed 'Results of a Successful Campaign in Vietnam' and the other headed 'Results of an Unsuccessful Campaign in Vietnam'. Use the material you have covered so far in Chapters 13 and 14 and your own ideas to fill out the table. It might be useful to think of success and failure in economic, political and social terms as well as the international relations aspect.

The Tet Offensive

As the war dragged on domestic opposition grew, hastened by the use of **the draft** to fill the demand for more troops. Throughout the escalation the Johnson White House maintained the argument that progress was being made and that the war would soon be over but early in 1968, an election year, the North Vietnamese launched the Tet Offensive, a co-ordinated attack on dozens of cities which destroyed the idea that the North Vietnamese were in disarray. Nearly 60,000 North Vietnamese died in the five weeks of the Offensive but during that time the US Embassy in Saigon fell for six hours before being captured. The symbolism of this successful conquest of American soil (embassies are regarded as the territory of the nation that holds the embassy, not that of the hosting country) was not lost on the viewing public and American opposition to the war soared as a result.

KEY PROFILE

Fig. 3   *Humphrey was vice president under Lyndon B Johnson*

Hubert Humphrey (1911–78) was a Democratic Senator for Minnesota. He was the Democratic majority whip in the senate from 1961 to 1964 and the principal author of the 1964 Civil Rights Act and so a natural choice for vice president. He received the Democratic nomination for president in 1968 but lost to Nixon.

KEY TERM

hawks and doves: in US foreign policy those who see weakness as dangerous and advocate an aggressive use of American power are often known as 'hawks' and their action as 'hawkish'. Those who see provocative behaviour as dangerous and advocate negotiation are often known as 'doves' and their action is, therefore 'dovish'

KEY TERM

the draft: the Selective Service and Training Act of 1940 provided for the army to 'draft' men in to fill vacancies in the armed services if there were insufficient volunteers. Exemptions existed including being in full-time education, working as a priest or rabbi or having a criminal record

The end of Walter Cronkite's CBS News broadcast, 27 February 1968. Cronkite was the most respected news anchor on US TV and had previously suggested he was in favour of the war:

Tonight, back in more familiar surroundings in New York, we'd like to sum up our findings in Vietnam, an analysis that must be speculative, personal, subjective. Who won and who lost in the great Tet Offensive against the cities? I'm not sure. The Vietcong did not win by a knockout but neither did we. For it seems now more certain than ever, that the bloody experience of Vietnam is to end in a stalemate. To say that we are closer to victory today is to believe in the face of the evidence, the optimists who have been wrong in the past. To say that we are mired in stalemate seems the only realistic, if unsatisfactory conclusion. It is increasingly clear to this reporter that the only rational way out will be to negotiate, not as victors, but as an honorable people who lived up to their pledge to defend democracy, and did the best they could. This is Walter Cronkite. Good night.

ACTIVITY

Evaluating primary sources

How useful is Source 2 for an historian studying the consequences of the Tet Offensive?

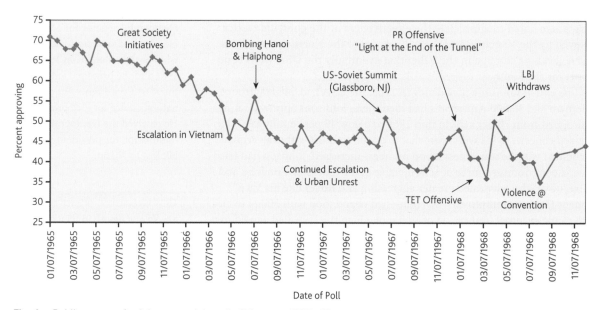

Fig. 4   *Public support for Johnson and the toll of Vietnam 1965–68*

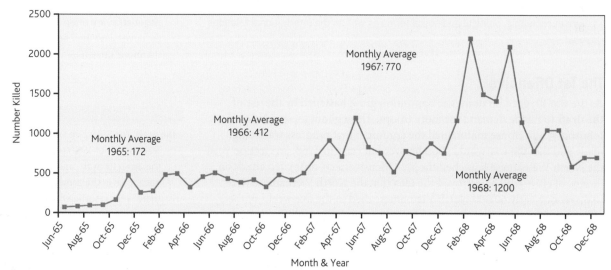

Fig. 5   *US personnel killed in action, June 1965 – December 1968*

Johnson decided not to stand in the 1968 presidential election, mostly due to the situation at home regarding involvement in Vietnam. Not only were there ongoing battles between the 'hawk' and 'dove' factions but anti-war activists began to demonstrate publicly against US involvement and Johnson in particular, the chant 'Hey, hey, LBJ! How many kids did you kill today?' haunted his public appearances. Meanwhile another Democrat, Eugene McCarthy announced his intentions to stand for the nomination for president against the **incumbent** Johnson.

CROSS-REFERENCE

Anti-war movements are examined in Chapter 16, pages 137–138.

KEY TERM

incumbent: meaning currently holding office. Although Johnson had served the end of Kennedy's term and then won the election of 1964 he was eligible to stand for election in 1968 as the incumbent

Fig. 6 *LBJ listens to a tape recording from Vietnam sent by his son-in-law Capt. Charles Robb, 31 July 1968*

The Khe Sanh base

At the same time as Tet, a second major battle had been going on in North Vietnam since January 1968. It began as part of the North Vietnamese Army's (NVA's) Tet Offensive but turned into the bloodiest battle of the war. Khe Sanh had been a US base since 1962 and lay close to the border with North Vietnam, enabling US forces based there to patrol the nearby **Ho Chi Minh Trail**. On 21 January 1968 **General Giáp** surrounded the base with 20,000 men and a 75-day siege began. The strategic importance of the base was the initial reason for the staunch defence undertaken by the US but as the siege developed it became impossible for Johnson to contemplate losing Khe Sanh. As a result, Johnson approved the dropping of 80,000 tons of bombs during the siege. Westmoreland was outraged by any suggestion of surrendering Khe Sanh and determined that the base should be held, even suggesting the use of tactical nuclear weapons. However, after Westmoreland was replaced by General Creighton Abrams, Johnson was more willing to accept that Khe Sanh was a liability and the decision was taken to close it down despite the fact that the siege had been broken. The retreat was kept from the US public for as long as possible but the North

KEY TERM

The Ho Chi Minh Trail: a route from North to South Vietnam that had sub-routes that went through both Laos and Cambodia. The trail allowed supplies to be moved to the Vietcong and was covered by jungle from the air. Disrupting the trail was seen as essential in starving the Vietcong of supplies

Vietnamese revelled in a propaganda victory; three-quarters of Hanoi radio broadcasts for a week after 5 July, the date of the closure, were devoted to their 'victory'.

A CLOSER LOOK

The American combat soldier in Vietnam

The average age of a combat soldier in Vietnam was 19, many really were just 'kids'. Eighty per cent had volunteered and were motivated by a twin sense of patriotism and anti-communism. Their experience of the realities of war was limited to a diet of Second World War films and the tales of their fathers. Once in Vietnam they found a very different war of heat, danger, and the impossibility of fighting an enemy who looked like the civilian population.

KEY PROFILE

General Võ Nguyên Giáp (1911–2013) fought against the Japanese then served as leader of the Vietminh in the war against the French. He was the logical choice as leader of the **NVA** when the civil war broke out. His logistical and strategic skill as well as his understanding of the nature of the war that was being fought contributed to the US defeat. He became Minister of Defense in the new Vietnam and then Deputy Prime Minister.

A month after Tet the New Hampshire **primary** took place and McCarthy took 41 per cent of the vote. Seeing Johnson's weakness Bobby Kennedy chose to enter the race throwing the party into turmoil. The country seemed to follow suit with the assassination of Martin Luther King, Jr in April and then Bobby Kennedy in June (by a 24-year-old Palestinian, Sirhan Sirhan who claimed the killing was in retaliation for Kennedy's support of Israel in the 1967 six-day war) and a bloody confrontation between police and protesters at the Democratic Convention in Chicago in August. With Nixon leading in the opinion polls Johnson halted the bombing campaigns in a desperate bid to salvage some legacy of peace. However, the unfailing optimism of the American people won out and it was Nixon's claim that he had a 'secret plan' to end the war that swayed the electorate rather than the tired and tainted Humphrey who could do little more than promise more of the same. Vietnam had broken Johnson and the Democrats who had lost heavily in the midterm elections of 1966, barely retaining control of the Senate and House. More damningly it had ended Johnson's hopes of a 'Great Society' and replaced them with a heavy debt in economic, political and human terms.

(A LEVEL) PRACTICE QUESTION

'Johnson's handling of the Vietnam War was disastrous.' Assess the validity of this view.

SOURCE 3

Black Power Address at UC Berkeley by Stokely Carmichael in October 1966:

The war in Vietnam is an illegal and immoral war. And the question is, what can we do to stop the people who, in the name of our country, are killing babies, women, and children? The only power we have is the power to say, "Hell no!" to the draft. We have to say to ourselves that there is a higher law than the law of a racist named McNamara. There is a higher law than the law of a fool named Rusk. And there's a higher law than the law of a buffoon named Johnson. It is the law of each of us saying that we will not allow them to make us hired killers. We will not kill anybody that they say kill. And if we decide to kill, we're going to decide who we going to kill. And this country will only be able to stop the war in Vietnam when the young men who are made to fight it begin to say, "Hell, no, we ain't going."

Relations between the USA and its Western allies

Fig. 7 *Johnson's car is pelted with paint during a visit to Australia in 1966*

When news reached Johnson that Harold Wilson had called an election in the UK in 1966 he responded, 'I suppose I'll have that little creep camping on my doorstep again.' Meanwhile when Wilson was questioned on why he wouldn't speak out publicly against the war despite his private reservations, his response was 'Because we can't kick our creditors in the balls.' It is safe to say the '**Special Relationship**' was affected by the war. Meanwhile Charles de Gaulle in France, after failing to persuade Kennedy of the danger of getting dragged into Vietnam, gave a speech to 100,000 people in Phnom Penh, the capital of Cambodia, denouncing US policy in Vietnam and urging Johnson to pull troops out of Southeast Asia. Despite the vehemence of this speech de Gaulle did talk frequently with George Ball, the Under Secretary of State. Ball used de Gaulle's arguments in an October 1964 memorandum to Johnson, but it had little effect.

In reality, the contribution made by other countries to the US cause in the Vietnam War was miniscule; South Korea had nearly 50,000 troops deployed in 1968, the greatest number at one time in the war as a whole. Thailand never mustered more than 11,570, Australia 7700 and the Philippines and New Zealand less than 3000 between them. The war exposed the weakness of **SEATO** and the international isolation of the USA, despite the professed goal of containing communism.

KEY TERM

Special Relationship: the idea that relations between the US and UK were different and superior to those between the US and its other allies

ACTIVITY

Could Johnson's foreign policy be deemed a success if Vietnam is not included in the debate? Can this ever be a fair way to view a president?

CROSS-REFERENCE

Revisit the Key Term definition of SEATO in Chapter 7, page 60.

Summary

ACTIVITY

Summary

The previously indefatigable Johnson was visibly drained by Vietnam. When his advisers began to urge him to consider retreat, reflecting the arguments of Congress and the results of opinion polls that suggested 78 per cent of Americans believed Vietnam was a stalemate and nearly three-quarters felt he was handling it badly, he took it to heart but was unwilling to admit he had been wrong. Johnson's attempts to negotiate, through Poland in 1966 and through Britain in 1967, had also failed and the Peace Talks that began in Paris in May of 1968 were hampered by the fact that Johnson was clearly a lame duck president. In the end his presidency limped to a halt, crippled by Vietnam.

Put the following reasons why Johnson failed in Vietnam into an order of importance. You must be able to justify your decisions.

- A South Vietnamese state was not viable without a long-term American commitment
- Johnson was hampered by a fear of inciting Soviet and Chinese retaliation
- Criticism at home damaged morale
- The quality of the forces at America's disposal was not good enough to win
- The military failed to appreciate the nature of the war and of the opposition
- Johnson's advisers lacked an understanding of war and an appreciation of history
- The cost of the war made it increasingly unpopular politically
- the American media coverage brought home the realities of war in a way never seen before in the US.

STUDY TIP

There are three strands to opposition here, one from Johnson himself, one from the media, and one from Carmichael. Obviously all three must be weighed up by their provenance, tone and emphasis, and content and argument. Consider other factors to provide a rounded answer.

 PRACTICE QUESTION

Evaluating primary sources

With reference to Sources 1, 2 and 3 and your understanding of the historical context, assess the value of these sources to an historian studying opposition to Johnson's policy in Vietnam.

African-Americans in the North and South

Developments in the Civil Rights Movement

> **LEARNING OBJECTIVES**
>
> In this chapter you will learn about:
>
> - developments in the Civil Rights Movement 1963–68
> - Johnson's role in passing civil rights legislation
> - the impact of change in the Civil Rights Movement, including urban riots.

Fig. 1 *Police protecting protesters at a St Augustine 'wade-in'*

Kennedy's death had come after the successes of **Birmingham** and the March on Washington, so King and the **SCLC** were aware of the need to pressure Johnson into reviving the Civil Rights Bill Kennedy had introduced. Their plan was to continue targeting cities that would produce the maximum media response. In early 1964 the SCLC went to St Augustine in Florida where they helped the local NAACP organise sit-ins, swim-ins and wade-ins at segregated facilities, provoking violence from locals and the Klan that kept pressure on Johnson.

> **CROSS-REFERENCE**
>
> For more information about what happened at Birmingham, see Chapter 11, pages 91–92.

Increasing the black vote

In Mississippi during the summer of 1964 the **SNCC** and **CORE** extended their involvement in the Deep South to draw the nation's attention to the violent opposition faced by African-Americans trying to vote; only 6.2 per cent were even on the voting rolls. SNCC activist Robert Moses proposed that northern white student volunteers join black activists for simultaneous local campaigns in Mississippi during the summer of 1964. Despite the likelihood of arrest, violence and the cost, over a thousand students joined the campaign and, after receiving training in Ohio, travelled to Mississippi to register black voters, teach literacy and civics at 41 Freedom Schools, and promote the Mississippi Freedom Democratic Party's (MFDP) challenge to the all-white Democratic delegation at that summer's Democratic National Convention in Atlantic City, New Jersey. After one week of the campaign three civil rights workers were reported missing in Mississippi. James Chaney, a black Mississippian, and Michael Schwerner and Andrew Goodman, two white northerners, disappeared while visiting Philadelphia, Mississippi, and were later found dead after

> **CROSS-REFERENCE**
>
> To recap on the SNCC and Core, look back to Chapter 11.

> **ACTIVITY**
>
> **Extension**
>
> Watch the film *Mississippi Burning*, based on a true story of the disappearance of three civil rights workers in Mississippi during the Freedom Summer. Some liberties have been taken with the plot but as an evocation of life for African-Americans in small towns in the South it is invaluable.

Fig. 2   *Hamer at the Democratic National Convention in 1964*

Fannie Lou Hamer (1917–71) was sterilised without her consent in 1961 as part of a programme to reduce the poor black population but after attending SNCC meetings she became active as an inspiring speaker. She was a delegate of the MFDP in 1964 and was active in both the anti-war movement and the feminist movement. Her grave is marked with her quote, 'I am sick and tired of being sick and tired'.

CROSS-REFERENCE

The failures of the Civil Rights Act of 1964 are discussed later in this chapter.

See Chapter 11, page 91 for information on Bull Connor.

For information on The Voting Rights Act/Bill, see later in this chapter, page 124.

CROSS-REFERENCE

See the Closer Look feature in Chapter 4, page 31 for detail on the Nation of Islam.

an FBI investigation. The killings outraged the SNCC who felt that the federal government had offered no protection to the Freedom Summer participants.

Approximately 17,000 black residents of Mississippi attempted to register to vote in the summer of 1964, but only 1600 were approved, highlighting the need for further legislation. The MFDP, led by **Fannie Lou Hamer,** travelled to Atlantic City and succeeded in getting some of its members seated at the Democratic Party Convention. During the campaign as a whole there were 1062 arrests, 37 churches were bombed and 80 workers reported being beaten. SNCC members became frustrated by government inaction and the focus on King who, in October 1964, was awarded the Nobel Peace Prize.

Selma

The failure of the Civil Rights Act of 1964 to address voting and the Freedom Summer led the SCLC to target voting and triggered a 1965 campaign in Selma, which the historian Stephen Oates described as 'the movement's finest hour'. Half of Selma's 30,000 population was black, but only 23 of them were registered to vote. The town Sheriff, Jim Clark, was as combustible as **Bull Connor** in Birmingham and when King led a march for would-be voters to the Selma County Court many were beaten and even had live snakes thrown at them. A young black man was shot trying to protect his mother. Three thousand were arrested, including King who quipped that there were more black people in jail in Selma than on the voting rolls. To further the pressure, King planned a march from Selma to Montgomery but it was attacked by state troopers using clubs and tear gas. This 'Bloody Sunday' brought national attention just at the right time to push Congress to pass the **Voting Rights Act**.

Opposition to the mainstream Civil Rights Movements

King and the SCLC were also being criticised. SNCC activists accused them of leaving a 'string of embittered cities' through their policy of extracting maximum media attention from an event before moving on. Some accused King of having a messiah complex and the SCLC of 'leader worship'. Still others criticised the fact that King and the SCLC received most of the donations that were forthcoming into the movement and were increasingly choosing to spend them on campaigns in the North.

In the North, the **Nation of Islam** (NOI) had lost influence after Malcolm X had left the organisation. Having been suspended by Elijah Mohammed after comments he made following the death of Kennedy about 'chickens coming home to roost' Malcolm X chose to leave after learning of Mohammed's extra-marital affairs and coming into conflict with his fellow ministers over his high media profile. Malcolm X then embarked upon a pilgrimage to Mecca, converted to Sunni Islam and toured Africa and Europe promoting two new organisations, Muslim Mosque Inc. and the Organisation of African-American Unity. He appeared to be coming towards a compromise position with southern civil rights groups, renouncing his previous criticisms of them and King in particular and attacking the Nation. Malcolm X, who had by this stage changed his name to el-Hajj Malik el-Shabazz, was then assassinated in February 1965 onstage in front of his children at a meeting of the Organization of Afro-American Unity (OAAU) by two gunmen from the NOI. Elijah Mohammed denied that the NOI was involved in the killing but stressed that Malcolm got what he deserved.

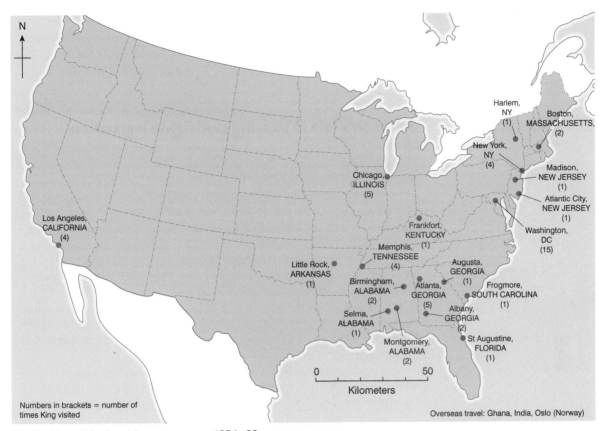

Fig. 3 *Map of King's public appearances, 1954–68*

SOURCE 1

Extract from the eulogy at Malcolm X's funeral delivered by actor and activist Ossie Davis, 27 Feb 1965:

There are those who will consider it their duty, as friends of the Negro people, to tell us to revile him, to flee, even from the presence of his memory. Many will ask what Harlem finds to honor in this stormy, controversial and bold young captain – and we will smile. Many will say turn away –away from this man, for he is not a man but a demon, a monster, a subverter and an enemy of the black man – and we will smile. They will say that he is of hate – a fanatic, a racist – who can only bring evil to the cause for which you struggle! And we will answer and say to them: Did you ever talk to Brother Malcolm? Did you ever really listen to him? Did he ever do a mean thing? Was he ever himself associated with violence or any public disturbance? For if you did you would know him. And if you knew him you would know why we must honor him.

SOURCE 2

Martin Luther King in a telegram to Malcolm X's widow, Betty Shabazz, after the assassination:

I was certainly saddened by the shocking and tragic assassination of your husband. While we did not always see eye to eye on methods to solve the race problem, I always had a deep affection for Malcolm and felt that he had a great ability to put his finger on the existence and root of the problem. He was an eloquent spokesman for his point of view and no one can honestly doubt that

ACTIVITY

Criticism of King was common from pro-segregation white people, radical black people and those in organisations other than the SCLC, along with the FBI's COINTELPRO special operation and historians in the decades that followed his death. Find a quotation from each of these groups and see if you can mount a defence of their accusations against him.

Fig. 4 *Downtown Chicago slums in around 1962*

Malcolm had a great concern for the problems that we face as a race. While I know this is a difficult hour for you, I am sure that God will give you the strength to endure. Always consider me a friend and if I can do anything to ease the heavy load you are forced to carry at this time, please feel free to call on me.

Johnson's role in passing civil rights legislation

As a southern senator Johnson had a mixed record when it came to civil rights, he didn't sign the 1956 Southern Manifesto but as Senate majority leader he ensured that Eisenhower's 1957 Civil Rights Bill was examined and diluted by a committee headed by the racist Senator for Mississippi James Eastland. However when Johnson became president, with Kennedy's Civil Rights Bill struggling through Congress, he showed enormous levels of commitment and political skill to get the bill through. He continued to support civil rights throughout his presidency despite the increasingly violent turn the movement took after 1965. Johnson showed his understanding of human nature in an aside to one of his staff in 1960 'I'll tell you what's at the bottom of it. If you can convince the lowest white man he's better than the best colored man, he won't notice you're picking his pocket. Hell, give him somebody to look down on, and he'll empty his pockets for you.'

The civil rights legislation passed by Johnson should be seen in the wider context of his 'Great Society'. It was, definitely the most difficult legislation to pass, requiring all his political skill in bullying and cajoling congressmen to support and not amend the bills. Johnson called in every favour, used every device, even suggesting to the staunchest Dixiecrats that by levelling the playing field it would leave African-Americans with no excuses left for their inferiority. Despite 68 per cent of the public supporting the first Civil Rights Bill it was subject to a 54 day **filibuster** attempt by Dixiecrats including Johnson's former mentor Richard Russell. However, the bill was eventually signed into law by Johnson in July of 1964. Johnson feared this would mean that the South would not vote Democrat for a long time and to some extent he was correct: Mississippi, Alabama and South Carolina have only voted for a Democratic candidate in a presidential election once since, for the Georgia-born Jimmy Carter in 1976.

The 1964 Civil Rights Act made all forms of *de jure* segregation a federal crime, meaning perpetrators would no longer benefit from the bias of the state courts. It furthered school desegregation and established an Equal Opportunity Commission. As a result the killers of Goodman, Chaney and Schwerner were convicted of 'denial of civil rights' rather than murder, which was a crime dealt with in-state. The 1964 Act failed to address problems with voting however, which Johnson wanted to leave until a later date. Events in Mississippi and Selma, Alabama, forced him to reconsider and Johnson then proposed and passed a Voting Rights Bill in 1965 which abolished literacy tests and poll taxes along with 'constitutional interpretation tests' and established federal registrars. This meant that all that was needed to vote was American citizenship and a registration form, and as the registrars were now federal employees, anything they did to deny a black citizen the right to vote made them answerable to the federal system rather than to local politicians. Its effect was immediate and dramatic. By the end of 1966, only four of the Southern states had less than half of their African-American population registered to vote, even Mississippi had 59 per cent registered. Over the next decade the number of elected black officials increased twelve-fold. Johnson's third Civil Rights Act, in 1968, outlawed racial discrimination in the sale or

CROSS-REFERENCE

See the Key Term definition of filibustering in Chapter 8, page 68.

rental of houses. Johnson delivered the most effective civil rights legislation in American history despite the political difficulties involved in trying to win over the Dixiecrats, and the risk of splitting his party and losing the South. Little wonder that after his death, 70 per cent of those that came to see him lying in state were black.

The impact of change including urban riots

The fight for economic equality

The achievements of the 1964 and 1965 legislation and the divisions in the NOI, following the assassination of Malcolm X, led the SCLC and King to look north for their next intervention and to focus on economic justice. King told **Bayard Rustin** that now the movement needed to focus on economic opportunity to allow black people to afford to eat in the restaurants they could now sit anywhere in. The new direction led King to Chicago in 1966, America's second largest city with a population of 3 million, 700,000 of whom were black. City Mayor Richard Daley was a skilful Democrat and close ally of Johnson who was wary of King's intentions. This lack of political support along with poor planning meant the Chicago campaign saw a succession of failures:

- King moved his family into a ghetto apartment which the landlord quickly refurbished to prevent media attention.
- A July 1966 rally only gathered 30,000 supporters instead of the hoped for 100,000.
- Daley met frequently with King but the meetings were unproductive.
- After arrests following a police intervention to turn off a fire-hydrant that had been opened in the sweltering summer heat, Daley blamed King for the disturbances which caused $2 million in damages.
- A march through the white working-class area of Cicero saw violent opposition with cries of 'apes', 'savages' and the police protecting the marchers derided as 'nigger lovers'. King was hit by a rock and made the decision to leave Chicago and concentrate his efforts elsewhere. His deputy, Jesse Jackson took over a more limited campaign of economic boycotts known as 'Operation Breadbasket'.

Chicago failed because there was no clear plan of action. King's tactics did not suit the territory and his focus wasn't on the real concerns of Northern African-Americans, such as police brutality, a lack of skilled jobs and the poor ghetto conditions. Johnson made $4 million of federal funds available but it was a drop in the ocean of what was needed and the president was wary of criticising his ally Daley whilst also being increasingly alienated by King's outspoken stance on the Vietnam War.

King had also failed to fully commit to Chicago because of problems elsewhere. In June 1966 James Meredith, the first black student to have attended the University of Mississippi embarked on a 200-mile walk from Memphis to Jackson, Mississippi. On the second day he was shot and unable to continue; civil rights leaders vowed to complete his march. King led an SCLC group but **Stokely Carmichael**, the new leader of the SNCC, was also on the march and was determined to express the discontent of black groups at the failings of the national government. Whilst SCLC marchers chanted 'Freedom Now' Carmichael demanded black power and some SNCC campaigners altered the words of a Christmas carol to become 'Jingle Bells, Shotgun shells / Freedom all the way / Oh what fun it is to blast a trooper man away'. The increased militancy of the SNCC alarmed King who feared it would alienate both white moderate support and Johnson, but he had few answers, epitomised by the rhetorical title of his 1967 book *Where Do We Go From Here?*

ACTIVITY

Extension

Look back at the 'Great Society' programmes Johnson introduced in Chapter 13, page 106-108. Which of these would have disproportionately aided African-Americans?

CROSS-REFERENCE

Look back to Chapter 11, page 92 for the role Bayard Rustin played in the civil rights rally in 1963.

KEY PROFILE

Stokely Carmichael (1941–98) had an uncompromising style, and a willingness to suffer beatings and arrest. His rhetorical skill saw him rise from being a participant in the Freedom Rides in 1961 to heading the SNCC by 1966. Here he coined the phrase 'Black Power' on the Meredith March but left the group in 1968 having become the Prime Minister of the Black Panther Party.

For King the answer was to Washington and an even more poorly planned campaign than in Chicago the previous year. King proposed an occupation of Washington by poor people of all colours and races, who would create a shanty town in the heart of the capitol to put pressure on legislators. Bobby Kennedy, by now a senator with designs on the White House in 1968, sent a message to King encouraging him to 'bring the poor people to Washington to make hunger and poverty visible since the country's attention had turned to the Vietnam War and put poverty and hunger on the back burner'. The logic of the idea was simple.

SOURCE 3

Extract from an article in The Baltimore Afro-American newspaper 25 May 1968:

The scenic side of the Lincoln Memorial's reflecting pool will be the home of some 10,000 poor people who have begun converging in Washington in protest against poverty. Planners were attracted by the availability of water, sewage, recreational and electrical facilities. But the present 'Resurrection City is planned to accommodate only 3000 poor people - a figure far below what the SCLC expects. James Peterson, the Poor People's Campaign administrative assistant, said they have had good responses from middle class whites who have donated sums ranging from $1000 and over. It might be a sense of guilt. They are beginning to feel that the world they are living in and the world of the poor people are quite different. They feel they have neglected their brothers and sisters and this campaign has given them the opportunity to assist the poor' he said. Peterson remarked that quite a number of white people are still adamant and not moved by the efforts of the poor people to communicate their needs to the entire nation.

ACTIVITY

Evaluating primary sources

Source 3 highlights some of the problems with mass occupation of a major city by the poor. If you were preparing a report on these problems, what other issues would you highlight?

Before the campaign could even get underway, King was assassinated on 4 April 1968 in Memphis, Tennessee, by a drifter and petty criminal called James Earl Ray. The previous night, King had given a speech to a group of sanitation workers which suggested he was prepared for death but had no fear for what it held. King's death sparked eulogies and riots that lasted several days and can be seen as another era defining moment. The flaws in his character which had led the FBI to blackmail him may have run deep, but his achievements in keeping a movement that was born in outrage and injustice peaceful for so long were considerable.

Riots

During the four summers from 1965 to 1968 ghettos all across America erupted in an orgy of violence, looting and arson. Beginning with Watts, Los Angeles in 1965 where 34 deaths, 3500 arrests and $40 million of damage set the tone. In the following years leading up to the riots that occurred after King's death, there were disturbances in over 200 cities and if the sporadic rioting that took place up to 1972 is included, there were 250 deaths, 10,000 serious injuries and 60,000 arrests. Some of the most serious rioting took place in Detroit, a city that had previously been seen as a model of inter-racial relations. Many argue that the decline of Detroit can be traced back to the effect of the riots and, such was their severity, Johnson commissioned Otto Kerner, the Governor of Illinois, to investigate the causes and report back. In February 1968 the Kerner Commission's report included the damning sentence 'This is our basic conclusion: Our nation is moving toward two societies, one black, one white – separate and unequal.' echoing the language of the **Plessy v. Ferguson** decision of 1896. The commission established 12 reasons for the rioting which were gathered from hundreds of interviews with those involved.

ACTIVITY

Evaluating primary sources

Look back at Source 3. Why do you think some white people opposed the Poor People's Campaign?

CROSS-REFERENCE

Look back to Chapter 8, page 65 for detail on the *Plessy v. Ferguson* ruling of 1896.

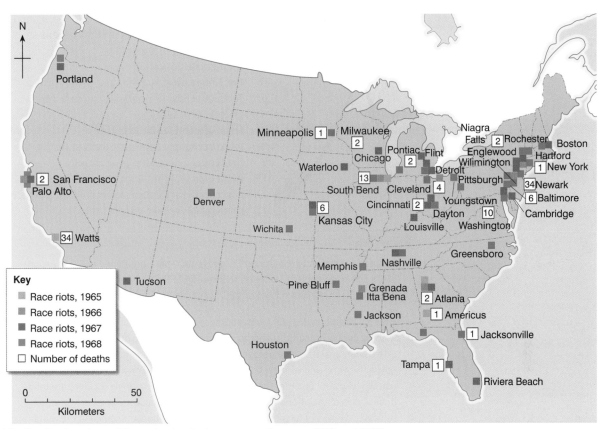

Fig. 6 *The locations of the major riots in the summers between 1965 and 1968*

Fig. 7 *A police patrol vehicle in Detroit next to burned-out furniture stores following the riots of 1967*

First Level of Intensity	1.	Police practices
	2.	Unemployment and underemployment
	3.	Inadequate housing
Second Level of Intensity	4.	Inadequate education
	5.	Poor recreation facilities and programmes
	6.	Ineffectiveness of political structure and grievance resolution
Third Level of Intensity	7.	Disrespectful white attitudes
	8.	Discriminatory administration of justice
	9.	Inadequacy of federal programmes
	10.	Inadequacy of municipal services
	11.	Discriminatory consumer and credit practices
	12.	Inadequate welfare programmes

SOURCE 4

Adapted extract from the Kerner Commission report, published on 29 February 1968 commissioned by Johnson to investigate the causes of the riots from 1965– 67, and the Detroit riot of 1967 in particular:

The civil disorders of 1967 involved Negroes acting against local symbols of white American society, authority and property in Negro neighborhoods – rather than against white persons. Disorder generally began with rock and bottle throwing and window breaking. Once store windows were broken, looting usually followed. Disorder did not erupt as a result of a single incident. Instead, it was generated out of an increasingly disturbed social atmosphere, in which typically a series of tension-heightening incidents became linked in the minds of many in the Negro community with a reservoir of underlying grievances. The typical rioter was a teenager or young adult, a lifelong resident of the city in which he rioted, a high school dropout. What the rioters appeared to be seeking was fuller participation in the social order and the material benefits enjoyed by the majority of American citizens. Rather than rejecting the American system, they were anxious to obtain a place for themselves in it.

ACTIVITY

Extension

Read up on the 'Broken Window' theory in sociology. How far does this theory go in explaining the riots of 1965–68?

The riots angered Johnson who felt that he had done more than any previous president to help African-Americans. Their exposure in the media both nationally and internationally challenged the progress many felt the US had been making in social justice during the post-war years by seeming to point to an explosive tension between the races and between the rich and poor in US society. It was a tension that Johnson would not be able to resolve and would be left to his successor. However, at a time when Vietnam and the other rights movements were demanding the attention of the media and voters, radicalisation kept the issue of black civil rights at the forefront of national attention. This focus exposed the economic problems that were so prevalent in the ghettos, once again showing that the poor in America were often hidden from the rest of society, and denied access to the 'Dream'.

Summary

ACTIVITY

Summary

Draw up a table of the actions Johnson took that either hindered or helped the Civil Rights Movement.

Johnson completed a legislative revolution for African-Americans despite enormous problems. He was helped by the unrelenting pressure of the Civil Rights Movement and the all-seeing eye of the now ubiquitous media coverage. But, despite the progress, Johnson's civil rights legacy began to unravel, as did the Movement. Political gains were difficult to achieve but at least they were cheap. When African-Americans could express their dissatisfaction politically it became clear that economics were the principal issue and addressing those problems would be enormously costly. Johnson knew the country needed time to heal after Kennedy's death and the civil rights struggle. What it got was an explosion in the ghettos as loud and as fiery as those being rained on the people of Vietnam. His unremitting faith in his own ability to deliver was being tested to its limit and Johnson was to find that his personality couldn't carry the weight of a country increasingly disenchanted with it.

 PRACTICE QUESTION

To what extent did Johnson's civil rights legislation meet the demands of the Civil Rights Movement?

 PRACTICE QUESTION

Evaluating primary sources

With reference to Sources 1, 3 and 4 and your understanding of the historical context, assess the value of these three sources to an historian studying the effectiveness of the Civil Rights Movement in the North during Johnson's presidency.

STUDY TIP

The focus of this question is on the demands of the movement so this is your starting point. Look at the different groups involved and try to establish what demands they shared and what demands were unique to one or two groups. This will enable you to analyse whether their broad demands were met and whether their specific demands were too disparate and if this affected Johnson's ability to address them. You can then look at other factors that prevented Johnson engaging with civil rights as a whole.

STUDY TIP

There are lots of interesting issues raised by this question. Carefully examine the content and provenance of each source and judge how valuable they are to an examination of the Civil Right Movement. You should aim to evaluate the effectiveness of each source and try to define this concept in order to frame your answer.

 PRACTICE QUESTION

Evaluating primary sources

With reference to Sources 1 and 2 and your understanding of the historical context, assess their value to an historian studying Malcolm X.

STUDY TIP

Malcolm X polarised opinion and was often highly critical of King, but the tone of those who talk about the deceased can change and this should be considered in assessing these two sources. The eulogy on the other hand tackles criticism of Malcolm X head-on. Try to use contextual evidence to balance your views on the sources.

16 Social divisions and protest movements

ACTIVITY

Evaluating primary source

What does Source 1 suggest were the main concerns for the SDS?

CROSS-REFERENCE

For more information about the Peace Corps, see Chapter 12, page 98.

KEY TERM

counterculture: an anti-establishment movement that was spawned by the Civil Rights Movement. Widespread social tensions also developed concerning other issues, and tended to flow along generational lines regarding human sexuality, women's rights, traditional modes of authority, experimentation with psychoactive drugs, and differing interpretations of the American Dream

KEY TERM

fraternities and sororities: social organisations for students in the United States; fraternities comprise young men and sororities are for young women

Social divisions

SOURCE 1

An extract from the Port Huron Statement, drafted by **Tom Hayden** on behalf of the Students for a Democratic Society (SDS), Port Huron, Michigan, 15 June 1962:

When we were kids the United States was the wealthiest and strongest country in the world: the only one with the atom bomb, the least scarred by modern war, an initiator of the United Nations that we thought would distribute Western influence throughout the world. Freedom and equality for each individual, government of, by, and for the people – these American values we found good, principles by which we could live as men. Many of us began maturing in complacency. Others declare that the people are withdrawn because compelling issues are fast disappearing – perhaps there are fewer breadlines in America, but is Jim Crow gone, is there enough work and work more fulfilling, is world war a diminishing threat, and what of the revolutionary new peoples? But why should business elites help decide foreign policy, and who controls the elites anyway, and are they solving mankind's problems? Others, finally, shrug knowingly and announce that full democracy never worked anywhere in the past.

The Kennedy presidency had promised a great deal for the young people of America, and although the **Peace Corps** could be seen as fulfilling some of that promise in reality little was achieved. Kennedy's death left a sense of dislocation and dissatisfaction which was fuelled by the emergence of a **counterculture**. This counterculture was fed by Hollywood, drugs, television, books, and particularly music. Its effect was to give rise to outraged and worthy protest movements, incredible art, brilliant entrepreneurs and ludicrous posturing.

Education and youth

A CLOSER LOOK

The US education sector in the 1960s

The size of the education sector in the USA had exploded after the Second World War. Before 1941 the average grade reached by Americans was 8 (Grade 8 is the end of middle school, reached at the age of 13–14. High school runs from Grade 9 to Grade 12, or age 15–18). Thirty years later the average grade was 12, and 50 per cent of young people of college age went on to higher study with over 20 per cent graduating. The expansion of post-high school provision was also spectacular, with many new institutions created and others expanding to accommodate the influx of students.

Student life in the growing universities centred around lectures, **fraternities, sororities** and sports, with social issues largely ignored. However as the 1960s began, the election of Kennedy stimulated youth interest in politics. Kennedy seemed to be the embodiment of hope, from his 'New Frontier' programme to his promise to put a man on the moon by the end of the decade. As a result, students became more politicised. Left-leaning groups such as SDS began to gather support but many more were engaged with the civil rights demonstrations that were taking place throughout the South, most notably the sit-ins and freedom rides. In 1963 Malcolm X was the second most sought-after speaker on US college campuses after Republican presidential candidate Barry Goldwater.

However, although there was a rise in political engagement among young people, they were by no means a majority and nor were they all necessarily liberal. The students who had opposed James Meredith at Ole Miss in 1961 or Autherine Lucy at the University of Alabama in 1956 hadn't given way to a left-wing majority. Just 12 per cent of students identified themselves as part of the 'New Left' movement in 1970. What the youth protesters did have on their side was the prestige that came from attending elite institutions and the ability to express themselves in the language of the ruling class. When there was conflict at southern state universities it wasn't big news but when students barricaded themselves into the president of Columbia University's office in 1968 it was. In the first half of 1968 alone there were 221 major demonstrations at universities such as Stanford, Yale, Harvard and UC Berkeley, which often featured slogans such as 'Don't trust anyone over thirty.'

Fig. 1 *Protestors burn a US flag during an anti-Vietnam War demonstration in Washington DC; the banner on the left reads 'Troops home NOW'*

KEY TERM

'the man': a catch-all term referring to the government, corporations or some form of authority usually in a derogatory manner. For many young protesters the nebulous idea of 'sticking it to the man' embodied resistance to authority or even sabotage

ACTIVITY

Extension

Research the counterculture and compile a top ten events list for the period 1960 to 1976, and then see how much agreement there is in your class.

ACTIVITY

If you were curating an exhibition on 1960s counterculture what five images would you choose to sum up the period?

CROSS-REFERENCE

See Chapter 12, pages 101–103 for the beginnings of the 1960s feminist movement.

Unlike its counterparts in Paris, Hungary, London and across China, the youth protest of 1968 lacked a dominant issue. Causes it campaigned about included the African-American Civil Rights Movement, environmental protest following the growing opposition to pesticides begun by Rachel Carson's 1962 book *Silent Spring*, and, of course, the war in Vietnam. However some of the student protest was directed inwards at the very institutions in which they were studying. Criticisms of teaching methods and gaps in the curriculum, notably the absence of black studies programmes, morphed into protests about how universities were buying up land and evicting poorer residents to build plush new labs (such as at Harvard) and then to a wider sense of disenchantment that students were being processed to fit in a role in the 'rat race' and work for **'the man'**.

This disenchantment had its roots in popular culture. The 1955 James Dean film *Rebel Without a Cause* had portrayed the alienation and generational conflict between young people and their parents and grandparents and the allure for the new and exotic was powerful. As young people had found jobs in the service economies they had disposable income and this allowed them to buy music made by the new wave of artists which had replaced the likes of Johnny Cash and Elvis Presley. Foremost amongst these new artists were The Beatles who led a 'British invasion' that led to the Rolling Stones and The Who becoming hugely successful. These groups explored sexuality and drug taking in their music which encouraged young people to experiment. Their success fed the US music scene with bands like 'The Doors' coming to prominence alongside the established acts from the earlier 1960s like Bob Dylan, Joan Baez and Janis Joplin.

Although many who lived through the 1960s would confirm that their decade was just as conservative as their parents' youth, the opportunities it provided were undoubtedly significant in changing the USA. It is a measure of the flexibility of the concept of the 'American Dream' that it could as easily embrace events as diverse as dropping out in the 1967 'Summer of Love' in Haight-Ashbury, San Francisco, or working your way from poverty in California to become president as Richard Nixon did. It seemed that a 'generation gap' had emerged where the group who had lived through the war could no longer understand the music, the movies, the poetry, the intoxicants, the art, the clothes, the hairstyles, the literature or the politics of the young. In New York, Andy Warhol turned Campbell's Soup tins, Coca-Cola bottles and even images of Mao into high art while patronising avant-garde bands like The Velvet Underground. In 1965 the poet Allan Ginsberg coined the term 'flower power' and argued that wearing flowers was the antidote to military fatigues, the concept of 'free love' became much talked about (if not often enacted) and events like the huge Woodstock music festival of 1969 were heralded by the media as the dawn of a new age driven by youth. Alfred Kinsey had shown in his rigorous reports on sexual behaviour in 1948 and 1953 that Americans were not as conservative as many believed and *Playboy*'s circulation of 7 million in the early 1970s suggested some amongst the older generation were subscribers. However, the assault on traditional values seemed largely to be an assault of the new ideas of the young against the traditions of the older generation, led by students, encouraged by the media and embracing a huge variety of forms.

Feminism

SOURCE 2

Taken from an article in *New York* magazine by **Gloria Steinem** from April 1969 entitled, 'After Black Power, Women's Liberation':

At the Students for a Democratic Society (SDS) Convention in 1967, women were still saying such integrationist things as 'The struggle for the liberation of women must be part of the larger fight for freedom.' Many Movement women still are. But members of groups like the Southern Student Organizing Committee and New York Radical Women [a loose coalition of various radical groups whose representatives meet once a month] withdrew to start concentrating on their own problems. They couldn't become black or risk jail by burning their draft cards, but they could change society from the bottom up by radicalizing [engaging with basic truth] the consciousness of women; by going into the streets on such women's issues as abortion, free childcare centers, and a final break with the 19th-century definition of females as sex objects whose main function is to service men and their children.

ACTIVITY

Evaluating primary sources

How useful is Source 2 for establishing the aims and techniques of feminists in the 1960s?

In 1964 the sociologist Alice Rossi suggested that there was no 'feminist spark' left in American women. Rossi was blind to the signs. In 1962 Helen Gurley Brown's book *Sex and the Single Girl* had sold two million copies in three weeks, Betty Friedan's *Feminine Mystique* had an initial print run of 2000 but its first paperback run sold 1.4 million. Female activists were leaving the Civil Rights Movement because of the sexist attitudes of campaigners like King, Rustin and Carmichael. In another connection with the Civil Rights Movement, the Supreme Court seemed to be coming onside, in the 1965 *Griswold v. Connecticut* decision to strike down the last state law banning the use of contraception, freeing up access to the contraceptive pill.

KEY PROFILE

Fig. 2   *Steinem was a spokeswoman for the feminist movement in the late 1960s and early 1970s*

A CLOSER LOOK

The contraceptive pill

Licensed in 1960, by 1962 1,187,000 women were using the Pill which was distributed by doctors as part of President Johnson's 'Great Society'. By giving women control over their own fertility it had a considerable effect on their career potential and was also associated with the 'free love' movement of the sixties.

By 1966 Rossi's assertion seemed laughable as Betty Friedan and 27 other women, including Anna Roosevelt Halstead (the daughter of FDR) and **Shirley Chisholm**, founded NOW (National Organisation for Women). Over the next five years the organisation was to win $30 million in back pay for women from companies who had ignored the 1963 Equal Pay Act.

A CLOSER LOOK

NOW was founded in June 1966 by 28 women. It aimed to organise women to campaign for full equality of the sexes by putting pressure on employers and government and increasing the number of women in higher education and the professions.

Gloria Steinem (b. 1934) was a journalist, feminist and activist whose 1969 article 'After Black Power, Women's Liberation' linked the two movements. Steinem co-founded the National Women's Political Caucus in 1971 and *Ms.* magazine before becoming an outspoken critic of the Vietnam War. She also popularised the slogan 'A woman needs a man like a fish needs a bicycle.'

CROSS-REFERENCE

For a Key Profile of Shirley Chisholm, see Chapter 18, page 155.

Parallels with the Civil Rights Movement abounded. Feminist organisations employed tactics guaranteed to attract media attention. In September 1968 a group called 'Radical Women' picketed the Miss America beauty pageant in Atlantic City. They crowned a sheep as Miss America and declared a series of reasons why they wanted to see the pageant ended including: the upholding of a prescriptive and impossible standard of beauty, the fact that objectification of women harmed all women, a charge of racism on the grounds of there never having been a black Miss America, an anti-war agenda given that one of Miss America's duties would be to go to Vietnam to 'entertain' the troops.

KEY TERM

draft card: a card sent to someone telling them they have been drafted into the US military and must report for duty to a specified location

It was at this protest that the myth of 'bra burning' developed after protesters discarded items of female oppression into a 'freedom trash can' including dishcloths, bras, a copy of *Playboy* and make-up, whilst an overly creative sub-editor drew parallels with the burning of **draft cards** by conscripted men in a headline. The image played into an increased level of militancy in the feminist movement, the radical feminist Valerie Solanos founded SCUM (the Society for Cutting Up Men) and attempted to assassinate the artist Andy Warhol while the brilliantly named WITCH (Women's International Conspiracy from Hell) acted as an umbrella group for various independent feminist organisations who came together for protests including staging a 'hex' of Chase Manhattan Bank and hosting an 'un-wedding' at a 'Bridal Fair' at Madison Square Garden, New York, while chanting 'Here come the slaves / Off to their graves'.

These media grabbing actions raised attention for women's rights issues but the political successes for the movement largely came in the following decade. What they did achieve however was the syphoning away of attention from the African-Americans' Civil Rights Movement as editors clamoured to liberally sprinkle their coverage of the protests with pictures of attractive young women in the same way as many British tabloids still do today. A more academic side to the women's rights movement came in the works of Germaine Greer and Erica Jong who expanded on the work of Betty Friedan and wrote frankly about sexual liberation for women while also discussing the rampant **misogyny** of the time. The climate of protest and demands for equality, heightened by media interest, prompted Johnson to sign Executive Order 11375 in 1968 which added 'sex' to the list of 'race, color, religion, or national origin' that the Civil Rights Act of 1964 had barred organisations from discriminating on. Though bigger issues were to come for women's rights, Johnson had begun to engage the federal government far more closely with the issues women had been increasingly protesting about since the decade began.

KEY TERM

misogyny: contempt for or hatred of women; the equivalent term for men is misandry

Fig. 3 *Protest banners for the feminist movement*

The radicalisation of African-Americans

In 1965 SNCC worker **Stokely Carmichael** had led a voter registration drive in Lowndes County, Alabama. Here he formed a separate organisation, the Lowndes County Freedom Organization who took as their emblem a snarling Black Panther. Meanwhile CORE had also been active in campaigning for voter registration in the South, protected by an offshoot of their organisation, the self-titled 'Deacons for Defense and Justice' were the first organised and armed black group in the South.

While youth protest embraced freedom and love, black people were turning away from it. The riots in Watts in 1965 showed how combustible the ghettos were and the failure of the federal government to protect either the Freedom Summer workers or enforce the Civil Rights Acts of 1964 and 1965 had led many to conclude that non-violence had taken them as far as it could. Carmichael was elected as head of the SNCC in May 1966, replacing John Lewis and he began to radicalise the group. Floyd McKissick had taken a similar route after replacing James Farmer as head of CORE in January of the same year.

As CORE and SNCC members took more confrontational and militant stances, hastened by the assassination of Malcolm X in 1965, King struggled to control the movement as seen in the 1966 Meredith March where Carmichael's chant **'Black Power'** was taken up with considerably more enthusiasm than King's 'Freedom Now'. King quickly recognised the power of the slogan calling it a 'psychological call to manhood' but was keenly aware of the damage increased militancy could do to his aims for the movement. It could decrease white sympathy and funding at a time when the path was unclear and other groups were gaining the attention of the media.

Black Power is most often associated with the threat of violence and, in particular, the rise of the Black Panthers. However it did have a positive side, leading young African-Americans to celebrate their heritage and equate black with beautiful. In 1968 the 'Godfather of Soul' James Brown released a song titled *Say it Loud I'm Black and Proud* catching the mood of young black people who had begun to wear their hair in the Afro style and campaign for Black History to be taught in schools and colleges.

The Black Panthers

The more militant side of Black Power echoed Malcolm X's most vitriolic speeches, such as 'The Ballot or the Bullet' delivered in 1964 and in particular his declaration 'We declare our right on this earth [...] to be a human being, to be respected as a human being, to be given the rights of a human being in this society, on this earth, in this day, which we intend to bring into existence by any means necessary.' **Roy Wilkins** described Black Power as 'the mother of hatred and the father of violence' but there was no denying its appeal to black youth, particularly those born in the cities of the North, North East and West Coast.

The most notable of these were **Huey Newton** and Bobby Seale, founders of the 'Black Panthers' who took their name from the symbol of the Lowndes County group founded by Carmichael. Founded in Oakland, California, in 1966 with specific aims the Panthers used aggressive rhetoric, an intimidating paramilitary style uniform and staged media attracting stunts to gain attention. Their most notable act was invading the California State Assembly Chamber armed with guns to protest against the 1967 Mulford Act, which proposed to make the public carrying of loaded firearms illegal.

CROSS-REFERENCE

For the Key Profile of Stokely Carmichael, revisit Chapter 15, page 125.

KEY TERM

'Black Power': a term variously used to describe both empowerment of African-Americans and their communities and the latent ability of black people to exercise their physical power to claim their rights

CROSS-REFERENCE

Look back at the Key Profile of Roy Wilkins in Chapter 11, page 92.

ACTIVITY

Extension

Though the Panthers were a small group they have had a disproportionate influence on African-American culture and boast some famous names amongst their alumni and their alumni's children. See if you can discover which two famous rappers had parents who were Black Panthers and which actor was a Panther himself.

Fig. 5   *Newton was a political activist and revolutionary*

Fig. 4   *Black Panthers, in full regalia, demonstrating in New York, 1969*

Huey Newton (1942–89) was the co-founder of the Black Panthers with Bobby Seale. He taught himself to read using Plato, Marx, Che Guevara, Mao and Lenin whilst supporting himself in college through robbery. He was targeted by COINTELPRO and imprisoned for murder in 1968 and arrested on further charges in 1977 before fleeing to Cuba.

SOURCE 3

The Ten-Point-Program of the Black Panther Party 15 May 1967. All subsequent 537 issues of the *Black Panther* newspaper contained the party's ten-point manifesto and programme:

What We Want Now!

1. We want freedom. We want power to determine the destiny of our Black Community.
2. We want full employment for our people.
3. We want an end to the robbery by the white men of our Black Community.
4. We want decent housing, fit for shelter of human beings.
5. We want education for our people that exposes the true nature of this decadent American society. We want education that teaches us our true history and our role in the present day society.
6. We want all Black men to be exempt from military service.
7. We want an immediate end to POLICE BRUTALITY and MURDER of Black people.
8. We want freedom for all Black men held in federal, state, county and city prisons and jails.
9. We want all Black people when brought to trial to be tried in court by a jury of their peer group or people from their Black Communities, as defined by the Constitution of the United States.
10. We want land, bread, housing, education, clothing, justice and peace.

ACTIVITY

How realistic were the aims in Source 3? Do you think the Panthers genuinely expected their programme to be fulfilled or were there other reasons behind its launch?

CROSS-REFERENCE

For the Key Profile of J Edgar Hoover see Chapter 20, page 167.

J Edgar Hoover described the Panthers as the greatest internal threat to the security of the USA however they also carried out substantial aid programmes offering free breakfasts, free health clinics and legal advice to members of the ghetto community. Hoover was adamant the group should be infiltrated and destroyed and by 1970 most of its leaders had been killed, imprisoned or had fled the country. However, this was not before their raised fist salute had become known globally through the actions of Olympic sprinters Tommy Smith and John Carlos who chose to employ the gesture having come 1st and 3rd in the Mexico Olympic 200 metres. Their posture while the Stars & Stripes was being raised and the *Star Spangled Banner* was being played brought home to millions how far away the American Dream remained even for some of the country's brightest talents.

Fig. 6   *George Harris, 18 years old, placing flowers into the rifle barrels of National Guardsman outside of the Pentagon, 21 October 1967*

Anti-war movements

Protests against the Vietnam War began even before Johnson put troops on the ground with marches in San Francisco, Boston, Madison and Seattle in 1964, led by students from the Progressive Labor Party and the Young Socialist Alliance. On 12 May young men in New York publicly burned their draft cards in protest against the growing US presence, an act which led to copycat gestures across the country and led Congress to criminalise anyone who 'knowingly destroys, knowingly mutilates' the card. Strom Thurmond moved the bill through the Senate, calling draft card burning 'contumacious [wilfully disobedient] conduct'.

The protest movement grew quickly, helped by the experience of black and white civil rights workers who knew how to generate maximum publicity for their new cause. In 1965 the SDS organised a 'teach-in' at the University of Michigan at Ann Arbor which again became a popular method of protest with universities across the country being picketed and boycotted. Later that year Norman Morrison, a 32-year-old Quaker and father of three, stood outside the window of Robert McNamara's office in the Pentagon and burned himself to death in protest at the escalation of the war. In 1966 Muhammad Ali refused the draft and declared 'My conscience won't let me go shoot my brother, or some darker people, or some poor hungry people in the mud for big powerful America. And shoot them for what? They never called me nigger, they never lynched me, they didn't put no dogs on me, they didn't rob me of my nationality, rape and kill my mother and father [...] Shoot them for what? How can I shoot them poor people? Just take me to jail'.

Johnson could only look on in despair as crowds of students chanted 'Hey, hey, LBJ! How many kids did you kill today?' at all his public appearances in response to the draft figures going through the roof: from 5000 a month in 1965 to 50,000 in 1967. In Berkeley that year protesters used smoke bombs against the police while smoking joints of their own and vandalising cars. In October 1967 the largest rally yet, held in Washington by a coalition of protest groups, saw 70,000 anti-war activists involved in running battles with the police and national guard leading to 625 arrests. After casting around for a cause, the student-led youth protest movement began to coalesce around Vietnam and can be seen as a key reason behind Johnson's decision not to run for a second term in 1968.

The role of the media

By 1968 24 per cent of households had colour TVs and over 100 million sets had been sold in the US. This made it practical to bring real-time footage of events into the homes of millions and the more sensational these events were, the higher the viewing figures and the more money the stations could charge for advertising. As a result, TV news focused on the sensational and controversial giving substantial airtime to scenes from Birmingham in 1963 and Selma in 1965, to feminist protests and, most tellingly, to both the war in Vietnam and the protests against it. Academics like Marshall McLuhan began to question the role of television but the relentless pressure for news and comment created a new environment for politics as well as protest which pushed the newspapers to keep up and made them more dependent on photos to sell a story.

Summary

By the end of the Johnson presidency the media had held a mirror up to America and shown that the American Dream was not an ubiquitous inheritance for all. Clear social divisions had emerged, not just between rich and poor, but between young and middle-aged, between men and women, between students and blue-collar workers and even within ethnic groups. While African-Americans had seen their political rights entrenched, the question of economic justice had barely been addressed while disproportionate numbers of their young men were sent off to die in Vietnam, the cost of which was partly responsible for the unlikelihood that they would see economic justice in the near future. Meanwhile the successes of their protests had inspired other groups with grievances against the government and taught them the importance of the camera as a weapon. These groups, women and young people in particular were media-literate enough to play the game and garner attention at the expense of other minorities, particularly homosexuals, Native Americans and Hispanic Americans, but the message was very clear to anyone who turned on the television news. The golden era of the 1950s was very much over and perhaps it hadn't been so golden after all.

But protest was only part of the picture. The growing wealth of the US had created more time for leisure and recreation and a new demographic, the teenager. Those born after the Second World War had been saved from the privations of the Depression and the war itself and were free to take advantage of technological change to explore a world of music, films, travel and, to a lesser extent, sex and drugs, which created a landscape for them that was genuinely different to anything their parents or grandparents had experienced. The Generation Gap, which had always existed, now yawned wider than ever and the old bonds of family life were weakening in every community as individualism and consumerism became the version of the American Dream that companies repackaged and sold to newly wealthy consumers.

PRACTICE QUESTION

'The media was responsible for the growth in protest movements in the 1960s.'
Assess the validity of this view.

STUDY TIP

A good way to start is by looking at all the other reasons that protest movements grew in the 1960s. These should then be evaluated in terms of how the media portrayed them.

 PRACTICE QUESTION

Evaluating primary sources

With reference to Sources 1, 2 and 3 and your understanding of the historical context, assess the value of these three sources to an historian studying whether the American Dream was exposed as an illusion in the 1960s.

STUDY TIP

It would be useful to think about what you understand by the 'American Dream' before you attempt this question. In many ways Source 1 suggests that the Dream was alive for many and that its allure had stopped them questioning whether the Dream applied to all Americans. The other two sources highlight dissatisfaction among women and African-Americans. It is worth considering whether some of the demands, particularly in Source 3, are compatible with the idea of the Dream at all.

5 Republican reaction: the Nixon presidency, 1968–1974

17 The presidential election of 1968 and the reasons for Nixon's victory

ACTIVITY

Evaluating primary sources

What events and groups is Nixon referring to in Source 1? Why might he be invoking them?

KEY TERM

gubernatorial: meaning relating to a governor, it is most frequently used in relation to the elections for governors held in US states, i.e. 'the gubernatorial race', or 'gubernatorial contender'

CROSS-REFERENCE

See Chapter 13, page 108 for the Key Profile of Barry Goldwater.

The presidential election of 1968 and the reasons for Nixon's victory

SOURCE 1

Richard Nixon's address accepting the Presidential Nomination at the Republican National Convention in Miami Beach, Florida, 8 August 1968:

America is in trouble today not because her people have failed but because her leaders have failed. The great question Americans must answer by their votes in November is this: Whether we shall continue for four more years the policies of the last five years. When the strongest nation in the world can be tied down for four years in a war in Vietnam with no end in sight; When the richest nation in the world can't manage its own economy; When the nation with the greatest tradition of the rule of law is plagued by unprecedented lawlessness; When a nation that has been known for a century for equality of opportunity is torn by unprecedented racial violence; And when the President of the United States cannot travel abroad or to any major city at home without fear of a hostile demonstration – then it's time for new leadership for the United States of America. The time has come for honest government in the United States of America.

Nixon's defeat to Kennedy in 1960 was extremely close but his **gubernatorial** defeat in California in 1962 to the incumbent Pat Brown was widely believed to have ended his political career. Nixon even declared in a press conference after his defeat, 'You don't have Nixon to kick around anymore, because, gentlemen, this is my last press conference.' After the 1962 failure, Nixon became a senior partner in a New York law firm and travelled to Europe but he couldn't shake the desire to be involved in politics and his Manhattan office became an outpost of Republican Party planning. Nixon campaigned vigorously and loyally on behalf of Barry Goldwater against Johnson in 1964 and for other Republicans in the congressional elections whilst privately believing that Goldwater couldn't win. The landslide defeat and loss of 36 seats in the House of Representatives tarnished many in the Republican Party whilst leaving Nixon looking selfless and blameless. The year 1964 had seemed to spell an end for conservatism and a nationwide endorsement of the liberal domestic policies that could be traced back through Johnson and Kennedy to Roosevelt. The one chink of light was the success Goldwater had in the South where he won Alabama, Georgia, Louisiana, Mississippi and South Carolina as the South rejected Democrats thanks to the Civil Rights Act.

Nixon was not the only Republican to emerge from the Goldwater campaign with credit. The B-movie actor Ronald Reagan had been developing a political platform and his televised speech entitled 'A Time for Choosing' raised $1 million for the Goldwater campaign. However Reagan had never held public office and had to run for Governor of California before he could be seen as a credible presidential candidate. Nixon had a head start, leveraging his loyalty and connections and cultivating key Republicans. Johnson referred to Nixon as a 'chronic campaigner', but the 1966 congressional elections saw the Republicans storm back, aided by the growing dissatisfaction over Vietnam and the riots. Nixon's team crafted television interview programmes with Nixon answering questions posed by 'ordinary' Americans whilst protecting him from press questioning. Gradually this tactic worked with Nixon's new image, party loyalty and reputations as a safe pair of hands seeing off his opponents, both declared and possible.

Helped by the growing disarray within the Democrats, Nixon won the nomination on the first ballot at the Republican National Convention in Miami in August. His support base was wider than the Republican Party had been able to boast for over 30 years, from leading evangelist preacher **Billy Graham** to the staunch segregationist Strom Thurmond who helped secure the growing Republican vote in the South after switching parties. Nixon seemed to offer hope to a country in chaos.

KEY PROFILE

Billy Graham (b.1918) was a Christian evangelist preacher and friend of King who acted as spiritual adviser to Johnson, Nixon and Eisenhower, (who asked for him on his deathbed). Graham had enormous influence over the evangelical movement and was outspoken both on issues of civil rights and foreign policy. Graham appeared for 49 consecutive years on Gallup's list of most admired men and women.

Fig. 1   *Graham held large Christian rallies*

Divisions within the Democrats

The anointing of Richard Nixon was in sharp contrast to the divisions within the Democratic Party. The quagmire of the Vietnam War had sharply divided Democrats whilst Johnson's handling of the riots had led to criticism of his social policies. This in turn was combined with criticism of his civil rights legislation by Democrats in the South. Stung by a loss to Eugene McCarthy in the first primary, and the growing antipathy to him in the country and by the decision of Bobby Kennedy to announce his intention to seek the nomination, Johnson withdrew from the race in late March. Kennedy won the California primary but on the same night, 6 June 1968, he was shot dead by Sirhan Sirhan, a 24-year-old Palestinian. For a nation still grappling with the meaning of the death of Martin Luther King, Jr in April of that year it appeared that America was in the midst of a crisis.

In August 1968 the Democrats were due to meet in Chicago, the stronghold of **Richard Daley**. Johnson's vice president Hubert Humphrey had chosen to stand in April 1968 and delegates loyal to Johnson ensured that he won the nomination against a field that by this stage included McCarthy, George McGovern standing in place of Bobby Kennedy, the segregationist Governor of Alabama George Wallace and others. Daley was determined that the Convention would go off without incident but this led to a greatly increased police presence from a force not noted for its patience and understanding. In total Daley had 23,000 police and National Guardsmen on duty for the Convention.

A CLOSER LOOK

The plot against Johnson

In late 1967 Allard Lowenstein a delegate to the Democratic National Convention began a campaign to 'Dump Johnson'. Having failed to persuade Bobby Kennedy or George McGovern to run against an incumbent president, Lowenstein approached Senator Eugene McCarthy of Minnesota who agreed to run on an anti-war platform. McCarthy declared he was running because of the crisis of American ideals brought about by the Johnson presidency and went on to win 41 per cent of the vote in the first primary in New Hampshire.

KEY PROFILE

Richard J Daley (1902–76) was the Irish-American working class Mayor of Chicago from 1955 to 1976. He was a key figure in the Democratic Party as an ally of Johnson who out-manoeuvered King in the 1966 Chicago Campaign. The 1968 Democratic National Convention in Chicago was designed to highlight Daley's achievements but heavy-handed policing earned comparisons with the Gestapo from Senator Abraham Ribicoff.

SOURCE 2

Yippie Manifesto Abbie Hoffman and Jerry Rubin, 1968:

Come into the streets on Nov. 5, election day. Vote with your feet. The American election represents death, and we are alive. Come all you rebels, youth spirits, rock minstrels, bomb throwers, bank robbers, peacock freaks, toe worshippers, poets, street folk, liberated women, professors and body snatchers: it is election day and we are everywhere. Freak out the pigs with exhibitions of snake dancing and karate at the nearest pig pen. Release a Black Panther in the Justice Department. Wear costumes. Take a burning draft card to Spiro Agnew. Stall for hours in the polling places trying to decide between Nixon and Humphrey and Wallace. Take your clothes off. Hold block parties. And then on Inauguration Day Jan. 20 we will bring our revolutionary theater to Washington to inaugurate Pigasus, our pig, the only honest candidate, and turn the White House into a crash pad. Every man a revolution! Every small group a revolutionary center! We will be together on election day. Yippie!!!

ACTIVITY

Evaluating primary sources

If you were asked to suggest what the Yippies stood for from the manifesto in Source 2, what could you say?

The opposition that the police were drafted to patrol amounted to 10,000 mostly young demonstrators from a variety of groups including the Students for a Democratic Society, the Yippies and the National Mobilization Committee to End

Fig. 2 *Police hold back protesters outside the Hilton Hotel in Chicago where delegates for the 1968 Democratic National Convention are staying*

the War in Vietnam who had announced their determination to shut down the Convention. On 28 August police tried to break up a protest rally in Grant Park, the ensuing riot led to beatings and extensive use of tear gas which even reached the Convention hotel. The scenes were filmed by the media with protesters shouting 'The whole world is watching'. NBC news chose to switch between shots of Humphrey celebrating his nomination and the protests outside possibly in response to the treatment of the press which had led CBS anchor Walter Cronkite to describe security staff within the Convention centre as 'a bunch of thugs'.

In the aftermath of the Convention Daley boasted that he had received over 130,000 letters of support over his handling of the protesters. Worse was to come for those involved in the protests as Daley ensured eight of the leaders were charged with conspiracy and incitement to riot, including Abbie Hoffman, Tom Hayden, Jerry Rubin and Bobby Seale of the Black Panthers. Five were convicted on the charge of intent to incite a riot and received heavy prison sentences.

The debacle of Chicago increased Nixon's lead in the polls to double-digits and he was helped further by the growing popularity of George Wallace in the South since his decision to stand as an independent candidate who was both segregationist and highly critical of anti-war demonstrators. Nixon refused to debate Humphrey but courted big business bringing in substantially more in donations than Humphrey could manage and spending heavily on advertising. It appeared that the only thing that could stand in his way was a significant development in Vietnam so when the North Vietnamese accepted Johnson's proposal for peace talks in Paris in return for a bombing halt, Nixon was faced with a dilemma. Publicly he had to support any measures that could bring about peace but privately he knew that failed peace talks would go a long way in securing the White House for him by further tarnishing Humphrey. In secret conversations, the Nixon campaign team urged contacts in South Vietnam's government to refuse to take part in the talks promising them better terms when Nixon won, and this delay helped ensure that Johnson's final flourish achieved little in boosting Humphrey.

ACTIVITY

By 1968 the Democrat Party was in disarray. Use a mind-map to highlight the reasons behind their internal conflicts and try to categorise these into short- and long-term factors.

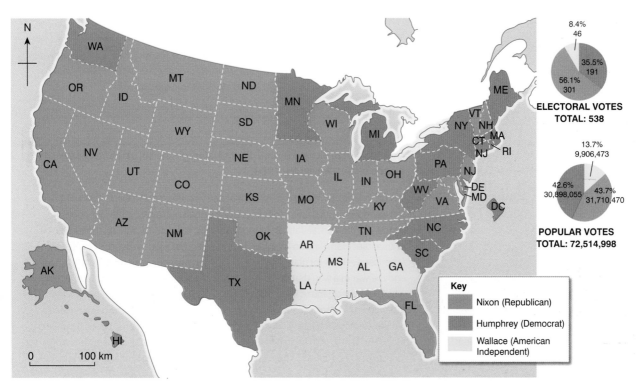

Fig. 3 *Results of the 1968 elections; the letters represent states/constituencies*

Only 43 per cent of voters supported Nixon, and 2.5 million less people voted for him than in 1960, but Wallace's hoovering up of nearly 10 million votes damaged Humphrey more and demonstrated how many in the South still opposed desegregation. The Democrats remained in control of both the House and the Senate, meaning Nixon became the first president elected without his party winning either House or Congress since the nineteenth century. The presence of Billy Graham in the White House both for Johnson's last night as president and for Nixon's first suggested that both presidents felt in need of divine guidance over their actions both future and past.

Policies of the Nixon Administration

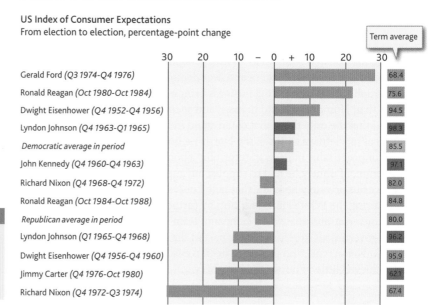

US Index of Consumer Expectations
From election to election, percentage-point change

Fig. 4 *The University of Michigan has been surveying consumer confidence since the 1940s; the chart shows the change from the month before the presidency is decided to the month before the next president is determined – in other words, how much has each president lifted expectations?*

ACTIVITY

What does the chart in Fig. 4 suggest about the Nixon Presidency in terms of the American consumer? How do the other presidencies compare?

SOURCE 3

An extract from Richard Nixon's '**Silent Majority**' speech, part of an Address to the Nation on 3 November 1969:

Let historians not record that when America was the most powerful nation in the world we passed on the other side of the road and allowed the last hopes for peace and for the freedom of millions of people to be suffocated by the forces of totalitarianism. And so tonight – to you, the great silent majority of my fellow Americans – I ask for your support. I pledged in my campaign for the presidency to end the war in a way that we could win the peace. I have initiated a plan of action which will enable me to keep that pledge. The more support I can have from the American people, the sooner that pledge can be redeemed; for the more divided we are at home, the less likely the enemy is to negotiate in Paris. Let us be united for peace. Let us also be united against defeat. Because let us understand: North Vietnam cannot defeat or humiliate the United States. Only Americans can do that.

CROSS-REFERENCE

Look back to Chapter 13, page 109, for the Key Term, definition of 'Silent Majority'.

From a letter to Richard Nixon signed by 32 US soldiers who had served in Vietnam, 26 November 1969:

As for those of us in the 'vocal minority' who have demonstrated for peace, most of us are neither basically anti-American nor even anti-Nixon. Despite the harsh language in your speech, we do not seek to 'defeat' or 'humiliate' America. We want our country to be strong. And we believe wholeheartedly that the policies we advocate will benefit America by extricating her from a war which is sapping both her international and domestic strength. Furthermore, we support your pledge to change the Johnson Administration's policies. We don't want our country to 'bug out' on her foreign commitments. We wish to affirm American support for free government and to continue our commitments to our allies if they are subject to external aggression. However we do not see how it is in our national interest to commit US troops for putting down internal rebellions or for supporting corrupt and repressive governments.

 PRACTICE QUESTION

Evaluating primary sources

Using Sources 4 and 5 and your understanding of the historical context, assess the value of these two sources to an historian who was trying to identify Nixon's Vietnam policy when he became president.

STUDY TIP

There are a number of points to make here by considering the audience for the sources and how they relate to each other. How are the soldiers engaging with Nixon's speech, and how has Nixon sought to portray opponents of the war?

Clearly the biggest issue facing Nixon was **Vietnam and the problems associated with it**. These ran the full range of issues from the military matters of winning the war to the economic costs of continuing to fight and the social costs of protest and the damage that was being done to the national self-image.

CROSS-REFERENCE

The issues surrounding Vietnam and its problems are detailed further in Chapters 18 and 19.

Fig. 5 *In July 1968 after Nixon emerged as the Republican candidate he was invited to the White House for discussions with President Johnson about the war in Vietnam*

Nixon inherited an economy that had boomed under Kennedy and Johnson with an unemployment rate of 3.3 per cent when he entered the White House in January 1969. However inflation was running at 4.7 per cent, its highest rate since the end of the Korean War. Nixon decided to focus on reducing inflation but without ending the war this was an extremely difficult task and one he failed to achieve.

CROSS-REFERENCE

See pages 155–157 in Chapter 18 for more on the US economy under Nixon.

In constitutional issues Nixon sought to introduce a 'New Federalism' backing up the rhetoric of his election campaigns with proposals to roll back some of the power of the federal government that had accrued since Roosevelt's 'New Deal'. His biggest success here was the State and Local Assistance Act of 1972 which provided $4 billion per year in funds to states and municipalities and amounted to $83 billion dollars before it was cancelled by Ronald Reagan in 1986. This act aside, further eroding the power of the federal government was always going to be a demanding task for a president whose party didn't control Congress and much of Nixon's work in this area failed to pay dividends.

Perhaps surprisingly (for a Republican) Nixon's heaviest area of legislation concerned the environment (even though environmental issues had not featured heavily in his campaign). This was an issue that was popular with many of the young protesters that Nixon so derided. Rachel Carson's 1962 book *Silent Spring* had highlighted the damage being done to the environment by powerful businesses, particularly in their production of pesticides but little had been achieved to curb pollution before 1968. After seeing the success of the first Earth Day in 1970 Nixon announced the formation of the Environmental Protection Agency (EPA), discussed environmental issues in his State of the Union speeches and passed the Clean Air Act of 1970.

Nixon's election rhetoric had made extensive reference to the breakdown of law and order, citing the riots of 1964 to 1968 and pointedly emphasising the events of the 1968 Democratic Party Conference. It might have been expected then that draconian new legislation would have been brought in to try to address issues of civil disobedience but this would have trodden on the toes of the governors and mayors and compromised the ideas of the 'New Federalism'. Instead Nixon contented himself with reshaping the drugs policy after a series of reports highlighted the growing threat of illegal substances. Nixon began with the October 1970, Comprehensive Drug Abuse Prevention and Control Act, but after a 1971 report suggested that 15 per cent of Vietnam veterans had returned with an addiction to heroin, President Nixon declared drug abuse to be 'public enemy number one' and created the Drug Enforcement Administration (DEA) in 1973.

ACTIVITY

How would you characterise Nixon's policies? Was he a traditional Republican president or something new?

Key personalities of the Nixon Administration

Fig. 6 *Earl Warren, Richard Nixon Conrad Hilton and evangelist Billy Graham at the international Christian leadership conference*

Nixon was never a man to form close friendships and the advisers and appointees he brought on board to help him rarely got close to the president himself, especially when faced with the 'Berlin Wall' of White House Counsel John Ehrlichman and White House Chief of Staff Bob Haldeman. His key political ally was his National Security Adviser **Henry Kissinger**, one of the few of Nixon's team who avoided the reshuffles he frequently undertook. During the six years of Nixon's presidency he went through four Secretaries of the Treasury, three Secretaries of Defence, four Attorney Generals and even two Vice Presidents, **Spiro Agnew** and **Gerald Ford**.

KEY PROFILE

Spiro Agnew (1918–96) was the son of Greek immigrant parents. He won the traditionally Democratic state of Maryland as governor in 1966 and as a popular, charismatic and sufficiently Southern politician he balanced the Nixon ticket well in 1968. Initially he was seen as Nixon's enforcer but the president grew to resent Agnew's self-confidence and lack of vision. He resigned over unchallenged accusations of tax evasion which saw him slide back into obscurity.

Nixon's non-executive appointments were more revealing. He appointed 231 federal judges, more than any previous president and including four Supreme Court justices, notably Warren Burger as Chief Justice in 1969 after Earl Warren stood down. The conservative Burger held the role for the next 17 years ushering in a more conservative period for the court than it had had under Warren.

Nixon did make a point of cultivating celebrity friendships however and never missed a photo opportunity, including appearing with Elvis and Sammy Davis Jr, whilst at the White House. He had even appeared on the TV sketch show *Laugh-In* during the presidential campaign, an appearance credited with making Nixon seem more in touch with the people than Humphrey. Nixon is perhaps best remembered in terms of the personalities around him; less for his cabinet and celebrity 'friends' than for his 'Enemies List'. The paranoid side of the president came out in a list compiled in advance of the 1972 presidential election of those who opposed him. White House Counsel John Dean said in a memo that the purpose of the list was to see how the Administration could use its power to 'screw our political enemies'. Those on the list included the Democrat Allard Lowenstein, actor Paul Newman, journalists Daniel Schorr and Mary McGrory and the financier Howard Stein. The list became public knowledge after it was mentioned by Dean in his testimony to the Watergate committee and was further evidence of the divide between the recreated persona of Nixon and the reality.

From being seen as a serial loser Richard Nixon was, perhaps, the beneficiary of the greatest fortune of any victorious president. To have the Democratic Party split by internal factions, some of which were of their own making through the Civil Rights Act, others of which were the fault of Vietnam, was fortunate. To have the legacy of Kennedy devalued by Johnson's failings and then the heir apparent to it shot dead before he had the chance to stand, was fortunate. To be faced with a vice president tarnished by the previous Administration but not politically skilled nor media-savvy enough to turn it around was also fortunate. And to have the entire messy business of choosing a Democratic nominee played out with violence in the media eye was remarkably lucky.

Within his own party he benefitted from Reagan's lack of preparedness, Rockefeller's vacillations over standing, Romney's mute reaction to the riots that had wracked Detroit and the absence of any other rising stars.

KEY PROFILE

Fig. 7 *Kissinger was secretary of State for Presidents Nixon and Ford*

Henry Kissinger (b. 1923) is a former Harvard professor who came to politics through his support of Nelson Rockefeller. This brought him to the attention of Nixon for whom he fulfilled the role of both National Security Adviser and Secretary of State. Kissinger and Nixon operated a secretive foreign policy based on the ideas of **realpolitik** which allowed them to pursue détente with the USSR, rapprochement with China and peace in Vietnam without recourse to problems of ethics. The humourist Tom Lehrer once said 'Political satire became obsolete when Henry Kissinger was awarded the Nobel Peace Prize.'

CROSS-REFERENCE

Gerald Ford is the subject of a Key Profile in Chapter 21, page 175.

KEY TERM

realpolitik: a term given to diplomacy based on pragmatic considerations about what is most advantageous to a power rather than on ethical or ideological considerations

ACTIVITY

Nixon surrounded himself with advisers who were loyal to his ideas. Why is this potentially problematic for a president?

Summary

ACTIVITY

Summary

Draw up a table that covers the state of the Republican and Democratic parties in 1968 in terms of their policies on foreign affairs, economic affairs and social policy using the material you have covered so far for that year. How far apart were they?

Nixon showed resilience and brilliance in equal measure to bounce back from the disappointments of 1960 and 1962 and win an election despite a relatively healthy economic situation. He played the prospect of peace in Vietnam to great political effect even if he could be accused of endangering lives for political ends. He used the media superbly to stay ahead of the game and was willing to take advice where previously he had been pig-headed. Most importantly he identified a constituency that was crying out for representation and gave them a voice. In winning the election he had a golden opportunity to rebuild the American Dream, end the war in Vietnam, protect the environment, reach a détente with the Soviets, prevent the tide of drug use, complete the work of civil rights and keep the economy on an even keel. It could be argued that, without Vietnam, Nixon may have achieved all of these. It could also be argued that without Watergate, his final two years could have seen him craft a legacy that would burn brighter than any of the post-war presidents. But for a man who could have been a nearly man 'could haves' were small recompense for the events that were to follow.

STUDY TIP

This question requires you to compare not only Nixon's campaign with Humphrey's but also to look at the context in which the campaigns were fought. You will need to look at the promises Nixon made and how he presented his campaign and assess Humphrey's failings as a candidate. You should also look at the wider issue of divisions within the Democrats along with other vital factors.

PRACTICE QUESTION

'The Democrats lost the 1968 presidential election more than Richard Nixon won it.' Assess the validity of this view.

STUDY TIP

These sources cover a very broad range of opinion. You should consider tone, along with the argument put across in each source. Consider also the provenance and how this affects each source's message. You will also need to refer to your contextual knowledge of the key issues that had a significant impact on ordinary Americans and their idea of the 'American Dream'.

PRACTICE QUESTION

Evaluating primary sources

With reference to Sources 1, 2 and 4 and your understanding of the historical context, assess the value of these three sources to an historian studying the 'American Dream' in 1968.

The restoration of conservative social policies

SOURCE 1

Taken from Nixon's Labor Day message to the nation, 3 November 1972:

We are faced this year with the choice between the 'work ethic' that built this Nation's character and the new 'welfare ethic' that could cause that American character to weaken. The work ethic builds strong people. The welfare ethic breeds weak people. It's human nature for a person who works hard for a living to want to keep most of what he earns, and I think it is natural for a worker to resent seeing a large chunk of his hard-earned wage taken by Government to give to someone else who may even refuse to work. The people who advocate the welfare ethic spend their time discussing how to cut up the pie we have, but those who believe in the work ethic want to bake a bigger pie, and I'm for baking that bigger pie. Putting a ceiling on the opportunity of those who work is not the way to provide a floor for the support of those who do not work.

ACTIVITY

Evaluating primary sources

From Source 1 alone what would you expect Nixon's attitude to taxation, welfare and business would be?

The silent majority

Fig. 1 *Millions of the 'Silent Majority' marched against the Vietnam War outside the White House*

KEY PROFILE

Fig. 2 *Friedman taught at the University of Chicago for 30 years*

Milton Friedman (1912–2006) was a University of Chicago economist who opposed Keynes' theories and predicted 'Stagflation'. Friedman went on to be an economic adviser to Reagan who adopted his policies of 'monetarism', the idea that controlling the economy should be done primarily by controlling the amount of money in circulation.

Nixon's 'silent majority' weren't a group of people who would be impressed by the **neo-liberal** monetarist policies of **Friedman**. Rather they were a group that was predominantly white and working class, who felt appalled by the erosion of traditional values and a perceived lack of respect both for America and for the moral teachings of the Protestant Church, the very things they

KEY TERM

neo-liberalism: an economic philosophy that encourages minimal government spending and supports a free market

Roe v. Wade, 1973

The *Roe v. Wade* case made abortion legal in the US and created legal, moral, and political controversy that has persisted to the present day. The two arguments, a woman's right to 'choose' vs a child's right to life, ossified into opposing factions whose importance in US politics remains significant. The abortion issue was to become a key factor in the 'moral majority' movement that emerged in 1979.

KEY TERM

caucus: a meeting of members of a political party to select candidates or decide policy

---

ACTIVITY

Pairs task

In pairs, discuss why it was politically astute of Nixon to address the 'silent majority'.

felt the 'American Dream' was based upon. The 'silent majority' felt like they had no rights movement, no group to protest for them, to act as a counter to groups who advocated change. And change seemed to be all around them, the Generation Gap between young and old was greater than at any time, African-Americans, Hispanics, Native Americans, homosexuals and women were all expecting to be counted. Technology was advancing rapidly from the Pill to the record player and the Supreme Court, once a bastion of conservatism had moved on from issues of civil rights to controversial issues of prisoner rights in *Gates v. Collier* (1974) and even the rights of unborn children in *Roe v. Wade* (1973). Faced with this onslaught the 'silent majority' felt no one was arguing that things could and should stay the same, that there were tweaks that could be made but that revolution was not necessary. In many ways they were the group that believed in the America as it had been and they were increasingly concentrated in the 'Sunbelt', the region of the US predominantly in the growing South West, West and the old South where the climate was more appealing and where liberal ideas hadn't yet spread. Together with the 'Solid South', the conservative leaning southern states that Johnson had alienated with his 1964 Civil Rights Bill, they made up a **caucus** of voters that were sufficient to overcome the 'vocal minority' in presidential policy considerations.

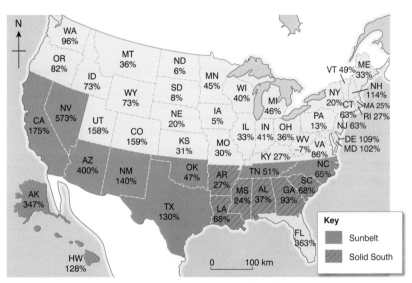

Fig. 3 *Map of the US showing the Sunbelt and Solid South which were targeted by Nixon along with population growth by state from 1950 to 1990*

Welfare and taxation

In his first inaugural address Nixon declared that 'The American Dream does not come to those who fall asleep. But we are approaching the limits of what government alone can do.' and certainly the tone was far more 'self-help' than 'welfare', a tone that rang more clearly as his presidency evolved. Following his second election victory in 1972 Nixon told the *Washington Star News* that the average American was like a child who should either be trusted with responsibility or be spoiled and become weak. The 'silent majority' Nixon courted before 1968 and named in 1969 were those who had grown up in the Great Depression and fought in the war, making sacrifices so their children could have more opportunities. Many of them saw the growth in government welfare schemes as hand-outs which would make people lazy and dependent. It helped of course that 'lazy' and 'dependent' were two of the epithets most often deployed when disparaging ethnic groups like Native Americans, Hispanics and African-Americans. The support of the 'silent majority' enabled

Nixon to talk tough on welfare. The key plank in Nixon's welfare reform was a proposal to use a **negative income tax**, a favourite idea of conservative economist Milton Friedman, whose work was later to influence the Reagan Administration (and Thatcher in the UK).

The purpose of the negative income tax was to provide both a safety net for the poor and a financial incentive for welfare recipients to work. Nixon also proposed an expansion of the Food Stamp program, renaming it the Family Assistance Program (FAP), a pet idea of **Patrick Moynihan**. FAP called for the replacement of bureaucracy-heavy aid schemes like **food stamps** with direct cash payments to those in need, including single-parent families and the working poor. All recipients of FAP, except mothers of preschool children, would have to either work or undergo training. FAP was heavily criticised by a variety of groups.

1. Welfare advocates said that $1600 pa for a family of four was insufficient.
2. Conservatives disliked the idea of a guaranteed annual income for the 'workshy'.
3. The Unions saw the proposal as a threat to the minimum wage.
4. Bureaucrats within the various organisations FAP would replace feared for their jobs.
5. Many of the public felt the addition of the working poor would expand welfare by millions.

Given that the bill was struggling and unpopular, Nixon was willing to let it die in 1972, however Haldeman later suggested that Nixon wanted the Democrats to kill the bill as it was unaffordable.

KEY PROFILE

Daniel Patrick Moynihan (1927–2003) was an American politician and sociologist. In 1965 he wrote the controversial report *The Negro Family: The Case For National Action* which blamed the poverty of African-Americans on the breakdown of the black family unit. He was Democratic Senator for New York four times from 1976 and served four successive presidential Administrations from John F Kennedy to Gerald Ford.

One area where Nixon did succeed in reforming Welfare was in the introduction of Supplemental Security Income (SSI) which provided a guaranteed income for elderly and disabled citizens, very possibly because of polling that suggested the elderly were the demographic most likely to vote. The Nixon years also brought substantial increases in Social Security, Medicare, and Medicaid benefits. In 1971, Nixon proposed health insurance reform and the federalisation of Medicaid for poor families with dependent children which was followed in 1974 by a proposal for even more comprehensive health insurance reform. Such substantial reform and creation of new organisations seemed to fly in the face of the neo-liberal rhetoric that Nixon used in his election campaigns and inaugural speeches.

Business

A series of acts that imposed more bureaucracy on business also seemed to ignore the principles of Nixonian rhetoric. Nixon created the Occupational Safety and Health Administration (OSHA) in 1970, the Environmental Protection Agency (EPA) and a National Oceanic and Atmospheric Administration (NOAA), along with the 1972 Noise Control Act, the 1972 Marine Mammal Protection Act, the 1973 Endangered Species Act, and the 1974 Safe Drinking Water Act. While some of this was to curry favour with the environmental lobby, who inevitably felt it did not go far enough, Nixon also recognised that big business was ripe for criticism while the 'silent majority' needed to be left alone.

The reaction to protest movements and forces of social change

Anti-war protests

Nixon in an informal conversation in a corridor at the Pentagon on 1 May 1970, reported in *The Public Papers of the Presidents of the United States: Richard Nixon*, 1970:

You think of those kids out there. I say kids. I have seen them. They are the greatest. You see these bums, you know, blowing up the campuses. Listen, the boys that are on the college campuses today are the luckiest people in the world, going to the greatest universities, and here they are burning up the books, I mean storming around about this issue – I mean you name it – get rid of the war; there will be another one. Out there we've got kids who are just doing their duty. I have seen them. They stand tall, and they are proud. I am sure they are scared. I was when I was there. But when it really comes down to it, they stand up and, boy, you have to talk up to those men. And they are going to do fine; we've got to stand back of them.

Evaluating primary sources

In Source 2, what is Nixon's attitude towards young people and the war? How does the tone of the speech convey this?

Both Nixon and Kissinger were convinced that keeping protests quiet at home was part of the key to bringing North Vietnam to negotiate. Nixon adopted four strategies to achieve this:
1. withdrawing troops
2. altering the criteria for the draft
3. concealing the most damaging realities of Vietnam
4. using speeches to question the patriotism of anti-war protesters.

However, anti-war protests continued despite the removal of 25,000 troops in June 1969 and a further 60,000 in December of that year. Changes were also made to the draft so it didn't affect those over 20, and Nixon made brilliant speeches invoking peace while criticising protest and replying to protesters personally.

Extension

Research each of these tactics and draw up a table covering the details and their effectiveness.

Reply from Richard Nixon to student Randy J Dicks, 13 October 1969. Dicks had written to Nixon criticising the president's statement that he would not be affected by anti-war protests:

First, there is a clear distinction between public opinion and public demonstrations. To listen to public opinion is one thing; to be swayed by public demonstrations is another. A demonstration – in whatever cause is an organized expression of one particular set of opinions, which may or may not be shared by the majority of the people. If a President – any President – allowed his course to be set by those who demonstrate, he would betray the trust of all the rest. Whatever the issue, to allow government policy to be made in the streets would destroy the democratic process. It would give the decision, not to the majority, and not to those with the strongest arguments, but to those with the loudest voices. It would reduce statecraft to slogans. It would invite anarchy. It would allow every group to test its strength not at the ballot box but through confrontation in the streets.

Evaluating primary sources

How valuable are Sources 3 and 4 in explaining why it was difficult for Nixon to deal with opposition to the war in Vietnam?

While congressional wrangling over Vietnam occasionally made the news, especially in the form of the sustained opposition of Senator **William Fulbright** and testimonies from Vietnam veterans like John Kerry, it was the visibility of the protesters that most damaged the war effort thanks in no small part to the presence of celebrities amongst them. John Lennon and Yoko Ono staged a 'bed-in' for peace as part of their honeymoon in 1969 and Lennon recorded the anthemic *Give Peace a Chance* which was taken up by half a million protesters during the second Vietnam Moratorium March on 15 November 1969 (the first had occurred a month earlier) in Washington. The Actress Jane Fonda visited the Vietcong in 1972, earning the derisory nickname 'Hanoi' Jane. Musicians including Bob Dylan, Jimi Hendrix, Joan Baez, Joni Mitchell, Phil Ochs and countless others were joined in their opposition by intellectuals like Howard Zinn and Noam Chomsky. Even amongst this august company one of the most eloquent opponents of the war was the heavyweight boxing champion, Muhammed Ali.

Fig. 5 *Actress Jane Fonda visits an anti-aircraft gun position near Hanoi, Vietnam, in 1972*

KEY PROFILE

Fig. 5 *Ali became World Heavyweight Boxing Champion three times*

Muhammad Ali (b. 1942) was born Cassius Clay and won the World Heavyweight Boxing title in 1964. He became friends with Malcom X in 1961 and Ali renounced Clay as his slave name and was renamed by Elijah Mohammed. Ali and X fell out over the latter's split from the Nation, an incident Ali later regretted. He was stripped of his boxing title in 1967 for refusing the draft.

KEY PROFILE

Fig. 4 *Fulbright became known for his opposition to American involvement in the Vietnam War*

J William Fulbright (1905–1995) was the Junior Senator for Arkansas 1945–74. He was a Dixiecrat who signed the Southern Manifesto but became a critic of US Foreign Policy. Fulbright opposed McCarthyism and HUAC and initially supported the Tonkin Resolution, but in 1966 Fulbright published *The Arrogance of Power*, attacking the Vietnam War, and Congress's failure to set limits on it.

But at the forefront of the protests were the students. Three factors led to student leadership of protest. Firstly, college enrolment had reached 8.5 million by the end of the 1960s as the baby boom generation began to leave school, this meant there were substantial numbers willing to get involved. Secondly students had what the Stanford Sociologist Doug McAdam calls 'Biographical Availability' meaning the social, economic and psychological freedom to involve themselves in high-risk activism, and finally there was the fact that rallies and marches were a great way to listen to music and meet with members of the opposite (or same) sex.

The most visceral example of the Administration's response to protests came with the shootings at Kent State University in Ohio. On 4 May 1970 the National Guard shot dead four students who were protesting Nixon's incursion into Cambodia and chanting '1,2,3,4 we don't want your fucking war'. Ronald Reagan, now Governor of California, closed all the state colleges in response. On 8 May in the 'Hard Hat riot' 1000 students in New York protesting the Kent State shooting were attacked by 200 construction workers for their lack of patriotism. New York Mayor John Lindsay criticised the police response and himself became the target for pro-Nixon rallies which culminated in 130,000 people marching through New York on 20 May.

1970 marked the high point of protest, Nixon's **drawdown** continued, and the protests became fewer. On 23 April 1971, Vietnam veterans threw away over 700 medals on the steps of the Capitol building in Washington as the prelude to a 500,000 strong march. On 5 May 1971, 1146 people were arrested for trying to shut down Congress including Abbie Hoffman. After May 1971 the Gallup opinion polling company stopped doing monthly surveys to establish how many people were in favour of the war after hitting a low of 28 per cent.

KEY TERM

drawdown: the removal of troops from a conflict region, usually in a gradual and staged manner

Finally in December 1971, 15 anti-war veterans occupied the Statue of Liberty, flying a US flag upside down from her crown. Further protests including 'kneel-ins' to pray for the war and 'bleed-ins' to donate blood for the Vietcong continued but the public opinion argument had been won.

Nixon had failed to control the protests partly because of the clear case they had but also because his own tactics failed. These tactics varied from cancelling protesters' permits, to encouraging pro-war protests and repeatedly declaring that the war was nearly over, which he did in 1969, 1972 and again in 1973. In 1971 Nixon even dispatched his vice president, Spiro Agnew, to brand opponents and critics as 'traitors' – a tactic he himself formerly employed as Eisenhower's vice president. However nothing seemed to work. Public opinion increasingly turned against the war with every news report and veterans' protest and eventually Nixon's rhetoric turned to withdrawal and the question of whether to end the war was reduced to an issue of when the war would be ended.

Civil rights protests

SOURCE 4

Extract from Nixon's first inaugural address, 20 January 1969:

To lower our voices would be a simple thing. In these difficult years, America has suffered from a fever of words; from inflated rhetoric that promises more than it can deliver; from angry rhetoric that fans discontents into hatreds. For its part, government will listen. Those who have been left out, we will try to bring in. Those left behind, we will help to catch up. In this past third of a century, government has passed more laws, spent more money, initiated more programs, than in all our previous history. In pursuing our goals of full employment, better housing, excellence in education; in rebuilding our cities and improving our rural areas; in protecting our environment and enhancing the quality of life--in all these and more, we will and must press urgently forward. We shall plan now for the day when our wealth can be transferred from the destruction of war abroad to the urgent needs of our people at home.

CROSS-REFERENCE

See page 126 of Chapter 15 for more information on the Kerner Report.

For a definition of *de jure* see Chapter 4, page 28.

KEY TERM

busing: the practice of using school buses to move students around between schools ensuring schools are racially mixed even when the surrounding area is dominated by one ethnic group. Busing was upheld by the Supreme Court as a legitimate way to ensure desegregation in *Swann v. Charlotte-Mecklenburg Board of Education*, 1971

Nixon inherited a federal relationship with a Civil Rights Movement fractured beyond all recognition. The **Kerner Report** had stressed the need for action to prevent *de facto* economic segregation replacing the *de jure* segregation in the South. The funds available for Johnson's 'Great Society' had been bled dry, white liberal sympathy had also drained away following the riots of 1964–68 and the radicalism of groups like the Black Panthers and the SNCC. Always keenly aware of the political ramifications of his actions Nixon chose to tread a careful line which pleased no one but moved desegregation forward at a pace Eisenhower would have appreciated.

Bayard Rustin, the organiser of the 1963 March on Washington, believed that Nixon was destroying the victories of Kennedy and Johnson but it is difficult to see where this took place. On desegregation of schools he tasked Spiro Agnew with completing the desegregation of public schools and by September 1970 fewer than 10 per cent of black students were attending segregated schools. The key to this success was a practice known as **busing** which Nixon privately disapproved of but was willing to endorse publicly. Many white groups reacted angrily to busing and forced integration with protests, propaganda and sometimes even rioting. In addition to busing, George Schultz, the Secretary of Labor to whom Agnew delegated the desegregation role, ensured that federal aid was made available to school committees who complied with desegregation plans.

Perhaps Nixon's most significant achievement in civil rights was the introduction of the first federal **affirmative action** programme in 1970, known as the Philadelphia Plan. Executive Order 11246 put the Philadelphia Plan into effect requiring government contractors in Philadelphia to hire minority workers until stated targets were reached. Affirmative action has remained controversial but in attacking institutionalised discrimination it confirmed the Federal Government's support for integration and was upheld by the courts in *Contractors' Association of Eastern Pennsylvania v. Shultz* in 1971 as Affirmative Action was rolled out nationwide.

While the Federal government was under less pressure to legislate on civil rights issues an explosion of elected African-Americans and university courses dedicated to Black Studies occurred. Courses were founded at prestigious institutions like Duke, Cornell and Harvard while **Shirley Chisholm** became the first black woman elected to Congress in 1968 and the Congressional Black Caucus was founded by the 13 black members of Congress sitting in 1971. Civil rights groups like the SNCC and Black Panthers reduced dramatically in size and influence as donations dried up and questionable policies such as Eldridge Cleaver's visits to Pyongyang in North Korea in 1969 and 1970 drained their popular support.

Feminism

Feminists like Gloria Steinem repeatedly stressed how little the Nixon Administration had done for women's issues and sought to encourage the First Lady, Pat Nixon, to come to their aid. This appeared to shock Nixon into action despite the fact that feminist-specific protest was largely lost in the anti-war movement. Nixon used presidential power, as Kennedy had, to increase the number of female appointments to the Administration and created a Presidential Task Force on Women's Rights. He also instructed the Justice Department to bring sex discrimination suits under Title VII of the Civil Rights Act and encouraged the Department of Labor to add sex discrimination provisions to the guidelines for its Office of Federal Contract Compliance. Advances in women's rights is of the most positive aspects of Nixon's legacy.

Economic change and an end to the post-war boom

Nixon had the dubious honour of being the first president to have the suffix -nomics applied to his name to describe his economic policy and it could be argued that this was a result of its incoherence. He inherited a low unemployment rate of 3.3 per cent but rising inflation, and chose to employ a policy of monetary restraint to cool the overheating economy. This '**gradualism**', worked on the principle of restricting the growth of the money supply advocated by neo-liberal economists such as Milton Friedman.

However this policy did not produce results quickly enough and Nixon chose to refocus for political reasons arguing that elections were lost because of recessions and unemployment rather than inflation. Nixon's political instincts were right as by the end of 1970, unemployment rose to 6 per cent and the Republicans lost 12 seats in the House of Representatives. Nixon appointed his chief economic adviser, Arthur Burns, as chairman of the Federal Reserve. He promptly demanded the president hold federal spending under $200 billion in order to address the problem of inflation without having

Fig. 6 *Chisholm was a politician, teacher and author*

Shirley Chisholm (1924–2005) was a former teacher who became the first black woman in Congress and the first to stand for president. Chisholm was a powerful advocate for both the poor and women. She consistently supported spending increases for education, healthcare and reductions in military spending. She also co-founded the National Women's Political Caucus in 1971 and the National Organisation for Women in 1966.

to resort to tax increases, but this required pay freezes which led to strikes, notably from the postal workers. Vietnam was still sucking huge sums out of the budget and unemployment and inflation were both rising. They were now in 'stagflation', as predicted by Friedman, where a stagnant economy is accompanied by inflation. Nixon had to act. In August 1971, the president gathered his economic advisers together and adopted a New Economic Policy which reversed most of his economic principles. Nixon announced a wage-and-price freeze, tax cuts, a 10 per cent import tax to protect American business and ending the 1944 Bretton-Woods Accord which linked the value of the dollar to the price of gold. Public approval was immediate and a boom began which offset some of the damage of Vietnam and which Nixon rode to his re-election in 1972.

Fig. 7 *Cars lining up for gasoline during a shortage in 1974*

ACTIVITY

How big a part did the price of oil play in Nixon's presidency compared to the presidents that preceded him?

A CLOSER LOOK

OPEC and the US

OPEC members included Iraq, Kuwait, Iran, Saudi Arabia, Venezuela, Libya, the United Arab Emirates, Qatar, Indonesia, Algeria and Nigeria. By operating together they offset the power of the big oil companies which were dominated by the US, UK and France. The OPEC members were predominantly Arab countries that were dependent on oil sales for their national income. US support of Israel was a continuing source of contention and the OPEC countries frequently used the spiralling US demand for oil as a way of putting pressure on the US.

However inflation then began to bite again, exacerbated by massive sales of US wheat to the USSR and the oil price rises brought about by **OPEC** in response to the US abandoning the Bretton-Woods Accord. This had served to lower the price of oil and, combined with the US support for Israel in the 1973 Yom Kippur war, the policy angered the predominately Arab states in OPEC. For the first time since the Second World War a US president was faced with a financial crisis to which US economic superiority was not the answer, not least because the US had passed its own point of '**peak oil**' in 1970. Mired in the Watergate scandal Nixon was powerless to change matters and inflation climbed to 12.1 per cent in 1974, pushing the US economy into recession. Even worse, TV footage of queues to buy gasoline combined with rising unemployment and inflation and a crashing stock market left the country looking as destitute financially as it felt politically.

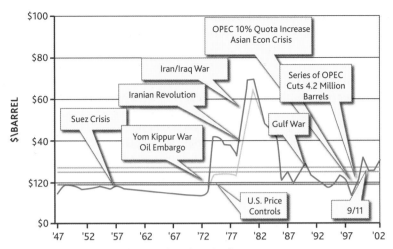

Fig. 8 *The fluctuations in the price of crude oil*

Summary

Nixon appealed to the 'silent majority' who voted for him in huge numbers on two separate occasions but he failed to do much for them. The social fragmentation that they opposed continued apace through, music, cinema, drugs and sex. The economic stability of the golden years of Eisenhower was cast aside to be replaced by 'stagflation' and the decline of American industry. To some extent the last factor was out of Nixon's hands, the rebuilding of Europe and Japan had taken 20 years but their economies were now beginning to take off and it was inevitable that US supremacy would decline. Likewise it was inevitable that the US couldn't act with impunity in foreign affairs once it became dependent on the oil of others. But in purely domestic matters, Nixon failed to be the truly great president he aspired to be, even without the anchor of Watergate. Perhaps he was eight years too late for his time, perhaps if Nixon had won in 1960 he too could have ridden out the last of the post-war economic boom, led the way in civil rights without having to worry about the reaction of the South and used Kissinger and diplomacy to avoid entanglements over Cuba and Vietnam.

 PRACTICE QUESTION

How successful was Richard Nixon in tackling US domestic problems?

 PRACTICE QUESTION

Evaluating primary sources

With reference to Sources 2, 3 and 4 and your understanding of the historical context, assess the value of these three sources to an historian studying Nixon's response to protests?

ACTIVITY

Summary

Draw a spider diagram showing the problems Nixon faced domestically, including protest movements, the state of the economy and political opposition as a minimum. How do these domestic problems compare to those faced by other presidents you have studied?

STUDY TIP

In order to assess 'success' you will need to establish your criteria and consider Nixon's aims. Your essay should aim to focus on social, political and economic problems, with protest movements fitting into the social issues section and the political section incorporating a discussion of how effectively Nixon handled his re-election.

STUDY TIP

Here tone, provenance and argument are pivotal. You should aim to compare and contrast these aspects of each of the sources and evaluate what this can tell us about how Nixon responded to protests. Finally, you should make a judgement on the extent to which the sources are valuable to an historian, explaining your reasoning.

19 The limits of American world power

ACTIVITY

Evaluating primary sources

Considering the principles outline in Source 1, draw a table containing other presidents you have studied and make notes on how far they stuck to these principles with regard to foreign affairs, and in what instances?

KEY TERM

impugned: called into question; disputed

ACTIVITY

Extension

Many of the events of the Nixon presidency are covered both in depth and with great subtlety in the 1994 film *Forrest Gump*. Watch the film and look for the many references to real events, notably the origins of John Lennon's song *Imagine*.

SOURCE 1

Taken from the book *Nixon's Ten Commandments of Statecraft* by James C. Humes and Richard Nixon, published in 1998:

A president needs a global view, a sense of proportion and a keen sense of the possible. If I could carve ten rules into the wall of the Oval Office for my successors in the dangerous years ahead, they would be these:

1. Always be prepared to negotiate, but never negotiate without being prepared
2. Never be belligerent, but always be firm
3. Always remember that covenants should be openly agreed to but privately negotiated
4. Never seek publicity that would destroy the ability to get results
5. Never give up unilaterally what could be used as a bargaining chip
6. Never let your adversary underestimate what you would do in response to a challenge
7. Always leave your adversary a face-saving line of retreat
8. Distinguish between friends who provide some human rights and enemies who deny all human rights
9. Do at least as much for our friends as our adversaries do for our enemies
10. Never lose faith. Faith without strength is futile, but strength without faith is sterile.

Nixon had always aimed to be a foreign policy president. As vice president his overseas itineraries took him to places other politicians didn't venture, including Saigon, Hanoi, Montevideo, Lima, Caracas, Moscow and Panama City. Nixon was an astute student of foreign affairs but also made sure he had good advisers, hand-selecting the Harvard academic Henry Kissinger to be his National Security Adviser. Despite mutual mistrust which sometimes bordered on contempt the two worked so closely together that they were sometimes referred to as 'Nixinger'. When he became president, one thing everyone agreed on was that Nixon was as anti-communist as a president could be and this gave him the political capital required to play the game of international diplomacy without having his actions **impugned** at home. Nixon saw opportunities to improve relations with the Soviet Union and establish relations with the People's Republic of China whilst playing the two off against each other. But in order to do this he had to fulfil an election promise and deliver a peace with honour in Vietnam.

Peace negotiations and the continuation of the war in Vietnam and Cambodia

In 1985 Nixon told the *New York Times* that the Vietnam War was misreported at the time and misremembered afterwards. Although his legacy has been overshadowed by Watergate it was clear that Richard Nixon still felt his role in Vietnam was not given sufficient credit.

In the election campaign of 1968 Nixon had talked about his 'secret plan' to end the war in Vietnam, but had insisted he couldn't reveal this to avoid compromising the peace talks that were ongoing in Paris. Nixon attempted to play a complicated game with the North Vietnamese, initially trying to settle the war on favourable terms to the US but warning in secret negotiations conducted by Kissinger that if major progress was not made by 1 November

1969 there would be great consequences. These measures were to include resuming the bombing of North Vietnam and the mining of Haiphong Harbor. In addition Nixon took a calculated risk in ordering the secret bombing of communist supply lines on the **Ho Chi Minh Trail** in Cambodia. Most riskily of all Nixon chose to take Kennan's advice to its extremes; if communists would only respond to the threat of force they would be most likely to respond to the threat of force wielded by a man on the edge of madness. As Nixon explained the idea to **Harry Robbins 'Bob' Haldeman** in 1968: 'I call it the Madman Theory, Bob. I want the North Vietnamese to believe I've reached the point where I might do anything to stop the war. We'll just slip the word to them that, "for God's sake, you know Nixon is obsessed about communism. We can't restrain him when he's angry – and he has his hand on the nuclear button" and Ho Chi Minh himself will be in Paris in two days begging for peace'. To make the 'Madman Theory' seem more realistic Nixon not only bombed Cambodia, but also talked about bombing the dikes that protected North Vietnam's agricultural lowlands, an action that might have drowned upwards of a million people.

In a further act of brinksmanship and unbeknownst to the American people Nixon moved the military to full global war readiness alert and gave instructions to bombers armed with thermonuclear weapons to fly practice missions along the Soviet border for three consecutive days. October 1969 was a dangerous time.

CROSS-REFERENCE

For more information on the Ho Chi Minh Trail, see Chapter 14, page 117.

KEY PROFILE

Fig. 1   *Haldeman was a political aide and businessman*

Harry Robbins 'Bob' Haldeman (1926–93) was a former advertising man and loyal servant to Nixon since 1956. He was chosen by the new president as his Chief of Staff and earned a reputation as a stern taskmaster and the conduit to Nixon. Haldeman reorganised the White House into a system still used today. He eventually served 18 months in prison for his role in Watergate.

ACTIVITY

In retrospect, Nixon's actions in October 1969 seem ridiculously reckless, how do you think he could justify behaving in such a way given that in his election campaign he had sought to portray himself as a president who would de-escalate the war.

Ho Chi Minh was not taken in however and as he lay on his death bed in August of 1969 he rejected Nixon's threats. The North Vietnamese did not yield and Nixon's secret plan didn't bring America the closure Nixon had hoped for.

Publicly however, Nixon had to have a policy that didn't revolve around pretending to be insane enough to start a nuclear war and the strategy he settled on was known as 'Vietnamization'. This was a policy of building up and training the South Vietnamese to take over responsibility for their own defense, enabling a **drawdown** of American troops which Nixon knew would be politically popular.

CROSS-REFERENCE

The definition of a drawdown is given in Chapter 18, page 153.

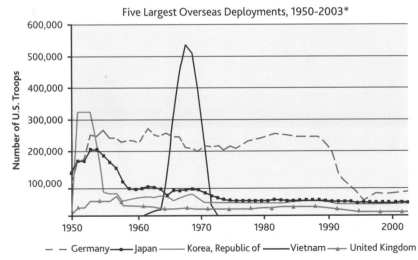

Fig. 2   *The number of US troops deployed overseas, 1945 to 1980*

This seemed a sensible tactic to achieve the peace with honour that Nixon craved in order to end the nightmare of Vietnam while he still enjoyed the political confidence of the American electorate. However, events in Cambodia, where a *coup d'état* had replaced the increasingly anti-American leader Prince Sihanouk with a pro-American military government led by General Lon Nol, gave him an opportunity. Nixon took advantage of the Cambodian change in allegiance by ordering an incursion into Cambodia by American troops to attack the Vietcong there and destroy the Ho Chi Minh Trail, thus strangling the supply lines to the Vietcong in the South.

SOURCE 2

Nixon's address to the nation on the situation in South East Asia, 30 April 1970 announcing the start of operations in Cambodia:

In cooperation with the armed forces of South Vietnam, attacks are being launched this week to clean out major enemy sanctuaries on the Cambodian-Vietnam border [...] During my campaign for the presidency, I pledged to bring Americans home from Vietnam. They are coming home. I promised to end this war. I shall keep that promise. I promised to win a just peace. I shall keep that promise. We shall avoid a wider war. But we are also determined to put an end to this war. I have rejected all political considerations in making this decision. Whether my party gains in November is nothing compared to the lives of 400,000 brave Americans fighting for our country and for the cause of peace and freedom in Vietnam. I would rather be a one-term President and do what I believe is right than to be a two-term President at the cost of seeing America become a second-rate power and to see this Nation accept the first defeat in its proud 190-year history.

Fig. 3 *A time exposure shot of gunfire from 173rd Airborne Brigade Admin Compound as they try to flush out a sniper*

ACTIVITY

Evaluating primary sources

In what ways does Nixon seek to justify the incursion into Cambodia in Source 3?

CROSS-REFERENCE

See Chapter 18 page 153 for information on the largest anti-war protests in American history where National Guardsmen fired on protesters at Kent State University in Ohio, killing four. A fortnight later, police fired on students at Jackson State University in Mississippi, killing two more. The anti-war cause now had martyrs.

Faced with **growing opposition at home** Nixon wanted to complete the US withdrawal from Vietnam by the middle of 1971 but Kissinger talked him out of it because it might create problems ahead of the 1972 presidential election. In 1971 the South Vietnamese army, operating with the benefit of American air support, took part in Lam Son 719, an offensive against the Ho Chi Minh Trail in Laos and Cambodia. Lam Son was considered a test of the success of **Vietnamization**. In a televised speech on 7 April 1971 Nixon announced 'Tonight I can report that Vietnamization has succeeded.' However Lam Son was a failure. Despite the huge amount of US air support the **ARVN** had received they had been unable to do more than delay the use of the Ho Chi Minh trail for a few weeks. Meanwhile, fierce fire fights such as the one shown in Fig. 3 and the guerrilla tactics of the Vietcong with their sophisticated tunnel systems, as shown in Fig. 4, continued to inflict heavy casualties on US troops.

After failing with the Madman theory, Vietnamization and continuing with Johnson's tactics Nixon and **Kissinger** anticipated a communist offensive in 1972. In March 1972 the North Vietnamese regular army began to infiltrate the South in larger and larger numbers. Nixon responded by mining Haiphong Harbor and using B-52s to intensively bomb the North. These actions held up the North Vietnamese offensive but more territory had been lost before the tactics could take effect.

KEY TERM

Vietnamization: Nixon's policy of pulling US troops out of Vietnam but providing financial support to the South Vietnamese army (the ARVN)

KEY TERM

ARVN: the Army of the Republic of Vietnam, i.e. the South Vietnamese army. Formed in 1955 and active until 1975 they suffered over 1.3 million casualties during the Vietnam War

CROSS-REFERENCE

See page 147 in Chapter 17 for more on Henry Kissinger.

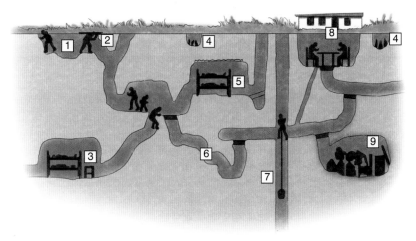

Key

1	Firing post	6	Blast deflection wall
2	Airtight trapdoor	7	Well
3	First aid post	8	Meeting room
4	Punji stake trap	9	Storage cache for weapons and food
5	Reinforced sleeping chamber		

Fig. 4 *Examples of tunnels used by the Vietcong to fight their guerrilla war*

With money, morale and political goodwill draining from the presidency the desire of the North Vietnamese to reach a peace deal was now Nixon's only hope. In October 1972 North Vietnam proposed a peace deal which would preserve the territory they currently held. Kissinger was in favour but the South Vietnamese were horrified. Cleverly the North Vietnamese began broadcasting provisions of the agreement to intensify the pressure on Nixon at home to override the South's objections. The promise of peace contributed to Nixon's landslide victory in the 1972 election far more than did the information gleaned from Watergate. Kissinger's press conference announcement that 'peace is at hand' giving Americans genuine hope that the seven year nightmare might be about to end.

After the election, Nixon gave South Vietnamese President Thieu an ultimatum. If he did not agree to the settlement, Congress would end aid to his government. The carrot was a promise that the US would retaliate militarily if the North violated the agreement. Just to emphasise the point Nixon launched a 'Christmas Bombing' campaign in the winter of 1972. Finally a Nixon tactic worked. When negotiations resumed in January, the few outstanding issues were quickly resolved. The Paris Peace Accords were signed on 23 January 1973, bringing an end to the participation of US ground forces in the Vietnam War and finally fulfilling Nixon's 1968 election promises.

ACTIVITY

Draw up a table of Nixon's tactics in Vietnam with columns for successes and failures. Try to categorise the actions covered in this chapter and those from your wider reading.

STUDY TIP

A balanced response will consider the impact of the Vietnam War on US military power and the perception of it, and on the reputation of US alliances.

A CLOSER LOOK

The Paris Peace Accords

The accords recognised the independence, sovereignty, unity, and territorial integrity of Vietnam as per the 1954 Geneva Agreements on Vietnam and provided for a ceasefire from 27 January 1973. Finally the accords suggested that the eventual goal of the peace was for reunification of Vietnam to be 'carried out step by step through peaceful means'.

 PRACTICE QUESTION

How significant was the Vietnam War in eroding US power internationally?

The influence of Kissinger on US foreign policy

Kissinger was profoundly influenced by his experiences during the war and his study of the Cold War that followed it. He felt that the US had wasted its power under Truman, Eisenhower, Kennedy and Johnson by allying with weak regimes like South Vietnam and South Korea, and pursuing vague ideas of 'development'. Instead, Kissinger emphasised the effective use of American power for the defence of national interests by negotiating directly with the major powers of China and the USSR. Kissinger felt that if the US chose its battles more wisely and elevated national security above hazy ideas like justice and rights it could use its undoubted economic and military superiority to force its rivals to come to terms. Initially Nixon found himself in agreement with this policy but he was always aware of the need to portray decisions in a moral light for their electoral appeal. Eventually this was to divide the two men, with Nixon also privately questioning Kissinger's loyalty and attitude. Despite this, together they pulled off an audacious foreign policy success in dividing the Soviet Union and China.

China

SOURCE 3

ACTIVITY

Evaluating primary sources

What can Source 3 tell us about Kissinger and Nixon's reasons for seeking to improve relations with China?

KEY TERM

Sino-Soviet: Chinese-Soviet; Sino means relating to China

Winston Lord, special assistant to Kissinger in 1972 and later US Ambassador to China, speaking in 1998:

First, an opening to China would give us more flexibility on the world scene generally. We wouldn't just be dealing with Moscow. We could deal with Eastern Europe and we could deal with China, because the former Communist Bloc was no longer a bloc. Kissinger wanted more flexibility, generally. Secondly, by opening relations with China we would catch Russia's attention and get more leverage on them through playing this obvious, China card. The idea would be to improve relations with Moscow, hoping to stir a little bit of its paranoia by dealing with China. Thirdly, Kissinger and Nixon wanted to get help in resolving the Vietnam War. By dealing with Russia and with China we hoped to put pressure on Hanoi to negotiate seriously. With Nixon going to China in February, 1972, and to Moscow in May, 1972, the Russians and Chinese were beginning to place a higher priority on their bilateral relations with us than on their dealings with their friends in Hanoi.

Since the death of Stalin there had been a deterioration in **Sino-Soviet** relations culminating in an undeclared seven month war in 1969 known in China as the Zhenbao Island incident. Nixon and Kissinger saw an opportunity to drive a wedge between the two major communist powers which had the potential to enhance trade links with China and help resolve the situation in Vietnam whilst also pushing the USSR back to the negotiating table over arms talks. Nixon knew that his reputation as a staunch anti-communist gave him the **political capital** to begin to build bridges with the Chinese without the danger of being accused of 'turning red'. To this end, he secretly began to explore the possibility of a rapprochement through messages, then the exhibition matches of the US ping pong team in Beijing, then a secret trip by Kissinger.

Kissinger's trip paved the way for China to join the UN and take the seat that Taiwan had held on the Security Council on 24 October 1971 and for Nixon to become the first US president to visit the People's Republic. Nixon's visit to China in February 1972 was a media sensation and the phrase 'Only Nixon could go to China.' became part of the political and cultural lexicon. It was the first time US audiences had seen the Chinese in two decades. Nixon met Mao for an hour and discussions were also held on a solution to the problem of Taiwan, over Vietnam and over beginning trade links. Nixon described his trip, in typically self-congratulatory style, as 'the week that changed the world' and certainly the press attention and plaudits Nixon received suggested the trip was a success. However recently, historians such as Niall Ferguson have suggested that the actual winner was Mao and China given that they continued to pose a threat to Taiwan, the North Vietnamese emerged victorious and Chinese patronage began to dominate South East Asia most notably in the barbarous regime of Pol Pot in Cambodia.

The Soviet Union

Nixon's policy of drawing closer to **China** produced the desired result of improving relations with the USSR who feared being isolated by the two other powers. Nixon left China on 28 February 1972, and went to Moscow on 22 May of the same year, becoming the first US president to visit the city. He signed two agreements that limited the growth of nuclear armaments: Strategic Arms Limitation Treaty (SALT 1) and an Anti-Ballistic Missile treaty, both were the first of their kind and paved the way for a reduction in armaments. The eight-day visit also saw Nixon conclude deals in the field of environmental protection, trade and a deal for a joint US–Soviet space mission.

CROSS-REFERENCE

For an explanation of political capital, see Chapter 1, page 3.

ACTIVITY

In what ways did Kissinger differ from his predecessors who advised on foreign relations?

KEY PROFILE

Leonid Brezhnev (1906–82) was a Major General in the Second World War. He joined the Central Committee in 1952 and replaced Khrushchev in 1964. Brezhnev failed to address the economic woes of the USSR leading to stagnation exacerbated by increased defence spending. His reactive foreign policy meant no active role in Vietnam but he was forced to negotiate with the USA after Nixon's approach to China.

Fig. 5 *Kissinger meets with minister Ismael Fahmy in Egypt in 1975*

Cold War competition

July 1972 saw the 29-year-old American Bobby Fischer defeat the Russian Boris Spassky in a 24-game chess match in Reykjavik. Fischer was the first American Chess World Champion and such was the interest that the games were televised and newspapers printed extra editions with the latest scores. Later that year in August the USSR basketball team beat the USA in controversial circumstances to win the gold medal at the Munich Olympics.

ACTIVITY

Evaluating primary sources

How does the relationship between the two men seem in Source 4? Find the rest of the conversation online. Has this source been taken out of context?

Kissinger was proving himself to be a master of diplomacy, manoeuvring to bring the Soviets to the table and gaining substantial concessions from **Brezhnev**. And all of this was occurring in a climate where the Cold War seemed to be being played out with more passion everywhere except between the two leaders, with intense rivalry in the space race and in sport. In such a febrile environment, Kissinger's promotion of negotiation and skill at creating a climate where it could happen, was laudable.

SOURCE 4

Extract from a transcript of a meeting between Nixon and Brezhnev on 3 May 1973 in the Oval Office. The only other person present was a translator:

Brezhnev: Now, I believe that our personal relationships and the respect which I certainly harbor, very sincerest regard for you and I know it's reciprocal, can be confirmed by two events and that is: your arrival to Moscow last year, and mine in Washington this year. This is not in any way to remember the bad past or to emphasize anything out of the present, but, simply, I'm giving an answer in substance and what is, I think, is realistic. Yesterday, I had a very pleasant conversation with Dr Kissinger and I guess he must have told you at least about it in general terms, but I want to say now – I said this to him yesterday, and I do want to say it now – that it is certainly my very earnest desire that you should pay another visit to the Soviet Union some time next year, in 1974. I think that would be very good –
Nixon: For the election?

Brezhnev visited Washington in 1973 and plans were discussed for the exchange visits to become an annual event as the two men's relationship deepened. In the end, however, Watergate put a stop to Nixon's vision of détente with the Soviet Union and Brezhnev was never to form the same bond with Ford, Carter or Reagan that he had enjoyed with Nixon.

Latin America

Once again in Latin America the election of a socialist leaning president, this time Salvador Allende in Chile in 1970, was causing concern to the US president. Following Allende's election, Nixon authorised the CIA to obstruct his government and explore the possibility of removing him. Nixon cut $70 million of American aid to Chile and the CIA's efforts bore fruit in a military *coup d'état* on 11 September 1973 which brought a dictatorship under General Augusto Pinochet that was condoned by the US. One thousand of Allende's supporters were summarily executed. After Pinochet took power, Kissinger informed Nixon that while the CIA 'didn't do it' they had 'created the conditions' in which a *coup d'état* could take place.

Summary

ACTIVITY

Summary

Truman had the most famous doctrine as far as school history is concerned. Having read this chapter, if you were asked to define what the Nixon Doctrine was, what would you describe it as?

Nixon's efforts to be seen as a global statesman had been unstinting since he was elevated to the vice presidency by Eisenhower. His wife, Pat, was dragged along to 53 countries and countless visits to orphanages and palaces but by the time her husband was forced to step down did Pat have reason to be proud of how he had changed the world?

ACTIVITY

Summary

How far did Nixon keep to his foreign rules outlined in Source 1?

The Nixon Foundation's top ten foreign policy achievements certainly sound more impressive than their domestic top ten. Ending the Vietnam War, bringing a billion people out of isolation, signing SALT 1 and avoiding a second Cuban Missile Crisis are all listed but these assertions require questioning. How effective were Nixon's solutions in Vietnam? What were the consequences of the rapprochement with China in the rest of South East Asia? Foreign policy has so many variables and so many players that success can often be more of a matter of luck than judgement. Nixon was unlucky to have inherited a costly, unpopular and unwinnable war and he played his hand in Vietnam poorly. Elsewhere however he avoided entangling the US in further conflict whilst also standing up to communism but always allowing for negotiation. Whilst his policies in Latin America may have been dubious he is hardly unique in this. What can be said with certainty however is that his foreign policy achievements were far more notable than his achievements at home.

 PRACTICE QUESTION

Evaluating primary sources

With reference to Sources 1, 2 and 3 and your understanding of the historical context, assess the value of these three sources to an historian studying Nixon's foreign policy.

STUDY TIP

Dates are important here, Source 1 is retrospective, Source 2 is the prelude to a highly damaging change of tactic and Source 5 deals with Nixon as he begins to look towards his legacy. You may want to discuss the relationship between private conversations (Source 3), public pronouncements (Source 2) and memoirs (Source 1).

20 The Watergate Affair and its aftermath

KEY TERM

subpoena: a demand by a court that compels a witness to appear and provide evidence

ACTIVITY

Evaluating historical extracts

What reasons does Kutler give for the reliability of the Nixon tapes as historical source?

The events of the Watergate Affair

In 2013 the final tapes from the Nixon Oval Office were released. The tapes contained all of Nixon's private conversations while he was president and were critical in bringing about his resignation.

EXTRACT 1

SK: The difference between these tapes and Lyndon Johnson and John F Kennedy and Dwight Eisenhower is that, say Kennedy, when Kennedy taped, he pushed a button to tape. Nixon, being such a klutz, they were voice activated. You lose track of the fact you're being taped. You just talk. That's the beauty of these. It's a fundamental difference, because in many ways the tapes of the others are carefully controlled and contrived. They controlled the button, so they controlled the taping.

Interviewer: I would think that Nixon could hold his own among the controllers and contrivers.

SK: I've found examples where somebody would come in and tell him something, like [Chief of Staff H.R.] Haldeman, in very great confidence. Two visitors later you might get (counsel to the president) John Dean, who wasn't trusted as much, and John Dean would tell him the same thing, and Nixon would say, 'You're kidding. I'm surprised. That can't be true.'

Historian Stanley Kutler in an interview with a television reporter (2013)

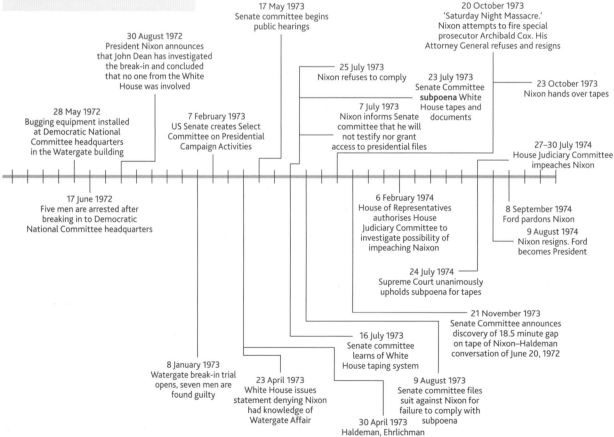

Fig. 1 *Timeline of the Watergate Affair*

Watergate has become so synonymous with political scandal that the suffix '-gate' is now erroneously added to the topic of a new scandal as if that was enough to explain it. The affair was a complex tangle of intrigue that resolved in such a classic Hollywood fashion that it was the subject of the 1976 film *All the President's Men* which won four Oscars.

The Watergate Affair

The Watergate Hotel was the location of the Democratic Party's Washington DC offices where the party was preparing for the 1972 presidential election. On 17 June 1972 five men were arrested inside the Democratic Party's offices shortly after 2:30am. The story of how they got there ended Richard Nixon's presidency and shattered many American's illusions about the trustworthiness of their politicians.

SOURCE 1

Adapted from an interview by the British journalist David Frost with Richard Nixon, aired in May 1977. The Frost: Nixon interview, the first the disgraced president had given, became the subject of a stage play and film:

David Frost [initially addressing the camera]: The wave of dissent in America, occasionally violent, which followed the incursion into Cambodia prompted President Nixon to demand better intelligence about the people who were opposing him on the domestic front. To this end a series of meetings were arranged with representatives of the **CIA**, the FBI, and other police and intelligence agencies. These meetings produced a plan, the Huston Plan, which advocated the systematic use of wiretappings, burglaries, mail openings and infiltration against anti-war groups and others. Some of these activities were clearly illegal. Nevertheless, the president approved the plan. Five days later, after opposition from the FBI director, **J Edgar Hoover**, the plan was withdrawn, but the president's approval was later to be listed in the articles of impeachment as an alleged abuse of presidential power.

David Frost: [now addressing Nixon] Would you say that there are certain situations where the president can decide that it's in the best interests of the nation, and do something illegal?

Richard Nixon: Well, when the president does it, that means it is not illegal.

KEY TERM

CIA (Central Intelligence Agency): the international intelligence and security agency in the USA

ACTIVITY

Evaluating primary sources

Watch David Frost's interview with Richard Nixon. If you had to defend Nixon's assertion in the above source that the president's actions can never be illegal how would you go about it?

KEY PROFILE

J Edgar Hoover (1895–1972) was Director of the FBI from 1935 until his death in 1972 at the age of 77. Hoover built up both the Bureau and his personal power, prompting Truman to suggest that all politicians feared him. He was fiercely anti-communist, and both Truman and Kennedy considered dismissing him, but they decided that the political fallout would be too great. Johnson waived the federal retirement age to allow Hoover to continue indefinitely as director of the FBI.

A year earlier, Nixon had been alarmed by the release of the **Pentagon Papers** by Daniel Ellsberg which revealed secrets of the Johnson and Kennedy Administrations. Fearful that a conspiracy to leak some of his own secrets was underway Nixon approached FBI Director J Edgar Hoover. Hoover couldn't be persuaded to investigate so Nixon set up his own investigative team who became known as 'The Plumbers', because its role was to fix leaks. One of the first jobs the plumbers carried out was part of a **smear campaign** against Ellsberg. Two of the plumbers, ex-CIA agent Howard Hunt and

KEY TERM

smear campaign: a smear campaign is an orchestrated effort to discredit an individual or organisation by questioning their morality, mental-health, behaviour or attitudes. Usually it is achieved through exposing their private activities in the press

CROSS-REFERENCE

See Chapter 10, page 82 for the Bay of Pigs invasion.

ex-FBI agent Gordon Liddy put together a team to burgle the offices of Ellsberg's psychiatrist. Some of this team were Cuban expats that Hunt knew through his past-life with the CIA who had been involved with the Bay of Pigs invasion.

A CLOSER LOOK

The Pentagon Papers

More correctly known as 'United States–Vietnam Relations, 1945–1967: A Study Prepared by the Department of Defense', The Pentagon Papers were secret documents discovered and released by military analyst Daniel Ellsberg in 1971. They showed that the Johnson Administration had lied to the public and Congress about the bombings of Cambodia and Laos and other aspects of the war. Ellsberg was initially charged with conspiracy, espionage and theft of government property.

Two of those Cuban expats were amongst the five men caught repairing bugging equipment and in possession of cameras in the Watergate Hotel on 17 June 1972. There is considerable debate as to how much Nixon knew about the initial bugging operation. In 2003 Jeb Magruder, a White House aide to Nixon, told an interviewer that he personally heard Nixon authorising the placing of bugs in the Democrat Campaign offices as a way of gaining information on the Democrat campaign and backers. Magruder had been interviewed before and not revealed this. Regardless of the issue of authorisation President Nixon instructed Bob Haldeman, his White House Chief of Staff, to head off a possible FBI investigation by getting the CIA to argue that it might interfere with their operations. On 15 September the five arrested men, along with Howard Hunt and Gordon Liddy, were indicted for conspiracy, burglary, and violation of federal wiretapping laws. $500,000 in funds from the Committee to Re-elect the President (CRP) were used to pay the legal expenses for the five men but this only aroused more suspicion as Nixon's former Attorney General John Mitchell was now running the CRP. Liddy and Hunt had also been part of the CRP and Nixon became increasingly concerned about how other activities might become part of further investigation of the Watergate break-in. He was right to be concerned; Howard Hunt went on the record to say that Watergate was the tip of the iceberg and that there had been a number of illegal activities carried out on behalf of senior White House staff.

On 23 June, a few days after the break-in, Nixon met with Haldeman to discuss how to prevent the investigation uncovering more evidence of wrong-doing. The conversation, as with all conversations in the Oval Office since Kennedy, was recorded onto tape. In this exchange, Nixon decided to ask the CIA to tell the FBI not to push ahead with the investigation in order to prevent bringing up the Bay of Pigs affair. The White House managed to prevent Watergate's **political fallout** from affecting the 1972 election.

But a Washington Post journalist, **Bob Woodward**, who had been present when the Watergate burglars were charged, was also investigating. He had heard the initials 'CIA' from one of the charged men and another had given his occupation as 'anti-communist'. Woodward discovered that James McCord, one of the five, was responsible for security for the CRP. A second link to the White House came when Howard Hunt's phone number was discovered in a second burglar's notebook. Woodward began to receive classified intelligence from a very well informed source with access to one of the investigations into Watergate, the source was anonymous but became known as 'Deep Throat'.

KEY TERM

political fallout: fallout is the term given to the polluting radioactive particles that disperse through the atmosphere after a nuclear explosion. In the context of politics it refers to the negative effects of an event which can linger for a substantial time after that event

KEY PROFILE

Bob Woodward (b. 1943) and Carl Bernstein (b. 1944) were investigative journalists for the *Washington Post* newspaper which broke the story of Watergate and pursued it despite a seeming lack of interest from other media. The story won the Pulitzer Prize in 1973 and the book *All the President's Men* became a bestseller, whilst the 1976 film starring Dustin Hoffman and Robert Redford won four Oscars and made the two men celebrities.

In 2005 the Associate Director of the FBI at the time of Watergate, Mark Felt, revealed himself as Woodward's source.

Fig. 2 *A window display showing posters relating to Nixon and Watergate*

Nixon had won by a landslide in November 1972 against the Democrat George McGovern, helped in some ways by the material that had been gleaned from the listening equipment that had been planted in the Democratic Party's offices. However, in February 1973, L Patrick Gray revealed that John Dean, a White House lawyer, whose role was to advise the president on legal matters relating to the presidential role, had been given classified information about the investigation. Gray was Nixon's nominee to succeed Hoover as head of the FBI and had been Acting Head since May 1972, after Hoover's death. This brought the investigation even closer to Nixon, especially when he refused to allow Dean to testify in front of the separate Senate Watergate investigation committee.

A CLOSER LOOK

The 20 figures at the centre of the Watergate scandal were: James McCord; Dwight Chapin; H.R. Haldeman; John Mitchell; John Erlichman; Maurice Stans; Eugenio Martinez; C. Gordon Liddy; Charles Colson; Herbert Kalmbach; John Dean; Robert Mardean; Jeb Magruder; Richard Nixon; Bernard L. Barker; Virgilio Gonzalez; Donald Segretti' Frank A. Sturgis; E. Howard Hunt Kr.; Hugh Sloan Jr.

ACTIVITY

The Watergate Affair is one of the most complicated and far-reaching scandals in American history because of the number of strands the numerous investigations took. 'Deep Throat's' advice to Woodward and **Bernstein** was to 'follow the money' as a way of linking things together. Try using the names in the Closer Look above to link the key players to each other as the police do in a criminal investigation.

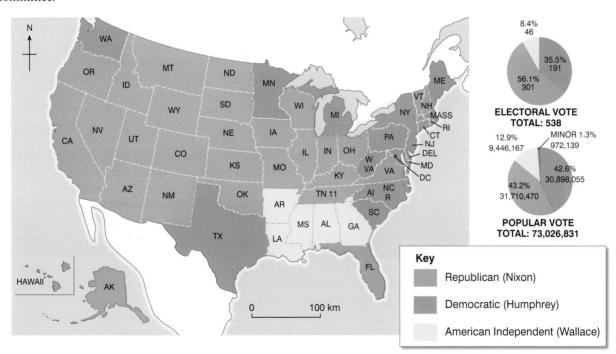

Fig. 3 *The election results of 1968; the letters represent states/constituencies*

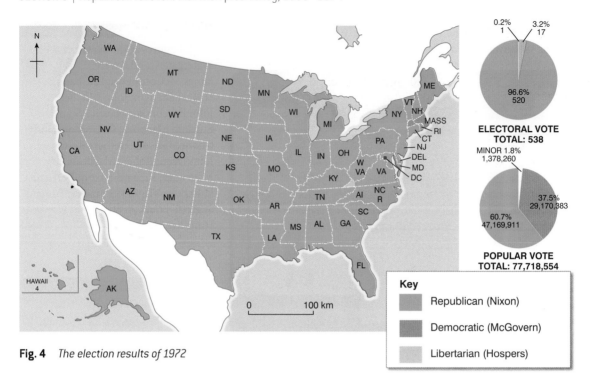

Fig. 4 *The election results of 1972*

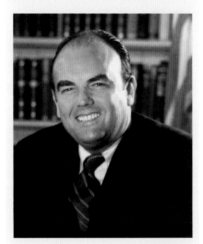

Fig. 5 *Ehrlichman was a key figure in the Watergate scandal*

John Ehrlichman (1925–99)
worked on the Nixon campaign
in 1960. After Nixon's win in 1968
he became White House Counsel
then Chief Domestic Advisor for
Nixon and part of Nixon's inner
circle. Ehrlichman was responsible
for initiating the 'plumbers' and for
advocating keeping information
about the early phase of Watergate
unclear. He served 18 months in
prison for his part in the scandal.

SOURCE 2

**An extract from an Address to the Nation About the Watergate Investigations
by Richard Nixon, 3 April 1973:**

For the fact that alleged improper actions took place within the White House or
within my campaign organization, the easiest course would be for me to blame
those to whom I delegated the responsibility to run the campaign. But that would
be a cowardly thing to do. I will not place the blame on subordinates. In any
organization, the man at the top must bear the responsibility. That responsibility,
therefore, belongs here, in this office. I accept it. And I pledge to you tonight,
from this office, that I will do everything in my power to ensure that the guilty
are brought to justice. Some people, quite properly appalled at the abuses that
occurred, will say that Watergate demonstrates the bankruptcy of the American
political system. I believe precisely the opposite is true. It was the system that has
brought the facts to light and that will bring those guilty to justice. It is essential
now that we place our faith in that system – and especially in the judicial system.

On 23 March 1973 the Watergate intruders were due for sentencing. Before
sentencing the judge read a letter from James McCord which provided
more evidence of a cover up and said that the defendants had been paid to
plead guilty and stay silent. Dean had decided to co-operate with the Senate
investigation but continued to work for Nixon without informing him
until the end of April, when Nixon announced the firing of Dean and **John
Ehrlichman** and the resignation of Bob Haldeman but by this time it was
too late to salvage anything. In May the televised Senate Watergate hearings
began and witness after witness revealed details of corruption in the White
House. Nixon's approval rating plummeted. One revelation was to be key to
Nixon's final humiliation: the existence of the taping system. Watergate special
prosecutor Archibald Cox subpoenaed the tapes. Nixon fought the subpoena
to the Supreme Court citing Executive Privilege and National Security, leading
the House of Representatives to vote to impeach him for obstruction of justice

and abuse of power. On 24 July 1974 in *United States v. Richard Nixon* the court upheld the subpoena 8–0 saying 'the President's generalised assertion of privilege must yield to the demonstrated, specific need for evidence in a pending criminal trial'. On 30 July 1974 3500 hours of conversations were released by Nixon to the prosecutors to go through.

The role of Congress in the Watergate Affair

Edward Kennedy pushed for a Senate Committee to investigate Watergate. Republicans were prepared to defend Nixon and they controlled the Senate in 1973 and pushed for an even split of Democrats and Republicans in the Committee which was to be headed by Sam Ervin, the Democrat Senator from North Carolina. Ervin was one of the foremost constitutional lawyers in the Senate and had a passion for civil liberties and checking executive power. The parties' nominations to the Committee were unusually balanced and this helped considerably in their task for which there was no constitutional precedent. The seven-senator Committee was supported by a large investigative team of talented lawyers and this helped smooth over the inter-party tensions. However, it was Nixon's intransigence over handing over the tapes that effectively ended the Republican interest in defending their president. As it became increasingly clear that Nixon had considerable knowledge of the break-in and other nefarious activities, the Senate Committee rose to the challenge of holding the Executive to account, clearing the way for the House Judiciary Committee to begin impeachment hearings. In acting in such a bipartisan fashion the two parties achieved their goals. The Democrats finally slayed Nixon and the Republicans managed to put enough distance between themselves and the president that the taint of his corruption didn't last longer than a one-term Carter presidency.

The resignation of the president

Fig. 6 *Cartoonist Herblock on the missing minutes*

200 hours of the tapes related directly to Watergate and one key part had a gap of 18 and a half minutes that was explained away by a convoluted story involving a secretary inadvertently erasing it but there was still more than enough information to convict Nixon in the court of public opinion

CROSS-REFERENCE

For the Key Profile of Barry Goldwater, revisit Chapter 13, page 108.

and to virtually guarantee he would be impeached. **Barry Goldwater**, the conservative leader in the Senate, told the President that there were a maximum of 15 senators who might vote against his conviction, not nearly enough to save him from humiliation. Nixon was left with no choice and announced his resignation on 8 August 1974. His vice president, Gerald Ford, who had been in the job less than a year, following the conviction of the previous vice president, Spiro Agnew, for accepting bribes while Governor of Maryland, sought to heal the divisions that had afflicted the previous two years. In his inaugural address Ford declared, 'Our long national nightmare is over'. and one month later, he granted Nixon a full pardon.

A CLOSER LOOK

Presidential pardons

Article 2 of the US Constitution gives the president the power to grant a full pardon, to commute a sentence, or to rescind a fine for individuals of their choice, effectively freeing them from their punishment. Truman pardoned 2044 people, Eisenhower 1157, Kennedy 575, Johnson 1187, Nixon 926, Ford 409 and Carter 566.

SOURCE 3

Adapted from a speech by President Gerald R. Ford – September 8, 1974:

The facts, as I see them, are that a former President of the United States, instead of enjoying equal treatment, would be cruelly and excessively penalized either in preserving the presumption of his innocence or in obtaining a speedy determination of his guilt in order to repay a legal debt to society. But it is not the ultimate fate of Richard Nixon that most concerns me, my concern is the immediate future of this great country. My conscience tells me clearly and certainly that I cannot prolong the bad dreams that continue to reopen a chapter that is closed. My conscience tells me that only I, as President, have the constitutional power to firmly shut and seal this book. My conscience tells me it is my duty, not merely to proclaim domestic tranquility but to use every means that I have to insure it. Now, therefore, I, Gerald R. Ford, President of the United States have granted a full, free, and absolute pardon unto Richard Nixon.

ACTIVITY

Class debate

Hold a class debate to try to establish a consensus on whether Ford was right to pardon Nixon.

Nixon's political legacy

Richard Nixon broke the relatively liberal consensus that had dominated the presidency since Roosevelt by becoming the first practising Republican to win the Presidency since Hoover in 1929. The Nixon Foundation website suggests his ten greatest domestic achievements include:

1. ending the draft in 1973
2. founding the Environmental Protection Agency and introducing the Clean Air Act, the Clean Water Act, and the Mammal Marine Protection Act
3. appointing 4 Supreme Court justices who ushered in an era of judicial restraint
4. dedicating $100 million to begin the War on Cancer
5. signing Title IX in 1972, preventing gender bias at colleges and universities receiving federal aid
6. overseeing the peaceful desegregation of southern schools
7. overseeing the Apollo XI lunar landing
8. extending the right to vote to 18- to 20-year-olds

9. authorizing joint work between the FBI and Special Task Forces, resulting in over 2500 convictions for involvement in organised crime by 1973

10. ending the policy of forced assimilation of American Indians, returned sacred lands, and became the first American President to give them the right to tribal self-determination.

Nixon was an arch politician and was always willing to adapt his media presence and his message for political gain and take credit wherever possible. He privately admitted that if he hadn't created the Environmental Protection Agency the Democratic Congress would have forced more liberal environmental legislation on him. He opposed wage and price controls philosophically, privately believing they would not work, but still introduced them in an election year. Towards the end of his time in office came the moment where the difference between image and reality was laid bare in the American presidency. Roosevelt's illness, Truman's racism, Eisenhower's penchant for golf, Kennedy's philandering, Johnson's vulgarity had all been kept from the public to a greater or lesser extent but the release of the Nixon tapes has provided, and continued to provide up to the last tranche in 2013, evidence of the veneer. When the first transcripts of the tapes were released, the words "[Expletive deleted]" appeared again and again next to Nixon who had always studiously avoided swearing throughout his political career. The relatively mild revelation of this difference shocked conservative supporters but worse was to come as subsequent revelations from the tapes have demonstrated shockingly un-PC attitudes including racism, sexism, anti-Semitism and a penchant for stereotypes about Irish and Italian people.

Fig. 7 *Nixon announces his resignation as president*

An extract from Richard Nixon's resignation speech, 8 August 1974:

We have ended America's longest war, but in the work of securing a lasting peace in the world, the goals ahead are even more far-reaching and more difficult. We must complete a structure of peace so that it will be said of this generation not only that we ended one war but that we prevented future wars. We have unlocked the doors that for a quarter of a century stood between the United States and China. We must now ensure that the one quarter of the world's people who live in the People's Republic of China will be and remain not our enemies but our friends. In the Middle East, 100 million people in the Arab

Extension

Draw up a table comparing Nixon's achievements in domestic affairs with those of the other presidents you have studied. Your columns might include; Economy, Environment, Political Change, Minority Rights, Health Care, Transport, Scientific Advances. How does Nixon compare?

Class debate

One of the thorniest issues in politics is whether we should expect our politicians to have high moral standards. Debate the motion 'This house believes a politician's effectiveness is more important than their personal views and morals' in relation to the presidents you have covered so far.

Evaluating primary sources

Compare the achievements that Nixon claims he has been responsible for in Source 4 with the information you have read in Chapter 19 on his foreign policy. How far does this support the idea that Nixon was more successful in his foreign policy than his domestic policy?

Nixon's foreign policy is covered in more detail in Chapter 19.

countries, many of whom have considered us their enemy for nearly 20 years, now look on us as their friends. We must continue to build on that friendship so that peace can settle at last over the Middle East and so that the cradle of civilization will not become its grave.

Summary

The lure of politics and the chance to prove people wrong was always too great for this most idiosyncratic and flawed of presidents. His ability to pick himself up and start again was his greatest skill and he developed an arsenal of techniques involving media manipulation, blue-sky thinking, selecting brilliant colleagues and subterfuge to achieve it. According to Gallup opinion polls his lowest rating was lower than any post-war president except Truman in 1952. His highest rating was the lowest of any post-war president too. In surveys of historians he never comes higher than 23rd 'greatest' and more regularly features in the bottom quartile. Even his biographers are split on his place in history. Perhaps the most generous is Jonathan Aitken who summarised the president as having been excessively criticised for his faults and inadequately credited for his virtues. Ironically, Aitken was to have his own torrid downfall from his position as a British MP, receiving an 18-month prison sentence for perjury in 1999.

Nixon could never shake the epithet of 'Tricky Dicky' as is often the case when an epithet is well deserved, but his importance in providing an end to the problems he inherited and a new start for the Republican Party should not be overlooked. For many liberals he was the summary of everything that had gone wrong since Kennedy died: a failed war and a corrupt political system. But for Republicans with a sense of history it was Nixon that created the 'Solid South' that has been so vital to subsequent Republican party success. It was Nixon that reached out to the religious right and it was Nixon that refocused the party isolation onto the importance of foreign affairs and created a climate in which Reagan could feel that he could win the Cold War and George W Bush could feel that he could democratise the world. For better or, most often, for worse the Nixon presidency casts a long shadow.

 PRACTICE QUESTION

'Watergate overshadowed all of Nixon's other achievements in politics.' Assess the validity of this view.

 PRACTICE QUESTION

Evaluating primary sources

With reference to Sources 1, 2 and 3 and your understanding of the historical context, assess the value of these three sources to an historian studying the consequences of the Watergate Affair?

21 Ford and Carter as presidents

ACTIVITY

Evaluating primary sources

This British obituary for Ford is very critical of him. Try to rewrite it to cast Ford in a more positive light (the *New York Times* obituary might be a good place to start).

KEY PROFILE

Fig. 1   *Ford was a high school and university American football star*

Gerald Ford (1913–2006) served in the Navy in the Second World War and then became a lawyer and, eventually, a member of the House of Representatives for Michigan. Renowned as an honest and open politician, but not a great mind, he replaced Spiro Agnew as Nixon's vice president and then Nixon himself after Watergate. His presidency was tainted by Nixon and he was defeated by Carter in 1976. His wife, Betty Ford, founded the famous Betty Ford Centre for addiction.

Ford and Carter as presidents

Gerald Ford

SOURCE 1

Extract from **President Gerald Ford's** obituary in the British newspaper, *The Guardian*, 27 December 2006. Ford served as president from 9 August 1974 to 20 January 1977:

Gerald Ford will be remembered for exposing an extraordinary constitutional weakness unforeseen by the founding fathers of the United States. Having been a notoriously mediocre congressman, he went on to fill the country's two principal executive posts without the benefit of a single electoral vote. When voters were eventually given a chance to legitimise his presidency, he became the first White House incumbent in 44 years to be defeated. Opinion polls showed that a critical factor had been his decision to issue the former president Richard Nixon with a 'full, free, and absolute pardon for all offences against the United States' committed during the Watergate cover-up. The seal was finally set on his presidency in the 1976 campaign against Jimmy Carter. In one of their televised debates he offered the unbelievable judgment that 'there is no Soviet domination of eastern Europe'. It brought home sharply to his audience how slim was his understanding of the world he was supposed to lead.

After taking the Oath of Office on 9 August 1974 Gerald Ford aimed to put Vietnam, Watergate, the riots and the spluttering economic situation behind him and draw a line under the period since Kennedy's assassination. However, though he could see an end in sight to both the Watergate scandal and Vietnam, inflation and unemployment were rising and social issues such as busing, abortion and women's rights, along with Native American and Hispanic rights were proving divisive. Ford had risen through the Republican ranks in Congress because of his reputation for decency, integrity, and fairness. He cultivated a 'man of the people' image helped by his status as an Eagle Scout and as a former university American Football star who had been offered a contract with both the Detroit Lions and Green Bay Packers. However the start of the satirical late night show *Saturday Night Live* in 1975 coupled with the effect of Watergate in diluting the prestige of the president, allowed comedian Chevy Chase to impersonate Ford every week by stumbling and falling down stairs, saying the wrong thing at the wrong time, and accidentally injuring himself and innocent bystanders.

A CLOSER LOOK

Saturday Night Live

An irreverent topical weekly sketch show on NBC which parodied American popular culture and politics. It debuted in October 1975 and marked a shift in public attitudes to previously revered figures including the president. It paved the way for shows like *The Colbert Report* and *The Daily Show* and introduced many of the most notable US comedians and movie stars of the last 40 years.

Fig. 3   *Haig served in both Korea and Vietnam*

Alexander Haig (1924–2010) became military adviser to Kissinger in 1969, before becoming Deputy Assistant to the President for National Security in 1971. He was Chief of Staff for Nixon and then Gerald Ford when Ford promoted him to Supreme Allied Commander in Europe in 1974. He resigned on 3 January 1979 but returned to government service when President Reagan selected him to be Secretary of State.

Fig. 4   *Carter was originally a peanut farmer*

Jimmy Carter (b. 1924) is a Democrat who was raised in rural Georgia and served two terms as a Georgia State Senator followed by one as the Governor of Georgia, from 1971 to 1975. He defeated incumbent president Gerald Ford in 1976 promising an outsider's insight and a return of morality but struggled with the economy and foreign affairs.

Fig. 2   *Gerald Ford falling down the stairs of Air Force One*

Journalists joined in, quoting Johnson's comment that Ford had played too much football without his helmet and that 'Jerry Ford is so dumb he can't fart and chew gum at the same time.' But Ford helped the critics by making what many saw as an error of judgement in pardoning Nixon 'for all offenses', telling Americans on 8 September 1974 that Nixon had suffered enough and the threat of prosecution was damaging his health. The decision led to outrage with opinion polls suggesting most Americans wanted Nixon punished and the decision disastrously affected Ford's own polling. In a nationally televised appearance on 17 October 1974, in front of the House Judiciary Committee, Ford admitted that pardoning Nixon was an option discussed with Nixon's chief of staff, **Alexander Haig** but declared 'There was no deal, period, under no circumstances'.

Carter as president

Jimmy Carter defeated Ford in 1976 through clever tactics and media support. Positioning himself as a devout Christian and a Southerner he gathered up the supporters of George Wallace in the South and established himself in the North East through relentless campaigning. Carter had travelled over 50,000 miles, visited 37 states, and delivered over 200 speeches before other candidates announced their candidacy. Carter portrayed himself as a Washington outsider throughout his campaign and early presidency and remains the only US president to have been interviewed by *Playboy*. He walked to the White House from the Capitol building following his inauguration and en route made the 'I Love You' sign language gesture to a group of deaf supporters. The US media latched on to his differences during the campaign and the favourable coverage he received propelled him into the White House.

Carter saw himself as a reformer and a progressive in the spirit of Woodrow Wilson, and he tried to make his policy priorities clear right from the start as the country and the press willed him to be a success. His first policies were marked by a desire to heal divides; he pardoned Vietnam-era

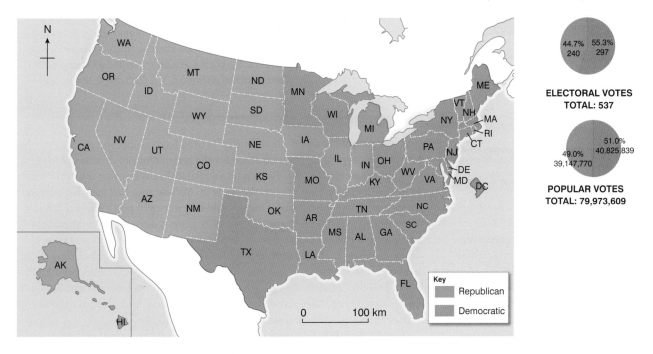

ELECTORAL VOTES
TOTAL: 537

44.7%
240

55.3%
297

POPULAR VOTES
TOTAL: 79,973,609

49.0%
39,147,770

51.0%
40,825,839

Key
Republican
Democratic

Fig. 5 *Presidential election results, 1976; the letters represent states/constituencies*

draft resisters, ended funding for the B-1 bomber airplane, and pushed for a comprehensive consumer-protection bill. However, Carter was unwilling to use his position to win friends in Congress through the usual method of promising federal spending in certain states and districts. This led Congress to become unwilling to cooperate, perhaps sensing the shallowness of his support in the country. A pattern of mutual contempt and distrust had been established, which saw little achieved by either side and left a country feeling let down.

Carter's initial popularity with the media faded quickly as he proved to be only marginally more media savvy than Ford and certainly lacking the charisma of Kennedy or Reagan. Carter wasn't helped by the fact that his successes were difficult for the population as a whole to grasp in an increasingly **sound bite**-driven media landscape, the **Energy policy**, **SALT II** talks and **Camp David Accords** lacked the punch of a Civil Rights Act or a victory in war. Television had made it harder for Americans to look in depth at the actions of their government, making it harder to make a case for the political usefulness of complex legislation.

CROSS-REFERENCE

To see how the election results of 1980 compare to these of 1968 and 1972 see Chapter 20, pages 169–170.

KEY TERM

sound bite: a short extract from a speech or policy announcement that serves as a handy summary of the speaker's position in a two minute news article. Reagan's expertise here eclipsed Carter, for example 'Recession is when a neighbor loses his job. Depression is when you lose yours'

SOURCE 2

Jimmy Carter's 'malaise' speech, 15 July 1979. The speech was very popular and saw Carter's opinion poll ratings rise by 11 per cent despite its apparent criticism of Americans:

I want to talk to you right now about a fundamental threat to American democracy. The threat is nearly invisible in ordinary ways. It is a crisis of confidence. We've always had a faith that the days of our children would be better than our own. Our people are losing that faith. But just as we are losing our confidence in the future, we are also beginning to close the door on our past. In a nation that was proud of hard work, strong families, close-knit communities, and our faith in God, too many of us now tend to worship self-indulgence and consumption. What you see too often in Washington and

CROSS-REFERENCE

See Chapter 22, pages 186–187 and page 189 for more information on the SALT II talks and Camp David Accords.

ACTIVITY

Evaluating primary sources

If you were a Republican seeking to criticise Carter how could you use this speech?

A CLOSER LOOK

The Three Mile Island Accident

A combination of human and mechanical errors at the Three Mile Island nuclear generator in Pennsylvania, resulted in a partial meltdown of the reactor core and the release of radioactive gases into the atmosphere. The accident played on public fears of a nuclear catastrophe and led to the shutdown of several plants. Massive demonstrations in the aftermath of the accident culminated in a 200,000 strong rally in New York.

CROSS-REFERENCE

Detail on the corruption within Carter's Administration and family can be found later in this chapter on pages 180–182.

elsewhere around the country is a system of government that seems incapable of action. You see a Congress twisted and pulled in every direction by hundreds of well-financed special interests. You often see a balanced and a fair approach that demands sacrifice abandoned like an orphan. You don't like it, and neither do I. What can we do?

As Carter sought to assert his authority he fired four cabinet secretaries, transferring several others, and asked for the resignations of dozens of lower ranking White House staff. The media and Republicans leapt on the opportunity to associate Carter himself with the sense of 'malaise' that had been highlighted in his speech. Perceptions became key and two stories in particular damaged Carter's public image; firstly in August 1979 when a story about the president being attacked by a rabbit began to do the rounds in Washington, and then in October Carter collapsed from heat exhaustion while jogging in full view of the nation's press. Events were not kind to Carter in the final year of his presidency either and the disasters were summed up by a serious nuclear accident in March 1979 at the **Three Mile Island** reactor in Pennsylvania. It now appeared that the Carter Administration was suffering a similar meltdown.

Perceptions didn't do justice to Carter whose success rate in getting legislation through Congress was higher than Eisenhower, Nixon and Ford, and close to the success rates of the arch manipulator of Congress, Johnson. In total, the Carter Congress passed 29 new pieces of legislation including three significant energy acts, five environmental acts and several pro-business acts including a commitment to deregulation in transport. None of these were landmarks of the magnitude of Johnson, however, one thing that Carter could always cling to was his promise to Americans during his election campaign that 'I'll never tell a lie. I'll never make a misleading statement. I'll never betray the confidence that any of you had in me. And I'll never avoid a controversial issue.' Unfortunately key members of his **Administration and even his family** chipped away at this moral rectitude.

Responses to social divisions

Ford's two years in power coincided with perhaps the quietest period since the mid-1950s for social unrest. As a Republican without a mandate, Ford was not inclined to push issues of minority rights whilst ignominious ending to the Vietnam War had left protesters vindicated. With African-American civil rights making clear, if slow, progress Ford at least was blessed with some respite.

The same could not be said for Jimmy Carter. In his July 1976 speech at the Democratic Convention, Jimmy Carter tried to address America's growing distrust of government and the divisions that had emerged in society. However, the activism that had been inspired by the black Civil Rights Movement and Vietnam had diversified and a series of cases were again making their way to the Supreme Court that would demand difficult decisions from a president who lacked a solid base of party support.

In *Bryan v. Itasca County* in 1976, the Supreme Court ruled that a state did not have the right to assess a tax on the property of a Native American living on a reservation, paving the way for considerable new freedoms for tribes including the lucrative practice of operating casinos on their land. However other minority groups were still campaigning for what they saw as their constitutional rights, notably Mexican-Americans under Cesar Chavez, and homosexuals who had successfully campaigned for the removal of homosexuality from the *Diagnostic and Statistical Manual* of the American Psychiatric Association in 1973. In 1977 14 gay and lesbian activists were invited to the White House for the first official visit of its kind, but in March

1980 Carter formally refused to issue an Executive Order banning anti-gay discrimination in the federal government. It was clear that Carter was unwilling to risk his political capital in a first term to make a stand of the same magnitude that **Lyndon Johnson** had in the mid-1960s, particularly when it came to groups whose support was not electorally advantageous.

CROSS-REFERENCE

For detail Johnson's actions, see Chapter 13.

Fig. 6 *Betty Ford speaking at a luncheon sponsored by Republican Women Power of Illinois in 1976*

When it came to the position of women, legislation was easier to pass, especially as by 1980 more women than men voted in the presidential election. Ford had signed the Equal Credit Opportunity Act which outlawed credit discrimination on the basis of race, colour, religion, national origin, sex, marital status or age, though it had been introduced by Nixon. In the 1975 *Taylor v. Louisiana* case, the Supreme Court ruled that excluding women from the jury pool was illegal because it violates a person's right to a fair trial by a representative segment of the community. Ford was pro-women's rights but again had little time to make a difference; indeed his wife, **Betty Ford**, probably made more of an impact speaking out about issues as diverse as abortion and addiction always with the interests of the disadvantaged at heart.

For Carter there was more time and in 1978, he managed to pass the Pregnancy Discrimination Act, making employment discrimination on the basis of pregnancy illegal, a considerable legislative and moral success. There were parallels with Truman when in 1976, the five United States Service academies were required to admit women, more than 300 of whom enrolled in 1976. Under Carter shelters for female victims of domestic violence began to be created, states began adopting domestic violence laws, and activists worked to change the laws which stated that there had to be a witness other than the woman herself to charge a man with rape, and that a woman's sexual history could be brought up at trial, while the alleged rapist's could not. Also, due to feminist activism the first law against marital rape (raping one's spouse) was enacted by South Dakota in 1975, however it took until 1993 for marital rape to be a crime in all 50 states. Carter was not a crusading president when it came to women's rights but he was a supportive one both by morality and because he saw the political advantages. Indeed it would have been a stubborn and misogynistic man not to be keenly aware that the issue of women's rights was following a very similar path to that of African-American rights in the decade before.

KEY PROFILE

Betty Ford (1918–2011) was a former model and dance teacher. She was divorced from her first husband before marrying Gerald Ford in 1948. As First Lady her influence was substantial and she had approval ratings of over 75 per cent for her openness about drug use, psychiatric treatment and pre-marital sex. She was a passionate supporter of women's rights including being pro-choice. Later in her life she founded the Betty Ford Clinic for the treatment of drug addiction.

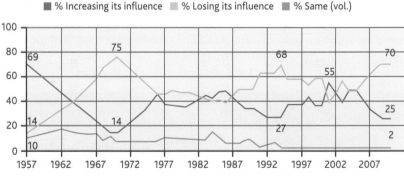

■ % Increasing its influence   ■ % Losing its influence   ■ % Same (vol.)

Fig. 7 *Belief in the importance and influence of religion in US society*

Carter and Ford were trying to adapt to a changing and diverse country and their support for women's rights is a clear example of this whilst carrying the benefits of electoral appeal. However, ranged against the interest groups was a growing right-wing Christian lobby that Nixon had tapped into and that Reagan mobilised. With fundamental beliefs on matters as varied as abortion, homosexuality, gun ownership and the teaching of evolution, this group was more than willing to see anything that deviated from the norm as truly deviant and hence a blot on their version of the American Dream.

The perception of political corruption

The Nixon Administration had not only seen the Watergate scandal but also the resignation of Spiro Agnew and even the prosecution of Teddy Kennedy for his actions in the death of a young woman at Chappaquiddick in Massachusetts in 1969. As a result, the faith of the electorate in politicians was severely shaken and the enthusiasm of newspapers for investigative journalism was enhanced. The result was a period of forensic focus on government for any examples of corruption and the expectation that it would be found. For both Ford and Carter these perceptions of corruption affected their poll ratings and subsequent electability.

Corruption under Ford

The **pardoning of Richard Nixon** tainted Ford's presidency although it is difficult to see what else the new president could have done to help the country move on. Worse was to come though when the **Church Committee** revealed that the CIA had been acting in a fashion that undermined many of the perceptions that Americans had about the honesty of the country's overseas engagements almost since its creation in 1947. There were also scandals involving racist comments by Ford's Secretary of Agriculture Earl Butz and the imprisoning of Otto Kerner, the main author of the **Kerner Report** for bribery whilst Governor of Illinois.

The sense of a corrupt ending to Watergate rankled with the American people and press and there was more than a whiff of corruption when it came to Ford's choices for his White House team. Ford kept Alexander Haig on before appointing him commander of NATO in Europe, Donald Rumsfeld became Ford's new chief of staff, Roy Ash stayed as head of the Office of Management and Budget and Kenneth Cole as head of the Domestic Council. Ford did bring in Nelson Rockefeller, the former governor of New York and leader of the moderate wing of the Republican Party, to fill the vacant office of vice president but this role no longer had the same importance that it had held when Nixon and Johnson had held it, tainted as it was by Spiro Agnew's own corruption.

Rockefeller's selection alienated many conservative Republicans who would have preferred Ronald Reagan. In addition, Rockefeller and Rumsfeld despised

ACTIVITY

To what extent did US politics become more corrupt after the Second World War? Were the failings of politicians just more apparent because of the media when previously they had been hidden?

CROSS-REFERENCE

For more information on the pardoning of Richard Nixon, see Chapter 20, page 172.

For an explanation of the Church Committee see Chapter 22, pages 184–185.

To read more about the Kerner Report, see Chapter 15, page 126.

each other, making life difficult in the Executive Office. Ford quickly realised the danger of keeping the Nixon team in place and began to put his own men into key positions.

Fig. 8 *Some of over 16,000 telegrams sent to the White House protesting President Ford's full and unconditional pardon of Richard Nixon*

Despite his 24 years in the House of Representatives Ford also had difficulty in working with Congress. The pardon of Nixon led to substantial Democrat gains in the 1974 midterm congressional elections giving them a 291 to 144 advantage in the House and a 61 to 39 advantage in the Senate. Republicans too were keen to reassert their role in policymaking after the debacles of Vietnam, Watergate and the Church Committee had left them looking impotent in the face of an executive that did what it liked. Newcomers to Congress in 1974 were referred to as 'Watergate Babies' and promised to clean up Washington politics.

Corruption under Carter

SOURCE 3

Extract from 'Carter's Broken Lance' an article by William Safire for the *New York Times*, 21 July 1977. Safire won a Pulitzer Prize for the article which attacked the president's judgement:

Jimmy Carter is trying to sell the Senate a dubious bill of goods about his long-time friend, Office of Management and Budget Director Bert Lance. Here we have a situation in which the man in charge of the nation's books is deeply, dangerously, in hock; who goes home every night not knowing whether the Labor Department will find out about his teamster connections, or the SEC will look into his assurance to 45 people about a stock issue, or the bank examiners and First Chicago stockholders will expose a sweetheart loan, or the man on whom he depends for financial solvency will exert some subtle pressure for political advantage. Jimmy Carter's broken Lance is a walking conflict of interest. The complaisant Senate subcommittee now glancing at his wheeling and dealing should stop making an exception and start making an example.

ACTIVITY

Evaluating primary sources

Safire's article is full of complex terminology that many readers of the *New York Times* wouldn't fully understand. What message would they be able to get from this extract?

Bert Lance, who filled the role of Office of Management and Budget Director and had worked on Carter's campaign, was fired a year into the Administration when he was connected to some dubious banking practices in Georgia. Despite being

Fig. 8 *Flynt has fought several prominent legal battles*

Larry Flynt (b. 1942) was a publisher of pornography. He grew up poor before drifting through various jobs and eventually publishing the magazine *Hustler*. The magazine was at the centre of series of court cases culminating in a Supreme Court case over whether the First Amendment's freedom of speech provision covers pornography. Flynt was confined to a wheelchair in 1978 after being shot by white supremacist Joseph Paul Franklin for publishing interracial pornography.

ACTIVITY

Draw up a table with two columns headed 'Bad Luck' and 'Bad Judgement' and try to categorise Carter's domestic misfortunes covered in this chapter into the columns. How important is luck to a president?

found not guilty Lance tainted the impression of the Carter Executive. Rumours also circulated that Carter's young chief of staff Hamilton Jordan was a cocaine user; again the charges proved false but the accusations were difficult to shake. While the Executive was shaken by hints of corruption, Congress was facing a far more serious scandal in 'Koreagate', in which 30 Congressmen were accused of taking bribes from the South Korean government for working to reverse Nixon's decision to remove troops from South Korea. The Democrat Richard Hanna eventually served a year in prison as part of the fallout. To many Americans these allegations and trials merely proved that Washington stank of money and corruption and eroded their faith in the democratic process. As a result, voter turnout in the midterm elections in 1974 and 1978 hit a 30-year low.

While Congress floundered, Carter was suffering from the attention of the press on his own family. His sister, Ruth Carter Stapleton, was pictured in public with **Larry Flynt**, the owner of the pornographic magazine *Hustler*. Billy Carter, the president's younger brother was even more of a gift to the media. He marketed his own brand of beer, 'Billy Beer' and had received a sum of $250,000 for an unspecified reason from the Libyan government after visiting the country three times in 1978 and 79, leading to a Senate investigation dubbed 'Billygate'.

Political corruption inevitably became a national obsession after Watergate. The attentions of the press and the disapproval of the electorate reflected a loss of national self-confidence that had been evident since the Vietnam War turned sour. It was in this climate that only Hollywood could provide an answer.

The loss of national self-confidence in the pre-Reagan years

The sixties cast a long shadow; the advances that had occurred in civil rights had not seemed to many to have delivered a better country but rather had exposed the inequalities that had always existed in the American Dream. Internationally, the self-confident USA of the Second World War years had been replaced by a USA that had been humiliated by a Third World nation in war, forced to negotiate as an equal with communists over trade and weapons whilst becoming dependent on the whims of Arabian Sheiks to keep the lights on at home. In major cities like New York and Detroit blackouts became common and housing stock degenerated as factories closed and graffiti proliferated. Even the quintessential American pastime of movie going was in decline.

For many Americans, this led to an overwhelming feeling that America had lost its direction, as if the very future of the 'American Dream' might be in question or at least out of the reach of 'normal' people. The evidence seemed to support this: increasing divorce rates, with up to half of marriages ending in divorce, were deemed responsible for a rise in juvenile delinquency and corresponding rises in drug use and crime. Those who could find work were often underpaid with 70 per cent of all new jobs created in the 1970s in low-paying service industries where salaries were eaten away by 10 to 15 per cent inflation per year.

But in addition to confidence being damaged both domestically and internationally there was a global fear that democracy itself was in danger. In 1975, the Trilateral Commission, an international organisation of leading politicians, academics and industrialists from the USA, Europe, and Japan, released a report entitled, *The Crisis of Democracy*, which concluded that a democratic political system benefits from some measure of apathy and non-involvement on the part of some individuals and groups. Samuel P Huntington, one of the report's eventual authors, summed up the message for the US by saying, 'The vitality of democracy in the United States in the 1960s produced a substantial increase in governmental activity and a substantial decrease in governmental authority.' In other words, the country had lost confidence in its government because when it had been called upon to act, it had increased the ways in which it could let the electorate down. To many, Ronald Reagan, with his film star confidence and a promise to cut government back down to size, would make a compelling candidate.

Summary

ACTIVITY

Summary

Use the 'Diamond Nine' system to categorise the key domestic events during the Carter and Ford presidencies in order of importance.

STUDY TIP

A 'Diamond Nine' template is provided in Chapter 7, page 55, which you can copy to help you complete this Activity.

Ford and Carter both suffered domestically from a series of misfortunes; some of their own making, some caused by the changes going on in America and others caused by the turmoil of the previous 15 years. Neither man had the charisma to win over a press that had been galvanised by the Watergate Affair into seeing itself as the voice of popular criticism. Their failure to appreciate the importance of presentation in winning over an American public increasingly raised on TV and advertising, was important in reducing their honeymoon period with voters. In the end Carter failed to take advantage of the damage done to the Republican Party by Watergate and Ford's limp presidency, and was swept away by the Reagan juggernaut of celebrity, free market principles and a new vision of what Republicanism meant. In a climate where assassination attempts seemed to be a regular occurrence, John Lennon was shot dead in New York in December 1980 and there had been five school shootings in the previous two years. Carter seemed to have lost control. In the end Carter's presidency can be judged to have been ineffectual and his defeat represented a rejection of liberal principles by the US electorate that continues to this day.

STUDY TIP

This is a very broad question that requires a keen understanding of the concept of the 'American Dream' and some careful selection of evidence. You can draw on many aspects of the Dream (economic success, the provision of justice and equal opportunity, the ideas of 'manifest destiny') but you must be able to justify your arguments in each of these categories and provide a balanced assessment.

 PRACTICE QUESTION

To what extent was the American Dream over by 1980?

 PRACTICE QUESTION

Evaluating primary sources

With reference to Sources 1, 2 and 3 and your understanding of the historical context, assess the value of these three sources to an historian studying the problems facing Ford and Carter at home.

STUDY TIP

Domestic policy questions should always focus heavily on the economy. Consider other factors in this period and note where the sources address these issues.

22 The position of the USA as a world power

ACTIVITY

Extension

Watch some of the footage available online of the evacuation of US personnel from Saigon. Turn the volume down and do a brief news report that sums up for audiences in different parts of the world what the evacuation means.

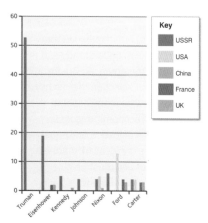

Fig. 2 *Use of the veto in the UN Security Council by the five permanent members during the terms of various US presidents, 1946–80*

Final withdrawal from Vietnam

Fig. 1 *Fleeing Americans board a US marine helicopter in Saigon, Vietnam, in April 1975*

Ford's two years saw little in the way of new initiatives in foreign policy. He kept Secretary of State Henry Kissinger (who also served as National Security Adviser) and Secretary of Defense James Schlesinger but later was to reduce Kissinger's role before firing Schlesinger. He did so for the latter's failure to dispatch more aircraft to help with the evacuation of Saigon. He also fired Director of Central Intelligence William Colby because of his openness when testifying before Congress. The two were replaced, respectively, with Ford's Chief of Staff Donald Rumsfeld, and the American Envoy to China, George H W Bush, names that have dominated Republican presidencies ever since.

Ford presided over a humiliating final retreat from Vietnam as even an infusion of $700 million in military and humanitarian assistance to the South Vietnamese failed to stem the progress of the communist forces towards Saigon. In late April 1975 communist forces entered Saigon and Ford ordered the evacuation of all US personnel and South Vietnamese citizens with connections to the US. This led to the humiliating spectacle of US helicopters taking off from the Embassy in Saigon as desperate South Vietnamese tried to break into the compound and join the evacuation. Meanwhile, May 1975 saw Ford order US marines to retake an American cargo ship, the *Mayaguez*, which had been seized by the Khmer Rouge, the new communist government in Cambodia. Despite the death of 40 Americans in the operation the ship was retaken and Ford's approval soared. Ford also faced problems as revelations of US covert activities by the CIA came out in the press.

A CLOSER LOOK

The Church Committee

Two committees were ordered to look into the CIA's conduct following the fallout of the Watergate affair and revelations about their role in assassinations of foreign leaders. Senator Frank Church of Idaho, investigating on behalf of Congress castigated the agency for its actions. CIA director William Colby paid with his job in late 1975. Congress agreed with Church's findings and enforced greater congressional oversight of the CIA.

Relations with the USSR

Ford and Kissinger continued Nixon's goals of **détente with the Soviet Union**, which was proving to be a more effective way of containing Soviet ambitions than Kennedy and Eisenhower's faith in **Mutually Assured Destruction**. In August 1975 Ford joined with Soviet leader Leonid Brezhnev and the heads of other European nations to sign the Helsinki Accords, which recognised the existing boundaries of European countries established at the end of the Second World War, a key demand of the Soviet delegates who had initiated the discussions and wanted to confirm their standing in Eastern Europe. In return, the Accords also included statements in support of human rights, to which the Soviets reluctantly acquiesced. In fact, both Ford and Kissinger saw the Accords as superficial. Kissinger privately claimed that 'we never wanted it but we went along with the Europeans' and Ford argued that the conditions that had been agreed were nothing more than the current basis of US foreign policy: respect for sovereign states, a commitment to peaceful settlement of disputes and respect for human rights. Ford had already agreed in November 1974 to the Vladivostok Accords, which provided a general outline for a successor treaty to SALT 1 (Strategic Arms Limitation Treaty) but this was to be the limit of Ford's success in détente and led to criticism from Ronald Reagan who was determined that the US should take a stronger line.

CROSS-REFERENCE

Look back to Chapter 19, pages 163–164 for more on détente with the USSR.

To revisit detail on Mutually Assured Destruction, look back to Chapter 7, page 55.

Jimmy Carter's foreign policy

KEY CHRONOLOGY	
June 1977	SEATO alliance is dissolved
Sept 1977	Carter agrees to hand over Panama Canal to Panama by 2000
Sept 1978	Camp David Accords, Carter helps negotiate a peace treaty between Egypt's President Anwar Sadat and Israel's Menachem Begin
Jan 1979	US recognises People's Republic of China and passes the Taiwan Relations Act
March 1979	CENTO alliance is dissolved
Nov 1979	US hostages taken in Tehran, Iran
Dec 1979	Soviet Union invades Afghanistan
Jan 1980	US Boycott of Moscow Summer Olympics announced

Jimmy Carter's foreign policy experience when he entered the White House was gossamer thin. Carter believed in the rule of law in international affairs, in the principle of **self-determination** for all people and that the United States should take the lead in promoting human rights while avoiding military intervention. In 1977 Carter declared, 'Our policy is based on an historical

CROSS-REFERENCE

To recap on the concept of self-determination, look back at the Key Term in Chapter 2, page 17.

vision of America's role. Our policy is derived from a larger view of global change. Our policy is rooted in our moral values, which never change. Our policy is reinforced by our material wealth and by our military power. Our policy is designed to serve mankind.' Carter certainly sought to bring human rights into the foreign policy debate and promote peace in areas of tension such as the Middle East and East Asia. However, he wanted to prevent any reconciliation between Beijing and Moscow in order to continue the work of Nixon and Kissinger in putting pressure on the Soviets.

SOURCE 1

Jimmy Carter outlining the reasons behind his decision to change the nature of US foreign policy towards communist countries in a speech at Notre Dame University in January 1977:

For too many years, we've been willing to adopt the flawed and erroneous principles and tactics of our adversaries, sometimes abandoning our own values for theirs. We've fought fire with fire, never thinking that fire is sometimes best quenched with water. This approach failed, with Vietnam the best example of its intellectual and moral poverty. But through failure we have now found our way back to our own principles and values, and we have regained our lost confidence. Our rise to world eminence dates from 1945, when Europe and the old international order lay in ruins. Before then, America was largely on the periphery of world affairs. But since then, we have inescapably been at the center. Our policy during this period was guided by two principles, a belief that Soviet expansion was almost inevitable but that it must be contained, and the corresponding belief in the importance of an almost exclusive alliance among non-Communist nations on both sides of the Atlantic. That system could not last forever unchanged.

The electorate had hoped that Carter would govern in a different way and he had pledged not to appoint Washington insiders to top positions, however he knew he was out of his depth with foreign policy and turned to **Zbigniew Brzezinski** as his National Security Adviser and **Cyrus Vance** as Secretary of State. The two were to clash repeatedly during the Carter presidency over the tactics, strategies, and even the goals of foreign policy.

KEY PROFILE

Cyrus Vance (1917–2002) was a talented manager and was known for his cautious and patient diplomacy. As Deputy Secretary of Defense under Johnson he had resigned over Vietnam. He advocated closer economic ties with the USSR and negotiation as a tactic of first choice. His successes over the Camp David Accords were considerable but he resigned over Carter's decision to order Operation Eagle Claw.

Brzezinski's strongly anti-communist views made him a critic of détente and he argued that the economic stagnation in the USSR that was the hallmark of the Brezhnev years made the USSR a less dangerous foe than under Khrushchev and Stalin. Brzezinski encouraged Carter to adopt a new approach and was willing to allow both SEATO and CENTO to dissolve as well as dismissing détente. The end of these encircling alliances had little effect on relations as NATO remained the principal fear of the USSR but Brzezinski was keen for Carter to pursue further arms reduction talks. Unlike Vance, however, he wanted these to be linked to human rights discussions. In June 1979 Brezhnev and Carter signed the SALT II agreement which had been under negotiation since 1972. The agreement

ACTIVITY

Evaluating primary sources

Use Source 1 to draw a spider diagram of the principles of Jimmy Carter's foreign policy and the reasons behind these. As you read through this chapter, add examples of where these principles were followed (or ignored) to your diagram.

KEY PROFILE

Fig. 3   *Brzezinski was National Security Advisor*

Zbigniew Brzezinski (b. 1928) was born in Warsaw and became a US citizen in 1958. He taught at Harvard and Columbia University. Brzezinski was an adviser to Kennedy and Johnson and a committed anti-communist. He disagreed with aspects of Kissinger's policy when succeeding him as the principal presidential spokesperson on foreign affairs but his policies had mixed success in Poland, Afghanistan and Iran.

promised limitations on development of future missiles and a reduction by both sides to 2250 usable weapons of all categories, still more than enough to make the planet uninhabitable. SALT II was a potentially historic achievement for Carter. However, **events in Afghanistan** meant that the agreement was not ratified.

Human rights

Carter's desire to differentiate his Administration from those that had brought the US self-conception so low crystallised in his declaration that his foreign policy would support human rights. This was not only politically pragmatic at home but also reflected his moral stance as a staunch Baptist. Early in his presidency, Carter explained that he wished to support 'human freedom' and protect 'the individual from the arbitrary power of the state', two ambitions that were contingent with the United Nation's 1948 'Universal Declaration of Human Rights', drafted by Eleanor Roosevelt. Carter believed that he had to hold America's allies to the same standards demanded of its enemies and went on to criticise both the Soviet Union, where Brezhnev had ignored the human rights aspect of the 1975 Helsinki Accords, and the Eastern European governments as well as allies like South Korea. Military and economic aid were suspended to Chile, El Salvador, Nicaragua, and Uganda as part of the policy.

Carter was accused however of hypocrisy in not pushing harder for human rights in the Soviet Union and China. Brezhnev threatened to end arms control talks over the issue, Deng refused to discuss it and Carter failed to halt military aid to the Shah in Iran whose human rights record had been condemned by Amnesty International who accused the Iranian leader of carrying out over 300 political executions. The criticism of Carter came from two sides, the peace lobby and conservative Republicans like Jeanne Kirkpatrick and Ronald Reagan, who suggested Carter's failure to understand the nature of diplomatic relations was damaging US allies. While Carter deserves credit for bringing the issue of human rights to the fore of US foreign policy, his deviation from the realpolitik of Nixon and Kissinger never paid the political dividends he might have hoped for.

Relations with China

Fig. 4 *President Carter with former President Nixon talking to Chinese leader Deng Xiaoping at a State Dinner at the White House, 1979*

CROSS-REFERENCE

Events in Afghanistan are covered in more detail later in this chapter, on pages 191–192.

ACTIVITY

'This house believes that foreign policy should be based on considerations of Human Rights.' This is a debate topic that goes far beyond the boundaries of this course and takes in both philosophical and economic ideas. List arguments on either side to establish the three best arguments and counterarguments then hold a class vote to see how the everyone feels.

CROSS-REFERENCE

For more on Nixon in China see pages 162—163 in Chapter 19.

Carter continued the work of **Nixon** and Kissinger by formally recognising the communist regime in China on 1 January 1979. Brzezinski encouraged this as part of the effort to put pressure on the Soviet Union and because the opportunity to normalise relations was too important to be squandered. This opportunity was particularly precious as after Mao's death in 1976 a power struggle had gripped Beijing resulting in the rise of **Deng Xiaoping** as Mao's unanointed replacement. Deng was keen to push forward economic reform in China, having famously declared in 1961 'it doesn't matter whether a cat is black or white, as long as it catches mice'.

KEY PROFILE

Deng Xiaoping (1904—97) was a Chinese communist leader. He was instrumental in addressing the economic problems caused by Mao's Great Leap Forward but this brought him into conflict with Mao. After becoming China's leader in 1978, Deng pursued a policy of opening China up to foreign companies including Boeing and Coca-Cola. He travelled to the US in early 1979, making it clear that China's new priorities were technological and economic development.

CROSS-REFERENCE

For information on the US relationship with Taiwan, see Chapter 7, page 59.

KEY TERM

to revoke: to officially cancel a promise, agreement or, in this case, a Treaty. Carter believed he had a constitutional right to do this

However recognising China required severing ties with **Taiwan**. Carter **revoked** the 1955 Mutual Defense Treaty with Taiwan but was challenged in court by conservative Republicans leading to the 1979 Supreme Court case of *Carter v. Goldwater*. The Supreme Court threw the entire case out on a technicality and Carter's recognition of China reduced tension in South East Asia allowing trade relations to flourish. Carter's desire not to fully abandon Taiwan led to relations with the Republic of China (Taiwan) continuing on an unofficial level through Congress passing the Taiwan Relations Act and creating an American Institute in Taiwan staffed by retired US diplomats. The pretence annoyed the Chinese but the increasing trade and the successful decoupling of the People's Republic of China and the USSR, begun by Nixon and Kissinger, were enough to mollify both sides.

ACTIVITY

Sino-US relations are now seen as key to a stable and prosperous world with the historian Niall Ferguson arguing that the two countries are so connected that he christened them 'Chimerica' Who deserves most credit for the restoration of relations with China: Nixon or Carter?

The response to crises in the Middle East

The Middle East had become vital to US interests in the post-war period for two principal reasons. Firstly, Truman's recognition of the state of Israel in 1948 had committed the US to a defence of Israel that antagonised its Arab neighbours. Secondly, the US had become increasingly dependent on Middle Eastern oil supplies to supplement its own dwindling stocks. Wars between the Arab nations and Israel had occurred in 1948, 1967 and 1973 without conclusive victories for either side but Israeli success was seen in the Arab world as the direct result of US financial, military and diplomatic support.

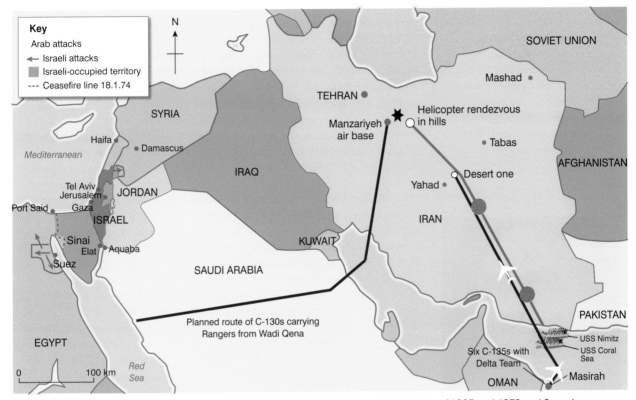

Fig. 5 *The disputed territory in the Sinai peninsula between Egypt and Israel in the wars of 1967 and 1973 and Carter's attempt to liberate the hostages in Tehran, Iran in 1980*

The Camp David Accords

Carter's foreign policy legacy was defined more by his actions in the Middle East than any president before him. It was the scene both of his greatest triumph and his biggest disaster. Following the **Yom Kippur War** of 1973, Israel was still occupying Egyptian territory in the Sinai Peninsula. In Autumn 1978, Carter invited Israel's Prime Minister Menachem Begin and Egypt's President Anwar Sadat to Camp David and, with Carter as the intermediary, Begin and Sadat reached a historic agreement that became known as the Camp David Accords and was signed in Washington on 26 March 1979. It stipulated that:

1. Israel would withdraw from the entire Sinai Peninsula
2. the US would monitor to ensure neither side attacked the other
3. Israel and Egypt would recognize each other's governments and sign a peace treaty
4. Israel pledged to negotiate with the Palestinians for peace.

This was the first time since 1905 that a US president had mediated effectively in a major dispute between two other nations. Begin and Sadat received the Nobel Peace Prize in 1979 whereas Carter received no recognition.

Iran

Recognition for Carter's achievements at Camp David was already dissipating when a hostage crisis occurred in Iran. The King (Shah) of Iran, Mohammad Reza Shah Pahlavi, was widely seen as a puppet of the West following the CIA orchestrated *coup d'état* against Mossadegh in 1953. The Shah had handed over the rights to 80 per cent of Iran's oil and with US support had gone on to ban all political parties, created a

A CLOSER LOOK

The Yom Kippur War, 1973

In a surprise move, a coalition of Arab states led by Egypt and Syria had attacked Israel on the Jewish holy day of Yom Kippur. Egypt's goal was to expel Israeli forces who had been occupying the Sinai peninsula since 1967. Initial Arab success was short-lived and a US ceasefire was required to end the conflict.

CROSS-REFERENCE

Look back to Chapter 7, page 60 for the CIA orchestrated coup against Mossadegh.

personality cult: a term often associated with dictators especially Mao and Stalin; a cult of personality arises when a leader controls propaganda to create an idealised and heroic image of themselves, which can almost veer into religious worship

KEY PROFILE

Fig. 6   *Khomeini was the Supreme Leader of Iran*

Ayatolla Khomeini (1902–89) was an Iranian religious leader who was exiled for 15 years for his opposition to the Shah, who himself was a puppet of the US. He returned to lead the revolution against the Shah in 1979 and instituted theocratic rule in the country and described the US as 'the great Satan'.

ACTIVITY

Draw up a table of successes and failures of Carter's foreign policy in the Middle East with separate rows for the different countries he was involved with.

personality cult and build up a terrifyingly brutal secret police known as SAVAK. As Carter came to power, discontent with the Shah was increasing in Iran led by a radical Islamic group who believed that a fundamentalist Muslim government was necessary. Their supreme religious leader, **Ayatollah Khomeini**, had been in exile in Paris for 15 years but returned in 1979 after the Shah was forced to flee Iran by the strength of feeling against him. On his return the Ayatollah became the nation's undisputed ruler and condemned the Shah. Carter made a fundamental misjudgement in allowing the Shah to be treated for cancer in the US. This action outraged the followers of the Ayatollah who were demanding his return to stand trial in Iran. Carter had expected the Shah's stay to be short but complications following his surgery led to a six week stay, which further angered Tehran. In November 1979, Islamic student militants took control of American embassy in Teheran and took 66 Americans hostage, demanding the Shah's return to stand trial along with money and property that the Shah had stashed outside Iran, and an apology from America.

Carter was faced with a foreign policy disaster; negotiating would make him look weak, attacking Iran would potentially provoke further fundamentalist Islamic resentment in the Middle East and risk the deaths of the hostages. While he vacillated, US news stations ran continuous footage of Iranian mobs burning the Stars and Stripes and chanting 'Death to America'. Carter tried freezing billions of dollars of Iranian assets in the United States, he tried secret negotiations but by day 88 of the siege with his chances in the forthcoming election seeping away, Carter approved a secret military incursion to free the hostages using eight helicopters. Unfortunately none of the helicopters even reached Teheran with three developing mechanical problems and one crashing into a transport aircraft in a remote desert in Iran, killing eight soldiers. The Ayatollah claimed divine intervention and the hostages were split up around the country to prevent a second attempt. Carter was doomed, Reagan's campaign which had concentrated on the president's weakness could not have asked for a clearer vindication of their argument. Towards the end of his term Carter agreed to unblock all Iranian funds and promised not to interfere in the internal affairs of Iran in return for the release of the hostages. The US Embassy building in Teheran remains a training camp for the Revolutionary Guards, the most militant group in the Iranian armed forces.

SOURCE 2

In his memoir, *Keeping Faith*, Carter reflects on how he felt when the hostages finally left Iran after 444 days in captivity, 30 minutes after Reagan had been inaugurated as President:

Of course, their lives, safety, and freedom were the paramount considerations, but there was more to it. I wanted to have my decisions vindicated. It was very likely that I had been defeated and would soon leave office as President because I had kept these hostages and their fate at the forefront of the world's attention, and had clung to a cautious and prudent policy in order to protect their lives during the preceding fourteen months. Before God and my fellow citizens, I wanted to exert every ounce of my strength and ability during these last few days to achieve their liberation. In spite of the fact that I turned over the reigns of a great nation, as President, to my successor, it (the release of the hostages) was one of the happiest moments, one of the happiest days of my life.

Afghanistan

Fig. 7 *The Soviet Army in Kabul, Afghanistan, in December 1979*

In April 1978, the communist People's Democratic Party of Afghanistan (PDPA) had seized power in Afghanistan. A guerrilla opposition, '**the mujahideen**' fought back, plunging the country into civil war. In response, the Soviet Union invaded Afghanistan on Christmas Day 1979, ostensibly in support of the Communist government in the capital Kabul, in line with **the Brezhnev Doctrine.**

SOURCE 3

Carter's National Security Adviser, Zbigniew Brzezinski in an interview with CNN, June 1997, describes the Carter government's reaction to the Soviet invasion of Afghanistan:

We immediately launched a twofold process. The first involved direct reactions and sanctions focused on the Soviet Union, and both the State Department and the National Security Council prepared long lists of sanctions to be adopted, of steps to be taken to increase the international costs to the Soviet Union of their actions. And the second course of action led to my going to Pakistan for the purpose of coordinating with the Pakistanis a joint response, the purpose of which would be to make the Soviets bleed for as much and as long as is possible; and we engaged in that effort in a collaborative sense with the Saudis, the Egyptians, the British, the Chinese, and we started providing weapons to the mujahideen, including some Soviet arms from the Egyptians and the Chinese. We even got Soviet arms from the Czechoslovak communist government; and at some point we started buying arms for the mujahideen from the Soviet army in Afghanistan, because that army was increasingly corrupt.

The invasion of Afghanistan took many by surprise although Brzezinski claimed he had predicted it six months in advance. Brzezinski encouraged Carter to retaliate with **embargoes** on grain sales to the USSR and with a boycott of the 1980 Moscow Summer Olympic Games by American athletes. He also began to channel funds to the opponents of the USSR in Afghanistan, the mujahideen. Because much of the public considered the public response to be more punitive towards American swimmers and runners than Soviet leaders, Carter only reinforced his weak image; an image that was to haunt him in the run-up to the election of 1980.

A CLOSER LOOK

The mujahideen

Ethnically diverse, the mujahideen included Afghans and radicals released from Middle Eastern prisons known as 'Afghan Arabs'. US money, arms and their guerrilla skills helped the mujahidin to victory in 1989 when the Soviets withdrew, having lost 15,000 troops plus 500,000 injured. The political chaos that ensued allowed a fundamentalist group known as the Taliban, comprising many former mujahids, to take power in Kabul.

KEY TERM

counterfactual history: this term refers to a type of historical thinking sometimes known as virtual history, that attempts to answer 'what if' questions. Such as 'what if Carter had defeated Reagan in 1980?'

STUDY TIP

This question makes an assertion that Carter's foreign policy was in some way 'ruined' by his caution. There are, therefore, a number of aspects to consider. Firstly, was Carter's foreign policy 'ruined' in its entirety or, indeed, at all? Secondly was it his caution that was at fault and finally can Carter's foreign policy legitimately be said to have been consistently cautious? With so many aspects to juggle this is a tricky question and requires very careful planning.

STUDY TIP

Identifying principles from these three sources is tricky. Isolate the argument of each source and then make a judgement about the relative value of what each tells us about Carter's foreign policy. For this question, your understanding of the historical context is vital, both in terms of what the sources say and the areas of foreign policy not touched on by the sources.

Summary

Both Carter and Ford struggled to impose themselves in foreign policy. Ford, of course, inherited the last spasms of the Vietnam War but Carter inherited a foreign policy arena devoid of Vietnam, the first president in 30 years who could claim such a luxury. Instead his problems were of his own making in setting out a stall so clearly tied to human rights that he ended up being seen as hypocritical.

The Republicans, and even some Democrats, were vociferous in their criticism of Carter's handling of key issues such as the Iran Hostage Crisis and the ongoing negotiations with the USSR. In the 1980 presidential election it was to the Cold Warrior militarism of the Hollywood hero Ronald Reagan, that they turned, leading to an eight-year presidency that, in Republican eyes to this day, broke the Soviet Union and won the Cold War. Unfortunately it is impossible to know what would have happened if Carter had won in 1980 without resorting to **counterfactual history**.

 PRACTICE QUESTION

'Carter's foreign policy was ruined by his caution.' Assess the validity of this view.

 PRACTICE QUESTION

Evaluating primary sources

With reference to Sources 1, 2 and 3 and your understanding of the historical context, assess the value of these three sources to an historian studying the principles of Carter's foreign policy.

23 African-Americans in the North and South

The impact of civil rights legislation

SOURCE 1

Extract from *The Declining Significance of Race: Blacks and Changing American Institutions,* by William J Wilson (1978). Wilson was a University of Chicago sociologist who put forward the controversial thesis that race was becoming less important than class in America:

In the first half of the twentieth century the efforts of whites to construct racial barriers profoundly affected the lives of black Americans. Racial oppression was easily documented, ranging from slavery to segregation, from the endeavours of the white economic elite to exploit black labour to the actions of the white masses to eliminate or neutralize black competition. As the nation has entered the latter half of the twentieth century many of the traditional barriers have crumbled under the weight of the political, social and economic changes of the civil rights era. A new set of obstacles has emerged from structural shifts in the economy. These obstacles may prove to be even more formidable for certain segments of the black population. Specifically, whereas previous barriers were usually designed to control and restrict the entire black population, the new barriers create hardships essentially for the black **underclass**; whereas the old barriers were based explicitly on racial motivations, the new barriers have racial significance only in their consequences, not in their origins.

LEARNING OBJECTIVES

In this chapter you will learn about:

- the impact of civil rights legislation
- change and continuity in the 'New South'.

ACTIVITY

Evaluating primary sources

What do you think the new barriers are that Wilson is talking about in Source 1?

KEY TERM

underclass: the lowest social group in a country which tends to include the very poor, particularly those who are long-term unemployed and dependent on benefits. The term is now seen as pejorative

Fig. 1 *An anti-busing demonstration in Boston, Massachusetts*

ACTIVITY

How do these protesters seek to undermine the idea of busing? Who are they trying to appeal to?

Despite the legislative advances and Supreme Court victories of the 1950s and 1960s African-Americans still did not feel they had achieved equality and William Wilson had identified how civil rights legislation had led to further barriers for many black people. The *Brown* decision of 1954 had ruled that desegregation of schooling must take place but the sheer size of some American cities meant that certain areas had school systems that were dominated by the racial demographic that lived in that area. To get around

CROSS-REFERENCE

See page 154 in Chapter 18 for more on the *Swann v. Mecklenburg case.*

KEY TERM

white flight: the ongoing move of middle-class white people away from the city and into the suburbs

CROSS-REFERENCE

To remind yourself of the meaning of 'affirmative action', see Chapter 18, page 155.

CROSS-REFERENCE

See Chapter 15 for more on the 1964 Civil Rights Act.

this problem and ensure that desegregation was taking place to meet federally prescribed targets, some districts began to use a system of school buses to take students from one geographical area to a school in another in order to provide a better racial mix. In the 1971 Supreme Court case ***Swann v. Charlotte-Mecklenburg Board of Education***, the NAACP had successfully argued that six-year-old James Swann had a right to an integrated education even though his geographically closest schools were all predominantly black. The city of Charlotte became a model for busing and integration but elsewhere the policy caused enormous tension. In 1974, a Boston judge ordered the city school system to begin busing, but mobs of white parents and students made the arrival of black students reminiscent of scenes from Little Rock 17 years earlier and riots eventually broke out. The only black member of Ford's cabinet, Secretary of Transportation William Coleman, asked the president to intervene but, following Eisenhower's example Ford chose to stay silent on the issue claiming it was a state matter. Ford was no racist, his best friend and roommate on the University of Michigan American Football team, Willis Ward, was black and Ford had refused to play when Georgia Tech asked that Ward be dropped for a game at their stadium. However Ford felt that Boston schools were not segregated because of legal mandate, so the federal government had no role to play.

By July 1974 attention had switched to Detroit, one of the most geographically segregated cities in America and in the Supreme Court decision *Milliken v. Bradley*, the Court narrowly voted 5 to 4 that districts where *de facto* segregation was occurring could only be forced into an integrated busing plan if there was clear evidence that the segregation in schooling was part of a pattern of violation on behalf of the districts. The *Milliken* decision hastened the trend of **white flight** as white parents realised they could ensure their children attended predominantly white schools merely by moving to predominantly white areas.

Away from High School education, the Supreme Court found in favour of **affirmative action** again in June 1978 in *University of California v. Bakke* which rather counter-intuitively barred racial quota systems in admissions to universities but also affirmed the constitutional validity of the affirmative action programmes which had been designed to give equal access to minorities. Allan Bakke, a white former marine had sought entry to the University of California at Davis' medical programme but found the existence of a quota of 16 out of 100 students being black had prevented his admission despite his meeting the criteria. Bakke was admitted but the court held true to the principles of the **Civil Rights Act of 1964** which it did again in 1979 in *United Steelworkers of America v. Weber* where Brian Weber, a white employee, failed to gain a position on a training programme that he claimed was disproportionately filled with black employees. The court again held that affirmative action was legal as the Civil Rights Act of 1964 did not bar employers from favouring women and minorities.

That the repercussions of the legislative victories of the 1950s and 1960s were still being played out as the 1980s approached, illustrates just how convoluted the issue of racial equality remained in the US, but the actions of the court in upholding the Acts, despite the supposedly conservative beliefs of Chief Justice Burger, demonstrates just how well entrenched they had become in a short space of time.

Cultural gains by black Americans

With the political gains made by African-Americans in the 1960s now largely entrenched in the constitution if not established across the land, the struggle for equality and acceptance for African-Americans moved into other areas.

Acceptance was hastened by the increasing presence of African-Americans in the media and, specifically in Hollywood. Sidney Poitier had blazed a trail for black actors and the 1970 film *Watermelon Man* echoed the 1961 book *Black Like Me* in which the white journalist John Howard Griffin had travelled in the South after darkening his skin pigment to pass for an African-American. In *Watermelon Man* a bigoted white man wakes up one morning to discover that his skin pigment has changed to black. **Blaxploitation** films such as *Shaft*, *Foxy Brown* and *Blackula* had become increasingly popular since 1970 but it was in April 1975 in the pilot episode of *Starsky and Hutch,* when black actor Richard Ward starred as the supervisor of white detectives, that a major step forward was made. The year 1976 also saw academic progress as Professor Carter Woodson founded Black History Month and Alex Hayley, who co-wrote Malcolm X's autobiography published the novel *Roots* which followed a family from its origins in Africa through capture and slavery. The book was turned into a hugely popular TV series in 1977 which won nine Emmy awards and saw popular white actors cast against type as slaves and slave masters.

However it was in music that black performers were most obvious, the early 1970s saw breakthroughs from artists as varied as Sly & the Family Stone, George Clinton, Isaac Hayes, Barry White, Stevie Wonder and the Jackson 5. The growth of disco music in the wake of Elvis Presley's death in 1977 and the film *Saturday Night Fever* made stars of Donna Summer and Gloria Gaynor whilst DJ Kool Herc and Frankie Knuckles led the development of hip hop and house music respectively. In 1979 *Rappers Delight* by the Sugarhill Gang became the first commercially successful hip hop release selling over 500,000 copies.

This growth of acceptance in the mass media masked a change in how segregation was pervading the black community which was recognised by the University of Chicago sociologist William J Wilson. Wilson described the issue as a 'spatial mismatch', no longer a problem of being black but rather of being born and living in a location which was distant from sources of employment. This problem was exacerbated by white flight from the inner cities in the 1950s and the flight of the growing black middle-class in the late 1960s, leaving areas like the Pruit-Igoe estate in St Louis as sinks of poverty, crime and isolation.

> **KEY TERM**
>
> **Blaxploitation:** a genre of films which emerged in the 1970s, with black actors and targeted at an urban black audience, which achieved crossover success

Fig. 2   *The Pruit-Igoe housing complex in St Louis, Missouri, designed by Minoru Yamasaki (the architect behind the World Trade Centre) first occupied in 1954 and demolished in 1972*

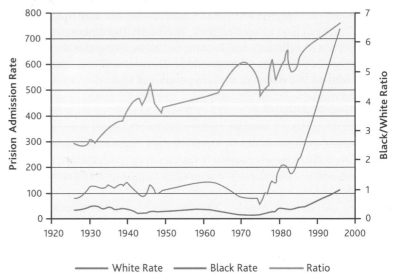

Fig. 3 *The increase in admission rates to prison per 100,000 people*

The growth of the prison system and African-Americans

Accommodation of another type was also becoming an issue for black Americans. Nixon had declared the 'War on Drugs' in 1971 which sparked an increase in the US prison population by 800 per cent up to the present day. The problems of the increasingly ghettoised inner cities meant that **incarceration** for drug offences began to affect young black men disproportionately and this was compounded in New York where Governor Nelson Rockefeller had introduced draconian sentences for drug possession and dealing in the state in 1973. There was a feeling amongst those in the ghettos that the black population was now being demonised, only ten years after the heroism of the Civil Rights Movement. For these people, poverty and police brutality remained a reality, despite the warnings of the 1967 **Kerner Commission**.

Economic change for African-Americans

Economically, little had improved for the worst off, as Wilson suggested. By the end of Carter's term African-Americans comprised 12 per cent of the population but made up 43 per cent of those receiving Welfare, 34 per cent of those in subsidised housing and 35 per cent of those receiving food stamps. In 1980 the Urban Institute calculated that there were 900,000 members of a black 'underclass' which it defined using five criteria:

- single female-headed households
- welfare dependent
- marginally educated (high school dropout or less)
- chronically unemployed
- criminal recidivists (those who were in and out of jail regularly).

Outside of the ghettos however, economic conditions had improved for black Americans through the 1970s. An emerging middle class was committed to education as a driver of change. In 1975 the percentage of 18- to 24-year-old African-Americans who had completed high school stood at 64.8 per cent and by 1980, 8 per cent of young black people graduated from college, up from 3 per cent in 1960.

KEY TERM

incarceration: to be put in prison

CROSS-REFERENCE

See page 126 in Chapter 15 for more on the Kerner Commission.

However, black Americans were aware that their presence in the middle class was not firmly established. They still tended to suffer from the old, **'last in, first out'** mentality at times of economic downturn, such as those that had occurred under Richard Nixon. Many saw the progress that had been made as closely tied to affirmative action with 90 per cent suggesting that it would still be necessary in 1990. Progress was clear in managerial positions; in 1958 only 2.8 per cent had been held by black people, by 1978 this was 6.4 per cent and the 1977 US Census reported that 31 per cent of black people could now be classified as middle class (having incomes over $15,000) with clear evidence of black women becoming more successful in employment.

The civil rights groups in the 1970s

Elsewhere the groups that had helped make such progress for black Americans in the 1950s and 1960s had suffered from relative decline:

SNCC – Largely disappeared in the 1970s with only a few chapters left, notably the one in San Antonio, Texas which shared operations with the Black Panthers.

SCLC – Ralph Abernathy became leader after King's death but argued with **Jesse Jackson** who many activists saw as King's successor. Jackson left in 1971 to form Operation PUSH (People United to Save Humanity) while Abernathy continued to campaign on both black and other minority rights including protesting against apartheid in South Africa and government spending on space exploration while poverty still existed.

CORE - Following the radicalisation of CORE by Floyd McKissick, Roy Innis took over in 1968 with CORE over a million dollars in debt. Innis refocused CORE on black economic development and community self-determination and supported Nixon in 1972.

NAACP – NAACP continued to fight and win cases including 1971 *Swann v. Charlotte-Mecklenburg Board of Education* as well as campaigning for voter registration and introducing education programmes.

Nation of Islam – After Elijah Mohammed's death in 1975 his son Wallace Mohammed took over leadership of the organisation dismissing much of his father's theology and bringing the organisation closer to Sunni Islam, renaming it as the American Society of Muslims. Louis Farrakhan broke away from this organisation in 1978 and reformed the NOI on the principles established by Elijah Mohammed.

National Urban League – Under Vernon Jordan from 1971 to 1981 the League pursued policies such as 'Street Academy', preparing high school dropouts for college and 'New Thrust', helping local black leaders identify and solve community problems. In 1980 an assassination attempt was made on Jordan's life by Joseph Paul Franklin.

Black Panthers – Disputes, splits, exile and a retrenchment to Oakland characterised the Panthers in the 1970s and its membership had declined to 27 by 1980.

KEY TERM

'last in, first out': the practice of sacking those who had most recently joined an organisation if employees had to be made redundant; this often affected black employees disproportionately

ACTIVITY

Try to put the civil rights groups in order of the significance of their achievements in the 1970s.

KEY PROFILE

Jesse Jackson (b. 1941) is a Baptist minister who worked closely with King in the 1960s, heading up Operation Breadbasket in Chicago after 1966. After splitting from the SCLC he founded his own civil rights group, Operation PUSH, and stood as a candidate for the Democratic presidential nomination in 1984 and 1988.

Fig. 4   *Jackson was a key supporter of Barack Obama in his 2008 election campaign*

Fig. 5   *Young was a supporter and friend of Martin Luther King*

Andrew Young (b. 1932) joined the SCLC in 1961 and was jailed for participation at both Selma and St Augustine. In 1964 he became executive director of the SCLC. He went on to serve in the House of Representatives for Georgia from 1973 to 1977 before Jimmy Carter appointed him as Ambassador to the United Nations.

A CLOSER LOOK

The Tuskegee syphilis experiment

From 1932 to 1972 the US Public Health Service (PHS) conducted a medical experiment on 600 poorly educated black men. 399 of the men had syphilis, but were not told in order for the PHS to follow its progression despite treatments being available. The study was ended following a report in the *Washington Star* in 1972 which led to a $10 million lawsuit.

ACTIVITY

Evaluating primary sources

Draw a comparison table looking at the tone, content, argument and provenance of Sources 2 and 3.

Civil rights and feminism

As the feminist movement had come to greater prominence, crossovers between civil rights and feminism had become more common. In 1975 the Combahee River Collective, a black feminist group, was established in Boston while New York boasted the National Black Feminist Organization. Salsa Soul Sisters, Third World Wimmin Inc Collective became the first organisation for black lesbians in 1974. While never boasting significant membership or achievements, the groups indicated both the fragmentation of civil rights as an issue and the inherent sexism that many women felt was prevalent in male dominated groups. The growth of demographically oriented pressure groups for African-Americans also indicated a lack of faith in the political leaders who had followed King. In 1980 Jesse Jackson and **Andrew Young** were voted as the most admired political figures by black Americans, perhaps not surprising given how under-represented they were in Congress with only Edward William Brooke, III in the Senate (from 1967 to 1979, representing the Republican Party in Massachusetts) and only 14 black members of the House of Representatives in office in 1980, all representing the Democrats.

SOURCE 2

A speech by Jesse Jackson to the Republican Party National Committee, 20 January 1978. Jackson was invited to address the convention to help the Republican Party in its plan to attract the black vote:

In thirteen short years, we have gone from 400 black officials to over 4000, but it is still less than half a per cent of all public officials. While much progress has been made to eliminate the external barriers denying our right to vote there are still some barriers remaining. The Democrats have no incentive to register us because we already comprise one-fourth of their total vote. The Republicans feel they have no incentive to register blacks because we tend to vote democrat. Since 1964 the Republican Party has turned its back on the black vote and black interests. Black people need the Republican Party to compete for us so that we have real alternatives for meeting our needs. The Republican Party needs black people if it is to ever compete for national office or, in fact, to keep it from becoming an extinct party. Hands that picked cotton in 1966 did pick the President in 1976. And they could very well be the difference in 1980.

SOURCE 3

Extract from the August 1980 edition of *Black Enterprise* magazine reporting a poll of 5000 of its readers:

A decade ago, our hopes for advancement seemed to lie in the hands of government, our allies, and ourselves. A Republican president had begun to dismantle the many programmes intended to help us progress towards an equality that often seemed as elusive as a phantom in a haunted house. Richard Nixon had adopted black capitalism as his solution to black oppression and our skepticism was nearly as deep as our dissatisfaction with government handouts. Our young people were dying in a war which seemed to have no purpose. Ten years later we find that our skepticism was justified but that we have made progress nonetheless – testimony again to the complexities of our times. Nixon and the war in South East Asia are now a part of our history but if many of us have moved forward into the American Dream more of us have slipped backwards into the American nightmare.

Change and continuity in the New South

Fig. 6 *A protest against the landfill site in Whispering Pines, Houston*

Through the late 1960s and into the 1970s, voters in the South began to elect governors who took on more progressive ideas on education and economic growth, whilst moving away from racist rhetoric even if not promoting integration wholeheartedly. These governors included Terry Sanford in North Carolina, Carl Sanders and Jimmy Carter in Georgia, Albert Brewer in Alabama and Bill Clinton in Arkansas who was elected as governor in 1979. This move away from the traditions of deeply segregationist governors such as George Wallace, who returned as governor of Alabama from 1971 to 1979 led to use of the term 'New South' which became a catch-all for the changes that were occurring in the South as a whole. The development of air-conditioning had made Southern summers less intimidating and led businesses to consider the South. In addition, new markets including retirees, immigrants from Hispanic countries of Latin America and students coming to the large state universities changed the economies of the South, while the manufacturing economies of the North and North East and agricultural economies of the Midwest declined.

The improvements in the position of African-Americans in the South remained piecemeal however. In 1979 the sociologist Robert Bullard highlighted environmental discrimination in where waste facilities were situated as an erosion of civil rights of black citizens in Houston. Bullard and his researchers found that African-American neighbourhoods in Houston were often chosen for toxic waste sites. All five city-owned garbage dumps, six of the eight city-owned garbage incinerators, and three of the four privately owned landfills were sited in black neighbourhoods, although African-Americans made up only 25 per cent of the city's population. Bullard's work exposed similar practices in Dallas, Texas, Alsen, Louisiana, Institute, West Virginia, and Emelle, Alabama. While the South had changed superficially, the experiences of Bullard and others seemed to echo **Thurgood Marshall's** assertion that the road remained long.

Summary

Neither Carter nor Ford can be said to have solved the problems of African-Americans or indeed any other minority interest group, however they did pay more attention to them than Nixon, at the expense of the 'Silent Majority' he had so successfully courted. Jesse Jackson's exhortations to

CROSS-REFERENCE

To recap on Thurgood Marshall, look back at his Key Profile in Chapter 4, page 33.

ACTIVITY

Extension

The 2013 film *The Butler,* starring Forest Whitaker and Oprah Winfrey, is loosely based on the life of Eugene Allen, an African-American who served as a butler in the White House for 34 years. It is worth watching for the exploration of the changes taking place for black Americans and the attitude of the older generation to these changes.

the Republican Party to attract black voters was successfully ignored by the Reagan campaign who were rewarded with a landslide victory in the 1980 presidential election. In spite of the lack of presidential engagement, a growing black middle class was asserting itself across the professions and appearing more frequently in the national media. Americans were being more accustomed to treating black co-workers as equals and having black families as neighbours. In many ways this period saw access to the American Dream transcend the control of the president and move into new fields. This was helped by affirmative action in the case of African-Americans, from an accommodation in the case of Native Americans and from hard work and educational attainment in the case of women. Inevitably some were left behind, trapped in urban ghettos and lured into lives of crime and the hazards of a growing drug culture, but this was increasingly because they were poor, rather than because they were black.

STUDY TIP

These sources suggest that some African-Americans were still trapped in poverty and disadvantage, whilst even successful ones struggled to get the attention of the Republicans. However, the sources also point to political progress, economic progress and social acceptance for some but not all African-Americans, and these nuanced considerations must be supported in your answer.

 PRACTICE QUESTION

Evaluating primary sources

With reference to Sources 1, 2 and 3 and your understanding of the historical context, assess the value of these three sources to an historian studying the changes to the position of African-Americans by 1980.

STUDY TIP

This question makes an assertion that the Civil Rights Movement 'fractured'. That must be addressed as well as looking at whether this fracturing was a consequence of progress. There are several issues here; try to address them in your answer.

 PRACTICE QUESTION

'The fracturing of the black Civil Rights Movement was due to the progress made between 1950 and 1965.' Assess the validity of this view.

Fig. 1 *Black people and white people queue together for the opening of* Star Wars: The Empire Strikes Back

LEARNING OBJECTIVES

In this chapter you will learn about:

- the US by 1980 as a Superpower

- the extent of social and economic change

- the reasons for Reagan's victory in the presidential election of 1980.

ACTIVITY

Does popular media reflect the times it is created in or does it contribute to their creation? See if you can find an example of a television show, song or film that was influential in some way on the events in the course.

In 1980 the population of the USA had reached 224,000,000, up 11 per cent from 1970 and GDP per capita stood at $26,085, up from $21,164 in 1970. However, the country was in recession thanks to the 1979 oil crisis and Carter's decision to embark on a grain embargo directed against the USSR in response to their **invasion of Afghanistan**. In this febrile atmosphere the US ice hockey team defeated the Soviet Union in the semi-finals of the Winter Olympics, in a game referred to as 'The Miracle on Ice'. The following month Carter announced a boycott of the Summer Olympics which were due to be held in Moscow, a decision that backfired as US viewers had to read about and watch Soviet athletes sweep the medals during the games while their athletes stayed at home.

CROSS-REFERENCE

For more information on the USSR's invasion of Afghanistan, see Chapter 22, pages 191–192.

In popular culture the big events of the year were the release of the second Star Wars film, *The Empire Strikes Back*, which grossed $239,000,000 and whose plot echoed the Cold War: being the battle between a heroic alliance made up of a disparate collection of creatures from across the galaxy and a monolithic Empire dominated by a single figure and backed by a powerful military. The media scene also expanded with the release of Pac-Man, the bestselling arcade game of all time. On television the cliff-hanging series finale of the soap-opera *Dallas* tantalised viewers, whereas back in the real world the third bomb from the terrorist known as the Unabomber injured the President of United Airlines. Far above the real world, the NASA space probe Voyager I passed Saturn and sent the first high resolution images of the planet back to scientists on earth. The latter two events perfectly encapsulated the two sides of the 'American Dream'. The pioneering scientific and technological brilliance of the space programme allied to the immense wealth of the federal government set against the radical dissatisfaction of an individual with a grudge.

ACTIVITY

Extension

Write a list of the five most significant events of the period 1945–80 in terms of their effect on the USA. How would you justify your choices? You might also draw up a list of heroes and villains and try to justify them.

The US position as a superpower

'Is America as respected throughout the world as it was? Do you feel that […] we're as strong as we were four years ago?' With this line in the final presidential debate with Jimmy Carter, Ronald Reagan highlighted the concerns of many Americans about America's standing in the world and managed to sweep Carter's achievements under the table. Reagan had been a staunch supporter of Containment and believed in Kennan's interpretation of the nature of the Soviet Union (he was later to refer to it as the 'Evil Empire' in a 1983 speech) and argued that the Soviets had taken advantage of the policies of détente that Nixon, Ford, and Carter had adopted. The clearest example was the Soviet invasion of Afghanistan that had taken place in December 1979 but Reagan also pointed to the SALT II nuclear treaty which seemed to him to impose greater limits on the US than on the USSR. The Iran Hostage Crisis also seemed to suggest that the US was no longer feared on the world stage, something that Reagan saw as reprehensible when the US could wield a greater nuclear arsenal than any other country.

Reagan also believed that the Soviet Union was teetering on the verge of economic collapse and thought the way to push it over the edge and, in effect 'win' the Cold War was to adopt a significant military build up. Carter's response to this aggressive rhetoric was to accuse Reagan of war-mongering.

In fact the US position was secure. The situation in Europe was stable and had been since 1968. Indeed the formation of the trade union Solidarity in Poland in 1980 was to be the prelude to the collapse of communism across the continent. In the Middle East, Carter had achieved a reconciliation of sorts between the Arabs and the Israelis, which importantly served to secure oil imports from the region. In China, Deng was proving to be a far less volatile and far more business friendly leader than Mao, and the rest of South East Asia, though communist, had not precipitated a **domino effect** across the whole continent. Finally, relations with the USSR had been damaged by the invasion of Afghanistan after a decade of détente but the relative power of the two countries had never been more tilted in the US's favour with a stagnant Soviet economy, presided over by out-of-touch leaders, which was embarking on a foolhardy and debilitating land war in Asia.

The US position was also enhanced by solid long-term alliances with the European powers through NATO, but in other international organisations her position was less secure. Despite providing over 25 per cent of the UN's funding, the US had suffered two significant defeats in the 1970s when the People's Republic of China was given the Chinese seat on the Security Council in 1971, and then again in 1975 when a Soviet-led resolution that declared Zionism was racism was passed, despite opposition from the US and Israel. Nevertheless, the fear of communism and MAD that had characterised the early post-war years had faded and been replaced by an acceptance of a status quo that was to collapse within the decade.

CROSS-REFERENCE

To recap on the domino effect/theory, revisit Chapter 10, page 84.

ACTIVITY

Draw up a table to show the similarities and differences between the Republican presidents' foreign policies (including Reagan's proposed foreign policy).

ACTIVITY

Evaluating primary sources

In what ways does Reagan use his response in Source 1 to undermine Carter's foreign policy?

SOURCE 1

Ronald Reagan's response to the question 'What are the differences between the two of you on the uses of American military power?', during the presidential debate of 28 October 1980:

I don't know what the differences might be, because I don't know what Mr Carter's policies are. I do know what he has said about mine. And I'm only here to tell you that I believe with all my heart that our first priority must be world peace, and that use of force is always and only a last resort. Now, I believe, also, that meeting this mission, this responsibility for preserving the peace, which I believe is a responsibility peculiar to our country, and that we cannot shirk our responsibility as a leader of the free world because we're the only ones that can do it. Therefore, the burden of maintaining the peace falls on us. And to maintain that peace requires strength. America has never gotten in a war because we were too strong. I don't ever want to see another generation of young Americans bleed their lives into sandy beachheads in the Pacific, or rice paddies and jungles in Asia or the muddy battlefields of Europe.

The extent of social and economic change

The US had changed radically in the years that followed the end of the Second World War but nowhere was that change greater than in the social make-up of the country where minority groups and women had successfully campaigned for many of the legal rights they enjoy today. However there remained considerable tension between those who believed that the progress had been sufficient and those that felt there was still a long way to go.

SOURCE 2

Ronald Reagan's response to the question 'What do you think is the nation's future as a multi-racial society?', during the presidential debate of 28 October 1980:

I believe in it. I am eternally optimistic, and I happen to believe that we've made great progress from the days when I was young and when this country didn't even know it had a racial problem. I know those things can grow out of despair in an inner city, when there's hopelessness at home, lack of work, and so forth. But I believe that all of us together, and I believe the Presidency is what Teddy Roosevelt said it was. It's a bully pulpit. And I think that something can be done from there, because a goal for all of us should be that one day, things will be done neither because of nor in spite of any of the differences between us – ethnic differences or racial differences, whatever they may be – that we will have total equal opportunity for all people. And I would do everything I could in my power to bring that about.

SOURCE 3

Jimmy Carter's response to the same question during the presidential debate of 28 October 1980:

It's obvious that we still have a long way to go in fully incorporating the minority groups into the mainstream of American life. We have made good progress, and there is no doubt in my mind that the commitment to unemployment compensation, the minimum wage, welfare, national health insurance, those kinds of commitments that have typified the Democratic party and are a very important element of the future. In all those elements, Governor Reagan has repeatedly spoken out against them, which, to me, shows a very great insensitivity to giving deprived families a better chance in life. This is a very important difference between him and me and I believe the American people will judge accordingly. There is no doubt that in the downtown central cities, with the new commitment on an energy policy, with a chance to revitalize homes and to make them more fuel efficient, with a chance for our synthetic fuels program, solar power, this will give us an opportunity for jobs which will pay rich dividends.

ACTIVITY

Evaluating primary sources

In Source 2 Reagan talks about 'equal opportunity'. What do you think he means by this and how does this idea contrast with Carter's answer?

Reagan's vague generalisations reflected a conservative belief that progress would now be a natural, even organic process in minority rights and this chimed with the deep seated conservatism that had grown amongst the politicised 'religious right'. Membership of religious groups and church funding had increased in the 1950s before coming under attack from the more extreme elements in the Civil Rights Movement, the "Sexual Revolution," Vietnam protests, Women's Liberation, and religions like transcendental meditation, Buddhism and Hinduism which had grown in popularity in California and were spreading.

However, the late 1970s saw this siege pushed back using some of the tools that had challenged the religious right in the previous decade. Nixon's 'Silent Majority' included a substantial number of Christians who had previously never exerted themselves as a political force. The growth of cable TV allowed for the development of 'televangelists' such as Pat Robertson. Robertson used his television station 'The Christian Broadcast Network' to deliver a conservative message to millions which challenged the liberal developments of the 1960s and 1970s. A coalition of opponents of liberalism began to form. Figures like **Phyllis Schlafly** began to speak out vociferously against the feminist movement, expressing ideas that seem prehistoric in the modern era but rang a chord with many Americans: they were fervently **pro-life**, shocked by sexual permissiveness in the media, against the Equal Rights Amendment and homosexuality and in favour of the traditional family unit.

> **KEY TERM**
>
> **pro-life:** a term ascribed to those who oppose abortion

> **KEY PROFILE**
>
> **Phyllis Schlafly (b. 1924)** was a constitutional lawyer and activist renowned for her conservatism and opposition to feminism. Schlafly campaigned against the ratification of the Equal Rights Amendment. Her self-published 1964 book *A Choice, Not an Echo* was issued in support of the Goldwater campaign and caused a rift in the Republican Party and her stance in favour of women at home has been criticised as hypocritical.

> **KEY PROFILE**

Fig. 2   *Milk's political activities were shaped by his experiences of counterculture in the 1960s*

Harvey Milk (1930–78) was the first openly gay person to be elected to public office in California when he won a seat on the San Francisco Board of Supervisors. He was killed on 27 November 1978 in an attack motivated by coincidence and internal politics rather than anti-homosexual fervour, but Milk became a martyr for the homosexual community because of his efforts to promote integration and acceptance before his death.

Fig. 3   *What does this typically sexist advert from the 1970s suggest about the success of the feminist movement?*

> **ACTIVITY**
>
> Bring in some quotes from Phyllis Schlafly and discuss as a group whether she can be criticised for her opinions at the time when society has moved on so dramatically since then.

Right-wing Republicans like Barry Goldwater aligned themselves with this new force in American politics, blaming Democrats and the liberal agenda for the rise in divorce and crime rates and a general 'moral decline' of the US, crystallised in the **Jonestown Massacre** of 1978 and evidenced in the death of **Harvey Milk** in the following days.

The Jonestown Massacre

On 18 November 1978, 918 inhabitants, including 276 children, of Jonestown – a commune in the Guyanan jungle established by cult leader Jim Jones – died of cyanide poisoning. This was the greatest single loss of American civilian lives in a deliberate act until 9/11. Jones, a former communist drug addict and self-proclaimed reincarnation of Gandhi, Lenin and Christ at various times, administered the cyanide by mixing it with Kool-Aid.

In 1979 the fundamentalist preacher Jerry Falwell founded the 'Moral Majority' which quickly became one of the most powerful lobbying groups in America, espousing the views of Pat Robertson and blaming the 'liberal' media for corrupting America's youth. The Moral Majority mobilised millions of Christians, including Catholic Americans in the support of the Reagan campaign, actively raising money to target liberal senators, representatives, and governors and seeking to control school boards on the local level to advance a conservative agenda and take back their own version of the 'American Dream'. This religious mobilisation in the support of a political goal paralleled King's ability to use the moral authority and organisational infrastructure of the church to put across a message that had mass appeal.

Reagan accepted and encouraged the support of the New Right even though the ideas of Falwell were also attractive to more extremist white groups such as the Ku Klux Klan and the American Nazi Party. Meanwhile Reagan's focus on small government found support from ultra-libertarian militia groups and survivalists who felt that the government had become too invasive, hence support for the right to bear arms was also a pivotal part of the New Republican agenda.

Class debate

The Silent and Moral Majorities could both lay claim to encompassing an actual majority of the US population. As a majority should they not have been entitled to a greater say in policy making during the period we have covered? Organise a debate covering the arguments for and against majority rule illustrated by examples from the period.

Economic progress

Economically, America in 1980 was not a vastly different place from America in 1945; it remained the wealthiest country in the world, a global leader in manufacturing and services, technology and entrepreneurship which facilitated the best funded military in the world. While the return to solvency of Japan and Western Europe had eroded the extent of US dominance, the country had certainly become wealthier and consumption of food, entertainment, leisure and technology had increased.

The relative economic stability and social changes it facilitated created a sense of optimism in the post-war years but for many there were underlying concerns about how the consumerisation of American life had affected American values. These concerns were exacerbated when the sustained prosperity of the post-war years came to a stuttering end under Nixon, Ford and Carter. Real wages had stopped climbing while even the mighty US corporations were struggling against foreign competition. Carter had been forced to bail out Chrysler, the nation's third largest car manufacturer in 1979. Unemployment and inflation had also continued to grow. To make matters worse the US was now dependent on imports of oil for the first time, making its economic success contingent on its foreign policy. For the first time, ordinary Americans who had become accustomed to a constant decade on decade rise in their standard of living, found themselves instead facing a new uncertainty. Inflation and unemployment had become serious considerations that challenged the cosy lives in the secure suburbs that middle-class America had become used to living and seeing reflected in the media. Carter had tried to galvanise the economy by increasing government spending which, as a percentage of GDP, had risen close to the Second World War highs of 35 per cent. In contrast Truman had brought government spending down to 19 per cent of GDP in 1949. Here was a clear change: the trend had been in government spending rising throughout the period, but Carter's failure to stimulate the economy gave Reagan the opportunity to condemn his excess and call for a return to the American tradition of a small government. It was one of many economic messages that appealed to voters as part of Reagan's promise to restore the lustre of the Dream.

The reasons for Reagan's victory in the presidential election

Reagan nearly unseated Gerald Ford from the Republican nomination in 1976 and Ford's spineless defeat to Carter left Reagan as the leading Republican candidate ahead of the 1980 presidential election. Reagan benefitted from his celebrity and ease in front of the camera but there were concerns about his age; he would turn 70 within a month of assuming the presidency. After Reagan won the nomination, Republican John Anderson launched his own independent campaign adopting a more liberal platform. Reagan's strategists worried that Anderson would syphon votes from Reagan in close states such as Ohio, but their concern was alleviated by a stellar performance from Reagan at the Republican National Convention in July 1980 which gave him a commanding poll lead over Carter.

Carter, who had defeated Senator **Edward Kennedy** to win re-nomination, at the 1980 Democratic National Convention in New York City, was able to claw back some of Reagan's lead in the following months as Democrats closed ranks around their president and Reagan made several ill-judged appearances such as affirming his support for State's rights in the very county where the

Edward Kennedy (1932–2009) was the fourth-longest-serving senator in US history, spending 47 years representing Massachusetts, formerly represented by JFK. He was a powerful orator and committed liberal in whom many saw a potential president. However a car crash in which a young woman died at Chappaquiddick in 1969 profoundly damaged his reputation and his chances of gaining the presidency were effectively ended.

Fig. 4 *Results of the 1980 election; the letters represent states/constituencies*

bodies of Goodman, Schwerner and Chaney had been found after their murder in the Mississippi Freedom Summer 16 years before. Then in a speech in Chicago to Veterans of Foreign Wars, Reagan proclaimed the Vietnam War to have been 'a noble cause'. Later he suggested creationism and Darwinism should be taught alongside each other in schools and that Carter's Georgia roots included connections to the Ku Klux Klan. Collectively these incidents raised questions about Reagan's competency and suggested that Anderson was right to be worried about Reagan as president. Carter had also been working on portraying Reagan as an 'extremist' who would divide America but Reagan's focus on the damage done to the American Dream was proving effective.

SOURCE 4

Extract from Ronald Reagan's Labor Day Address at Liberty State Park delivered 1 September 1980, Jersey City, New Jersey, a traditional Democrat stronghold, in the run up to the 1980 Presidential Election:

Today a President of the United States would have us believe that dream is over or at least in need of change. Jimmy Carter's Administration tells us that the descendants of those who sacrificed to start again in this land of freedom may have to abandon the dream that drew their ancestors to a new life in a new land. The Carter record is a litany of despair, of broken promises, of sacred trusts abandoned and forgotten. Eight million — eight million out of work. Inflation running at 18 percent in the first quarter of this year. Black unemployment at 14 percent, higher than any single year since the government began keeping separate statistics. Four straight major deficits run up by Carter and his friends in Congress. The highest interest rates since the Civil War, reaching at times close to 20 percent, lately they're down to more than 11 percent but now they've begun to go up again. Productivity falling for six straight quarters among the most productive people in the world.

Reagan regrouped, bringing in Stuart Spencer as his political consultant who refocused the campaign onto Carter's record, but by mid-October the race was too close to call. Carter was making headway in portraying Reagan as a dangerously belligerent war-monger when it came to foreign policy, but Reagan's attacks on Carter's domestic record were becoming increasingly stinging. The two candidates also differed on domestic issues. Carter promised further environmental regulations, Reagan contended that environmental regulations were hurting the economy. Carter stood up for the rights of women to have an abortion, Reagan outlined his opposition to abortion and his choice **George HW Bush** as vice president made an about turn on the issue from his speeches in the Republican primaries, switching to a pro-life stance more in line with Reagan.

Carter repeatedly claimed that the economy was on its way back to health but Reagan's promises to cut taxes, shrink the size of the federal government, and balance the federal budget seemed more concrete than Carter's. In addition, his consistent claims that the economy was in a recession, despite the fact that this wasn't strictly true, hit a chord with the public. Reagan also benefitted from being a Washington outsider, as Carter had been in 1976; the legacy of mistrust of Washington from the Nixon experience was still powerful. In the eyes of many Americans, Carter had promised much but delivered little and Reagan's optimism (which some alleged to come from the fact that he was partly deaf and had adopted smiling as a response to things he couldn't fully hear) seemed more clearly aligned with the perception that many had, of what America should be like. In the Reagan–Carter debate of 28 October, a week before the election, there was little to choose between the content of the two

KEY PROFILE

Fig. 5   *Bush's sons include George W Bush and Jeb Bush*

George HW Bush (b. 1924) is a veteran of the Second World War. Bush served in the House of Representatives for Texas then as Ambassador to the UN and China before heading up the CIA under Gerald Ford. Reagan chose him as VP candidate in 1980 and Bush followed Reagan into the White House as president in 1988 but lost to Bill Clinton in 1992.

men's answers but Reagan was more relaxed and confident as well as being over three inches taller. In the week after the debate Reagan began to extend his lead and with the hostages still stuck in Iran, Reagan overwhelmed Carter on election day winning 51 per cent of the vote to Carter's 41 per cent. Anderson took less than 7 per cent of the vote but his support came from states like New York and Massachusetts where he damaged Carter.

Fig. 6   *Carter and Reagan shake hands after a televised debate in 1980*

ACTIVITY

Draw up a table comparing the reasons behind Reagan's victory and Carter's defeat.

KEY TERM

long coat-tails: the coat-tail effect is the tendency for a popular political party leader to attract votes for other candidates of the same party in an election; to have 'long coat-tails' therefore suggests that lots of candidates benefit from the popularity of a leader

Carter's showing was the worst for any incumbent president since Herbert Hoover in 1932. This was largely because the frustrations with Carter outweighed reservations about Reagan in the public mind. Reagan also did well amongst Catholics, working-class Democrats and across the whole of the sun-belt which was the area Carter had won with in 1976. The country as a whole was in the mood for change, reflecting a global trend that had brought Margaret Thatcher to power in the UK the year before. The Republicans picked up 53 seats in the House of Representatives and twelve in the Senate, giving them a majority in the Senate for the first time since 1954. Some of the Republican gains were seen by Reagan's team as a sign that he had **long coat-tails**.

Reagan's victory in 1980 was partly a matter of good timing. Like Roosevelt in 1932 Reagan won the presidency at a time when many Americans felt a deep sense of disenchantment with the state of the economy, society, and politics in the country. At the same time, they had had to endure an ignominious defeat in Vietnam and the loss of 57,000 American lives which had also seemed to have unleashed deep cultural conflicts between young and old, rich and poor, black and white, and even men and women.

Summary

ACTIVITY

Summary

Rank the presidents you have studied by how far their actions enhanced or detracted from the American Dream. Remember to consider all aspects of this concept. Use your individual rankings to try to come to a consensus within the class.

The cumulative effect of these economic, social, and military setbacks was a sense of malaise that Carter had tried to address head on but lacked the political capital to put right. The reverence for Roosevelt's 'New Deal' policies had been eroded. As in Britain, the post-war consensus seemed to have broken down and Americans were willing to try something radically different which was sold to them as commensurate with the vision of the founding fathers. In many ways, the American children of today are the children of Ronald Reagan. Since 1980, free market capitalism, a powerful military, a small federal bureaucracy and significant influence for the religious right have been the norm in American politics.

 PRACTICE QUESTION

'Reagan's electoral promises were far more closely aligned to the American Dream than those of any other previous president.' Assess the validity of this view.

 PRACTICE QUESTION

Evaluating primary sources

With reference to Sources 1, 2 and 4 and your understanding of the historical context, assess the value of these three sources to an historian studying why Reagan won the presidential election of 1980.

STUDY TIP

This is a substantial question that asks you to consider the promises of all the presidents you have studied and match them against the concept of the American Dream. A sensible route might be to define the American Dream in terms of economic, social and political issues as well as US status overseas and then compare Reagan's promises with his presidential peers in each of these areas.

STUDY TIP

The three sources deal with different aspects of the Reagan message; you should aim to identify what these messages are. Then, along with a consideration of tone and provenance, you should aim to evaluate the extent to which the sources are valuable. A good answer will also consider other factors by drawing on contextual knowledge.

Conclusion

Fig. 1   *Reagan campaigning in Florida in 1980*

CROSS-REFERENCE

For more information on the ideas of James Truslow, see the Introduction, page xii.

The Reagan/Bush campaign slogan 'For a New Beginning' suggests that something had gone wrong with the American Dream but that, in the deeply entrenched optimism of the American mindset, the country could start over. Reagan's campaign therefore depended on fanning a feeling that the Dream was in danger, however much had gone right for America in the period from 1945 to 1980. The economy had grown, civil rights had been gained by minority groups and women, the political system had recovered from the shock of Watergate, nuclear war had been averted, Europe and East Asia were divided but stable and the USA remained the most powerful country in the world.

However, to analyse whether the Dream was a reality or an illusion by 1980, we must go back to the origins of the ideas it represents. This is the espousal of the ideas of equality, the right to 'Life, liberty and the pursuit of happiness' and the promise of 'a better, richer, and happier life for all our citizens of every rank' that **James Truslow** referred to in 1931.

Reagan himself certainly believed in the Dream (although even his own son described it as an 'overused cliché') and sought to realise it with an aggressive capitalism that addressed the failings he saw in foreign policy and the economy, and, to a lesser extent, the political system and social equality of the country. To evaluate the state of the American Dream in 1980 therefore it is sensible to look at these areas.

Foreign policy

The period 1945 to 1980 was dominated by the Cold War but need not have been. William Appelman Williams argued as early as 1959 that the US had made mistakes in the immediate period following victory over Japan and

Germany. Truman's decisions to drop the atomic bombs had ushered in a new age of warfare which brought civilians into unprecedented levels of danger and set the stage for an arms race between the major powers that increased tension and cost a huge amount of money. Meanwhile, the confrontational stance he took over the Berlin Blockade in 1948 to 1949 and later in the Korean War of 1950 to 1953 antagonised Stalin and introduced the idea of brinksmanship which was to be played out most dangerously in the Cuban Missile Crisis of 1962. Truman, affected by both the internal and external pressure faced by statesmen when conducting foreign policy, was keenly aware of the political need to look tough in standing up to communism that was made more pressing by the accusations of Joseph McCarthy. In so doing, his Truman Doctrine was to become the defining document of the period for subsequent presidents.

The Cold War also changed the nature of warfare for US presidents. Eisenhower was to warn in his 1961 farewell address of the danger of the 'military industrial complex': a group of interests combining politicians, manufacturers and the military who would always advocate for increased defence spending but his warning went unheeded and a huge build up of armaments resulted with only limited attempts to stem the spending under Kennedy and Carter. Alongside this growth in weapons of mass destruction came a new type of war, carried out by proxy between countries loyal to the Superpowers. These proxy wars in Greece, Afghanistan, the Middle East and initially, Vietnam, required covert operations and funding that weakened the US claim to be the leader of the free world and, in the case of Vietnam, brought large-scale social unrest and resentment when they escalated.

The US was drawn into becoming a genuinely global power intervening 26 times in total in nations as disparate as Indonesia, Guatemala, Iran, Albania, Congo and Chile as well as across the Middle East. Here their actions often undermined the heroic status the country enjoyed after the Second World War.

Society and civil rights

The defining domestic issue of the period was undoubtedly the various civil rights movements. Again, Truman took a lead while also creating problems. Black groups such as the NAACP, SCLC and SNCC created a system of protest that exploited the growing importance of the media as a way to get their message across and put pressure on the president. Their successes, through campaigns such as the 1963 March on Washington and at Selma in 1965 led to landmark court cases and legislation such as the 1954 *Brown* decision and the 1964 Civil Rights Act. However, these successes were tainted by the lack of progress black citizens made economically and the radicalisation of the movement saw civil unrest on a nationwide scale.

Other movements learned from the black civil rights campaigns but also made similar mistakes. Women's rights groups used the power of the media and tapped into an underlying sense of inequality that had been awakened during the Second World War. Here again, landmark court cases such as *Roe v. Wade* in 1973 enabled women to take more control of their lives, as did the growth in use of the contraceptive pill after it was first approved for use in 1960. However, progress stalled under the Nixon Administration as Republican's tapped into the 'Silent Majority', a disparate group united by the feeling that minorities had received a disproportionate amount of attention from government at the expense of hard working Americans whose wealth had been eroded by the expansion of taxes to cover the cost of Vietnam. Other minority groups such as Hispanics, Native Americans and homosexuals whose campaigns for rights in the late 1960s and through the 1970s were inspired by the African-American Civil Rights Movement, were forced to follow a political route as Vietnam and the counterculture drew media attention away from their causes. Though the submission to the 'Silent Majority' that characterised the 1970s certainly prevented minority groups making the huge strides blacks had in the 1960s, political engagement with the American Dream was certainly a characteristic of the wider period but, as in many areas, the Dream could remain illusory without the economic success to sustain it.

The economy

In 1945 with the economies of its competitors decimated by Second World War, the USA was, perhaps, in a stronger position than any other nation in history. With less than 2 per cent unemployment, no dependence on overseas oil and world-leading companies, the scene was set for a boom in consumer goods that transformed America. With this came a host of changes many of which were tied to the social changes that were to emerge in the 1960s and 1970s. Suburbanisation, along with the growth of a mass media, particularly in the ubiquitous possession of a television, saw an almost insatiable demand for manufactured goods which were initially virtually all 'Made in the USA'.

However, these advantages could not last. The decades after the war saw a rise in unemployment peaking at 8 per cent in 1975 as the major world economies recovered and began to challenge US dominance in manufacturing. Cheap products, notably from Japan, made American goods less competitive. Recessions followed in the subsequent decades with seven in total, including those precipitated by military involvement in Korea and OPEC's decision to quadruple oil prices in 1973. The US economy faltered leading to dissatisfaction as changes in taxation and monetary policy failed to address a perceived decline overall and a growing gap between the very rich and Michael Harrington's 'hidden poor'. By the time of the 1980 election, Reagan could use economic failure as a stick with which to beat Carter and the promise of an economic upturn as justification for his idea of a 'new beginning'.

Politics

The reverence in which Roosevelt was held by Americans following his successful management of both the 'New Deal' and the Second World War, was never replicated by subsequent presidents. Truman, Johnson and Ford were all affected in some way by succeeding to the presidency in difficult circumstances but it was the Watergate scandal that truly eroded faith in the political class. Kennedy's premature death allowed him to escape the vilification of sections of the press and electorate that beset his peers, but subsequent historians have sought to look more critically at his incumbency and set it in the context of both success and failure. For Carter, the novelty of being seen as an outsider eventually handicapped his ability to get things done as he lacked the political capital to influence a Congress that increasingly sought to assert itself following the Nixon presidency.

Congress had initially been marginalised by the presidency as the concerns of the Cold War placed media attention squarely on the president, and its role in key legislation such as the Civil Rights Act was perceived as being minimal. At the state level, despite the efforts of the Dixiecrats, the power of state governors and legislatures was increasingly eroded as the US political system began to revolve around the presidential elections, a consequence of the increasing role played by television in both campaigns and policy dissemination. Nevertheless, a career in politics became a more feasible option with increased representation for black people both in the Senate and the House of Representatives. There was a handful of Hispanics and no fewer than 17 women in the House in 1980. This was progress, slow but steady and reflecting the changes in society in spirit if not in numbers.

To evaluate fully the extent to which the American Dream was a reality or an illusion in the three and a half decades following the Second World War, there are several factors to consider. The definition of the Dream is, of course one, but there is also the question of its achievability. Politicians faced increasingly complex issues in dealing with civil rights, the Cold War and the changes in the demographics, ethnicity and economic strength of the US relative to the pre-war period and to its competitors. There is also the question of nostalgia. Those who believed that the Dream had turned into a nightmare by the late 1970s could be accused of choosing to ignore the sexism, racism, homophobia and poverty that had been a feature of the pre-war period and in many areas had continued through the 1960s and beyond. With these aspects in mind it is worth remembering that many still believed in the Dream both within the US and outside; over 4 million people emigrated legally to the US in the 1970s, up from less than 900,000 in the 1940s. Financially the country was still the dominant player in the world economy and rags-to-riches stories abounded across all professions. It had the most powerful military and a political system that was a stable democracy that regularly held politicians to account at the local, state and national level. Even in the battleground issue of civil rights there were few countries in the world that could boast legal equality for all their citizens. The subsequent decade was to see the self-confidence of America return resulting in victory in the Cold War and an economic boom that was described by Stanford's Martin Anderson, a Reagan adviser, as 'the greatest economic expansion the world has ever seen – in any country, at any time'. The 1980s also saw a growth in the gap between rich and poor and some questionable foreign policy adventures and decisions. The successes Reagan achieved did not emerge from nowhere; it is difficult to challenge the idea that the American Dream was as alive in 1980 as it had been triumphant in 1945.

Fig. 2 *Still from the film 'The Blues Brothers', one of the top ten grossing films of 1980. What does it suggest about the state of America?*

Glossary

A

affirmative action: usually a government programme that seeks to encourage positive discrimination in favour of under-represented groups

American execeptionalism: the idea that America is unique or exceptional, a popular tenet of conservative American thinking

appeasement: giving in to the demands of others as a way of stopping them from becoming more aggressive

ARVN: the Army of the Republic of Vietnam, i.e. the South Vietnamese army

Attorney General: head of the Department of Justice

attrition: the process of reducing something's strength through sustained attack

B

baby boom: the rapid rise in population that followed the Second World War

Bible Belt: an informal term referring to the prevailing socially conservative and protestant leanings of the Southern states and parts of the Midwest

big government: a critical term often used by right wing politicians to describe a government that they feel is too large or too inefficient or spends excessively

Bill of Rights: how the first ten Amendments of the US constitution, laying out the rights of all Americans, are collectively known

bipartisan: a term usually associated with a two party governmental system, this refers to when common ground is found between traditionally opposite sides

Blaxploitation: a genre of films which emerged in the 1970s with black actors and targeted at an urban black audience that achieved crossover success

blue-collar worker: a term given to those involved in manual work, particularly in industry

boycott: the refusal to purchase the products of an individual or company as a means to pressurise them to change

Brezhnev Doctrine, the: a policy outlined in 1968, equivalent to the Truman Doctrine, which suggested that the USSR would support communist governments where they were threatened

brinksmanship: pushing an opponent to the edge in the hope that they will concede first

busing: the practice of using school buses to move students around ensuring schools are racially mixed even when the surrounding area is dominated by one ethnic group

C

campaign: the process of persuading people to vote for a party or individual

capitalism: an economic and political system in which trade and industry are controlled by private organisations who aim to make a profit, rather than by the government

caucus: a meeting of members of a political party to select candidates or decide policy

commencement address: a speech given to graduating students at US Universities, usually by a speaker of considerable note

'conspiracy theory': a theory that suggests a group has covered up, through secret planning and deliberate action, an illegal or harmful situation

Constitution: the 'rule book' that states how a country or organisation is to be governed

convention: a formal meeting of a political party in the US for the purposes of choosing candidates and establishing policies

counterculture: an anti-establishment movement that was spawned by the Civil Rights Movement

D

de facto: Latin term meaning 'in reality/ in fact'

de jure: a Latin term meaning 'in law/ legally'

DEFCON: meaning Defense Readiness Condition, this is a measure used to estimate the imminence of nuclear conflict by the US armed forces ranging from 1 (nuclear war is imminent) to 5

demobilise: to take troops out of active service, usually after a war

destalinisation: the process of trying to remove the influence of Stalin by revising his policies and dislodging the cult of personality surrounding him after his death

disenfranchise: to deny the vote either through legal means, or by social or economic pressure

Dixiecrat: a Southern Democrat

domino theory: the idea that once one country fell to communism surrounding countries would inevitably fall 'like dominos'

Doomsday Clock: a symbolic clock face, housed in the University of Chicago, which represents a countdown to global catastrophe

Dow Jones Industrial Average: an average generated from the stock market performances of thirty top US companies, over a standard day's trading, seen as representative of the wider economic situation

draft, the: the Selective Service and Training Act of 1940 provided for the army to 'draft' men in to fill vacancies in the armed services if there were insufficient volunteers

drawdown: the removal of troops from a conflict region, usually in a gradual and staged manner

E

emancipation: the process of being set free from legal, social or political restrictions; in this context, the freeing of slaves by government order and the abolition of slavery

embargo: an official ban on trade with a particular country

entrenched: in political terms this means very well established and difficult to change

Ex-Comm: a group convened to manage the Cuban Missile Crisis

Executive: the branch of government designed to put laws into effect

Executive Order: issued by the president and has the full force of law even though it does not have to be approved by Congress

F

filibustering: a tactic used to delay a vote in Congress by prolonged speechmaking

food stamps: a system for subsidising food purchases for the poor provided by government

G

GDP (Gross Domestic Product): the total value of goods and services produced within a country

ghettoisation: the process of certain areas of cities becoming dominated by one ethnic group as others move out; usually this is linked to a decline in facilities like education, healthcare and housing

GI Bill, 1944: a scheme set up to help returning soldiers that provided low-cost mortgages, low-interest loans to start a business and funded university tuition

Gross National Product (GNP): the total value of goods and services provided by a country, equal to GDP plus income from foreign investments

GOP: 'Grand Old Party'; an alternative, informal name for the Republicans

grandstanding: seeking to attract praise or favourable attention from spectators or the media

Great Migration: the movement of over six million African-Americans out of the rural South to the urban Northeast, Midwest, and West that occurred between 1910 and 1970

gubernatorial: relating to a governor

guerilla: a form of warfare involving irregular fighting, especially against a larger force

H

Hawks and Doves: in US foreign policy those who see weakness as dangerous and advocate an aggressive use of American power are often known as 'hawks'; those who see provocative behaviour as dangerous and advocate negotiation are often known as 'doves'

homogenising: a process that makes things the same for wider and wider groups

HUAC: House Un-American Activities Committee, formed in 1938 to monitor extremist groups

I

impeach: to charge the holder of a public office, such as the president, with misconduct

inauguration: a formal ceremony to mark the beginning of a leader's office

incarceration: putting someone in prison

incumbent: currently holding office

inflation: the rise in the price of goods or services from one year to the next

intransigence: refusal to change one's view about something

Iron Curtain: Churchill's metaphor describing the border between the Soviet controlled Eastern European states and the states of Western Europe

IRS: Internal Revenue Service US government agency responsible for tax law enforcement

J

Jim Crow Laws: these were laws enacted in the South from 1876 to 1965 at the state or local level which made it illegal for black people to use the same public facilities as white people

K

Kremlin: the name, meaning 'fortress inside a city' given to the seat of the leader of the Soviet Union since the Bolshevik Revolution in 1917

Ku Klux Klan: a secret society based in the South that used terror tactics to assert white racial superiority

L

'lame duck' presidency: as a president approaches the end of their second term (or if they have announced they won't seek re-election) their ability to carry out policy is often hampered by a lack of co-operation from others

'last in, first out': the practice of sacking those who had most recently joined an organisation if employees had to be made redundant

long coat-tails: the coat-tail effect is the tendency for a popular political party leader to attract votes for other candidates of the same party in an election

lynching: a form of trial and execution carried out by an unofficial group or mob usually involving death by hanging

M

macroeconomics: the study of the whole economy

'the man': a catch-all term referring to the government, corporations or some form of authority, usually in a derogatory manner

Manifest Destiny: the phrase has come to mean both America's destiny to expand and spread its democratic capitalist identity and the special qualities of American people that enable it to do this

manifesto: a published declaration of intentions usually produced by a political party

Marshall Plan: an American initiative to offer financial support to European countries to help them rebuild their economies after the Second World War; named after Truman's Secretary of State, George Marshall

McCarthyism: campaign in the US against alleged Communists during the 1950s named after Senator Joseph McCarthy

microeconomics: the study of the financial state of individuals or small groups

misandry and misogyny: misandry is the hatred of men, misogyny is the hatred of women

miscegenation: the mixing of different races through marriage, cohabitation or procreation

Missile Gap: the name given to the perception that grew in the US after 1957 that the Soviets had passed the USA in terms of the number, range and power of their missile capability

N

National Guard: reserve soldiers of the US army who can be brought in by a state's Governor in emergency situations or federalised by the president to act on his authority

NATO: the North Atlantic Treaty Organisation signed a collective defence agreement in April 1949 that pledged that an attack on one of its members constitued an attack on all

negative income tax: in this model of taxation people whose earnings fall below a certain amount are taken out of the tax system altogether and receive supplementary income from the government

'New Frontier': a slogan used by Kennedy to describe his policies; he argued that achieving equality of opportunity for all was similar to pushing the frontier west in the nineteenth century

non-intervention: an ideological attitude where the government tries to minimise its involvement in the everyday lives of the population

NVA: the communist North Vietnamese Army

O

OPEC: the Organisation of the Petroleum Exporting Countries founded in 1960 by operating together these countries offset the power of the big oil companies which were dominated by the US, UK and France

P

Peak oil: the point at which oil production in a country hits its maximum after which production begins to decline

per capita income: the amount of money an individual earns in a year

Personality Cult: often associated with dictators, especially Mao and Stalin, a cult of personality arises when a leader controls propaganda to create an idealised and heroic image of themselves, which can veer into almost religious worship

political capital: the trust and influence a politician has with the public and other politicians, which forms a kind of currency that politicians can 'spend' to get things done

primary: between January and June in a presidential election year the parties hold 'primaries' to decide on who will become their nominee

pro-life: a term ascribed to those who oppose abortion

psephology: a branch of political studies which focuses on statistical analysis of voting patterns and habits across different demographics

R

realpolitik: a term given to diplomacy based on pragmatic considerations about what is most advantageous to a power rather than on ethical or ideological considerations

recession: if the economy growth figures for two consecutive quarters are negative, i.e. the economy has shrunk, the country is said to be in recession

revoke: to officially cancel a promise, agreement or treaty

rhetoric: persuasive speech making or writing

S

'silent majority': a large but unspecified group of people in a society who choose not to express their opinions publically

SEATO: a South-East Asian version of NATO created by John Foster Dulles in September 1954

Secretary of State: a senior appointment in the office of the president, primarily concerned with foreign affairs

segregationist: someone who supported the separation of the races

self-determination: the idea of letting the people of a nation decide on their own government

sit-in: a form of direct, non-violent protest where protesters occupy an area by sitting down

small government: non-intervention should lead to small government, meaning a limited number of administrators and hence lower taxation

smear campaign: an orchestrated effort to discredit an individual or organisation by questioning their morality, mental-health, behaviour or attitudes; usually achieved through exposing their private activities in the press

social mobility: people's ability to move between classes in society to go from being poor to becoming wealthier

State of the Union Address: a speech presented annually in January by the President of the United States to a joint session of the United States Congress outlining the challenges facing the US and the legislation the president would like to introduce

subpoena: a demand by a court that compels a witness to appear and provide evidence

subsidy: money granted by the government to help an industry or business keep the price of a commodity or service low

T

tertiary sector: the services sector of the economy where jobs are in finance, government, the media, hospitality, education and retail as opposed to primary (farming, etc.) and secondary (manufacturing) sectors

'The Ticket': a pair (or more) of candidates that will be elected in a single vote, for example, the president and the vice-president

Third World: originally a term to distinguish between those nations that were neither aligned with NATO or with the Warsaw Pact; its later use was related to the developing countries of Africa, Asia and Latin America

Truman Doctrine: declared by President Truman in 1947, a military commitment by the US to defend any country threatened with a takeover by an armed minority

U

underclass: the lowest social group in a country which tends to include the very poor, particularly those who are long-term unemployed and dependent on benefits

V

Vietcong: a Communist guerrilla force which operated in South Vietnam and was supported by North Vietnam

Viet Minh: 'League for Vietnamese Independence', formed in 1941 and led by Ho Chi Minh and Võ Nguyên Giáp

Vietnamization: Nixon's policy of pulling US troops out of Vietnam but providing financial support to the South Vietnamese army

W

Warsaw Pact: a defence agreement concluded between the Soviet-controlled countries of Eastern Europe in 1955 promising to respond collectively if one was attacked

white flight: the ongoing move of middle-class white Americans away from the city and into the suburbs

Bibliography

Students

Aldred, John, *The Cold War c1945–1991*, Oxford University Press, 2015

Bragg, Christine, *Vietnam, Korea and US Foreign Policy 1945–75*, Heinemann, 2006

Joanne, De Pennington, *Modern America: 1865 to the Present*, Hodder, 2005

Edwards, Oliver, *The USA and the Cold War 1945–63*, Hodder, 2002

Murphy, Derrick, *United States 1917–2008*, Collins, 2008

Hall, Mitchell K., *The Vietnam War*, Routledge, 2008

Rowe, Chris, *The Making of a Superpower: USA 1865–1975*, Oxford University Press, 2015

Sanders, Vivienne, *Civil Rights in the USA 1945–68*, Hodder, 2008

Scott-Baumann, Mike and Mark Stacey, *Civil Rights and Social Movements in the Americas*, Cambridge University Press, 2012

Teachers and extension

Branch, Taylor, *Parting the Waters: America in the King Years, 1954–1963*, Simon & Schuster, 1998

Cooke, Alistair, *America Observed*, Open Road Media, 2014

Farber, David, *The Age of Great Dreams: America in the Sixties*, Hill & Wang, 1994

Ferguson, Niall, *Colossus: The Rise and Fall of the American Empire*, Penguin, 2005

Gentry, Curt, *J Edgar Hoover*, Norton, 2001

Halberstam, David, *The Fifties*, Fawcett, 1994

Halliwell, Martin, *American Culture in the 1950s*, Edinburgh University Press, 2007

Moss, George Donelson, *Moving on: The American People Since 1945*, Pearson, 2004

Sandbrook, Dominic, *Mad as Hell: The Crisis of the 1970s and the Rise of the Populist Right*, Anchor, 2012

Zinn, Howard, *The Twentieth Century*, Harper, 2003

Presidents

Ambrose, Stephen E., *Nixon*, Simon and Schuster, 2014

Brinkley, Douglas, *Gerald R Ford*, Times Books, 2007

Dallek, Robert, *John F Kennedy*, Penguin, 2013

Dallek, Robert, *Lyndon B Johnson*, Oxford University Press, 2004

Edward Smith, Jean, *Eisenhower in War and Peace*, Random House, 2013

McCullough, David, *Truman*, Simon & Schuster, 1993

Perlstein, Rick, *Nixonland: The Rise of a President and the Fracturing of America*, Scribner, 2008

Zelizer, Julian E., *Jimmy Carter*, Times Books, 2010

The Cold War

Ferguson, Niall, *The War of the World*, Penguin, 2007

Hitchens, Christopher, *The Trial of Henry Kissinger*, Atlantic Books, 2002

Kissinger, Henry, *Diplomacy*, Pocket Books, 2003

Lewis Gaddis, John, *The Cold War*, Penguin, 2011

Schlosser, Eric, *Command and Control*, Penguin, 2013

The Vietnam War

Appy, Christian G., *Vietnam: The Definitive Oral History, Told From All Sides*, Ebury Press, 2008

Herr, Michael, *Dispatches*, Picador, 1991

Karnow, Stanley, *Vietnam: A History*, Pimlico, 1994

Kolko, Gabriel, *Anatomy of a War*, New Press, 1994

Civil rights

Dudziak, Mary, L., *Cold War Civil Rights*, Princeton University Press, 2011

Ling, Peter J., *Martin Luther King*, Routledge, 2002

Malcolm X and Alex Haley, *Autobiography of Malcolm X*, Penguin, 2007

Marable, Manning, *Malcolm X: A Life of Reinvention*, Black Classic Press, 2012

Marable, Manning, *Race, Reform and Rebellion 1945–82*, Pimlico, 1984

Williams, Juan, *Eyes on the Prize*, Longman, 1999

Social change

Anderson, Terry H., *The Movement and the Sixties*, Oxford University Press, 1995

Biskind, Peter, *Easy Riders, Raging Bulls: How the Sex-drugs-and Rock 'n' Roll Generation Changed Hollywood*, Bloomsbury, 1999

Dickstein, Morris, *Gates of Eden: American Culture in the Sixties*, Harvard University Press, 1997

Isserman Maurice, and Michael Kazin, *America Divided, The Civil War of the 1960s*, Oxford University Press, 2007

Acknowledgements

The publisher would like to thank the following for permissions to use their photographs:

Cover: Mary Evans Picture Library/Epic; **pxii**: Joe Rosenthal/Associated Press/Press Association Images; **p1**: Photo 12/Getty Images; **p2**: (l) Pictorial Press Ltd./Alamy, (r) ClassicStock/Alamy; **p5**: PF-(bygone1)/Alamy; **p7**: The Art Archive/Alamy; **p10**: Pictorial Press Ltd./Alamy; **p12**: Everett Collection Historical/Alamy; **p14**: akg-images/Alamy; **p16**: (l) Pictorial Press Ltd./Alamy, (r) World History Archive/Alamy; **p20**: Keystone Pictures USA/Alamy; **p23**: Underwood Archives/Alamy; **p24**: Everett Collection Historical/Alamy; **p25**: Everett Collection Historical/Alamy; **p29**: World History Archive/Alamy; **p31**: (l) Austin Hansen/The New York Public Library, (r) Everett Collection Historical/Alamy; **p32**: dpa picture alliance/Alamy; **p34**: Bettmann/Corbis UK Ltd.; **p37**: (l) Bettmann/Corbis UK Ltd., (r) dpa picture alliance/Alamy; **p38**: (l) GL Archive/Alamy, (r) Independent Picture Service/Alamy; **p43**: Everett Collection Historical/Alamy; **p47**: Jeff Morgan 01/Alamy; **p49**: (l) Bernard Hoffman/The LIFE Picture Collection/Getty Images, (r) Margaret Bourke-White/The LIFE Picture Collection/Getty Images; **p51**: (l) Bachrach/Getty Images, (r) Bob Adelman/Corbis UK Ltd.; **p54**: Keystone Pictures USA/Alamy; **p57**: Keystone Pictures USA/Alamy; **p58**: Everett Collection Historical/Alamy; **p59**: Hank Walker/The LIFE Picture Collection/Getty Images; **p63**: Everett Collection Historical/Alamy; **p64**: World History Archive/Alamy; **p65**: Everett Collection Historical/Alamy; **p67**: (l) Everett Collection Historical/Alamy, (r) World History Archive/Alamy; **p69**: World History Archive/Alamy; **p71**: World History Archive/Alamy; **p74**: Arnold Sachs/Getty Images; **p76**: (tl) Everett Collection Historical/Alamy, (tr) Everett Collection Historical/Alamy, (b) Stocktrek Images, Inc./Alamy; **p78**: Bettmann/Corbis UK Ltd.; **p81**: (l) Pictorial Parade/Archive Photos/Getty Images, (r) Heritage Image Partnership Ltd./Alamy; **p83**: Punch Cartoon Library; **p85**: Everett Collection Historical/Alamy; **p88**: (l) The Granger Collection/Art Archive, (r) Howard Sochurek/The LIFE Picture Collection/Getty Images; **p91**: Black Star/Alamy; **p92**: The Protected Art Archive/Alamy; **p93**: Everett Collection Historical/Alamy; **p97**: Hal Mathewson/New York Daily News Archive/Getty Images; **p101**: Bettmann/Corbis UK Ltd.; **p102**: Advertising Archives; **p103**: MixPix/Alamy; **p106**: George Tames/The New York Times/Redux/Eyevine; **p107**: Carl Mydans/The LIFE Picture Collection/Getty Images; **p108**: Keystone Pictures USA/Alamy; **p109**: A 1967 Herblock Cartoon/The Herb Block Foundation; **p110**: White House Photo/Alamy; **p113**: Everett Collection Historical/Alamy; **p115**: ZUMA Press, Inc./Alamy; **p117**: Everett Collection Historical/Alamy; **p119**: Everett Collection Historical/Alamy; **p121**: Stan Wayman/The LIFE Picture Collection/Getty Images; **p122**: Everett Collection Historical/Alamy; **p123**: Roger Viollet/Getty Images; **p127**: AFP/Getty Images; **p131**: Hulton Archive/Getty Images; **p133**: Hulton Archive/Getty Images; **p134**: David Fenton/Getty Images; **p136**: (l) Everett Collection Historical/Alamy, (r) David Fenton/Getty Images; **p137**: Bernie Boston/The Washington Post/Getty Images; **p141**: GL Archive/Alamy; **p142**: CBS Photo Archive/Getty Images; **p145**: Courtesy Everett Collection/Rex Features; **p146**: Bettmann/Corbis UK Ltd.; **p147**: Everett Collection Historical/Alamy; **p149**: (l) Associated Press/Press Association Images, (r) Chuck Nacke/Alamy; **p153**: (l) Tom Wargacki/WireImage/Getty Images, (tr) Associated Press/Press Association Images, (br) Keystone Pictures USA/Alamy; **p155**: George Rose/Getty Images; **p156**: Bob Kreisel/Alamy; **p159**: Associated Press/Press Association Images; **p160**: James Speed Hensinger/Rex Features; **p163**: David Hume Kennerly/Getty Images; **p169**: Joe Schilling/The LIFE Images Collection/Getty Images; **p170**: Everett Collection Historical/Alamy; **p171**: A 1974 Herblock Cartoon/The Herb Block Foundation; **p173**: Everett Collection Historical/Alamy; **p175**: GL Archive/Alamy; **p176**: (tl) Robert Clay/Alamy, (r) Keystone Pictures USA/Alamy, (bl) GL Archive/Alamy;

p178: Courtesy Everett Collection/Rex Features; **p181**: Everett Collection Historical/Alamy; **p182**: Ron Galella/WireImage/Getty Images; **p184**: Dirck Halstead/Getty Images; **p186**: Scott J. Ferrell/Congressional Quarterly/Alamy; **p187**: Everett Collection Historical/Alamy; **p190**: Gabriel Duval/AFP/Getty Images; **p191**: Francois Lochon/Gamma-Rapho/Getty Images; **p193**: Bettmann/Corbis UK Ltd.; **p195**: U.S. Geological Survey; **p197**: Ellisphotos/Alamy; **p198**: Danita Delimont/Alamy; **p199**: Courtesy Robert D. Bullard; **p201**: Ben DeSoto_HP/©Houston Chronicle. Used with permission; **p204**: (l) Bettmann/Corbis UK Ltd., (r) Lynne Sutherland/Alamy; **p207**: David Hume Kennerly/Getty Images; **p208**: Sipa Press/Rex Features; **p210**: Robert R. McElroy/Getty Images; **p213**: Universal Pictures/Kobal Collection

Artwork by OKS Typesetting.

We are grateful to the authors and publishers for use of extracts from their titles and in particular for the following:

Winston S. Churchill: extract from 'An Iron Curtain has descended' speech, 5 March 1946, Fulton, Missouri. Reproduced with permission of Curtis Brown, London on behalf of the Estate of Winston S. Churchill Copyright © The Estate of Winston S. Churchill. **Al From**: the founder and former CEO of the Democratic Leadership Council in an interview available from http://www.sargentshriver.org/sarges-legacy/war-on-poverty. Reproduced by permission of Al From. **David Frost**: adapted from an interview with Richard Nixon, in May 1977. Reproduced by permission of Wilfred Frost. **John Lewis Gaddis**: 173 words from p.173 *We Now Know: Rethinking Cold War History*, Clarendon Press, 1998. By permission of Oxford University Press. **J K Galbraith**: *The Affluent Society*, Pelican Publishing, © J K Galbraith 1958. Reproduced by permission of Abner Stein on behalf of the author. **Michael Harrington**: THE OTHER AMERICA: POVERTY IN THE UNITED STATES. Copyright © 1962, 1969, 1981 by Michael Harrington. Copyright renewed © 1990 by Stephanie Harrington. All rights reserved. Reprinted with the permission of Scribner, a Division of Simon & Schuster, Inc. **James C Humes and Richard Nixon**: *Ten Commandments of Statecraft* published in 1998 © James C Hughes and Richard Nixon. Reproduced by permission of the Carol Mann Agency. **Harold Jackson**: 'Obituary: Gerald Ford', Wednesday 27 December 2006, http://www.theguardian.com/world/2006/dec/27/guardianobituaries.usa. Copyright Guardian News & Media Ltd 2015. **Martin Luther King, Jr**: speech made 5 December 1955. Reprinted by arrangement with The Heirs to the Estate of Martin Luther King, Jr., c/o Writer's House as agent for the proprietor New York, NY © 1955 Dr Martin Luther King, Jr., © renewed 1983 Coretta Scott King. **Martin Luther King, Jr**: extract from a telegram to Malcolm X's widow, Betty Shabazz, February 1965. Reprinted by arrangement with The Heirs to the Estate of Martin Luther King, Jr., c/o Writer's House as agent for the proprietor New York, NY © 1965 Dr Martin Luther King, Jr., © renewed 1993 Coretta Scott King. **John L Lewis**: extract from a 'Labour and the Nation' speech made in 1937. Reproduced by permission of AFL-CIO. **James Meredith**: Extract from a letter to the Justice Department of the US Government, February 7, 1961. Copyright James Meredith 1961. Reproduced by permission of James Meredith. **Richard Nixon's ten greatest domestic achievements**, http://nixonfoundation.org/10-policy-achievements.php. Reproduced by permission of the Nixon Foundation. **Gloria Steinem**: extract from 'After Black Power, Women's Liberation' published in the New York magazine April 4, 1969. Reproduced by permission of the Office of Gloria Steinem. **Theodore White**: *Making of the President*, Atheneum Publishers, 1961. Reproduced by permission of David White. **William J Wilson**: *The Declining Significance of Race: Blacks and Changing American Institutions*, 1978. University of Chicago. Reproduced by permission. **Howard Zinn**: *A People's History of the United States*, Routledge 1980 © Howard Zinn 1980. Reproduced by permission of Taylor and Francis.

We have made every effort to trace and contact all copyright holders before publication, but if notified of any errors or omissions, the publisher will be happy to rectify these at the earliest opportunity.

Index

Topics available from
Oxford AQA History for A Level

Tsarist and Communist
Russia 1855-1964
978 019 835467 3

Challenge and
Transformation: Britain
c1851-1964
978 019 835466 6

The Tudors: England
1485-1603
978 019 835460 4

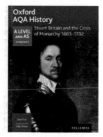

Stuart Britain and the
Crisis of Monarchy
1603-1702
978 019 835462 8

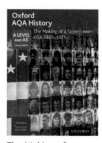

The Making of a
Superpower: USA
1865-1975
978 019 835469 7

The Quest for Polit
Stability: Germany
1871-1991
978 019 835468 0

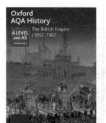

The British Empire
c1857-1967
978 019 835463 5

Industrialisation and
the People: Britain
c1783-1885
978 019 835453 6

Wars and Welfare:
Britain in Transition
1906-1957
978 019 835459 8

The Cold War
c1945-1991
978 019 835461 1

Democracy and Nazism:
Germany 1918-1945
978 019 835457 4

Revolution and
Dictatorship: Russia
1917-1953
978 019 835458 1

Religious Conflict and
the Church in England
c1529-c1570
978 019 835471 0

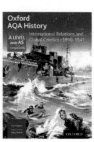

International Relations
and Global Conflict
c1890-1941
978 019 835454 3

The American Dream:
Reality and Illusion
1945-1980
978 019 835455 0

The Making of Modern
Britain 1951-2007
978 019 835464 2

The Crisis of
Communism: the USSR
and the Soviet Empire
1953-2000
978 019 835465 9

The English Revolut
1625-1660
978 019 835472 7

France in Revolution
1774-1815
978 019 835473 4

The Transformation of
China 1936-1997
978 019 835456 7

**Also available
in eBook format** *eBook
Available*

OXFORD